11 MAR 2002

The Open
University

D0230262

This Reader forms part of the Open University course *Studying Family and Community History: nineteenth and twentieth centuries* (DA301). If you enjoy active independent investigative work, want to compare your findings with those of other scholars, and would like to contribute to the developing understanding of family and community history, then write for details of the course to:

Central Enquiry Service
The Open University
PO Box 200
Walton Hall
Milton Keynes
MK7 6YZ

The core course books are:

Drake, M. and Finnegan, R. (eds) (1994) *Sources and Methods for Family and Community Historians: a handbook*, Cambridge, Cambridge University Press.

Finnegan, R. and Drake, M. (eds) (1994) *From Family Tree to Family History*, Cambridge, Cambridge University Press.

Golby, J. (ed.) (1994) *Communities and Families*, Cambridge, Cambridge University Press.

Pryce, W. T. R. (ed.) (1994) *From Family History to Community History*, Cambridge, Cambridge University Press

# TIME, FAMILY AND COMMUNITY

## Perspectives on Family and Community History

### Edited by Michael Drake

The Open University
in association with

BLACKWELL
Oxford UK & Cambridge USA

Selection, editorial and Articles 6 and 12
Copyright © The Open University 1994

First published 1994

Reprinted 1995, 1996

Blackwell Publishers Ltd
108 Cowley Road
Oxford OX4 1JF, UK

Blackwell Publishers Inc.
238 Main Street
Cambridge, Massachusetts 02142, USA

The opinions expressed in this book are not necessarily those of the Course
Team or of the Open University.

*British Library Cataloguing in Publication Data*
A CIP catalogue record for this book is available from the British Library

*Library of Congress Cataloging in Publication Data*
Time, family and community : perspectives on family and community
history / edited by Michael Drake.
p.   cm.
Includes bibliographical references and index.
ISBN 0-631-19236-0 (alk. paper). - ISBN 0-631-19237-9 (pbk: alk. paper)
1. Family - History.   2. Community.   3. Social history - 20th
century. I. Drake, Michael.
HQ515.T56        1994
306.85'09 - dc20
                                                    93-32895
                                                    CIP

Typeset in 10.5 on 12 Ehrhardt by Photoprint, Torquay, Devon
Printed in Great Britain by T. J. Press Ltd, Padstow, Cornwall

This book is printed on acid-free paper

# Contents

# Contributors

MICHAEL ANDERSON, Professor of Economic and Social History, University of Edinburgh.

STEPHEN J. DANIELS, Lecturer in Geography, University of Nottingham.

RICHARD J. DENNIS, Reader in Geography, University College, University of London.

MICHAEL DRAKE, Emeritus Professor in the Social Sciences, The Open University; Visiting Professor of History, University of Tromsø.

BRIAN ELLIOTT, Associate Professor, Department of Sociology, University of British Columbia.

JANET V. FINCH, Professor of Applied Social Science, University of Lancaster.

DAVID B. GRIGG, Professor of Geography, University of Sheffield.

TAMARA K. HAREVEN, Unidel Professor of Family Studies and History, University of Delaware; Adjunct Professor of Population Sciences, Harvard University; Editor of the *Journal of Family History*.

COLIN HOLMES, Professor of History, University of Sheffield.

JAMES H. JACKSON, Jr, Professor, Department of History and Political Science, Point Loma College, California.

LYNN JAMIESON, Lecturer in Sociology, University of Edinburgh.

DENNIS R. MILLS, former Staff Tutor and Senior Lecturer in Social Sciences, The Open University.

LESLIE PAGE MOCH, Professor, Department of History, University of Michigan, Flint.

SCOTT K. PHILLIPS, Assistant Director, Federal Department of Employment, Education and Training, Australia.

ELIZABETH A. M. ROBERTS, Research Fellow, Centre for North-west Regional Studies, University of Lancaster.

PNINA WERBNER, Senior Lecturer, Department of Anthropology and Sociology, University of Keele; Research Administrator, International Centre for Contemporary Cultural Research, University of Manchester.

# Acknowledgements

I wish to acknowledge the debt I owe to my colleagues on the *Studying Family and Community History* Course Team at the Open University, especially to Ruth Finnegan, for suggesting items for this Reader; also to my Open University editor, Kate Richenburg, for being a model of what an editor should be—painstaking, proactive, encouraging and forgiving. In addition, I greatly appeciate the cartographic skills of John Hunt of the Open University, and the careful work of David Green who copy-edited this book for Blackwell Publishers.

*Michael Drake*

The author and publishers wish to thank the following for permission to use copyright material.

Academic Press Ltd. for D. B. Grigg, 'E. G. Ravenstein and the "laws of migration"', *Journal of Historical Geography*, 3 (1977) pp. 41–51; Blackwell Publishers for Janet Finch, 'Do families support each other more or less than in the past?' from Janet Finch, *Family Obligations and Social Change*, Polity Press (1989) pp. 57–85; British Sociological Association and the author for Lynn Jamieson, 'Theories of family development and the experience of being brought up', *Sociology*, 21(4) (1987) pp. 591–607; Tamara K. Hareven for 'The history of the family and the complexity of social change', *American Historical Review*, 96(1) (1991), pp. 95–125; Helen Dwight Reid Educational Foundation for James A. Jackson, Jr. and Leslie Page Moch, 'Migration and the social history of modern Europe', *Historical Methods*, 22(1), (1989) pp. 27–36, Heldref Publications. Copyright © 1989; Macmillan Publishers Ltd. and St. Martin's Press for Brian Elliott, 'Biography, family history and the analysis of social change' from S. Kendrick et al, eds. *Interpreting the Past, Understanding the Present* (1990) pp. 59–82; New

Community for Pnina Werbner, 'Avoiding the ghetto: Pakistani migrants and settlement shifts in Manchester', *New Community*, 7(3) (1979) pp. 376–89; Office of Population Censuses & Surveys for Michael Anderson, 'What is new about the modern family?', Occasional Paper OPCS The Family, 31 (1983); Pinter Publishers Ltd. for Richard Dennis and Stephen Daniels, ' "Community" and the social geography of Victorian cities' from *Urban History Yearbook 1981*, Leicester University Press, pp. 7–23; Routledge for Colin Holmes, 'Historians and Immigration' in C. G. Pooley and I. D. Whyte, eds. *Emigrants and Immigrants: A Social History of Migration*, Routledge (1991), pp. 191–203.

Every effort has been made to trace all the copyright holders, but if any have been inadvertently overlooked the publishers will be pleased to make the necessary arrangement at the first opportunity.

# Introduction

'Family' and 'community' are two of the most evocative terms in the English language. Few people have a critical word to say about 'community'. Indeed, Raymond Williams is quoted here (p. 202) as saying that 'unlike all other terms of social organization (state, nation, society, etc.) it seems never to be used unfavourably'. It is a term often used to enhance less attractive ones, as in 'community charge' or 'community policing'. 'Family', on the other hand, has had a somewhat rougher ride in recent years, with some people pointing out its restrictive, even oppressive, role; an arena of conflict as much as consensus. Nevertheless this has not stopped a couple of British prime ministers and an American president from campaigning in the recent past on a platform of 'family values'.

As it happens, the dramatic growth in the numbers actively pursuing their interests in family and community history comes at a time when both institutions are changing rapidly. It has been suggested—for genealogical research at least—that one reason for this growth is a search for identity, for roots, in a rapidly changing, unpredictable, and somewhat scary world (Sayers, 1987). A more mundane reason may lie in recent demographic changes in the western world, specifically the vast increase in the retired population, many members of which, for the first time in history, are well educated, healthy, relatively prosperous, and have time on their hands.

Over the last quarter of a century, within the much smaller world of professional historians, there has been a notable increase too in those who, whilst often not labelled family and community historians, can be seen as such. Although a shift away from political and constitutional history towards social and economic history can be traced back for a century or more, it is only since the Second World War that the periodization and terminology of political and constitutional history, not to speak of the arena in which that history has been played out (the nation state), have been challenged. Thus many of the advances in historical demography, a precursor of academic family history as Hareven notes (p. 13), owe much to the deployment of social scientific techniques on local community sources.

What, then, distinguishes the different kinds of family and community historians, other than that some pursue their interests full time and others part time and that some are paid to investigate and others are not? Well, it certainly is not the *source material*. Family historians busy about their family trees draw just as much on census enumerators' books, parish registers, wills, electoral rolls, poll books, rate books, etc., as do historical demographers, social historians, students of household and family structure, to name but a few of the titles under which professional family and community historians operate.

And what of *language*. Here there are some differences. The use of specialized terms and concepts, so convenient for those who understand them and so bewildering for those who do not, is an obvious distinguishing feature. Some of the articles in this collection make more use of a specialized vocabulary than others, though none go very far in that direction. It is hoped that the glossary provided will overcome any difficulties (pp. 286–90).

When it comes to the *methods* employed by the various kinds of researchers there are both similarities and differences, as well as areas where one group can learn from another. Creating a family tree, for instance, calls upon genealogical techniques that are not far removed from the 'family reconstitution' technique used by historical demographers to create the family histories of as many of a community's inhabitants as possible in order to determine the population history of that community. Both sets of researchers draw upon parish registers of baptisms, marriages, and burials, and both adopt strict rules for deciding which event can be linked to which family. That the rules of linkage in family reconstitution are somewhat less tight than in genealogy does not affect their basic similarity.

Another technique increasingly favoured by both professional and amateur community historians, that of oral history, can also be used by those embarking on research into their family trees. Family historians are generally encouraged to get as much information as possible from living relatives before seeking to trace their dead ones, although exactly how to go about this—in terms of interviewing techniques—is not perhaps so well known in genealogical circles. In this volume you will find two articles based primarily on oral history, namely Jamieson (pp. 106–27) and Roberts (pp. 129–43); these show just how fruitful this approach can be. For a guide to the technique itself, see Thompson (1988) and the journal *Oral History*.

Some professional historians make considerable use of quantitative methods, ranging from simple percentages, ratios and rates, to sampling, time series analysis, correlation etc. It is hardly surprising that such methods are of little interest to family historians concerned with creating their family trees, nor do these techniques seem particularly relevant to community historians whose main purpose is to describe, in purely local terms, an institution (e.g. a church, school, fire station, charity), an annual event (e.g. a fair or parade), certain individuals (e.g. parsons, squires, schoolteachers, church wardens) or the work of local bodies (e.g. church vestry, town council, police force). When, however, an attempt is made to interpret the roles of these institutions, events, individuals, or bodies, or to assess their significance for a specific community by comparing them with others in different places or times, then one finds quantitative techniques come into their own. A single example drawn from Anderson's article (pp. 67–90 in this volume) is sufficient to illustrate the point. Many local historians have written about the operation of the workhouse in the community of interest to them, often reflecting the grim view of it held by those at risk of entering its portals. But how many of those historians have calculated the percentage of the local population, especially aged over 65, that did, in fact, go into the workhouse? And how many have gone on to compare the figures for different periods within the same community, or have contrasted them with other communities, or have even looked at the situation in a national context? The implications for our views on the role of the family in the past may be surprising. For example, 'in 1906 almost 6 per cent of [Britain's] population aged 65 and over were living in Poor Law institutions; in 1966 1.9 per cent were living in homes for the aged, 1.7 per cent in hospitals and 0.9 per cent in psychiatric institutions, an overall figure of 4.4 per cent' (Anderson p. 69). Yet in 1981 the overall figure was only 3.9 per cent. Incidentally, the related theme of support provided from within the family is taken up by Finch in another article in this collection (see pp. 91–105).

The use of quantitative methods and the adoption of specialized language are, therefore, features that may to some extent distinguish the different kinds of historians operating in the fields of family and community history. However, the major difference between that vast army of part-time family and local historians and the growing but, by comparison, tiny body of professional historians, who would seem to be exploring the same territory, lies in *the kinds of questions they ask*. There are at least two aspects to this. Whereas some historians seek answers to deeply personal and, set against the historical canvas as a whole, microscopic questions (e.g. Where and when did my great-great-grandfather die? Who sat on the Town Council in 1908?), others seek to enhance their understanding of essentially familial or local events by viewing them within a broader context. The figures given above for the proportion of people aged over 65 living in institutions represent one example of the latter, more wide-ranging approach. Another example is provided by Mills's discussion of the development of the Poor Law on the one hand and of hospitals and dispensaries on the other (pp. 261–85). In both examples wider issues are addressed: the extent to which the over-65s live in institutions leads to questions about what support families provide for their elderly members, whilst the discussion of how services came to be provided for the poor and the sick takes us into the various patterns of public sector growth. The second aspect of the difference between the types of questions asked is that the emphasis on the personal and the parochial tends to lead to repetition of basically the same questions (Where and when did my great grandmother die?) Who sat on the Town Council in 1918?), whilst the more analytical approach leads to new questions being asked as perspectives change, and so the research field develops. Hareven's review of research in her type of family history indicates this clearly:

> Over the two decades and a half of its existence, family history has moved from a limited view of the family as a static unit at one point in time to an examination of the family as a process over the entire lives of its members; from a study of discrete domestic structures to the investigation of the nuclear family's relations with the wider kinship group; and from a study of the family as a separate domestic unit to an examination of the family's interaction with the worlds of religion, work, education, correctional and welfare institutions, and with processes such as migration, industrialization, and urbanization.
> (*see p. 14*)

Several of these themes are covered, in greater detail, elsewhere in this volume. Thus Finch's examination of the support that families provide for each other is an example of the relationship between the nuclear family and the wider kinship group; Jamieson looks at the relationship between the family and the outside world and in so doing provides a useful corrective to what she calls the 'classical account' of family development; Roberts not only examines gender relations within the nuclear family but does so in the context of the family's interaction with the world of work and at the same time reveals possible flaws in contemporary feminist theory. Finally, Phillips discusses the relationship between people long resident in a community and those who have migrated to it in recent times.

Migration is, in fact, a theme that crops up in many of the articles; indeed it is a thread that runs through family and community history.

This is not simply because of the extent of migration, which was very considerable, as Anderson notes: in 1851 (the first year in which figures are available for Britain overall) 'well under half of the whole population was living in the place where they had been born . . . around two-fifths had moved from their places of birth by the time they were 15 and . . . one child in every six had been geographically mobile by the time of his or her second birthday' (see p. 68). The focus on migration is also justified by the impact it has had on the formation of new families (e.g. age at marriage, choice of marriage partners), on the growth and decline of communities, and on the interaction between host and migrant families (e.g. the degree to which the latter were accepted by the former and the extent to which they adopted the mores of the host community; see Holmes, pp. 240–60, and Werbner, pp. 165–80).

Research agendas and the kinds of questions asked by researchers are, of course, influenced by contemporary developments. Thus recent concern about the supposed 'break-up' of the family has led historians to examine some of the factors judged responsible for, or indicative of, such a break-up. Anderson, in the article reprinted here, refutes a number of long-standing assumptions: for instance, he points out that industrialization seems to have strengthened kinship relations rather than destroyed them (Hareven does likewise); and he notes that the scale of marital break-ups is not so dramatically different in the late twentieth century from that in the nineteenth century (though the number has risen somewhat since he wrote in 1983). Anderson also makes the point that illegitimate births, though higher today than at their previous peak in the mid-nineteenth century, are in large part 'a function of the drop in legitimate fertility [rather] than a reflection of a collapse in family life' (see p. 73). That pre-marital conceptions and births outside marriage have risen since he wrote in the early 1980s should be interpreted in the context of the high proportion of illegitimate births registered by both parents living at the same address. We are, in other words, dealing with 'paperless marriages', as the Scandinavians describe relatively stable and relatively traditional unions that exist without benefit of a marriage ceremony.

Likewise, alarm at the rise in the number of children living in 'one-parent families' in recent years, should be tempered by a closer look at the domestic circumstances of such children. It has been noted that in 1983–4, 41 per cent of single lone mothers occupied a household with kin outside the immediate family—nearly a third living with their own parents (Clarke, 1989, p. 9). It has been suggested by Clarke that the rise in the proportion of single mothers living alone (from 36 per cent in 1973–5 to 59 per cent in 1983–4) was probably a direct consequence of the Housing and Homeless Persons Act of 1977 (which included pregnancy as a ground for homelessness requiring local authority housing provision) rather than the consequence of a breakdown in kin relationships.

To return to the question of what distinguishes the different kinds of family and community historians, it is apparent that there has for too long been an unnecessary divide between the so-called amateurs and professionals. They operate in the same areas and share the same sources, many of the same concerns and, to some extent, the same methodologies. Only in the questions asked do major differences emerge. It is hoped that the articles in this book will help to close the gap here too, by indicating how the personal and parochial can be explored further and set in a wider context. By spanning the nineteenth and twentieth centuries, by covering a considerable range of issues, by including work by historians, geographers, sociologists and anthropologists, this book should provide insight and interest, no matter what your personal perspective might be.

You may have come to this volume as a historian wanting to know what your professional colleagues are up to in the twin fields of family and community history. You may be a social scientist wanting to view your interests in the family and community today from a historical perspective. Or, as a citizen concerned at what might seem to be the end of the western family and community as we know it, you may be hoping to find more substantial information than can be gained from newspaper headlines and television sound bites. My main hope, however, is that many of you will have come to this volume because you yourself want to participate in the production of family and community history. For one of the joys of that pursuit is that it requires neither expensive equipment nor a lengthy training. You can start at your own back door. And you can aspire, without fear of ridicule, to make a significant contribution.

With this last aim in mind what are some of the key points that can be drawn from this collection of articles? The first thing to note is that family and community history are, paradoxically perhaps, neither ethnocentric nor parochial areas of study. Quite the contrary; it could be claimed that they are among the most cosmopolitan fields of history. Examples testifying to this abound in the present volume. For instance, although Hareven's own research is based primarily in the USA, it is apparent from her article reprinted here that she has been inspired by the work of, among others, Laslett, Anderson, Wrigley and Schofield in England, Ariès, Henry, Ladurie and Segalen in France, as well as by scholars from Austria, Germany, Estonia, Sweden, Hungary, Japan and elsewhere. The *Journal of Family History*, which she edits, has devoted special issues to France, Latin America, Central and Eastern Europe, the Iberian Peninsula, and Sweden. Disciplines such as anthropology, demography, and sociology have all contributed to her area of interest.

As Hareven's article is a review, one naturally finds the cosmopolitan aspect of family and community history at its fullest extent there. Yet Elliott (pp. 44–63) can be seen to draw on the work of French, American, and British scholars, while German, French, British, and American citations are prominent in the article by Jackson and Moch (pp. 181–98).

It is hardly surprising, given the obvious advantages of sharing insights into the family and community histories of many places at different times, that the same themes are addressed in many different contexts and the same methodologies used—moreover, by historians, with their intellectual antennae tuned to the specifics of time and place. This can only be to the good. Elliott's classroom exercise on family history with his Canadian students could with profit be used on either side of the Atlantic (pp. 44–63). And, as if to underline this point, he draws attention specifically to what he hoped to gain from studies being carried on in the UK (p. 51). Jamieson used oral accounts from urban Scotland to study the process of growing up in the early 1900s (pp. 112–27); Roberts interviewed women in three Lancashire towns to study the role of women in the domestic economy in the years 1940–70 (pp. 137–42); Werbner worked on Manchester (pp. 240–60), Phillips on Muker in north Yorkshire (pp. 225–39), Dennis and Daniels on Huddersfield (pp. 201–24), and Mills on Lincoln. In every case, though the questions were put for a specific place and within a certain time frame, it is undeniable that were different places and times chosen our knowledge would be further enhanced.

The testing of hypotheses on different material, times, and places is a common feature of family and community history, each new test adding something to the existing corpus of knowledge. One theory or set of 'laws' that has been outstanding in this regard is discussed in this volume by Grigg (pp. 147–64). They were devised by Ravenstein, who was of German origin but spent his working life in England. Ravenstein's fame rests on two papers published in the *Statistical Journal*, in 1885 and 1889. In these he formulated a number of 'laws of migration' based upon a study of place-of-birth tables from not just British, but also North American and European censuses. These laws, which are presented as simple statements, such as 'The majority of migrants go only a short distance', have been tested again and again. That they are still being tested (see entries under migration in Mills and Pearce, 1989) is testimony to their continuing relevance.

Along with similar methods, similar source materials have been used in a variety of settings in different countries. Outstanding in this respect are census enumerators' books or householders' schedules (Mills and Pearce, 1989). The growth of international bodies concerned with census taking and vital registration from the middle of the nineteenth century led to many systems for both activities having much in common. Thus nominative census taking became the norm, with the household as the basic unit. Age, marital status, occupation and place of birth were details standardly requested. Less common, and all the more interesting for that, were questions about educational attainment, religious belief, language, ethnicity, standard of accommodation, etc. The increased activity of governments in the social and economic fields also led to vast numbers of enquiries conducted at the local level. These now provide us with information on the individual and the family from the cradle to the grave (living standards, occupations, cultural pursuits, education, religion, etc.), and reveal the growth and decline of communities, their economic and political activities, spiritual life, educational provision, tax base, etc. In addition, nominal listings such as directories, electoral registers, ratebooks, and religious records all contribute further details. Indeed, the bulk of the research in both family and community history is based on the patient exploration of the great variety of available documents.

Such research can, therefore, be seen as part of a larger, even international picture. As the articles in this book show, investigations can cut across academic boundaries, while common themes, methodologies and source materials promote debate and the exchange of information. But, perhaps most importantly for individuals engaged in unravelling a family or community history, the articles suggest broader questions and a range of methods whereby personal research can be carried forward and developed.


If, after reading this collection of articles, you too want to 'do' some family or community history, to make your own research contribution, what should you do next? I would suggest that you consider taking a course, subscribing to a journal or two and joining a society. Here are some suggestions about each of these proposals.

This collection of articles is part of the study material for the Open University's course *Studying Family and Community History: 19th and 20th centuries*. Some information about the course appears at the front of this volume. Many other courses are run by local authorities, university extramural departments and the Workers' Educational Association: for details of such courses enquire at your local library. Taught MA courses are available at some universities, notably Leicester, which has pioneered the academic study of local history in England.

A number of journals cover various aspects of family and community history, a fact not always apparent from their titles. Some are geared to the needs of people who are beginning or who are in the early stages of research. Amongst those that are particularly useful are *Local Population Studies*; *Oral History*; *Continuity and Change*; *Journal of Family History*; *Local Historian*; *Irish Economic and Social History*; *Scottish Economic and Social History*. For more details see the lists of references and recommended journals that follow.

Finally, a number of societies, through their day and weekend schools and their advisory services, provide a useful forum for full- and part-time family and community historians. Notable among these are the Local Population Studies Society; the Oral History Society; the Economic and Social History Society of Ireland; the Economic and Social History Society of Scotland. For more details about these see the listing below.

Family and community history, in all its forms, is a rapidly expanding field of enquiry. Tens of thousands have researched their family trees, or are in the process of doing so. A smaller, but still significant, number have worked in the field of community history. In doing so they have acquired some of the skills needed to carry those investigations further. My hope is that this volume will encourage many more to do just that.

*Michael Drake*
*Editor*

*Note*   The articles in this book have been edited: significant wording additions are shown in square brackets, and substantive deletions of text are indicated by ellipses (three points); however, minor changes are not flagged. Terms that appear in the Glossary are shown in bold type on their first occurrence in the text. Notes that have been omitted are indicated by [ ]; full footnotes can be found in original sources.

### References

Clarke, L. 1989. *Children's Changing Circumstances: recent trends and future prospects*, London, Centre for Population Studies Research Paper, 89–4.

Mills, D. R. and Pearce, C. 1989. *People and Places in the Victorian Census: a review and bibliography of publications based substantially on the manuscript census enumerators' books, 1841–1911*, Cheltenham, Institute of British Geographers, Historical Geography Research Group, Research Series no. 23.

Sayers, S. 1987. 'The psychological significance of genealogy', in G. Bennett, P. Smith and J. D. A. Widdowson (eds) *Perspectives on Contemporary Legend*, vol. 11, Sheffield, Sheffield Academic Press, pp. 149–68.

Thompson, P. 1988. *The Voice of the Past: oral history*, Oxford, Oxford University Press. [First published 1978.]

## Recommended journals

*Continuity and Change,* Cambridge University Press, Edinburgh Building, Shaftesbury Road, Cambridge CB2 2RU or 40 W 20th St, New York, NY 10011, USA.
*Irish Economic and Social History,* History Department, University College, Dublin, Ireland.
*Journal of Family History,* 55 Old Post Road, No. 2, P.O. Box 1678, Greenwich, Connecticut 06836–1678, USA.
*Local Historian,* British Association for Local History, Shopwyke Manor Barn, Chichester PO20 6BG.
*Local Population Studies,* Cambridge Group for the History of Population and Social Structure, 27 Trumpington Street, Cambridge, CB2 1QA. Two issues a year.
*Oral History,* Department of Sociology, Essex University, Wivenhoe Park, Colchester CO4 3SQ.
*Scottish Economic and Social History,* Department of History, University of Strathclyde, McCance Building, Richmond Street, Glasgow G1 1XQ.

## Recommended societies

*Economic and Social History Society of Ireland*
c/o Department of Modern History, Trinity College, Dublin 2, Ireland.
Annual conference; occasional day schools; pamphlet series.
*Economic and Social History, Society of Scotland*
Department of History, University of Strathclyde, McCance Building, Richmond Street, Glasgow G1 1XQ.
Meetings.
*Local Population Studies Society*
Secretary: Sir David Cooke Bt., 78 Harlow Terrace, Harrogate, North Yorkshire, HG2 0PN.
Conferences; regional contacts; project work.
*Oral History Society*
Secretary: Rob Perks, National Sound Archive, 29 Exhibition Road, London SW7 2AS.
Conferences; regional network of accredited individuals providing reliable advice and guidance on oral history methods.

# PART I

# APPROACHES TO THE HISTORY
# OF FAMILY OR COMMUNITY

# Recent Research on the
# History of the Family

*Tamara K. Hareven*

Recent historical research on the family has revised some widely held myths about family life in the past as well as generalizations about the impact of the grand processes of social change on the family and society. Family history has complex roots in both historical demography of the early 1960s and the 'new social history' of the same period. Particularly in the United States, it has shared with the latter a commitment to reconstructing the life patterns of ordinary people, to viewing them as actors as well as subjects in the process of change. Out of such concerns has come research that explores previously neglected dimensions of human experience such as growing up, courting, getting married, bearing and rearing children, living in families, becoming old, and dying, from the perspective of those involved. Contemporary historians of the family have sought to reintroduce human experience into historical research and to emphasize the complexity of historical change.[1]

The challenge for such scholars is the reconstruction of a multitiered reality—the lives of individual families and their interactions with major social, economic, and political forces. This enterprise is complicated by our increasing appreciation of the changing and diverse nature of 'the family', rendered fluid by shifts in internal age and gender configurations across regions and over time. The formidable goal is to understand the family in various contexts of change, while allowing the levels of complexity to play themselves out at different points in historical time. In short, it represents an effort to understand the

Recent research on the history of the family
Tamara K. Hareven

Abridged from an article originally published as 'The history of the family and the complexity of social change' in *American Historical Review* 96(1), 1991, pp. 95–124.

interrelationship between individual time, family time, and historical time.[2]

Before systematic historical study of the family began, various social science disciplines had generated their own myths and grand theories about continuities and changes in family behaviour in the past. Sociologists in particular argued that, in pre-industrial societies, the dominant household form had contained an extended family, often involving three co-resident generations, and that the 'modern' family, characterized by a nuclear household structure, family limitation, the spacing of children, and population mobility, was the product of **industrialization**. Associated with these generalizations was also the popular myth that industrialization destroyed familial harmony and community life. But historical research on the family has provided a perspective on change over time as well as on family behaviour within specific social and cultural contexts in discrete time periods. It has led to the rejection of these assumptions and to the resulting questioning of the role of industrialization as a major watershed for American and European history.[3]

Over the two decades and a half of its existence, family history has moved from a limited view of the family as a static unit at one point in time to an examination of the family as a process over the entire lives of its members; from a study of discrete domestic structures to the investigation of the nuclear family's relations with the wider **kinship** group; and from a study of the family as a separate domestic unit to an examination of the family's interaction with the worlds of religion, work, education, correctional and welfare institutions, and with processes such as migration, industrialization, and **urbanization**.[4]

More recently, efforts to explore decision-making processes within the family have led to an investigation of strategies and choices that individuals and family groups make. The life-course approach added an important developmental dimension to the history of the family by focusing on age and **cohort** comparisons in ways that link individual and family development to historical events. As historical research on the family developed further, new findings and approaches led to the revision of the pioneers' findings. . . . The cumulative impact of studies in the history of the family has been to revise simplistic views of both social change and family behaviour. These revisions have generated a host of new questions, which have been answered only in part. Given the richness and diversity of research in family history, it would be impossible to cover here all the aspects of this large volume of scholarly endeavour. I will try to follow the main strands of research and will illustrate them with select examples.[5]

The emergence of the history of the family as a special area of inquiry received its major impetus from the publication of Philippe Ariès's *Centuries of Childhood* (1960 in French; 1962 in an English translation). Ariès argued that childhood as we know it emerged only in the early modern period and that its discovery was closely linked to the emergence of the 'modern' or **conjugal family**, in which parents' private relationships with their children were more important 'than the honor of a line, the integrity of an inheritance, or the age and permanence of a name'. Looking back to pre-modern France and England, when the family was actively involved with the community and the household open to non-relatives engaged in familial activities, Ariès idealized the family's sociability in the 'big house'. 'The big house fulfilled a public function ... It was the only place where friends, clients, relatives and protégés could meet and talk.' In the big house 'people lived on top of one another, masters and servants, children and adults, in houses open at all hours to the indiscretions of the callers. The density of society left no room for the family. Not that the family did not exist as a concept', but its main focus was sociability rather than privacy. The 'modern' family, he argued, emerged as sociability retreated. In thus lamenting the loss of earlier sociability in the family, Ariès laid the foundation for a debate as to which family type best prepares children to function in a complex, modern society: the family of the past, which exposed children from a young age to a diversity of role models, or the contemporary, private, intimate family.[6]

By linking the 'discovery' of childhood to transformations in family and social structures as well as economic and demographic changes, Ariès inspired a whole new generation of scholars. His emphasis on sentiment and privacy as the defining characteristics of the 'modern family' was emulated by John Demos, Edward Shorter, and Lawrence Stone, among others. Equally influential was Ariès's integration of diverse, previously neglected sources with demographic data, especially his use of iconography and art. In recent years, however, historians have challenged Ariès's thesis that West European society before the eighteenth century was characterized by indifference to children. Shortly before his death, Ariès himself acknowledged that, had he looked at medieval sources, he might have modified his conclusions about the emergence of sentiment in the early modern period. His focus on attitudes toward children and the concept of childhood remains nevertheless the major reference point for studies of the historical transition to the 'modern family', especially for historians who employ cultural rather than socio-economic and demographic approaches. *Centuries of Childhood* has served as a catalyst for family history in the same way Henri Pirenne's *Medieval Cities* affected medieval and early modern European history.

While historians often point to Ariès's book as the first major work of family history, historical research on the family was rooted in several disciplines, such as psychology, anthropology, sociology, economics, and, most notably, in historical demography, which preceded it. In the early 1960s, historical demographers in France provided family historians with a powerful new weapon for the analysis of vital processes related to life and death in the past. Louis Henry and Pierre Goubert had developed a **family reconstitution** technique in the 1950s that, in E. A. Wrigley's words, enabled historians 'to assemble all the information about the vital events in a given family which can be gleaned from the register of a parish or a group of parishes'. The Institut National des Etudes Démographiques took the lead in the development of this new methodology. Using first genealogies and then marriage, baptismal, and death records from **parish registers**, demographers reconstructed aggregate patterns of fertility, nuptiality, and mortality for vast numbers of people and, in some instances, over several generations.

In France, historical demography and family history developed into two parallel but interrelated streams from the 1960s on. One stream continued to concentrate on demographic analysis, along the lines of Henry and Goubert; the other, influenced by Ariès, anthropology, and the French social history tradition, integrated demographic analyses with patterns of family and sexuality, linking community and social and cultural variables with *mentalité*, as exemplified in the work of Emmanuel LeRoy Ladurie, André Burguière, and Jean-Louis Flandrin, among others. Family reconstitution subsequently became a powerful tool in the hands of the Cambridge Group for the History of Population and Social Structure. Established in 1964, the Cambridge Group adapted the family reconstitution method to English parish registers, while also pursuing analysis of a seventeenth-century nominal household register for Clayworth, which Peter Laslett had discovered. In an analysis of Colyton from 1538 to 1837, Wrigley found—in the decline in seventeenth-century fertility and the eighteenth-century recovery— evidence that rural births and marriages responded to changing economic conditions. As Wrigley explained, the demographic transition did not involve a change from uncontrolled fertility to its reduction by the 'exercise of prudential restraint' but 'from a system of control through social institution and custom to one in which the private choice of individual couples played a major part in governing the fertility rate'. This family reconstitution for Colyton in east Devon and the analysis of the Clayworth household register became the base for Laslett's book *The World We Have Lost* (1965).[7]

Some demographic analyses for France and England revealed that, in the pre-industrial period, age at marriage was later than had been generally assumed, couples practised some form of family limitation and child spacing as early as the seventeenth century, households were predominantly nuclear rather than extended, and pre-industrial populations experienced considerable geographic mobility.[8] From today's perspective, it is difficult to recover the excitement of being able to recreate such patterns from the past. The evidence about the practice of family limitation in particular demonstrated the control that couples exercised over their own lives and the implicit choices (what Wrigley called 'unconscious rationality') that they followed in relation to changing social and economic conditions. Similarly, the discovery of late age at marriage helped explain the timing of household and family formation. Late marriage served as a method of family limitation. It was also closely related to the expectation that a newlywed couple would establish a separate household. Hence marriage was contingent on a couple's ability to accumulate resources that would enable them to live independently, as well as to contribute to their families of orientation. Linking late age at marriage to the nuclearity of the household, John Hajnal developed his thesis of the 'West European marriage pattern', which served as the basic model for the analysis of West European families until recently.[9]

Using nominal census records, Laslett found evidence of continuity in nuclear household structure in England, at least since the sixteenth century. In 1969 he convened a demographic conference on family and household structure, concentrating on Europe and North America but also including papers on Japan, China, and Africa. The conference essays were published in *Household and Family in Past Time* (1972), with an extensive introduction from Laslett that provided a classification scheme of household types. The essays from Western Europe and North America affirmed Laslett's findings for England that there has been little variation in mean household size and that there has been a continuity in the predominance of the small nuclear family since the sixteenth century. . . . The volume's conclusions, combined with those deriving from subsequent analyses of nominal censuses for urban communities in the United States and Canada, dispelled the previously held assumption that industrialization brought about a nuclear family form. The myth of what William Goode termed 'the great family of western nostalgia', namely the co-residence of three generations in a single household, was laid to rest. Subsequent studies showed that co-residence with extended kin tended to increase, not decrease, after the **'industrial revolution'**, because of the need of newly arrived migrants to industrial cities to share housing space.[10] . . .

Scholars' emphasis in the 1960s on the continuity of nuclear households and the subsequent wave of studies inspired by them had several limitations that left their mark on the new field for a decade at least. Although Laslett's early work implied that the nuclear 'family' persisted over historical time, the major unit discussed was the household, not the family. A nuclear household was not identical with a nuclear family, since the domestic group may have included non-relatives as well. Nor was a 'family' restricted to the household, since extended family ties transcended the household unit.[11]

Early generalizations also led to the formation of new stereotypes: by combining the findings about the nuclearity of the household with the Hajnal thesis on the western marriage pattern, Laslett developed the 'western family' type, which he characterized as having a nuclear family form or simple household, a relatively late child-bearing age, a relatively narrow age gap between husband and wife, with a relatively high proportion of wives older than their husbands, and the presence in the household of 'life-cycle servants' unrelated to the family with which they were residing. By contrast, he characterized the South European and Mediterranean family type as having a complex household structure and early marriage, in which nuclear households are formed by the break-up of extended households rather than through marriage. Recently, however, these generalizations about regional family forms have come in for criticism. For example, on the basis of research in Italy, David Kertzer refuted the thesis that links early female marriage to joint household organization as a characteristic of the 'South European' family pattern and claimed that household complexity was not universal; rather, it depended on variations in landholding and sharecropping. Similarly, Haim Gerber, on the basis of his analysis of households in the seventeenth-century Turkish city of Bursa, concluded that 'certain widespread notions about the traditional Middle Eastern family do not have a solid base'.

Scholars have also questioned the initial preoccupation with household structure and size and have seen the need to investigate internal family dynamics. Berkner has emphasized the fact that co-residence under the same roof was not the crucial variable. Of greater significance was whether family members cooked and ate together and the nature of their social and economic relations. Similarly, Hans Medick warned about the dangers of using structural criteria of household classification in isolation from the social–historical conditions:

> The danger arises of computing the incomputable. It is true that the industrial proletarian grandmother may have lived in an 'extended family' as did the peasant grandmother, but this apparent uniformity by no means indicates an identity of household structures. The 'extended family' of the proletariat primarily functioned as a private institution to redistribute the poverty of the nuclear family by way of the kinship

system. The extended family of the peasant, on the other hand, served as an instrument for the conservation of property and the caring of the older members of the family.[12]

When interpreted in the context of economic and social institutions (such as landholding, inheritance, religion, community structure, and religious attitudes), demographic patterns served as the backbone of family and community analyses. For example, in his 1970 analysis of the demographic patterns and household and family structure in Andover, Massachusetts, from 1650 to 1800, Philip Greven reconstructed multilayered family patterns. By relating age at marriage and household structure to landholding and inheritance, he revealed the power relations between fathers and sons and the limits of the sons' autonomy within a complicated web of kinship networks. The term 'modified extended family', which Greven borrowed from sociologist Eugene Litwak, best described the realities of family life in Andover, where households were primarily restricted to members of the nuclear family and non-relatives, but where a complex web of family connections, reinforced by proximity of residence, often on the same land, permeated the community. The strength of Greven's book also lies in his comparison of the generations. By the third generation, Andover society had stabilized considerably. The major change occurred in the fourth, when a land shortage led to the dispersal of sons and to outmigration, which in turn weakened patriarchal ties by the end of the nineteenth century.[13]

Demos's study of colonial Plymouth, Massachusetts, also published in 1970, uses family reconstitution, the analysis of nominal census records, and a great variety of other sources, such as wills and court records, architectural evidence, and sources of material culture, to reconstruct family and community patterns. It reminds us that even though households were nuclear, they differed considerably from those of contemporary society. Families were larger then and included non-relatives, such as servants, apprentices, and boarders and lodgers in the households. Families lived in small households with little chance to 'differentiate between various forms of living space . . . , individuals were more constantly together and their activities meshed and over-lapped at many points'. Age configurations were also considerably different. In some families, the oldest child in the household would be an adult while the youngest was still at the breast. Even though some disagreed with Demos's application of Eriksonian notions of develop-mental stages to the Puritans, his reconstruction of the stages of the life cycle is masterly in its own right. It provides a dynamic picture of individuals within families and households as they move from childhood to old age in relation to the prescriptions of their society.[14]

While the emphasis on the continuity of the nuclear household structure challenged the over-simplistic categories of modernization theory, it also sometimes obscured important historical differences between past and present family patterns. Nuclear households in the pre-industrial period were considerably different in their membership and age configurations from contemporary ones. Within medieval nuclear households, for example, family behaviour differed from that of the seventeenth- and eighteenth-century families. Pre-industrial households were larger because they included more children, as well as boarders, servants, apprentices, and other unrelated individuals; they also contained different age configurations because of later marriage, later child bearing, higher fertility, and lower life expectancy.

A major criticism of early studies of household structure was their reliance on 'snapshots' in the census household schedules. On the basis of his reconstruction of peasant households in the villages of Heiden-reichstein in northern Austria in 1763, Berkner provided evidence that household structure changed several times over the course of the families' lives. For example, stem family patterns (involving a household composed of a married couple living with their retired parents) recurred several times, as the family moved through its cycle in relation to the household head's retirement and to death and inheritance. A son first lived in a nuclear household; after his marriage and his father's retirement, he lived in a stem family; after his father's death, he lived in a nuclear family; but he found himself later in life again in a stem family, when he co-resided with his married son following his own retirement. Such phases of the family cycle were often of short duration because they were terminated by the death of the head. In contrast to Laslett's emphasis on uniformity, articles by anthropologists Eugene Hammel and Jack Goody in *Household and Family in Past Time* (1972) emphasized the fluidity in the structure of domestic groups as 'processes' in relation to agricultural production, migration, and the family cycle. Analysing the Zadruga—the large co-resident kinship groups in Serbia—Hammel warned that 'the Zadruga is not a thing but a process'. The Zadruga formed and reconstituted itself under the impact of demographic processes and external constraints, dictated by agriculture. Similarly, Goody pointed to the confusion in western scholarship between a 'family' and a 'dwelling group'. He proposed instead the concept of the 'domestic group' as the economic unit (meaning production and consumption). By documenting the changing configurations of domestic groups of the La Dagaba and the Lo Wiili in Ghana, he demonstrated the ways in which domestic groups change in their composition over their cycle and in relation to migration and agricultural production.

Even though Laslett may have contributed inadvertently to a static view of the household, he nevertheless focused attention on the massive movement of individuals from one household to the next at certain points in their lives. In his analysis of Clayworth, Laslett found the presence of 'life-cycle' servants—young men and women in their teens—who lived and served in other people's households in the transitional period between leaving home and marrying. Servants did not always come from a lower class; in many cases they were members of the same class, engaged in exchanges between households for educational purposes. Demos found a similar pattern in colonial Plymouth, where, significantly, the exchanges of young people as servants followed kinship lines.[15]

The case of the life-cycle servants, as well as the presence of other unrelated individuals in the household, proves the remarkable flexibility of households in the past. Nuclear family members engaged in exchange relations with non-relatives, servants, apprentices, boarders and lodgers, and, at times, extended kin. Households expanded and contracted in accordance with the families' needs. In American urban households, John Modell and I found a high proportion of boarders and lodgers, whose presence and functions within the household paralleled those of the life-cycle servants in an earlier period. Throughout the nineteenth century and the early part of this century, approximately one-half to one-third of all households had boarders and lodgers at some point; about the same percentage of individuals had lived as boarders and lodgers in other people's households in the transitional period between leaving home and getting married. Boarding and lodging provided young migrants to the city with surrogate family arrangements and the middle-aged or old couples who took them in with supplemental income and sociability. In younger families, the income from boarders contributed to the payment of a mortgage and, in some cases, enabled the wives to stay out of the labour force. Boarding and lodging represented an exchange across families by which young people who had left their own parents' households temporarily replaced their counterparts in other households.[16]

The discovery of boarders and lodgers in nineteenth-century households and of the overall fluidity of household structure led us to search for a framework that would allow us to capture the movement of individuals through various household forms over their lives and the changes in the composition of the family and the household in relation to these movements, under various historical conditions. Initially, the family-cycle approach proved satisfactory, for it helped explain changes in the composition of the family over its development. When applying the family-cycle approach, historians discovered that household patterns which appeared constant at one point actually varied significantly over the life of the family unit. Individuals living in nuclear households at one time in their lives were likely to live in households containing extended kin or non-relatives at other times. The family cycle proved especially valuable for identifying those stages in the family's development when it was economically vulnerable and prone to poverty.[17] Quickly, however, the shortcomings of the family-cycle approach became apparent. The stages of the family cycle were derived from contemporary American middle-class families, and they were not always appropriate for the study of families in the past. The *a priori* stages were based on the progression of the couple from marriage to parenthood, the launching of children, widowhood, and family dissolution. As sociologist Glen Elder explained, the family cycle identifies stages of parenthood rather than the more dynamic aspects of individual transitions into and out of various family roles.[18] . . .

The life-course approach has introduced a dynamic dimension into the historical study of the family, and it has moved analysis and interpretation from a simplistic examination of stages of the family cycle to an analysis of individuals' and families' timing of life transitions in relation to historical time.[19] The pace and definition of timing patterns are determined by their social and cultural context. On the familial level, timing involves the synchronization of individual life transitions with collective family ones. Because individual lives in the past were more integrated with familial goals, many decisions today considered 'individual', such as starting work, leaving home, and getting married, were part of collective family timing strategies.

Life-course research also illuminates the links between behaviour and perception. While the actual timing of life transitions can be reconstructed from demographic records, its meaning to the individual and family members undergoing these transitions hinges on the examination of qualitative, subjective sources. In his provocative book *Into One's Own* (1989), Modell examined twentieth-century changes in the timing of transitions to adulthood and found that these transitions have become increasingly well defined, more precisely timed, and more compressed in the time period it takes an age cohort to accomplish them. Using both demographic evidence and prescriptive literature, Modell found a major historical change from the erratic timing of life transitions governed by collective family needs to more individualized timing in conformity with age norms. He concluded that, over this century, the life course has become 'individualized' (especially since the Second World War) to the point that a young couple's decision to marry is contingent on finding a suitable partner at a suitable age rather than the requirements and constraints imposed by their families or orientation. Such individualization of the timing of life transitions first occurred in the native-born middle class; the process and pace by which various ethnic groups adopted similar attitudes still requires investigation.

A life-course perspective has made an important contribution to the study of kinship by directing attention to the changing configurations of kin with whom individuals travel together over their lives. Such configurations are formed and reformed; they change in their composition, their relationship to the individual and the nuclear family, and to each other over the life course.

During the second decade of the development of the field of family history, kinship ties outside the household received increasing attention. Studies now show that, rather than being isolated, nuclear households were embedded in kinship ties outside their confines. Members of the nuclear family were engaged in various forms of mutual assistance, collaboration, and rituals with extended kin. Even though ageing parents did not reside in the same household with their married adult children, they lived in the vicinity, often on the same land.

By applying network theory, Richard Smith effectively reconstructed kinship networks in a thirteenth-century Suffolk community. In his comparison of individuals' interaction with kin and neighbours, he found a strong embeddedness of nuclear households with non-resident kin. The intense interaction with kin led him to conclude that, on Redgrave Manor, 'the bulk of the rural population ... had a social structure that was for the most part familistically organized'. The contacts he identified, however, were not among groups of kin but between individuals. Suffolk may have had a higher concentration of kin because of **partible inheritance**. English villages in which impartible inheritance was practised showed a lower concentration of kin, because the non-inheriting sons tended to migrate out. On the basis of these findings, Alan Macfarlane concluded that kinship ties in medieval English villages did not resemble the characteristic 'clans' and lineages of peasant societies. He used this as proof of his much-disputed claim for the uniqueness of 'English individualism'. LeRoy Ladurie, however, found similar patterns of kin interaction in Montaillou. He found very little evidence subordinating the *domus* to a formal lineage. More important were the linkages between the *domus* and other kin, as well as non-kin. 'The *domus* was thus the center of a whole network of links of varying importance: they included alliance through marriage, family relationships, friendship.'

When trying to understand the kinship patterns in the villages discussed above, as well as in other communities in which kinship networks were not codified in clans and lineages, it is important to remember the fluidity of kinship networks over the life course and under the impact of migration. For example, a brother residing in a nuclear family becomes an extended kin member when he moves out. As Greven showed for Andover, it took more than two generations to form significant kin networks in the community, which then were disrupted again through migration in the fourth generation.

For nineteenth- and twentieth-century urban populations, Anderson and I, respectively, have documented the central role of family members and more distant kin in organizing migration from rural areas to industrial cities, in facilitating settlement in urban communities, and in helping migrants adapt to new working and living conditions. Most of the migration to industrial centres was carried out under the auspices of kin. Kinship networks in communities of origin were reinforced by the back-and-forth migration of individual members and the transfer of resources. Following '**chain migration**' routes, villagers who went to work in urban factories spearheaded migration for other relatives by locating housing and jobs. Those who remained in the communities of origin often took care of ageing parents and other relatives who stayed behind.[20]

In my study of late nineteenth- and early twentieth-century textile workers in Manchester, New Hampshire, I found that workers' kinship networks cushioned the adaptation of immigrant workers to new industrial working conditions. Kin acted as brokers between the workers and their industrial employers: they recruited new workers, placed them in work rooms where they could cluster together, initiated the young and the new immigrants into industrial discipline and the work process, taught them how to manipulate machinery, and provided protection inside the factory. At the same time, they socialized new workers to collective working-class behaviour, teaching them how to resist speed-ups in production through the setting of quotas on piece work and through the slow-down of machinery. These findings about the role of kin refuted those who argued that migration to industrial centres eroded kinship networks. Rather than disrupting kinship ties, migration often strengthened them and led to the development of new functions for kin in response to changing economic and employment conditions.

Kinship networks within the industrial community were most effective in mediating interactions with local institutions and in responding to immediate crises such as strikes and depressions. Their strength was in their accessibility and stability. But they also retained ties of mutual assistance with kin in the community of origin. The long-distance networks provided, in one direction, care to family members who remained behind and, in the other, back-up assistance from the communities of settlement, especially during crises. Thus kin networks in industrial communities retained both traditional functions as mediators between individual members of the nuclear family and public institutions and added new ones in response to the requirements of the industrial system.

Research on kinship awaits further development in several directions. First, one needs to examine systematically the interaction between the nuclear family and kin outside the household. To explore this question, Andrejs Plakans applied Meyer Fortes's model of '**structural domains**', which is based on the assumption that an individual participates in several domains simultaneously and fulfils a different role in each. Sometimes these roles are complementary; at other times they are in conflict. An individual can be engaged simultaneously in obligations to co-resident family members and to non-resident kin. How these roles have been negotiated and played out in various settings during different periods remains an important topic of research. Second, the question of why families in the West drew their household boundary at co-residence with kin but included unrelated individuals in the household has not been answered.

Pursuing these questions requires careful attention to the term 'kinship'. Scholars must distinguish between perceptual categories and definitions of kinship developed within a given society and the analytical categories used by social scientists. Reconstruction of kinship categories from within is extremely difficult, given the limitations of traditional historical sources, but essential. As Robin Fox put it, 'No Australian Aborigine sat down and worked out a blueprint for the complicated systems of kinship and marriage for which he is justly famous; but his ability to conceptualize and classify was as much a factor in this successful development as the claws of the tiger or the neck of the giraffe were in the survival and success of these species.'[21] Ideally, historians should juxtapose the actors' categories and definitions of kin with externally defined notions.

As in other areas of research in the history of the family, we need to find a comfortable equilibrium between quantitative analysis and 'thick description'. Too often, quantitative and qualitative methodologies have been presented as mutually exclusive. Analysis of kinship will be served best by merging the two. For example, while quantitative analysis identifies the composition or extensiveness of a kinship network, qualitative analysis reveals patterns of assistance or areas of conflict among kin.[22] Finally, we need to understand how kin relations changed over time in relation to the 'grand processes' of change.

An examination of the family's interaction with the process of social and economic change enables us to understand more precisely not only what occurred internally within the family but how such changes were accomplished on a societal level as well. It provides new insights into the process of industrialization and urbanization, into how labour markets functioned, and into how industrial work processes and labour relations were organized. These are only some of many areas in which the role of the family is critical for an understanding of social change and, conversely, for our understanding of societal influences on the family. Recent historical research on the family has led to the rejection of simplistic models of social change. How the family both initiates and adapts to change and how it translates the impact of larger structural changes to its own sphere are questions governing the richest area of intersection between the family and the process of social change. Much of this interaction still awaits thorough examination.[23]

The important principle underlying these questions is a view of the family as an active agent. The family planned, initiated, or resisted change; it did not just respond blindly. Historical research over the past two decades has provided ample evidence to reject stereotypes about the family's passivity. We have therefore widened questions such as 'What was the impact of industrialization on the family?' to include 'What was the family's impact on the industrial system?'[24] Some of the studies that reversed the stereotype of the family as a 'passive' agent have, in turn, generated new stereotypes that exaggerate the family's ability to control its environment. Since historical realities are better expressed in a process of interaction than in the reversal of unilateral processes, the question has been recast into a more complex form: under what circumstances was the family more able to control its destiny and to affect the larger social processes, and under what circumstances did the family succumb to declining markets, changing modes of production, business cycles, and other external forces? How did families interact with these processes and how did they react to opportunities or constraints? For example, how did they respond to technological developments and to new industries that were attracting a labour force? How did they save themselves from the decaying industries that had recruited them during their prime and that left them stranded when they were no longer needed?[25]

The family's interaction with the industrial system has received attention from two types of historical study: a study of family production systems in artisanal and proto-industrial settings, and the study of family and work in the context of large industrial enterprises. Proto-industrialization was a household-based form of production that preceded the 'industrial revolution' in the countryside and in some urban areas in England, France, Belgium, Switzerland, and Austria, from the seventeenth to the early nineteenth centuries. It was characterized by the production of goods in local cottages for a capitalist employer who controlled the means of production and sold the products in external markets. When Rudolf Braun first 'discovered' this process for Zurich, he emphasized its centrality as a household-based enterprise, which drew heavily on the labour of women and children and engaged the entire household unit. Braun and the historians who identified these patterns in other regions, especially Franklin Mendels, Hans Medick, and David Levine, developed a model of demographic behaviour they claimed was typical of proto-industrial families—an earlier age at marriage, higher fertility, and delays in children's departure from the home, all of which were conducive to maximizing a family labour force.[26] Marriage formed the key to the spread of the cottage industry, because it led to the formation of a new nuclear family unit, which was also a 'unit of labour'. As Medick explained it, 'Marriage and family formation slipped beyond the grasp of patriarchal domination; they were no longer "tangibly" determined by property relationships, but they did not lose their "material foundation" in the process of production.' The prevalent pattern became that of 'beggars' ' marriages between partners without any considerable dowry or inheritance, between 'people who can join together two spinning wheels but not beds.'[27]

Recently, the demographic model of proto-industrialization has come under criticism. On the one hand, scholars have questioned whether the demographic changes had been sufficiently widespread to warrant generalizations. For example, in their comparison of two proto-industrial regions in eastern Belgium, Myron Gutmann and René Leboutte concluded that high ages at marriage were sustained in some regions but not in others. Demographic behaviour in response to new economic conditions 'differed according to the environment (i.e. land ownership, social structure and inheritance), and the exact nature of the economic change which took place.' Shifting the analysis from demographic behaviour to the internal division of labour in proto-industrial households, Ulrich Pfister found considerable differences in the division of labour between men and women in relation to the type of manufacturing families engaged in various proto-industrial settings in Switzerland. Again, regional variation, interaction with the local agricultural structure, as well as the type of cottage industry (whether weaving or spinning), made a difference.[28]

On the other hand, despite these critiques, the concept of proto-industrialization has helped focus attention on the diversity of types of family-based production, some of which preceded the 'industrial revolution' and some of which coexisted with the factory system. As a transition, proto-industrial production prepared a family labour force for industrial work: in certain regions, women and children were first cast into the roles of 'industrial' labourers at the cottage production phase. Members of proto-industrial households who eventually entered factories brought their skills with them and may therefore have faced an easier adaptation to industrial work. The family had a central role in charting the transitions to various modes of industrial production by following diverse routes: from a rural economy to a proto-industrial or industrial one, or from a rural economy directly to an industrial one. Families of traditional craftsmen or artisans, in their struggle to survive in a changing economy, sent some of their members to work in new industries, while maintaining a crafts production system in their own households. Rural families released members through migration to work in urban factories or took in machinery and transformed their own households into proto-industrial domestic factories. Proto-industrial families as well as those of factory workers provided housing, employment, and training for new migrants in their households. In all these cases, while following its own priorities, the family facilitated the advance of industrialization by releasing the labour force needed for the newly developing factories and by organizing migration to industrial centres.[29]

Like research on the family in the proto-industrial system, the study of the family in the factory system has provided considerable evidence documenting the family's role as an active agent in its interaction with the process of industrialization. Such research effectively undermined the theory of 'social breakdown' that had haunted sociology and social history. According to this notion, throughout the history of industrial development migration from rural to urban centres had led to the uprooting of people from the traditional kinship networks. The pressures of industrial work and urban life caused a disintegration of the family unit, and adaptation to industrial life stripped migrants of their traditional culture.[30]

Historians and sociologists alike had challenged the assumption that families and kin groups broke down under the impact of migration to urban industrial centres and under the pressures of industrial work. Neil Smelser, in his pioneer study of the family in the early stages of industrialization in Britain, documented the recruitment of entire family groups as work units in the early textile factories. Fathers contracted for their children, collected their wages, and at times disciplined them in the factory. Entire families depended on the factory as their employer; the factories, in turn, depended on the recruitment of family groups to maintain a continuous labour supply. Beginning in the 1820s, however, as a result of factory legislation and technological change, economic and training functions were gradually removed from the workers' families. Child workers were separated from the supervision of their parents.

Smelser connected the increasing labour unrest, expressed in numerous strikes from 1820 on, to the workers' loss of control over their family members' work in the factory, which led to the break of the 'link between parent and child on the factory premises'. He viewed this process as the culmination of the differentiation of the working-class family, one 'involving a clearer split between home and factory, a split between the economic and other aspects of the parent–child relationship'.[31]

Michael Anderson disagreed with Smelser in his analysis of family work patterns in nineteenth-century Lancashire. He documented a continuity of recruitment in family units in the textile industry, at least through the middle of the nineteenth century. Most important, Anderson stressed the survival of kinship ties and the continuity of the vital role of kin in migration and in adaptation to industrial life. Thus the practice of family members working together in the factory, which Smelser identified for the early phase of industrialization, survived in different forms in Lancashire throughout the nineteenth century. It was carried over into the United States, as the factory system developed there, and was still present among immigrant workers in the twentieth century. Rural as well as urban families functioned as crucial intermediaries in recruiting workers from the countryside in the early phases of industrialization. The very success of the early industrial system depended on a continuous flow of labour from the countryside to the newly industrializing centres, which usually followed kinship lines.[32]

My study of family and work in the Amoskeag Mills in Manchester, New Hampshire, has documented the role of the family as an active agent in relation to the industrial corporation. The family type most 'fit' to interact with the factory system was not an 'isolated' nuclear family but rather one embedded in extended kinship ties. In cushioning the adaptation to industrial work without excessively restricting the mobility of individual workers, kin were instrumental in serving the industrial employer and, at the same time, in advancing the interest of their own members and providing them with protection. The active stance the family took in relation to the factory system does not imply that the family was in full control of its destiny, nor does it mean that workers and their families were successful in changing the structure of industrial capitalism. Workers' ability to influence their work environments greatly depended on the fluctuations within the factory system, on business cycles, and on production policies. In Manchester, control of kin over the factory weakened after the First World War, as the corporation shifted to a regime of labour surplus. As Smelser and Sydney Halpern observed, it has not been the steady or continued growth of industrial capitalism so much as its crises that have put strains on modern kinship networks.

The functions that kin fulfilled in their interaction with the factory system were not merely an archaic carry-over from rural society but a selective use of pre-migration kin assistance patterns in response to the needs dictated by industrial conditions. Among working-class and ethnic families, some pre-industrial family characteristics persisted, though in modified form. Even after the workplace had been separated from the household, the family continued to perceive itself as a work unit. Family members experienced a continuity between work outside the home and household production, especially where women were involved. Similarly, the survival of important functions of kin in the workplace suggests that the historical separation of family and work had not occurred throughout the society.

The encounter of immigrant workers with the modern factory system led neither to the abandonment of nor the rigid adherence to pre-migration family traditions. Rather, the workers adapted their customs and social organization to the new conditions they confronted. In doing so, they addressed the factory system on its own terms. Selectivity was the key principle in their adaptation. The family selected those aspects of traditional culture that were most useful in coping with new conditions and adapted them to new needs.

The patterns of selectivity in the transmission of pre-migration and family culture to the industrial system described here call into question the linear view of social change advanced by modernization theory. Modernization at the workplace did not automatically lead to the 'modernization' of family behaviour. Although the family underwent significant changes in its adaptation to new work roles and urban living, family behaviour did not modernize at the same pace as workers' conduct in the factory. The family was both a custodian of tradition and an agent of change. As a guardian of traditional culture, the family provided its members with a sense of continuity, which served as a resource to draw on when confronting industrial conditions. Familial and industrial adaptation processes were not merely parallel but interrelated as a part of a personal and historical continuum.

To understand the family's role in these processes better, it is necessary to examine how families charted their strategies in relation to external opportunities and constraints. Family strategies involved not only the decisions individuals or families made but also the actual timing of such decisions in response to opportunities or need: when to send a son or daughter to another community, for example, when to join other kin, when to change residence. Strategies involved, at times, calculated trade-offs in order to find employment, achieve solvency, buy a house, facilitate children's education or their occupational advancement, control or facilitate a child's marriage, save for the future, provide for times of illness, old age, and death. Strategies were part of a larger life plan. As people encountered new circumstances, they modified and reshaped their plans and strategies in the context of their own culture and traditions. As W. I. Thomas remarked, 'A family's behavior is influenced by what it brings to new situations, the demands and options or constraints of the situation, and situational interpretations ... The family is both the product and the producer of its career.'

Since very few ordinary people left behind diaries and correspondence, it has often been necessary to infer strategies from behavioural patterns. For instance, Daniel Scott Smith has inferred women's strategies of family limitation in early nineteenth-century New England from the gender of the last-born child and strategies of parental control over the timing of marriage through an analysis of marriage records and wills in the same period. Other historians have inferred strategies of children's and women's participation in the labour force from the census manuscript household schedules of the late nineteenth century. ...

More recently, historical research has begun to reconstruct consciously articulated strategies from ethnographies, autobiographies, oral history interviews, and other types of verbal testimony. Through these means, historians have uncovered conscious strategies underlying inheritance contracts in rural society, in which sons agreed to support ageing parents in exchange for inheriting property, or in the planning of marriages intended to serve the preservation or consolidation of family estates or lineages. Family work strategies in response to the industrial system, as discussed above, and the use of kin to organize and support migration to industrial communities have also emerged as significant areas of family strategies.

The most important contribution of recent research has been to emphasize the significance of cultural values both of the dominant culture and of the family's own culture in guiding family strategies. In contrast to economists, historians are much more inclined to examine the interrelationship between economic and cultural variables in the strategies families follow. As Stanley Engerman observed, 'Family decision making has peculiar aspects of jointness, since it affects, and is meant to affect, the entire family group. The family is, in essence, a group of individuals of varying ages with rather unequal decision-making power, and with a bond of "love" and "altruism" not generally thought to be found in other groups in our society.'

Strategies were not guided exclusively by economic needs but rather by the interaction of economic and cultural factors. On issues such as children's or wives' labour, or on expenditure patterns, even economically marginal families did not always make the most 'prudent' choices from a strictly economic point of view if such choices were inconsistent with their family history and their own cultural values. Labour-force participation by married women and children, for example, posed a critical dilemma for working-class families. The participation of women and children in a collective family effort was sanctioned by the cultural values that immigrant workers brought with them to the United States from their pre-migration communities. Even under conditions of economic marginality, the strategies of immigrant families were guided by their cultural values, which were sometimes in conflict with middle-class values in the dominant culture.

As in labour-force participation, family consumption patterns reflect strategies based on the interaction between the family's cultural values and economic opportunities. By comparing expenditure patterns in the family budgets of Irish and native-born workers, Modell found that, by the end of the nineteenth century, Irish workers had developed essentially the same consumption patterns as had Yankee working-class families, although the income of Irish working fathers still constituted only 85 per cent of the income of native-born working fathers. Conversely, new consumption patterns can lead to changes in values. This aspect, however, is still open to exploration.

In these beginning stages of the historical study of family strategies, the process of decision making within the family has not yet been sufficiently examined. The emphasis on the family as charting its own strategies raises the questions: whose strategies were family strategies? To what extent and in what ways did various family members participate in the collective decision impinging on their lives? Feminist scholars in particular have directed attention to the fact that an emphasis on the family as a collective entity might tend to obscure the respective roles of individual members in the decision-making process. The limited availability of historical sources containing conscious articulations of strategies has made it difficult to differentiate the respective roles and positions of various members in the charting of collective strategies. The use of oral history, however, has enabled us to reconstruct some of the internal dynamics of the family's collective decision-making process. Family collectivity did not necessarily imply mutual deliberation or 'democratic' participation in the process. It is possible that major decisions were imposed by the male head of the family on other members, although there is significant evidence that consultation and bargaining took place between husbands and wives and occasionally between parents and children.

Within nineteenth-century 'patriarchal' family systems, husbands may have officially held a dominant role in charting strategies pertaining to migration and family members' work careers, while wives made major decisions in areas more directly related to their responsibilities. For example, strategies of family limitation were commonly left to the initiative of women, especially at a time when such matters were not discussed openly. Wives also had a major role in deciding whether and when their children, especially their daughters, should go to work. As evidenced in the case of proto-industrial families, wives gained a greater role in family decision making because of their central place in household production.

Although men were considered to be the main breadwinners and were, therefore, expected to make the major economic decisions for the family, women were much closer to the routine management of household resources. Women made the daily decisions regarding the family budget, the allocation of household space, and family consumption. Since the responsibility of feeding and clothing family members was primarily theirs, women were more sensitive to shortages in food and supplies, and they pursued independent strategies to fulfil these basic needs. Strategies governing the care of relatives during critical life situations—childbirth, illness, infirmity, or death—were also primarily in the domain of women. Because women usually had nurturing responsibilities in all these areas, they had the main initiative in managing exchanges with kin. Thus women became the 'kin keepers', who maintained ties with kin over the life course and who held kinship networks together across geographic distances.

The extent to which children had an active role in family decision making has yet to be explored. The decision to send a child into the labour force was primarily, if not entirely, a parental one. Collective family values dictated that children follow their parents' decisions; however, the very dependency of the family on the earnings of children gave the latter considerable manoeuvrability in implementing these decisions. Under certain circumstances, children working and living at home had less latitude or bargaining power with their parents than children who left home to work in other communities. John Gillis found, for example, that mothers in proto-industrial households pressured their children to postpone marriage in order to retain them as workers in the family's collective enterprise. Louise Tilly and Joan Scott, countering Edward Shorter's claim that young women workers in urban areas became 'liberated' from obligations to their families of origin, emphasized the strong continuity of familial obligations for daughters, even for those who had left their rural homes to work in urban areas. Anderson has pointed out, however, that to continue to maintain control over faraway children and keep them more closely tied to the collective family economy, parents had to exercise greater flexibility in bargaining and tolerating these children's preferences, to the extent that they differed from their own.

The multidimensional research effort in family history has produced impressive results and identified new lines of investigation. At a 1986 conference convened to assess the state of research in family history, two interrelated future directions emerged. One is to pursue established topics that have not received sufficient or systematic attention, including the family's relationship to social space and also to religion, the state, and the legal system. Further study of kinship is needed, particularly with regard to friendship, family transitions over the life course, generational relations, especially in the later years of life, and family strategies, especially where the family's interaction with other institutions is concerned. Today, we could add to the list more systematic studies of the 'edges' of family life, such as solitary individuals, orphans and foundlings, and the process of family breakdown through divorce and death. Further research is also needed on the relationship of the family to foodways [the social and cultural construction of the preparation and consumption of food]. A second direction is the forging of more systematic exchanges between interrelated family patterns and processes: these would include a closer linkage of demographic patterns with household structure and internal family dynamics, a closer integration of the study of the household with non-resident kin, and a more careful linkage of kinship and household patterns with various processes such as work and migration. Another significant area to pursue is the linkage of demographic and structural family patterns with cultural dimensions and rituals. . . .

While Stone, like Ariès, has dated the emergence of the modern family in the late seventeenth and early eighteenth centuries, Shorter placed it in the late eighteenth and early nineteenth. Carl Degler dated the emergence of the American modern family in the late eighteenth or early nineteenth centuries as well. Following in Ariès's footsteps, Stone, Shorter, and Degler have focused on the rise of affective individualism as the major criterion of 'modern' family life. They generally agreed that the modern family is privatized, nuclear, domestic, and based on the emotional bonding between husband and wife and between parents and children. The correlates of its emergence were the weakening influence of extended kin, friends, and neighbours on family ties and an isolation of the family from interaction with the community. While there has been general agreement among these scholars on these characteristics, there is some disagreement and, at times, lack of clarity about which class initiated these changes. Ariès, Stone, and, more implicitly, Degler viewed the bourgeoisie and the gentry as the vanguard, while Shorter has assigned a crucial role to peasants and workers. Degler placed the origins of the 'modern' family in the middle class, although he generalized from the experience of that class to the entire society. Not only is there a lack of consensus over the relative importance of ideological or socio-economic causes in long-term changes in the family but also a greater need to know how the changes took place and what the nature of interaction among these different factors was. The 'grand' explanations of change are vulnerable, particularly in some of these studies' claims for linear change over time.

Related to the emergence of the family as a private, intimate entity is the widely accepted interpretation that this transformation was based on the family's surrender of earlier functions. As Demos put it, 'broadly speaking, the history of the family has been a history of contraction and withdrawal; its central theme is the gradual surrender to other institutions of functions that once lay very much within the realm of family responsibility'.

It is still an open question whether the loss of various functions had an impact on the quality of family relationships. The family's surrender of its functions of production, welfare, education, and social control to other institutions and its withdrawal into privacy have become standard clichés of family history and sociology. But the meaning of this generalization has not been fully explored. Did the functions left to the modern family retain the character they had exhibited in the past? To answer this question, we need to understand the process by which these functions were transferred to other institutions. The process has not been documented, however. A systematic exploration of the family's relationship to public agencies and institutions will help historians escape the trap of viewing the family as an isolated institution, completely divested of its earlier public functions. It will reveal areas where even middle-class families ensconced in domesticity retained some of their previous functions and added some new ones. Child rearing is a case in point. The family was already responsible for child rearing prior to becoming a specialized domestic unit. Following the transfer of its various functions to other agencies, the family's patterns of child rearing changed. The family became child-centred and motherhood emerged as a full-time career. Another such example is the family's role in health care. Even though hospitals assumed the major health-care functions once held by the family, the family continued to care for its own members during illnesses that did not justify hospitalization or when such services were not available.

We also need to examine the family's relationship to the institutions of education, welfare, and social control after its functions were transferred to these institutions. Historical studies of the family have generated several models governing this interaction.

The first model, articulated by Demos, emphasizes the family's integration with the community. In pre-industrial society, the family interacted closely with the community and authorities in the areas of education and welfare. The family served the community by maintaining social order, and, conversely, the community regulated family comportment. The family provided simultaneously for its members and the community in a variety of ways: it was a workplace, an educational institution, a house of correction, a welfare institution, and a church.

The second model plots the emergence of the private, domestic family that specializes in child rearing after the functions of welfare and social control have been transferred to other institutions. According to Jacques Donzelot, middle-class families enjoyed considerable privacy from public institutions, but working-class families, particularly the families of the poor, were subject to control and 'policing' by the state and various agencies of social control. Eventually, middle-class families became instruments of the state for controlling and manipulating lower-class families.

The third model, advanced by Christopher Lasch, expands the concept of social control of the family to all classes but uses evidence primarily from the middle-class family. After the family had transferred all its functions to external agencies, it became a 'haven in a heartless world'. Rather than being left alone in its retreat, the family was subjected to interference and control by government, social workers, efficiency experts, and even social scientists. 'Most of the writing on the modern family takes for granted the "isolation" of the nuclear family . . . It assumes that this isolation makes the family impervious to outside influences. In reality, the modern world intrudes at every point and obliterates its privacy. The sanctity of the home is a sham in a world dominated by giant corporations and by the apparatus of mass promotion.'[33]

The models of 'policing' the family proposed by Donzelot and Lasch share a view of the family as a passive entity *vis-à-vis* public agencies and the state. But, as historians of the 1990s return to an interest in the state and public policy as subjects of inquiry, it would be fruitful to re-examine the family's relationship to public agencies and bureaucracies as a dynamic process of interaction. . . .

Nevertheless, even if the family could not be an equal partner, it was by no means a passive agent. For example, Linda Gordon found that, under the worst cases of powerlessness, victims of child abuse and family violence struggled against their caretaking agencies and their abusers to retain control:

Even in the worst times, there were many family violence victims attempting to become the heroes of their own lives . . . Using the powers of the weak . . . attempting to replace with creativity and stubbornness what they lack[ed] in resources, they manipulated every device at their disposal to free themselves from abuse.[34]

A dramatic example of the family's resilience and resistance is its interaction with the most oppressive of all institutions—slavery. In this area, the lasting contribution of Herbert Gutman's work has been to document the vitality of family and kinship ties among slaves and their survival despite the break-up of families by the masters.[35]

Most recent historical studies have emphasized an integrated view of the family both as a private entity and an object of the state. *The History of Private Life*, a multivolume series under the general editorship of Philippe Ariès and Georges Duby, deserves particular comment. The fourth volume, *From the Fires of Revolution to the Great War*, edited by Michelle Perrot, presents the experiential history of the family in its diverse forms. The authors view the family's private life, its domestic life and sexuality, as inseparable from the state. 'The history of private life is more than anecdotal,' wrote Perrot in her introduction, 'It is the political history of everyday life.' Establishing an equilibrium between public and private was a delicate matter. 'The nineteenth century made a desperate effort to stabilize the boundary between public and private by mooring it to the family, with the father as sovereign: but just when things seemed firmly in place, they began to slip and slide.'[35]

A natural extension of the earlier explorations by French scholars, Perrot's volume does not merely use *mentalité* as an explanatory variable but treats it as a subject of investigation in its own right. The study goes beyond the earlier works on roles and attitudes within the family's domestic abode and reaches not only into the family's private life and activities but also into the realm of emotions. Inspired by the 'new cultural history' and by anthropology, this exploration of the internal dynamics of family life exploits an imaginative array of sources, including art, in its effort to reconstruct family rituals and relationships. What makes this ambitious approach particularly valuable is the authors' linking of patterns derived from cultural and literary sources and personal documents with demographic patterns.

It is important to note that privacy in the nineteenth century as documented in this volume does not connote individual privacy. Rather, the authors emphasize the privacy of the family as a collective entity. Ariès's original message runs through the entire script: the family enshrined itself in the privacy of the home and supported its domestic existence with various material props, myths, and rituals. The negative consequences of this process were predictable: the private family isolated its individual members from sociability and from diversity of role models and exercised excessive control over them. This powerful control by the family over the individual led eventually to the 'cries and whispers'—to rebellion and suffering, as expressed in emotional dysfunction, breakdown, impotence, neurasthenia, and psychosomatic diseases in individuals who felt trapped by the family and confused about their social identity. The next historical step was the emancipation of the individual from the oppression of the conformity-seeking private family.[37]

Perrot's and her contributors' emphasis on the family as the creator of its own lifestyle, history, and identity, even of its own documents (letters, for example), emerges as a significant theme in this study—one that historians have not sufficiently addressed. Perrot's characterization of the family contributes to a research agenda: 'The family describes itself, thinks of itself and represents itself as a unified entity maintained by a constant flow of blood, money, sentiments, secrets and memories.'[38] . . .

It is important to link the new dimensions of the family's private and inner life that emanate from the 'new cultural history' with the demographic patterns of household structure, kinship and economic activity reconstructed over the past two and a half decades. One would then be able to interpret the family's inner life in the past in a rich social-structural context.

As further research continues to emerge, it becomes necessary to develop a comprehensive model of change in family behaviour that does justice to its complexity. The main dissatisfaction with the studies of change over time that have emerged in the 1970s has been their linearity and their generalizations for the entire society based on the experience of one class, usually the middle class. The most important dimension still absent from studies of long-term changes in the family involves more systematic distinctions in family patterns and processes of change among different social classes. We need a more detailed understanding of the historical process by which other classes adopted middle-class family behaviour (if, indeed, that was the case) and what class differences have survived such a process. How did patterns of family behaviour that first emerged in the middle class transfer to other classes in society and by what processes? If one rejects simplistic models of a 'trickle down' theory, how did other social classes make their transition from a collective family economy enmeshed in a multiplicity of functions in the household to a domestic, child-centred, private family?

Equally important, at the end of that process, had rural and working-class families really adopted middle-class family forms, or did differences persist underneath apparent similarities? The intense focus on family history in Western Europe and in the United States has left similar questions about Eastern Europe and other parts of the world unanswered. A cursory comparison of changes in the family in the United States and Japan, for instance, suggests how profoundly different internal family relations are in the two societies, even though on the surface the Japanese family seems to be heading in the direction of the American family.

The question about when and how change takes place needs to be asked again. Various strands of change in family history still need to be traced individually, to the point of their culmination as visible transformations. The process is rendered more difficult by the fact that not all the strands undergo change at the same pace. Since the family is not a monolith, different members within it may initiate change or accept change at different points. For example, women were agents of change in certain aspects of family life, such as the introduction of family limitation, while men were innovators in others. Even children were innovators in certain areas. They may have brought literacy into the family, new perceptions of behaviour they learned in school, or new work habits and new technologies. Thus, when we examine the family's role in the process of social change, we need to distinguish the roles of members within the family in interacting with these processes. This is an important task for future decades.

When the historical study of the family first emerged, it drew its vitality and motivation from the need to link discrete family patterns to the community and to the larger processes of social change. That original impetus was shared by the pioneer generation of family historians, and it endowed the historical study of the family with its initial depth and energy. Doing justice to this goal and achieving the proper equilibrium between the reconstruction of time-specific family patterns and their linkage to larger social processes continues to be a major challenge.

## Notes

1 For other discussions of the state of the field, see Hareven, T. K. 1971, 'The history of the family as an interdisciplinary field', *Journal of Interdisciplinary History*, 2, pp. 399–414; Hareven, T. K. 1987, 'Family history at the crossroads', *Journal of Family History* (hereafter *JFH*), 12, pp. ix–xiii; Stone, L. 1981, 'Family history in the 1980s', *Journal of Interdisciplinary History*, 12, pp. 51–7; Tilly, L. A. and Cohen, M. 1982, 'Does the family have a history?', *Social Science History*, 6, pp. 181–99; Tilly, C. 1987, 'Family history and social change', *JFH*, 12, pp. 319–30; Plakans, A. 1986, 'The emergence of a field: twenty years of

European family history', Occasional Paper no. 1, West European Program, The Wilson Center, Washington DC.

2 Hareven, T. K. 1977, 'Family time and historical time', *Daedalus*, 106, pp. 57–70; Elder, G. 1978, 'Family history and the life course', in T. K. Hareven (ed.) *Transitions: the family and the life course in historical perspective*, New York; Elder, G. 1981, 'History and the family: the discovery of complexity', *Journal of Marriage and the Family*, 43, pp. 489–519.

3 Wrigley, E. A. 1977, 'Reflections on the history of the family', *Daedalus*, 106, pp. 71–85; Laslett, P. 1977, 'Characteristics of the western family over time', in P. Laslett (ed.) *Family Life and Illicit Love in Earlier Generations*, Cambridge; Wrigley, E. A. 1972, 'The process of modernization and the Industrial Revolution in England', *Journal of Interdisciplinary History*, 3, pp. 225–9; Goode, W. 1963, *World Revolution and Family Patterns*, New York; Laslett, P. 1972, Introduction, in P. Laslett and R. Wall (eds) *Household and Family in Past Time*, Cambridge, pp. 1–73; Smelser, N. 1959, *Social Change and the Industrial Revolution*, Chicago; Anderson, M. 1979, 'The relevance of family history', *Sociological Review Monograph*, 28, pp. 49–73.

4 Hareven, 'Family time and historical time', pp. 57–70; Stone, 'Family history in the 1980s', pp. 51–7; Hareven, 'Family history at the crossroads', pp. ix–xxiii; Vinovskis, M. 1977, 'From household size to the life course: some observations on recent trends in family history', *American Behavioral Scientist*, 21, pp. 263–87. [ ]

5 Hareven, T. K. and Plakans, A. (eds) 1987, *Family History at the Crossroads*, Princeton, NJ. For bibliographical coverage of the field, see Soliday, G. with Hareven, T. K., Vann, R. and Wheaton, R. (eds) 1980, *History of the Family and Kinship: a select international bibliography*, New York.

6 Ariès, P. 1962, *Centuries of Childhood: a social history of family life*, trans. R. Baldick, New York. On the debate concerning which type of family better prepares children to function in a complex society, see Sennett, R. 1970, *Families against the City: middle-class homes of industrial Chicago, 1872–1890*, Cambridge, Mass. [ ]

7 Laslett, P. 1965, *The World We Have Lost*, London; Laslett, 'Characteristics of the western family over time'; Wrigley, E. A. 1974, 'Fertility strategy for the individual and the group', in C. Tilley (ed.) *Historical Studies in Changing Fertility*, Princeton, NJ, p. 148; Wrigley, 'Reflections on the history of the family'; Wrigley, E. A. 1966, 'Family reconstitution', in P. Laslett et al. (eds) *An Introduction to English Historical Demography*, New York; Wrigley, E. A. and Schofield, R. S. 1981, *The Population History of England, 1541–1871: a reconstruction*, Cambridge; Wrigley, E. A. 1968, 'Mortality in pre-industrial England: the example of Colyton, Devon, over three centuries', *Daedalus*, 97, pp. 546–80.

8 Wrigley, 'Reflections on the history of the family'; Laslett, *The World We Have Lost*; Goubert, P. 1977, 'Family and province: a contribution to the knowledge of family structures in early modern France', *JFH*, 2, pp. 223–36.

9 Hajnal, J. 1965, 'European marriage patterns in perspective', in D. V. Glass and

D. E. C. Eversley (eds) *Population in History*, Chicago, pp. 101–43; Hajnal, J. 1983, 'Two kinds of pre-industrial household formation system', in R. Wall, J. Robin and P. Laslett (eds) *Family Forms in Historic Europe*, Cambridge, pp. 65–104. Recently Hajnal's thesis has been applied to Eastern Europe and to Japan, and there is now a serious question about how unique the model is for Europe and how general it is. Cornell, L. L. 1987, 'Hajnal and the household in Asia: a comparative history of the family in preindustrial Japan, 1600–1870', *JFH*, 12, pp. 143–62. For a reassessment of the Hajnal thesis see 'New perspectives on European marriage in the nineteenth century', a special issue of the *JFH*, 16 (1) 1991.
[ ]

10 Laslett and Wall, *Household and Family in Past Time*; Goode, *World Revolution and Family Patterns*, 6. On household extension following industrialization, see Anderson, M. 1971, *Family Structure in Nineteenth-century Lancashire*, Cambridge.
[ ]

11 Goody, J., 1972 'Evolution of the family', in *Household and Family in Past Time*; Hareven, T. K. 1974, 'The family as process: the historical study of the family circle', *Journal of Social History*, 7, pp. 322–9.

12 Berkner, L. K. 1975, 'The use and misuse of census data for the historical analysis of family structure, *Journal of Interdisciplinary History*, 5, pp. 721–38; Medick, H. 1976, 'The proto-industrial family economy: the structural function of household and family during the transition from peasant society to industrial capitalism', *Social History*, 1–2 (October), p. 295; Wheaton, R. 1975, 'Family and kinship in western Europe: the problem of the joint family household', *Journal of Interdisciplinary History*, 5, pp. 601–28.

13 Greven, P. J. Jr. 1970, *Four Generations: population, land and family in colonial Andover, Massachusetts*, Ithaca, NY, chapters 4, 6.

14 Demos, J. A. 1970, *Little Commonwealth: family life in Plymouth Colony*, New York.

15 Laslett, P. and Harrison, J. 1963, 'Clayworth and Cogenhoe', in *Historical Essays, 1600–1750, presented to David Ogg, H. E. Bell, and R. L. Ollard*, London, pp. 157–84; reprinted in Laslett, *Family Life and Illicit Love*; also in Laslett, *The World We Have Lost*; Demos, *Little Commonwealth*, pp. 124–5.

16 Modell, J. and Hareven, T. K. 1973, 'Urbanization and the malleable household: an examination of boarding and lodging in American families', *Journal of Marriage and the Family*, 35, pp. 467–79.

17 On the classic formulation of the family circle in relation to poverty, see Rowntree, B. S. 1901, *Poverty: a study of town life*, London; Hareven, 'Family as process'.

18 For a critique of the family cycle, see Hareven, T. K. 1978, 'Cycles, courses, and cohorts: reflections on the theoretical and methodological approaches to the historical study of family development', *Journal of Social History*, 12, pp. 97–109; Elder, 'Family history and the life course'.
[ ]

19 Hareven, T. K. 1974, 'Introduction: the historical study of the life course', in *Transitions*, pp. 1–16. The now classic formulation of the life-course approach is

in Elder, G. 1974, *Children of the Great Depression: social change in life experience*, Chicago.

20  Anderson documented the vital role of kinship ties in workers' migration from rural Lancashire and from southern Ireland to the industrial town of Preston: Anderson, *Family Structure in Nineteenth-century Lancashire*; Hareven, T. K. 1978, 'The dynamics of kin in an industrial community', in J. Demos and S. S. Boocock (eds) *Turning Points: historical and sociological essays on the family*, Chicago, pp. 151–82.

21  Fox, R. 1967, *Kinship and Marriage: an anthropological perspective*, London, p. 31.

22  Wheaton, R. 1987, 'Observations on the development of kinship history, 1942–1985', *JFH*, 12; Hareven, T. K. 1982, 'The subjective reconstruction of past lives', in Hareven, T. K. (ed.) *Family Time and Industrial Time: the relationship between the family and work in a New England industrial community*, New York pp. 371–82; For thick description, see Geertz, C. 1973, *The Interpretation of Cultures*, New York; Davis, N. Z. 1977, 'Ghosts, kin, and progeny: some features of family life in early modern France', *Daedalus*, 106, pp. 87–114; Segalen, M. 1986, *Historical Anthropology of the Family*, trans. J. C. Whitehouse, and S. Mathews, Cambridge.

23  Hareven, 'Family time and historical time', pp. 57–70.

24  Hareven, *Family Time and Industrial Time*. William Goode urged the reversal of the stereotype of the family as a passive agent to a view of the family as an active agent in the process of industrialization. He challenged historians to produce the evidence; Goode, *World Revolution and Family Patterns*, pp. 1–18.

25  Hareven, *Family Time and Industrial Time*; Hareven, T. K. and Langenbach, R. 1978, *Amoskeag: life and work in an American factory city*, New York.

26  Braun, R. 1960, *Industrialisierung und Volksleben: die Veränderungen der Lebensformen in einem ländlichen Industriegebiet vor 1800*, Zurich; Mendels, F. 1972, 'Proto-industrialization: the first phase of the industrialization process', *Journal of Economic History*, 32, pp. 241–61 (Mendels coined the term 'proto-industrialization'). Medick, 'Proto-industrial family economy'; Levine, D. 1985, 'Industrialization and the proletarian family in England', *Past and Present*, 6 (May), pp. 168–203; Levine, D. 1977, *Family Formation in an Age of Nascent Capitalism*, New York.

27  Medick, 'Proto-industrial family economy', p. 303.

[ ]

28  Gutmann, M. and Leboutte, R. 1984, 'Rethinking protoindustrialization and family', *Journal of Interdisciplinary History*, 14 (Winter), p. 589.

29  Smelser, *Social Change and the Industrial Revolution*; Tilly, L. A. and Scott, J. W. 1978, *Women, Work, and Family*, New York; Rose, S. O. 1988, 'Proto-industry: women's work and the household economy in the transition to industrial capitalism', *JFH*, 13, pp. 181–93; Scott, J. and Tilly, L. 1975, 'Women's work and family in nineteenth-century Europe', *Comparative Studies in Society and History*, 17, pp. 319–23.

[ ]

30  Thompson, E. P. 1963, *The Making of the English Working Class*, New York, p. 416; Parsons, T. 1955, *Family, Socialization and Interaction Process*, Glencoe, Ill.,

chapter 1; Ogburn, W. F. 1955, *Technology and the Changing Family*, New York; Wirth, L. 1938, 'Urbanism as a way of life', *American Journal of Sociology*, 44 (July), pp. 1–24; Thomas, W. and Znaniecki, F. 1918–20, *The Polish Peasant in Europe and America*, 3 vols, Chicago. The theories of social breakdown were translated into the historical experience by Oscar Handlin in 1951, *The Uprooted*, Boston.

31 Smelser, *Social Change and the Industrial Revolution*; Smelser, N. 1968, 'Sociological history: the Industrial Revolution and the British working class family', in N. Smelser (ed.) *Essays in Sociological Explanation*, New York, p. 34.

32 Anderson, *Family Structure in Nineteenth-century Lancashire*; Hareven, *Family Time and Industrial Time*, pp. 3–4, 85–100.
[ ]

33 Lasch, C. 1977, *Haven in a Heartless World: the family besieged*, New York, p. xvii. [See Jamieson in part II below, pp. 106–27, for a critique of this–Ed.]

34 Gordon, L. 1988, *Heroes of their own Lives: the politics and history of family violence, Boston, 1880–1960*, New York.

35 Gutman, H. 1976, *The Black Family in Slavery and Freedom, 1750–1925*, New York.

36 Perrot, M. (ed.) 1990, *A History of Private Life*, vol. 4, *From the Fires of Revolution to the Great War* trans. A. Goldhammer (Ariès, P. and Duby, G. gen. eds), Cambridge, Mass., p. 669.

37 ibid., pp. 453, 615–49.

38 ibid., p. 131.

# 2

# Biography, Family History and the Analysis of Social Change

*Brian Elliott*

In his book *Historical Sociology* Philip Abrams (1982) urged us to think about sociology and history as essentially the same enterprise. While there are some, particularly in history, who have reservations about this, there are plainly many scholars in both disciplines who, in recent years, have followed his prescription. Within history there has emerged a specialism—social history—that at its best combines the theories and methods of sociology with much of the historian's traditional craft. In sociology a focus upon long-run changes in the development of capitalism or in the processes of state-making, a concern with momentous events like social revolutions, the desire to make temporal rather than, say, cross-cultural comparisons or simply the ambition to set the actions, beliefs, and institutions of particular groups in context has given rise to a distinctive strand of writing—historical sociology. In Britain, as Calhoun (1987) observes, much of the interesting and exciting work which meets Abrams's objectives has been done by the historians but . . . within British sociology there is now a substantial and growing concern with history. The fruitfulness of historical sociology has certainly been well displayed in American sociology, . . . with many writers like Barrington Moore, Theda Skocpol, Tamara Hareven, and Charles Tilly exploring major processes of change, re-examining classic themes from the founding fathers of social science and bringing to bear a diverse array of techniques of investigation.

Tilly has shown, both in his books and articles and in his career, that it is indeed possible to combine the two crafts of history and sociology.

Biography, family history and the analysis of social change
Brian Elliott

From S. Kendrick et al. (eds), *Interpreting the Past, Understanding the Present*, Basingstoke and London, Macmillan, for the British Sociological Association, 1990, pp. 59–82.

And from his vantage point, as someone with a foot in both camps as it were, Tilly has had occasion to reflect upon the relations between the disciplines (Tilly, 1981) and from time to time to offer recommendations for the development of social history and (if we accept that there is no substantial difference in its objectives) of historical sociology. In the special edition of the *Journal of Family History* devoted to 'Family History, Social History and Social Change', for instance, we find him discussing what he sees as the two principal purposes of social history (Tilly, 1987). These he calls 'reconstitution' and 'connection'. Reconstitution is the effort to reconstruct 'a round of life as people lived it'. Connection refers to the attempts to show the links between 'life on the small scale and large social structures and processes'. Plainly, he sees the latter task as the more important for, laudable as much of the former may be, there is always the danger that if '. . . social historians devote themselves chiefly to reconstitution they will produce many bright fragments of dubious comparability and uncertain relationship' (1987, p. 319). . . .

If, then, good social history or good historical sociology involves this constant quest for connection between structures and everyday experience, and if what is required of us is real sensitivity to the ways in which the regularities, patterns, structures are continuously, subtly remade, how should we proceed? What methods and styles of research are needed? Since the task is evidently complex there can be no simple recommendation, no easy promotion, of a narrow range of methods. Recapturing the nature of the social life of peasants or nobility, tracing the impact of economic boom or slump or war or rebellion, describing the growth of states or whole socio-economic systems and the day-to-day adaptations of diverse populations require all the traditional techniques at our disposal. We need to scour the documentary sources, the papers and records of individuals and institutions, the statistical data of governments, churches, and businesses; we need the census and survey, the community studies, and the interviews with the powerful and the powerless. From all of these we may distil an appreciation of the broad regularities and structures; from these we should be able to construct theories and hypotheses of an increasingly refined kind. But in many cases—and the problem is more acute the further back in time we go, or the more we focus on the ordinary or on the poor populations who have left few records of their own making—we find it hard to capture the meanings of the decisions and choices that gave shape to people's lives, and the texture of their social existence. Exploring that 'dialectic' that Abrams referred to is extremely difficult.

However, in those cases where our interest is in relatively recent history, in the past of the last 50 or 60 years or less, then plainly we can, as sociologists or social historians, take advantage of the fact that our subjects (many of them at least) are still alive. Biography and history can be connected through detailed acounts of individual, family, and community life. And research in that vein has, of course, been growing in popularity. The impetus has come partly from those (and they are to be found in both history and sociology) who have been self-consciously developing *oral* history in the last few years—people like Raphael Samuel, Paul Thompson (1980), Trevor Lummis, and others in Britain; and partly from those who rediscovered the value of the life history approach pioneered by William Thomas and Florian Znaniecki (1918–20) and others in the 1920s—people like Norman Denzin, Hareven and Daniel Bertaux.

The advantages of the various oral and biographical styles of work are obvious. To those concerned to write 'history from below', to those who wish to ensure that the voices of ordinary men and women can be heard in the historical record, oral history is indisputably important. Among sociologists, particularly those who, during the 1970s, grew dissatisfied with conventional, **positivistic styles of research** and wanted to develop a more **phenomenological approach**, the collection of detailed life stories had much to offer. Critics of the oral history or life history approaches could, of course, challenge the validity and reliability of data collected in these ways or argue that substantial generalizations were difficult to make given the small-scale, in-depth nature of most investigations. And it would be hard to deny that work in these modes has, in Tilly's terms, produced much more by way of reconstitution than by connection. But it is by no means clear that these 'soft' methods can contribute little beyond description.

Reflecting upon and experimenting with the use of some of these biographical approaches suggests that they may be used very deliberately to explore the connections between major processes of change or great dislocative events and patterns of everyday life, and that they may have an important part to play in the refinement both of methods of research and our theories, hypotheses, and empirical generalizations. The key is to develop what we might call their 'forensic' potential.

## The forensic uses of biographical materials

The word 'forensic' conjures up the courtroom—denotes hard questioning, vigorous cross-examination. Thinking about the collection of life history data, the gathering of family histories, the construction of what Bertaux and Bertaux-Wiame (1986) call 'social genealogies' (or using such data where they are already available) can encourage us to do just that—call into question some of our conventional methods, data,

theories, and hypotheses about what we like to call 'structural change'.
. . . Starting our examination from the biographical perspective can lead
to more radical criticism, can help us to keep the image of social
structures as 'precipitates' of social action in the centre of our field of
vision, and should encourage us constantly to look for the connections
between big changes and the distinctive experiences of particular social
milieux.

The idea of using life history materials in something like this way is
not, of course, original. To take just one recent example: Lynn Jamieson
(see pp. 106–28 below) uses semi-structured interviews dealing with the
early life histories of a sample of elderly men and women in Scotland to
'interrogate', as she puts it, the generalizations and theories contained in
the classic accounts of the emergence of the modern family. Those
classic accounts were built up with the use of diverse demographic
information, census materials, or survey data (some, one would have to
say, were constructed with very little hard historical evidence at all).
Jamieson's collection of **experiential data** challenges commonly held
notions about the timing of changes in family form, about the varieties
of class-specific characteristics of family life, and, most importantly,
about the logical links between changes in economic, occupational, and
other broad features of modern society and the alterations in family life
that allegedly accompanied them. Her experiential data, drawn as they
are from a sample of less than one hundred interviews, cannot
thoroughly disprove theories about the modern family as a 'haven in a
heartless world', about the supposed emotional intensity or child-
centredness of the family; nor can they establish in an entirely
convincing way that important changes in family form and life took place
a good deal later than is frequently argued. But what they can and do
achieve is a radical questioning of the conventional theories and
methods, and in this way they can lead to new questions and more
precise and refined hypotheses.

Biographical materials—family histories, life histories, and social
genealogies—are difficult ones to work with, requiring considerable skill
and patience to collect and even more patience and imagination to
analyse. Transcription of long, tape-recorded sessions is expensive and
time-consuming, and for the researcher there is often a sense of being
overwhelmed by the sheer volume of material and the problems of
selection and interpretation. But their potential in the writing of
'sociology as history', as Abrams calls it, is substantial, and as yet only
partially realized. Among the many ways of employing such data and
developing their 'forensic' qualities those below seem particularly
important.

First, they can be used to trace those connections between major processes of change and the actual experience of specific social groups. There is still an enormous amount to be learned about the impact of what we can think of as the master processes—the development of capitalism and capitalist relations, the growth of industrialism, the spread of urbanization, the business of state-making. These, the central concerns of the founding fathers of social science, are not completed processes but ongoing ones. To be sure, studying the early phases of these processes in Europe takes us back well beyond the experience of any who are alive now, but capitalism, industrialism, urbanism have all altered their character substantially in the old countries where they began. ... In newer countries, in the peripheral regions of the old world, the dislocative effects of the master processes are only now being felt. And many of the most dramatic changes *have* occurred within the life spans of those whose personal or family histories we can collect. If, as is certainly the case, there have been major alterations in the occupational, communal, and family lives of our populations, if a distinctive modern life cycle has emerged, how and when did these changes occur and how can we best describe and analyse them? Evidence from the official sources, the censuses and diverse enquiries of the state, evidence from the market research organizations, commercial pollsters, and others, evidence from sociological surveys and case studies can teach us much, but they do not take us close into the real, lived experience and uncover the intimate dynamics of the social world. But the biographical studies can do that.

Secondly, biographical materials allow us to get beyond the **cross-sectional** quality of most official data and much of the survey evidence—the materials from which, in history and in sociology, we construct our models of changes and our portraits of family forms, life cycles, patterns of mobility, and so forth. Generally, these data do not allow us to trace groups or individuals through time or space. We know that to investigate processes of change we frequently require **longitudinal studies**, but these are technically difficult to manage, expensive, and, in consequence, rare. Biographical materials do not provide thoroughly adequate substitutes but they do take us much closer to the sequences we want to understand.

Thirdly, biographical materials allow us to overcome the overwhelmingly individualistic quality of much of the data we use by revealing the *collective* processes involved in, for instance, getting married, setting up households, getting a job or getting ahead. Thinking about and collecting life histories and family histories lead us to question our individualistic methodology.

Fourthly, . . . in the recounted experiences we hear our respondents recalling not only the facts of their lives but the meaning that events or decisions had for them. We learn about the values and beliefs that guided their actions, the salient ambitions, aspirations, and strategies that influenced them. And these, of course, are not simply *their* beliefs or values but are, in most instances, things derived from and shared with others in a particular milieu. Certainly we need to be cautious, sceptical, and sensitive in our interpretation of these reconstructions of their lives, for frequently they will be shaped by powerful myths embedded not only in their immediate social world but in the wider culture (myths of the self-made man or of the proletarian radical are two that commonly occur), as Jean Peneff (1986) has observed. But difficulties in interpretation notwithstanding, these life stories and family histories do give us an appreciation of the ways in which culture shapes action and how the myriad actions coalesce into the regularities we call structure.

The biographical approach then is rich in possibilities. Its more extensive use can lead to reappraisal and criticism of our methods of studying social change and of the models of change that we have built.

## The biographical approach and the study of social mobility

In order to illustrate more clearly the critical uses to which a biographical approach can be put we can draw upon ideas which Bertaux and Bertaux-Wiame have been developing and upon some preliminary findings from studies that they have conducted. These will be supplemented by some observations that come from essentially similar exploratory investigations that I conducted, initially with no knowledge of their work, but latterly with some deliberate reference to their concerns.

Patterns of social mobility have been extensively studied in sociology and there has been a good deal of work on the same topic by historians too. Such enquiries tend to follow a well-defined set of issues and employ very similar methods of investigation. The main focus is on occupational status changes. The researchers want to know about the rates of movement up and down a prestige hierarchy—sometimes the changes that occur during the course of individuals' working lives, but more often the changes that appear when we compare the occupations of sons with those of their fathers. The data are gathered from sample surveys and relate, of course, to individuals. Within sociology there is no doubt that such studies have long been regarded as important ones for they touch upon matters of profound social and political significance

—the relative openness of a society and the effects of efforts to achieve greater egalitarianism. They are also admired, at least by those with a quantitative bent, for the methodological elegance and sophistication that the best of them display.

But to Bertaux (and he is one who spent his early years as a sociologist working in this particular vineyard) the conventional mobility studies are seriously flawed. Their statistical sophistication, he argues, has far outstripped their real sociological insightfulness and their resolutely individualistic methodology has concealed the fact that mobility processes are far more profoundly social and collective than these studies allow us to see. Moreover, as attempts to look at a major social process, these investigations have an enormous deficiency: they look almost exclusively at men. This criticism has, of course, been made by many writers including, as one would expect, many feminists, but from the perspective of one like Bertaux, who has spent more than a decade encouraging the development and use of biographical methods, there are really two points to be made. Not only should we pay more attention to the rates and routes of mobility for women (as a recent study by Goldthorpe (1987) does) but we need also to explore the possibility that women—mothers especially—may have far more influence on the social mobility of their children than has been supposed. To explore these matters, especially the latter, will require studies of a quite different kind: of a biographical kind.

Life histories and other biographical materials, which are often rich in details about status ambitions and mobility, serve then to sharpen criticism of the conventional studies and underscore their methodological and conceptual shortcomings. If we think about social mobility on the basis of our own experience or that of groups and families and individuals we know well—if we start, that is, with an immediately familiar kind of biographical perspective—we are led to ask some questions that really challenge the commonplace sociological enquiries.

The Bertauxs begin by asking 'Who gets ahead? Individuals or whole sets of siblings?' (Bertaux and Bertaux-Wiame, 1986). The possibility that sets of brothers and sisters may have rather similar educations, may find themselves in occupations of broadly similar status levels, that in the marriage patterns the principle of homogamy is powerful, that a group of siblings may find themselves, in maturity, moving in rather similar social worlds—all that is intuitively appealing. Which is not to deny that we can think of counter-instances, of the case where one of the siblings became, say, a doctor while the others became routine white-collar or even manual workers. But the question is how common is it for whole sets of siblings to follow similar social trajectories? And where there are sharp differences among groups of brothers and sisters we can ask if these too are patterned. Do older siblings do particularly well or badly? Are there constraints in particular milieux that might influence this? Very quickly we are led to a new curiosity about the *process* of mobility, about the complex of social factors that may come into play. The design of the usual mobility studies rules out the exploration of all but a very limited number of these.

Thinking about factors that may influence the mobility prospects of groups of siblings leads to the recognition that these are of at least two broad kinds. There are 'external' factors like the structure of job opportunities and the buoyancy or depressed nature of local, regional, or national economies at particular points in time. Conventional studies do, of course, pay attention to these. They do so especially when they address the question of widespread shifts in the nature of the occupational structures and seek to take out their effects when measuring rates of mobility. And no doubt the current investigations of regional economies being carried out in the several Social Change and Economic Life projects in the UK will tell us more about these kinds of external factors. But there are plainly *other* influences that in a rather crude way we can think of as 'internal' ones. The Bertauxs suggest that there are distinctive 'microclimates' in families, cultural constellations that may encourage or inhibit social mobility or steer it along particular pathways. Certainly there seem to be major differences between families in terms of the kinds of projects and aspirations (and the specificity of these) that parents and perhaps other family members establish for the younger generation.

What we really need to know is what is transmitted to the young from within the family. Particular, describable attitudes and aspirations. Rooted in what? Religious commitments or perhaps special experiences of parents. Describing cultural transmissions is peculiarly difficult, but placed side by side the accounts that I have gathered leave no doubt that stark differences exist. . . .

Material transmission, of course, matters enormously—the wherewithal to support youngsters in their studies, money to buy private education, funds to support diverse lifestyles, property and capital assets to start a business—all have substantial effects.

Cultural transmissions, material transmissions—but there is also another kind that might simply be labelled 'social'. Parents invoke social ties, sometimes those of kinship but often looser ones to acquaintances made through business or leisure, in the process of helping their offspring to find colleges to go to or jobs to take. Life history and family history accounts focused on mobility seem to contain much that attests to the strength of those 'weak ties' that Granovetter (1973) drew to our attention.

If social mobility is really more of a family affair than we have so far shown in our sociological and historical studies, what role do women play in all of this? Do mothers do more than fathers to establish the Bertauxs' microclimate of the family? Is this a feature of certain social groups—the traditional working class in the UK, Jewish immigrant communities? Literary as well as sociological accounts suggest that this issue would certainly bear systematic investigation.

And what about other family members? The Bertauxs (1988) suggest that grandparents may play important roles in ensuring the advancement or at least the maintenance of the status positions of their grandchildren. Since more and more people live to see their grandchildren grow to maturity, transmission across three generations becomes a matter of more and more interest. As yet we know little about this.

There are ties too between older and younger siblings that are important. In some families we find older siblings supporting younger ones, assisting them with funds for education and social contacts that are of value in obtaining work. Sibling bonds seem especially significant in the process of migration, with elder siblings (usually males), acting as pioneers in the move from country to town, from region to region or indeed from country to country. Once established they sponsor brothers, sisters, parents, and other family members in making those moves in space that so often are the preconditions for changes, improvements, in economic and social fortunes. If we are to explore some of the links between geographical and social mobility we find in these accounts of family histories much evidence of kinship bonds as the 'auspices' of migration—to use a term employed in a paper written a good many years ago (Tilly and Brown, 1967).

Biographical materials then remind us or reveal for us the real complexity of social mobility. They force us to think not just about upward mobility but about those lateral moves across changing occupational structures and, as the Bertauxs insist, they make us recognize that simply maintaining social status, preventing downward movement, is a matter of interest not just to individuals but to wider social groups. Not just individual but family resources of the most diverse kind are mobilized in the struggle to offset illness, divorce, job loss and the host of eventualities that can threaten some sections or members of a family with social demotion. For most individuals, for most families, long-range mobility is rare. The common experience is a struggle to maintain respectability, to hang on to those things that guarantee a measure of comfort and security in an uncertain world.

These then are some of the issues thrown into sharp relief by accounts which describe the actual experiences of social change as they are recollected by family members. If we wish to gather biographical materials that provide useful data we can, as the Bertauxs suggest (1986, 1988), use several slightly different methods. We can collect individual life histories; we can by talking to several family members try to piece together a family history; or we can have our respondents construct a social genealogy—that is, a family tree on which is recorded a number of salient details about, for instance, education, jobs and careers, geographical moves of individuals. In the very limited, strictly exploratory kind of investigations that I have conducted the social genealogy was the most useful device. I began by asking each student to interview his or her parents and to record information about the two sets of grandparents—the countries, regions, and communities they were born in, the size and composition of the households of origin, principal occupations, geographical mobility. Similar information was then gathered for the parents—the nature of the families, economies, cultures, and communities in which they grew up, and then some data on the families and households they had established and the places in which they lived. Students were also asked to look for evidence of the impact on their families' lives of major social changes—the big events like wars, revolutions, depressions, and booms, and the more gradual shifts in occupational structures, patterns of educational opportunity, and the growth of the welfare state. The prime purpose, of course, was to get them to explore the relationships between biography and history. Most of them seemed to enjoy this exercise and in the end it achieved its main objective admirably. Discussion of broad structural changes suddenly took on real life when they could begin to trace the ways in which their grandparents and parents were part of history, the ways their lives had been affected by, say, the depression of the 1930s, a world war, revolutions in China and South-east Asia, or the new opportunities in education or jobs. Summarizing data on family size and household composition revealed major changes across the generations; information about geographical moves uncovered their families' parts in the process of urbanization. Didactically the very modest enquiry had highly rewarding effects, and small group discussions in which students described to each other their family profiles produced an interesting social effect in breaking down somewhat the anonymity and isolation of the learning experience in a class of 70.

Many weeks later I asked each student to read the Bertauxs' paper and consider the central hypothesis that social mobility was not so much an individual as a family affair. They then went back to the original social genealogies and refined these by collecting more detailed information on at least two branches of their family. (Most commonly they compared their own immediate family with that established by one of the siblings of their parents.) They then wrote essays appraising the strengths and weaknesses of the Bertauxs' approach (comparing it with a brief summary of a conventional mobility study) and considering the validity of the main hypothesis by cautious use of their own data.

The results were fascinating. A few rejected the biographical approach and defended the conventional style of research on various methodological grounds or by reference to social genealogies which seemed to show that social mobility *was* very much an individual matter. But the great majority found reasons to support the idea that social mobility does seem to be patterned at the level of the family.

The significance of the 'external' factors, the economic and social contexts in which families lived, emerged frequently and vividly as the students contrasted the educational and occupational trajectories of groups of siblings—those in the families that had stayed in the small towns of the prairies, say, with those who had moved to a large and rapidly growing city like Vancouver. Many in the class came from India, China, and other parts of South-east Asia, and for them the differences between their lives and those of their siblings were set against the experiences of and prospects for their cousins living still in very much less industrialized or still colonial social structures.

'Internal' factors—the cultural 'microclimates' of families—were sometimes brilliantly described, as in the cases in which students came from staunchly Protestant families within which strict codes of self-denial, hard work, and long-term educational and occupational projects were very deliberately enjoined. Many (though certainly not all) of those from Chinese backgrounds wrote about the discipline, application, and ambition that characterized their upbringing. There were discernible class-related differences in the cultural transmissions to whole sets of siblings, and in a few cases the real reasons behind parents' ambition for their children were revealed in moving ways. The clearest exploration of the roots, the real meaning of a family ethos, was provided by a Japanese Canadian student whose construction of the social genealogy had evidently prompted lengthy discussion of the family history and the revelation of much that had rarely been disclosed before. During the Second World War the Canadian government interned families of Japanese descent. Canadian citizens, Japanese Canadians, were shipped off to camps remote from the main centres of population. Families were split up, many privations endured, and when hostilities ceased there were government efforts to prevent these families from returning to British Columbia, from where most of them came. They were instructed to seek work 'east of the Rockies'. Worst of all, they lost all their property—their farms, fishing boats, and homes. The father of the student explained his own determination not just to acquire an education but to excel at university. Skills and qualifications were the only thing 'they couldn't take away from you'. Both mother and father in this case had experienced the internment and all the injustice that went with it. Small wonder then that in this family there was a strong emphasis on educational and occupational success!

About the role of women in the process of mobility it would be difficult to generalize with confidence from such a limited exercise, but there certainly seemed to be support for the idea that in the majority of families the mother's aspirations and ambitions for the children were more clearly articulated, more substantial than those of the father. The most definite exceptions to this were interesting. They seemed to be found either in farming families or in very wealthy families. Both of these might be seen as instances where productive property is most evidently and exclusively in the father's hands and where, certainly in the case of farmers, it will be transmitted principally along the male line. More detailed analysis of the deviant cases might prove instructive, but these should not distract us from what I think is the more important possibility: that mothers, and maybe grandmothers, for whom the family is still the principal focus of activity and responsibility, play a most important role in maintaining or advancing social status. One of the essays offered what seems like an unhoped for natural experiment on this theme. A Chinese Canadian student described her paternal grandfather, born in Shanghai in the early years of the century, as a wealthy merchant and a 'very traditional' Chinaman. He was poly-gamous. His three wives, though none from poor families, came from somewhat different backgrounds. Each bore two or three children and, while the evidence leaves much to be desired, it appeared that the offspring of the different mothers had distinctive social trajectories. The values of each mother, it seemed, patterned the lives of her children in discernible ways. (To test the proposition that mothers have more influence than fathers, hold father constant, vary wives!)

Finally, in this necessarily brief account, it is perhaps worth recording that the data gathered from the students at the University of British Columbia offered some support for a finding that Bertaux made in his early exploration of these matters, which he conducted at the University of Laval in Quebec. Among his respondents there were many from farm families, and the social genealogies and family histories they constructed suggested that birth order affected mobility patterns in a particular way. Eldest sons tended to stay at home to work on the farm (presumably with the expectation of inheriting it) rather than pursuing qualifications and seeking social mobility through a non-farm career. Younger siblings then received more education in these families and were more likely to display upward or lateral mobility. There were relatively fewer from farm backgrounds in the Vancouver group, but among those who did come from such families a similar pattern was evident.

Overall, of course, these little experimental investigations cannot provide us with confident generalizations, but one can legitimately say that they do encourage us to think about an important process in new ways.

## The biographical approach and the study of the modern life cycle

In his paper 'What is new about the modern family?' [see pp. 67–90] Michael Anderson describes and analyses major changes in the patterns of birth and death, of marriage and child-bearing from the early eighteenth century to the 1970s. Throughout he is addressing a number of key questions: 'How did the life cycle change and when did a distinctive modern pattern appear?', 'What factors brought about these changes?', and 'What were the wider social implications of these changes?' . . .

Anderson provides us with an interesting and important set of findings and ideas but, like all efforts to build good general inter-pretations of social change, they invite, indeed they deserve, criticism and refinement. His analysis is based upon a variety of official data—censuses, Household Surveys and the like—and it is certainly possible to question and qualify his research in its own terms, using essentially similar methods and data. An obvious step would be to disaggregate the data on key variables so that we could examine more closely the patterns for different social classes and other broad groupings. In practice this is not easy to do since most of the officially produced demographic data in Britain are not presented in ways that allow this. One requires access to the original materials and then has to make a special study. If we were to try to explore Anderson's idea about the 'fragility' of the modern life cycle and to assess the impact of recent changes in state policy we would confront the same problem, and it would be compounded by the fact that, as part of the Conservative government's effort to reduce public expenditures, there has been some attenuation of the gathering and publication of official statistics. All of which underlines Tilly's point about the irony that in trying to examine the links between big structures and individual experience we are very often dependent upon information from those very structures—in this case the state—whose influence we want to measure (Tilly, 1987, p. 323). Those who control the state tell us what they want us to know. They do not necessarily tell us what *we* want to know and, on occasion, as in recent years in Britain, they may go to some lengths to suppress information that might lead to genuinely critical appraisal of policies. With all these limitations and difficulties though, it is still possible to examine more closely Anderson's main arguments using data similar to his own.

However, if our goal is to establish the connections between broad structural changes and the actual experiences of groups and individuals we could usefully approach Anderson's findings about life-cycle changes not only by refining the statistical data; we could do so too by gathering and using biographical materials. Indeed, the need to do this is evident if we consider that he refers explicitly to life *experience*, yet experiential data are precisely what his account lacks. It is a deficiency which is entirely understandable where he is dealing with those who lived in the eighteenth and nineteenth centuries, but clearly it could be supplied for those who have lived through and whose experiences constitute the changes in which he is most interested: the relatively recent changes that give form to this specifically 'modern' life cycle. Family histories and social genealogies can be employed to give vital detail to those connections between aggregate birth, death, divorce, and other rates and the real lives of men and women, and at the same time they can be employed in a questioning, critical, 'forensic' way.

We could begin by considering the fact that while the life-cycle patterns for various groups of the population may show 'convergence' they do not display **synchronous change**. Within the aggregate regularities we know there are some significant differences. The shift towards the modern life cycle did not occur at the same time for, say, different classes. For example, the move towards two-child families occurred later for working-class than for middle-class groups. Kendrick et al. in their analysis of Scottish demographic data (1984) (and in recent times Scotland's demography has not been much different from that of England and Wales) show this clearly. As late as the 1950s and 1960s mean family size for Social Class I mothers (those married to professional and managerial men) was two while for those in the Registrar General's Social Class V (unskilled workers) it was three. More detailed information on the incidence of large families (more than four children) shows wide class differences persisting into the 1960s. The move towards the small, two-child family occurred as late as the 1970s for the working class. Similarly, ages at marriage also reveal class differentiated trends. Roughly, we can say that in the 1950s and 1960s the working class led the way towards earlier marriage, while in the 1970s and 1980s middle-class women pioneered a trend towards later marriage.

The point is that the *contexts* within which these kinds of demographic changes occurred were obviously different. Family histories and social genealogies provide not only evidence of these changes, as they record the varying numbers of offspring or different ages of marriage in successive generations, but they allow us to grasp something of the social, economic and historical settings in which they occurred. Anderson's analysis tells us about aggregate patterns at particular points in time. Using biographical materials moves us closer to the kind of life-course analysis outlined by Hareven (1978) and Glen Elder (1985), in which we can compare the transitions in family form and life-cycle experience across different social groups. In the family histories we learn how cumulative experiences of family life, of work, of community, shape decisions. We find ourselves once more, as with the social mobility instances, looking at not only external, structural constraints that help people's lives but also at cultural factors—at those aspects of the 'microclimate' of families—that help to establish conventions, plans, and aspirations. This time they attach to marriage, to child-bearing and child-rearing, to setting up house, to the desirability or necessity of women working outside the home, of having a career or a particular standard of living.

In his paper Anderson stresses the relative stability, predictability, and regularity of the modern life cycle compared with life cycles in earlier periods. His focus is on what, on average, people can expect. But life history and family history accounts reveal how, for some sections of the population—particularly the poorer ones—life is still full of uncertainty. Family histories collected by Straw (1985), for instance, contained frequent reference to the impact of illness, injury, and premature death among a working-class population, reflecting both the remembered misfortunes of those in the older generations and also the continuing inequalities of health (which current medical statistics corroborate). Employment prospects and experiences too, of course, show very substantial differences across the population if we disaggregate by class, gender, or ethnicity, and these too are starkly displayed in life and family histories.

Biographical methods then serve to qualify in important ways Anderson's observations about the relative predictability and security of the modern life cycle. To be sure, death, particularly the death of young children, is much less common today than was the case, say, in Victorian Britain. But what we see in the experiential accounts is evidence of the fact that such security as was attained by the working class, and especially by the poorest sections of that class, was reached only very recently and any trends towards more stability or predictability in the life cycle are by no means certain to continue.

Indeed, in the family histories currently being collected we shall surely see proof not just of persisting class-based differences but also of *divergencies.* Anderson's speculations about the 'fragility' of the modern life cycle will be borne out as we gather more information on the many families whose members, particularly young members, have lived through the years of the late 1970s and the 1980s in Britain. These were the years during which unemployment reached levels not seen since the 1930s and youth unemployment in some parts of the inner cities or other deprived areas reached 60, 70, and even 80 per cent. Elder wrote (1974) about the children of the Great Depression and while conditions in Britain in the early 1980s were not so bleak, the poverty not so abject or widespread, still the effects of recession will be deep and lasting and, like the crises of the 1930s, will mark a generation. The neo-conservative market-oriented policies have had a profound impact on the poorer sections of the community, not only through their effects on jobs but also through the reductions in the value of state-provided benefits for those who are workless and needy. Housing policies too have created terrible problems as prices have soared and public sector house building programmes have come almost to a halt. Homelessness is once again the plight of many thousands. Homelessness, joblessness: two conditions which are bound to have consequences for the modern life cycle, for they will prevent the establishment of independent households, will mean deferred marriages and, later perhaps, smaller families. If state policies during much of the post-war period contributed a good deal to the making of a distinctive modern life cycle, those of the years since 1979 have surely done much to undermine these trends of 'convergence', 'homogenization', and growing 'predictability'. Officially generated statistics will tell us something about that, but the fullest appreciation will come from data of another kind: from those that offer detailed experiential accounts. Family histories will give us a strong sense of what it has been like to live in a society that has become markedly more divided, more inegalitarian.

## Conclusion

Studies of the modern life cycle then, like studies of social mobility or accounts of changing family forms, can benefit greatly from the use of biographical approaches. These techniques offer more than mere description, more indeed than their original proponents, the Chicago School sociologists, foresaw. Clifford Shaw (1945), Edwin Sutherland (1937), Thomas and Znaniecki (1918–20) and others used life histories in illuminating but still relatively conservative ways to complement investigations of urban life, of crime, of migration and other processes: investigations carried out in essentially positivistic frameworks. The biographical accounts enriched the understanding of social processes but they were not employed seriously to challenge the methods, theories, and epistemology of the early sociology.

The claims made for the biographical approach by some of those who have engineered its recent revival are altogether larger. Franco Ferrarotti, for example, describes how his early interest in collecting life histories merely as 'background' for his studies of industrialization and technical change has developed to the point where he now sees biography as restoring a full appreciation of subjective meaning and providing 'a means of access—often the only possible one to the scientific knowledge of a social system' (1983, p. 67). Drawing upon Sartre, he argues that

> When we are dealing with the consideration of human practice, only dialectical reason allows us scientifically to understand an action, to reconstruct the processes which make behaviour the active synthesis of a social system, and to interpret the objectivity in a fragment of social history by starting from the non-evaded subjectivity of an individual history. Only dialectical reason allows us to attain the universal and the general (society) by emphasising the individual and the singular (man). (1983, p. 73)

The new enthusiasm for the biographical approach and the recent growth of historical sociology can be seen then as intersecting in some interesting ways. In both we find ourselves exploring the manner in which individuals simultaneously constitute and are constituted by society. In both we are encouraged constantly to move from the unique, particular experience of individuals or groups to the regularities that allow us to identify broad patterns of change. In this constant toing and froing we must, says Ferrarotti 'identify the most important spaces, those which serve as pivots between structures and individuals, the social field where the singularizing practice of man and the universaliz-ing effort of a social system confront each other most directly' (1983, p. 76).

Those 'pivots' are found in small primary groups, in peer groups at work, or in neighbourhoods, but above all in the family. And if that is true, then we can extend our biographical enterprises so that we collect not just personal biographies, but collective biographies—which is, of course, precisely what the Bertauxs recommend in their attempts to look afresh at social mobility processes.

Sociologists' reawakened interest in history, not only in a specialism called 'historical sociology' but more generally in writing 'sociology as history', raises inevitably all the old questions about how as sociologists or as historians we can recover the past. Paul Rock's comments (which reflect the impact of phenomenology or sociology in the 1970s) throw the familiar difficulties into sharp relief:

As mediator and creator of order, the historian produces a particular kind of description whose coherence and plausibility flow from his techniques of reconstructing that everyday reality. He can know the past, but the content and form of any knowledge he acquires are finally shaped by his **existential relationship** with the dead. The dead are not available to him, he cannot converse with them: he can know them only through fragmented and partial records. He cannot survey them as he would a contemporary, observing the detail of gesture, tone, expression and position. He cannot question them. He cannot assume any community of context of experience to unite him with the dead. (Rock, 1976 p. 354)

Pressing this kind of argument to its logical conclusion, Rock argues that 'subjective worlds are irrevocably inaccessible to the historian' (1976, p. 358) and therefore the whole historiographic enterprise is absurd. But to most historians and sociologists that would seem too extreme. Both historical and sociological description and explanation, as Rock suggests, rest upon assumptions that the past leaves imprints, residues, that are discoverable in the present, that between the dead and those alive today there is at least some coincidence of common-sense understandings and that there is some broad similarity of social forms. There are certainly 'great regions of experience and happenings that can never be recovered. Only a skeletal portrait of the past is possible' (1976, p. 367) but, with all its limitations, that portrait is worth painting.

When we reflect upon these difficulties of reconstruction and connection it is surely the case that, at least as far as the recent past is concerned, biography does offer a way of recapturing events and their meanings. Not only sociologists but historians too can interrogate men and women who have lived through periods of momentous change, whose actions and beliefs constituted (and constitute) major transformations which we need to know about. We can question them (and note all the nuances of speech, gesture, and expression) and (though we still require circumspection) we can assume some community of experience with them.

There are many alive today whose lives span the greater part of the twentieth century—a period of profound change with its revolutions and wars, its periods of rapid economic growth and others of depression and recession. These years (and these people) have seen the rise and fall of empires, global processes of industrialization and urbanization, transformations in the position of women in many countries, major demographic changes and great changes in the role of the state. Even if we take only the last 10 or 15 years and look, say, at what has been happening in just one country, Britain, we find much that we could usefully explore. We would be looking at a country that has experienced a rapid decline in political and economic power, a major recession and a government intent on transforming its economic, social and political arrangements. To examine such a country and such changes we need social history and historical sociology. And in both specialisms we require approaches that will take us close to the lived experience of all classes and generations, approaches that will enable us 'to understand how transformation at the national and local levels are experienced within families and neighbourhoods. Few foci of research are likely to be more practical or potentially more intellectually creative' (Smith, 1982, p. 297).

### References

Abrams, P. 1982. *Historical Sociology*, Ithaca, New York, Cornell University Press.
Bertaux, D. 1981. *Biography and Society*, Beverly Hills, Sage.
Bertaux, D. and Bertaux-Wiame, I. 1986. 'Families and social mobility', paper delivered to XIth World Congress of Sociology, New Delhi.
Bertaux, D. and Bertaux-Wiame, I. 1988. 'Le Patrimoine et sa lignée: transmissions et mobilité sociale sur cinq générations', *Life Stories/Récits de vie*, 4, pp. 8–26.
Calhoun, C. 1987. 'History and sociology in Britain', *Comparative Studies in Society and History*, 29 (3), pp. 615–25.
Denzin, N. 1978. *The Research Act: a theoretical introduction to sociological methods*, New York, McGraw-Hill.
Elder, G. H. Jr. 1974. *Children of the Great Depression*, Chicago, University of Chicago Press.
Elder, G. H. Jr. (ed.) 1985. *Life Course Dynamics: trajectories and transitions, 1968–80*, Ithaca, New York, Cornell University Press.
Ferrarotti, F. 1983. 'Biography and the social sciences', *Social Research*, 50 (1), pp. 57–79.
Goldthorpe, J. H. 1987. *Social Mobility and Class Structure in Britain*, Oxford, Clarendon Press.
Granovetter, M. S. 1973. 'The strength of weak ties', *American Journal of Sociology*, 78, pp. 1360–80.
Hareven, T. 1978. *Transitions: the family and the life course in historical perspective*, New York, Academic Press.
Hareven, T. 1982. *Family Time and Industrial Time*, Cambridge, Cambridge University Press.
Kendrick, S., Bechhofer, F. and McCrone, D. 1984. 'Recent trends in fertility differentials in Scotland', in H. Jones (ed.) *Population Change in Contemporary Scotland*, Norwich, Geo. Books.
Moore, B. Jr. 1968. *Social Origins of Dictatorship and Democracy: lord and peasant in the making of the modern world*, Boston, Beacon Press.
Peneff, J. 1986. 'Le Myth dans l'histoire de vie', unpublished paper, Université de Nantes.
Rock, P. 1976. 'Some problems of interpretive historiography', *British Journal of Sociology*, 27 (3), pp. 353–69.

Shaw, C. 1945. *The Jackroller*, Chicago, University of Chicago Press.

Skocpol, T. 1979. *States and Social Revolutions*, New York, Cambridge University Press.

Smith, D. 1982. 'Social history and sociology—more than just good friends', *Sociological Review*, 30 (2), pp. 286–308.

Straw, P. 1985. 'Times of their lives: a century of working class women', Ph.D. thesis, University of Edinburgh.

Sutherland, E. 1937. *The Professional Thief*, Chicago, Chicago University Press.

Thomas, W. I. and Znaniecki, F. 1918–20. *The Polish Peasant in Europe and America*, vols 1–5, New York, Knopf.

Thompson, P. 1980. *The Voice of the Past: oral history*, Oxford, Oxford University Press. [First published 1978.]

Tilly, C. 1981. *As Sociology Meets History*, New York, Academic Press.

Tilly, C. 1987. 'Family history, social history and social change', *Journal of Family History*, 12 (1–3), pp. 319–30.

Tilly, C. and Brown, C. H. 1967. 'On uprooting, kinship and the auspices of migration', *International Journal of Comparative Studies*, September, pp. 139–64.

# PART II

# THE FAMILY, PAST AND PRESENT

# 3

# What is New about the
# Modern Family?

*Michael Anderson*

The image of the family of the past which implicitly underlay most sociological writing as late as the early 1960s—and which still seems to inform most popular thinking about the topic—contrasted the 'modern' family with a very different past. It was a past full of affectively close and stable families, in which uncontrolled fertility produced large numbers of children within marriage (while strong morality inhibited their birth outside it), a past in which the population lived in large and complex households, set in stable communities and surrounded by large numbers of close and more distant relatives. These notions were given a considerable boost by the community studies of the 1950s, which discovered, living in 'urban villages', what came to be called 'traditional working-class communities', populations characterized by stability, large families, and apparently close and functional relationships within a wider kin circle dominated by and centred on 'Mum' (for summaries see, for example, Frankenberg, 1966; Klein, 1965). It was easy to believe that these areas were relics of a more widespread older style of life, one very different from what were seen as today's isolated, small, readily disrupted, and conflict-ridden families, living out their private lives in isolation from any close and meaningful wider social relationships. Intuitively, and by a superficial reading of a few selected nineteenth-century texts, it was easy to assume that 'industrialization' (or its vaguer associate 'modernization') was ultimately responsible for the change.

## The myth examined

Research over the past 20 years has significantly modified at least the academic if not the popular view of the past. It is clear that indus-

What is new about the modern family?
Michael Anderson

From *The Family* 31, 1983, pp. 2–16.

trialization as such cannot have been primarily responsible for many of the most salient features of the modern family if only because many of the most significant 'new' features are a product of the twentieth century (and some are, for much of the population, really a feature of the period after 1945). The 'traditional working-class communities' are now perhaps best seen as in part a function of a bogus stability produced by **sampling without replacement** and by relying too strongly on a few 'key' informants; and in part they were the result of a particular combination of economic and demographic conditions, which probably only really emerged in limited areas of the country in the late nineteenth century and which were already disappearing when first 'discovered' by the sociologists of the 1950s (Young and Willmott, 1973).

As far as the older myths are concerned, however hard we look, the stable community in which most of the population grew up and grew old together, living out their whole lives in one place, seems to have been very rare in most if not all of non-highland Britain at least since medieval times (Clark, 1979; Laslett, 1977, chapter 5). As for the nineteenth century, work on a national sample from the 1851 Census of Great Britain suggests that well under half of the whole population was living in the place where they had been born, that around two-fifths had moved from their places of birth by the time they were 15 and that one child in every six had been geographically mobile by the time of his or her second birthday. Perhaps even more interestingly, the migration behaviour of urban populations looks remarkably similar to that of those living in rural areas—though the proportion of the population who were long-distance migrants was rather larger in the towns (Anderson, 1985). With these rates of population turnover, the likelihood that people would have had many relatives living in the same village as themselves was quite low right into the twentieth century—even if they had the living relatives to live near, a point to which I shall return below. Contrary to the popular view it was in the twentieth century that rent restriction, council housing and a fall in population growth rates produced in many areas more stable communities than had probably been found for hundreds of years. Much pre-twentieth-century migration was, of course, of relatively short distance (even in the towns around half of all migrants had come from within the same county or less than 50 kilometres from their birthplaces); in a walking society, however, a distance of even 8 kilometres was the equivalent in journey times of 30 to 80 kilometres today and no mail service in the past was in any way a substitute for the telephone on which so many longer distance migrants today rely for much of their kin contact (Hubert, 1965).

The possibility of keeping in touch with kin and childhood associates is clearly, then, at least as good today as in the past. And volumes of research have over the past 20 years been devoted to demonstrating the widespread extent and functional importance of relationships with kin in the modern world (Bell, 1968; Shanas and Streib, 1965). In parallel with this, the work of the SSRC Cambridge Group for the History of Population and Social Structure has effectively exploded the myth of the large and complex household of the past. One set of estimates suggests that in 1970 the mean household size in England was 2.9, with the mean nuclear family size being 2.8. At around the same date about 8 per cent of households contained relatives outside the conjugal family group, at an average of about 0.1 persons per household (Wall, 1983), and around 4 per cent of households contained three or more generations. For the period 1650–1749 work on household listings suggests a mean conjugal group of around 3.4 though the mean household size once servants and other residents are included was around 4.4. At the same period, there were roughly 0.2 relatives per household (Wall, 1983, chapters 1 and 16); for the early modern period as a whole around 10 per cent of households contained kin (Laslett and Wall, 1972, chapter 4). Size and complexity seem to have risen a little during the eighteenth century and preliminary estimates from my own work on the mid-nineteenth century suggest a mean household size of 4.6, with a mean conjugal group of 3.7. Some 19 per cent of urban households and 27 per cent of households in rural areas contained relatives; there were 0.3 relatives on average per household and 8 per cent contained three or more generations.

In terms of residence patterns, then, as far as relatives were concerned the picture for the more distant past looks not unlike today's. The period of industrialization, seen by earlier scholars as a process highly disruptive of family relationships, seems to be emerging as a period when in residential terms—and indeed also in some other ways —kinship relationships may actually have been of rather more (and indeed of not inconsiderable) social significance; at least in some areas of the country mass migration, female employment outside the home in textiles, shortage of housing, and rising wage levels seem, in the absence of any effective welfare support, to have placed considerable functions on to kinship relations and to have accentuated especially relationships between married children and their parents (Anderson, 1971). But this should not be seen as supporting another popular myth: the notion that people in the past regularly and unquestioningly took care of aged relatives. The modern practice of placing the aged in institutions is not new: in 1906 almost 6 per cent of the population aged 65 and over were living in Poor Law institutions; in 1966 1.9 per cent were living in homes for the aged, 1.7 per cent in hospitals, and 0.9 per cent in psychiatric institutions, an overall figure of 4.4 per cent. Right back into the early nineteenth century and beyond it is clear that the aged normally depended on poor relief for their support and that large numbers were in institutional care. Overall, the evidence would strongly suggest that the aged were only likely to live with, and be supported by, relatives where either they had property, which gave them power over their relatives' future living standards, or where they could be useful, for example in child care, or where their support was heavily subsidized by charity or by poor relief (Anderson, 1977).

More generally, considerable doubt has in recent years been cast on the notion of the family of the past as a warm and altruistic institution. In some areas there seems evidence of a distinct calculative streak in relations between kin; one contemporary drew an analogy with attitudes to investment in a joint stock company. Some scholars have even gone so far as to argue that in Europe before the later eighteenth century little love and affection as we would know it existed in relations even between spouses and between parents and children (Shorter, 1976). This extreme view has been somewhat dubiously countered by references to contemporary literature and drama and rather more effectively by reference to working-class autobiographies (Vincent, 1981). Nevertheless, it would surely be hard on the basis of present evidence to sustain an argument that people were on average more affectionate towards their children or that children had a higher priority in the everyday lives of families than they have today.

One other point may be drawn from the household data just referred to: the small number of children found in the average home. For the period 1650–1749 the average household contained just 1.8 offspring of the head, a figure to be compared with the 2.0 of the 1851 Census sample and 1.1 of the 1970 sample. In part this reflects the fact that children left home earlier in the past (a point explored in a later section) but it also reminds us of two other things.

Firstly the figure is relatively low because family sizes in the past were seldom as large as is often popularly believed and the main reason for this, as John Hajnal pointed out (1965), is the relatively delayed marriage pattern characteristic not merely of Britain but of most of Western Europe. In fact, median ages at first marriage for women were not perhaps quite as high as is sometimes believed; recent estimates suggest a cyclical pattern over the past 300 years with high points at around age 25 in the later seventeenth and early twentieth century marriage cohorts and low points of around 22 in the early nineteenth and 21 in the mid-twentieth century marriage cohorts (see Appendix). Fluctuations of this kind were of considerable demographic significance producing at the margin very considerable changes in rates of

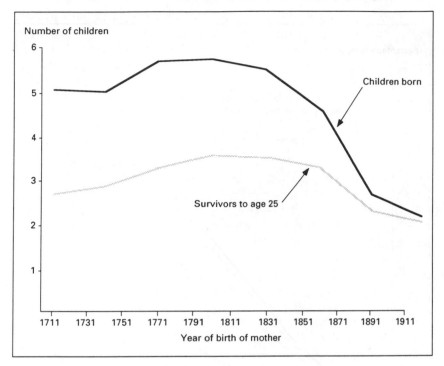

**Figure 3.1** Mean completed family size and number of survivors, by year of birth of mother, England and Wales from 1711 to 1911

population growth (Wrigley and Schofield, 1981), but for the historian of the family it is the relative constancy up to the late nineteenth century in numbers of children born that is perhaps of more interest (see figure 3.1; the Appendix gives details of calculations).

Even more significant, however, if we are trying to picture changes in the experiences of growing up, is the fact (also shown in figure 3.1) that pre-twentieth-century levels of infant and child mortality (to the implications of which I shall return more fully below) reduced the numbers surviving between generations to a much more constant figure peaking at only 3.59 in the 1801 maternal birth cohort and remaining at a high level for a considerable time in spite of the onset of the nineteenth-century fertility decline. While completed family sizes in the past were clearly larger than at present, the number of children surviving to become kin of the next generation or alive in a household at any time can clearly be exaggerated.

Another topic of considerable concern today, which also looks less characteristically modern if seen from a long-run historical perspective,

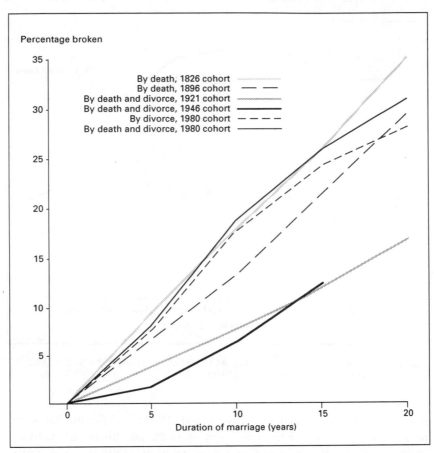

**Figure 3.2** Percentage of marriages broken, against duration of marriage, for various marriage cohorts, with projections for 1980 cohort, England and Wales

is marital dissolution and its effects on children. Figure 3.2 shows, for five different marriage cohorts, estimates of the percentage of marriages broken by death and/or divorce at 5, 10, 15, and 20 years' marital duration. The 1980 curve assumes current levels of break-up, the remainder are calculated from estimated cohort life tables combined where appropriate with published figures (see Appendix for details). Clearly, comparing the earlier twentieth-century marriage cohorts with the present reveals a marked increase in disruption through marital break-up of the lives of both adults and children (though once death is included the differences are perhaps less marked than some would have expected). But the earlier nineteenth-century marriage cohorts show current patterns in a very different light. For pre-twentieth-century marriages, at most marriage durations marital break-up rates closely paralleled modern ones (and, given that death in the past was probably largely independent of parenthood status while divorce is significantly correlated with childlessness, the proportion of children affected must have been considerably higher right through the nineteenth century and earlier). The problem of marital break-up is not, then, new; but we view it against a historical background where it was temporarily lower and we lack so far the institutions and attitudes which were available in the past to handle what was clearly, statistically, an equally or even more serious problem.

Finally, the myth of a new level of immorality in modern society is also one which needs handling with some care (at least if, as is frequently done today, we fall into the trap of using rates of behaviour as indicators of underlying values). Even at the high levels reached since 1960, the illegitimate birth rate was little if at all higher than in the mid-Victorian period; the recent rise in the rate (from an early 1960s figure at about the mid-nineteenth-century level) is clearly much more a function of the drop in legitimate fertility than it is a reflection of a collapse of family life. Few communities even today can match the level of illegitimate births of 19.3 per cent recorded for three inland Banffshire parishes in 1861–5 (Smout, 1976). And while we know that the percentage of couples engaging in premarital sex with their eventual spouses had reached 67 per cent even for the relatively staid group who married at ages 25–29 in the early 1970s (and it had exceeded 60 per cent for those marrying under 20 some ten years earlier) (OPCS, 1978), the modern figures have to be seen in a somewhat different long-run perspective when we note that in the early nineteenth century around 60 per cent of women bearing their first child seem to have conceived that child out of wedlock (Laslett, 1980). Again, the more recent past—when premarital sex was clearly somewhat less frequent—should not be taken as a guide to what may have happened in an earlier society.

## Some salient features of the modern family

I have so far suggested that many elements of the popular view of the family of the past are false. We should not, however, as some authors recently have tended to, conclude that there is a timelessness about modern familial patterns, that as it is now so has it always been.

Clearly the most marked—and the most easily measurable—changes have their roots in the demographic trends revealed in figures 3.3 and 3.4, the sources and methods of computation of which are briefly described in the Appendix. The high rates of infant and childhood death (the 1891 cohort being the first where three-quarters of those

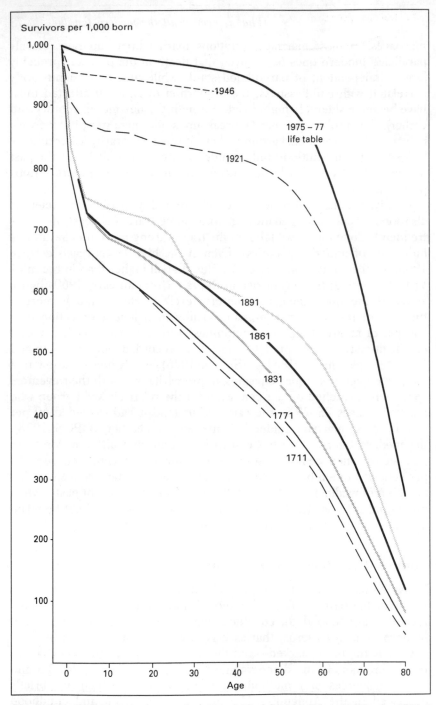

**Figure 3.3** Male survivors, by age, for various birth cohorts, with a projection for 1975–7 cohort, England and Wales

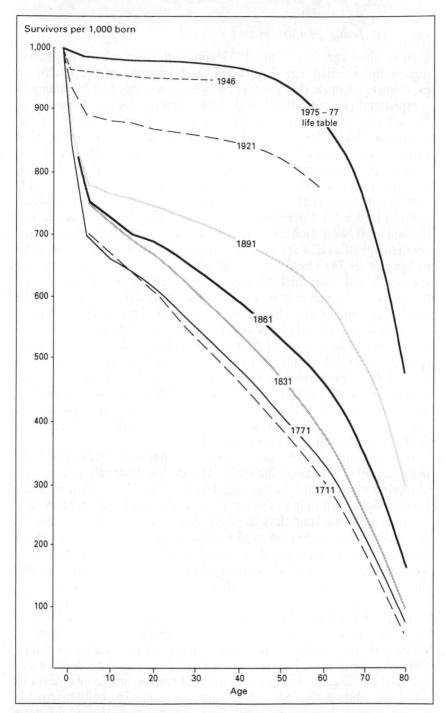

**Figure 3.4** Female survivors, by age for various birth cohorts, with a projection for 1975–7 cohort, England and Wales

born reached age 5, and the 1831 cohort the first where more than three-fifths reached age 25) clearly had impacts on the childhood experiences of those that survived, which we are only just beginning to comprehend (Vincent, 1981), and more arguably may also have limited the amount of affection that parents were willing to invest on any individual child. The impact of the continuingly high levels of adult mortality has already been noted in terms of their impact in marital break-up; put another way, it was only in the early 1770s that half of any marriage cohort could have even celebrated a silver wedding. At that date about 2 per cent of children were total orphans (had lost both parents) by age 10, 4 per cent by age 15, and 12 per cent by age 25 (for methods of calculation see Appendix). The approximate estimated **median** age of a child at the death of his or her father was 32 and of his or her mother 34. These figures did not change markedly over the next century. A child born in 1861 stood a 1 per cent chance of orphanhood by age 10 and 6 per cent by age 25, with father dying when he or she was 35 and mother when he or she was 36. But of the 'median' children of the 1921 cohorts only 2 per cent lost both parents by age 25 and such a child would have been 41 by the time father died and 47 when the mother died. Of the cohort born in 1946, about 1 per cent could expect to have lost one parent by age 25 and the median child of the first generation, a majority of which has an expectation of inheriting a substantial sum (as a result of the spread of owner-occupancy in the twentieth century), has to wait until age 45 for death of father, 53 for death of mother and 56 for death of both.

But it is not only changes in mortality that have transformed the demography of the family life cycle. The decline in family size and the clustering of children into the earlier years of marriage, both of which became significant only in the last years of the nineteenth century (and later for many working-class families), have been equally important. In figure 3.5 I have attempted to plot some of the more significant of the consequential changes as they would have been experienced by a women who herself and whose family had first and last children at, and died at, the median ages (for further details see the Appendix).

A number of points may be noted. The age of such a woman at the marriage of her last child has fallen over the period described by some 13 years and her age at the birth of her last grandchild by about 22 years; both these falls occurred almost entirely in the twentieth century. Over the same period a 'median woman's' age at the death of her husband has risen by around 12 years and her age at her own death by 14. Thus, while in the 1681 cohort such a woman's last child married in the same year that her husband died and she herself died 13 years before the birth of her last grandchild, women in the 1861 cohort could

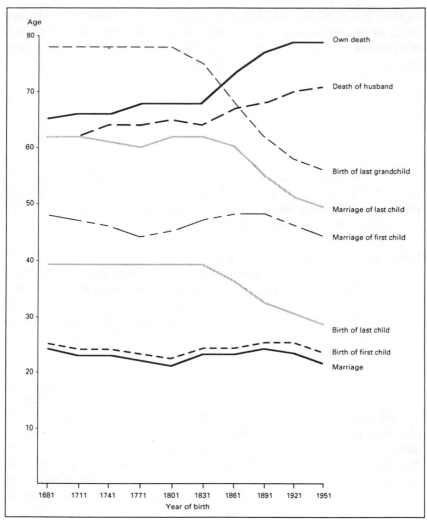

**Figure 3.5** Life courses of women whose vital events took place at median ages, by birth cohort, with projections for 1951 cohort, England and Wales

expect their husbands to live about seven years after the marriage of their last child and the women themselves to live five years beyond the birth of their last grandchild. The 1861 birth cohort, the grandparents of the interwar period, was the first of my cohorts in which a majority would know all their grandchildren. Subsequent events are equally dramatic. Even men can now expect, on the assumptions made here, to live some 14 years after the birth of their last grandchild and women can expect another 23 years of life; this is just long enough on average to see all their grandchildren married if they marry at the median age. Modern levels of life expectancy give a woman around 30 years of life after the marriage of her last child, compared with just three for the 1681 cohort and only six for the cohort born in the early 1830s.

The implication of these estimates for the likelihood of knowing and of relating to particular kin are considerable but they have, more speculatively, other possible implications. Whereas my 'typical' 1946 cohort woman will have some 17 years between the birth of her last child and the birth of her first grandchild, years in which she is likely to seek to follow the increasing post-war trend of returning to work once the family is established, a similar woman born in the 1860s had only 13 years and a woman born in 1831 only nine. In a very real sense for earlier generations it was possible to conceive of spending one's whole life caring first for one's own children and then, if they were accessible, helping in the care of one's children's children; and this was the pattern found in the 'traditional working-class communities', areas where this older demographic pattern continued for somewhat longer and where low mobility meant that children's children were frequently accessible. Thus, women growing old in the later nineteenth and earlier twentieth centuries did so at a period of life during which their own children were themselves child-bearing. A very real possibility of reciprocity (grandchild-care by grandparents, parent-care by children) could occur. As late as the 1861 cohort, for my 'median' families, the last grandchild reached the age of five in the same year that his or her maternal grandmother died. But the trends of the twentieth century have changed all that. Increasingly in the 1960s and 1970s, women, free of their own childcare responsibilities by their forties, returned to work, and worked right through the period when their grandchildren were born. And now that they themselves are entering old age, with around 20 more years to live, they find that their own children have in turn had their families and returned to work. The possibilities of reciprocity of the kind found in 'traditional working-class communities', which were surely in part encouraged by early twentieth-century demography, have now disappeared (compare with Rosser and Harris, 1965). Interestingly, however, this pattern of behaviour had itself been a relatively short-lived phenomenon. Whereas in the 1861 cohort the last grandchild reached age five in the year that his or her grandmother died, in the 1681 cohort the grandmother would have died 13 years before such a child was born, a pattern which changed little before the 1861 cohort. The possibility and need for a three-generation system of child and grandparental care was, before the later nineteenth century, much less present.

One other point may be noted. The 1921 cohort now entering old age will have had, on my estimates, about 2.1 children, on average, who will reach age 25. Women in this cohort can expect to live 14 years past age 65 giving a ratio of survival years to children alive of 6.7. By contrast, the 1831 cohort had some 3.5 children reaching age 25 and a median life expectancy of only eight years, a ratio of only 2.3. Therefore, not only has the demographic basis of the relationship changed, but the burden falling on each child has risen considerably. The possible policy relevance of these changes should not be ignored.

To simplify both the computation and the description I have up to this point assumed that the population as a whole behaved like my 'median' families; but this is clearly wrong. As figures 3.3 and 3.4 showed, a person's likelihood of dying in any year of childhood or of young to middle-aged adulthood was much higher before 1900 than it is today (and somewhat higher even in the earlier part of the twentieth century). The 1861 cohort was the first of my estimated cohorts in which half of all men reaching 25 could expect to live to 65, and as late as the 1831 cohort more than one in six of all children aged five could expect to die before the age of 25. Contemporary comment (Vincent, 1981) confirms an expectation that this would lead to a sense of insecurity, uncertainty, and reluctance to plan for the future among much of the population. This general sense of uncertainty, however, seems to have characterized many other areas of family life.

For example, figure 3.6 shows the percentage of the female population never married (by single years), derived from the published censuses for 1911 and 1971 and from preliminary estimates from the 1851 Census National Sample. The pattern for 1971 is clearly very different from that for 1911 and 1851. Not merely were overall levels of eventual marriage higher in 1971 but the rate of entry into marriage in the 20–29 age-group was much more rapid. If we eliminate the never-marrying population at the minimum figure for each census and treat the cross-section data as if they related to a cohort so as to estimate transition rates, it appears that the interquartile range (between the age at which one-quarter and three-quarters of the group were married) was just four years in the early 1970s, compared with eight years in 1911 and nine in 1851. The central 80 per cent of the distribution covered just eight years (from 17 to 25) in the 1971 data but 17 years in 1911 and 20 in 1851. The delayed entry into matrimony in the past can also be seen if one notes the rough estimates that more than 2 per cent of the single population married in 1971 at all ages between 16 and 32 compared with more than 2 per cent at all ages between 18 and 45 in 1851. More than 5 per cent of the single men married over a period of 14 years in the 1971 data (not illustrated here) compared with 24 per cent in the 1851 data, and over 2 per cent over a period of 16 years

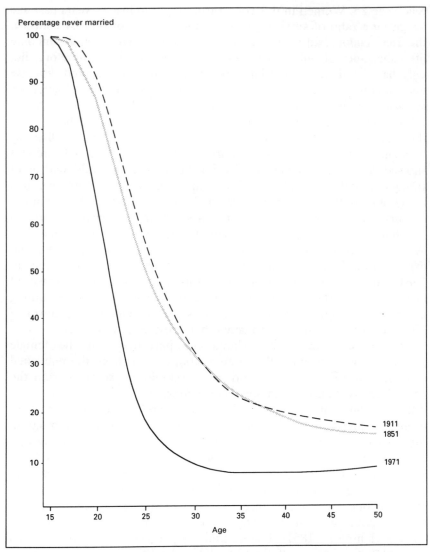

**Figure 3.6**  Percentage of females never married, by age, for the whole population at various census dates, England and Wales

compared with a period of 30 years; however, over these lengths of time some inaccuracy is introduced by genuine cohort effects . . . Nevertheless, the data seem robust enough to suggest that in a very real sense in the 1970s there was a right age to marry, in a way which was not found in any period before the Second World War (for the 1851/1911 pattern remains very little changed right up to and including the 1931 census but is clearly different by 1951).

Equally, in the nineteenth century and earlier, the passage between childhood status and household headship was statistically and probably culturally a much more protracted one. Figure 3.7, using the 1851 Census sample contrasted with **GHS** data for 1979, shows the percentages of the male population who were not living as offspring of the head and of those who were living as heads of households. Even allowing for **sampling error** the differences are clear.

At age 17 in 1979, almost all were still living in households headed by a parent and none were heads. (There is a small bias here since the GHS data do not include institutions, but the effect is very small.) By age 24 almost three-quarters had left home and almost 70 per cent were heads. By age 30 over 90 per cent had left home and around 90 per cent were heads. The average age gap between leaving home and entering headship was one year.

The mid-nineteenth-century pattern was quite different, much less rapid and much more tentative. Roughly 10 per cent of children at all ages from birth to early teens were separated from their parents. These residentially parentless individuals were mostly living with kin; some were undoubtedly orphans, others separated from parents by migration, others probably lessening overcrowding or keeping a sole person company or providing domestic services. From age ten onwards, however, the proportion who had left home rose rapidly. By age 25 over three-quarters of boys were no longer at home but under half were household heads. Indeed 30 per cent or more of boys between 17 and 27 were neither 'children' nor heads of households. At the peak age of 20 some 49 per cent of boys and 46 per cent of girls were in this 'intermediate' residential status. And even in their early thirties under three-quarters of men were heading households of their own (and not much more than 80 per cent at any age). This does not mean that at these ages only 75–80 per cent of men had *ever* headed their own households, for one aspect of this nineteenth-century pattern was a tendency, clear from autobiographical data, for people to move into and out of lodgings, as the uncertainties of employment, of frequent migration, and of demographic accident affected familial composition and the standard of living.

What all this seems to suggest is that another important new characteristic of family life—indeed of all life—in the years after the Second World War was its greater age-gradedness and predictability. A young person aged, say, 14, looking forward in the 1960s, could, with a reasonable probability of being right, have predicted within a very few years the timing of his or her future life course—leaving school,

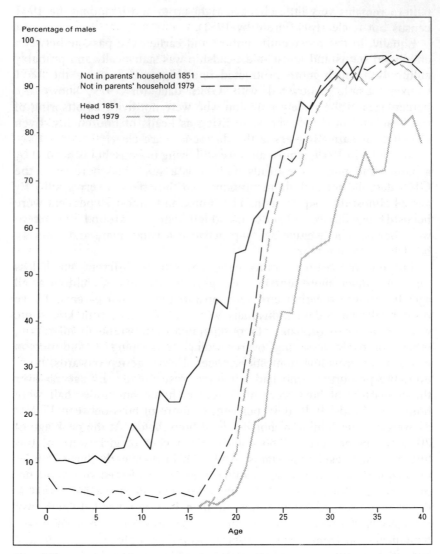

Percentage of males

Not in parents' household 1851 ————
Not in parents' household 1979 — — —

Head 1851 ᨨᨨᨨᨨ
Head 1979 ᨨᨨ  ᨨᨨ  ᨨᨨ

Age

**Figure 3.7**  Male residence patterns, by age, based on samples from the 1851 Census and the 1979 General Household Survey, Great Britain

entering employment, leaving home, marrying and setting up home, early patterns of child-bearing and rearing. None of this would have been possible in the nineteenth century; much would still have been difficult before 1945. Possibly we are again returning to a situation of much greater diversity of experience. Whatever the trends, an increased ability to 'plan' one's family life seems a feature of society over the past 30 years, and it may be not unimportant in allowing certain lifestyles to develop, in providing a stable basis for family formation, and even in increasing a willingness to behave in a more 'altruistic' way towards friends and kin (Anderson, 1971). It may perhaps even be one of many factors producing the instability of modern married life; how many people on marrying consciously realize that 'till death do us part' is now likely to mean, even on average, 45 years? And that it may mean 45 years in which shorter working hours and the ideology of 'private' family life will force the couple to spend more 'leisure' time together than ever before, supposedly 'having fun' and 'being happy together'?

But the data on residence patterns just referred to also point to another connected set of 'new' features of family life. The 49 per cent of boys and 46 per cent of girls aged 20 and over who were living in 1851 in houses other than those of their parents were living in an 'in-between' status which has now all but disappeared. In 1851 between one-fifth and one-quarter were living with kin, nearly one-third of the boys and one-fifth of the girls as lodgers, one-fifth of the boys as apprentices and living-in shopmen and journeymen, and the rest as servants. Some 21 per cent of all women aged 21 (27 per cent of all single women of that age) were living as domestic servants; there were some male domestic servants but above all boy servants were living-in farm servants—farm service as late as 1851 was still absorbing about 9 per cent of all boys, urban and rural together, in the 15–19 age-group.

This pattern of young men and women leaving home and going into service went right back into the early modern period, and it went into rapid decline from the late nineteenth century. But while it lasted it took young people away from their parents at what was by today's standards an early age; in spite of all the contemporary allegations to the contrary about the disruptive effect of industrialization on children's relations with their parents, it was in fact in the industrial areas that children stayed at home the longest. The pattern of leaving home early was also the most important reason why so many houses had 'extra' members beyond the conjugal family group. While it is wrong to see the households of the past as full of relatives, many contained other persons beyond the conjugal family. In all, in 1851 some 42 per cent of households had one or more additional persons resident on census night (38 per cent if visitors are excluded).

And these extra persons reduced considerably the possibility of the family achieving another characteristic which may be seen as a significant feature of 'modern' family life: privacy for the marital and familial life of the members of the primary residential unit. But it was not only these extra individuals that were important in this connection;

the small size of most homes, the crowding—for the mass of the population—of the whole family into one or two rooms, the sharing of beds not merely by couples and by children but by couples with children, and sometimes even with lodgers or servants as well, all these were equally constraining to personal and sexual privacy. Even the higher social classes, before the architectural revolution of the eighteenth century with its introduction of corridors, had little protection from the eyes and ears of servants and other family members; some scholars, indeed, have gone so far as to argue that privacy was actually seen as undesirable (Flandrin, 1979). Others have pointed to the intrusion of business into the households of even the most affluent, right up until the end of the eighteenth century (Davidoff and Hall, 1983). Among the poor it was much, much later before the household's living space ceased to be, for many, cluttered by the operations of mother's work. The home as a haven from the perils of the world is usually seen, probably rightly, as a nineteenth-century invention though—as some scholars have recently noted—the very group who most praised that ideal were at the same time beginning to devise new ways to control working-class family behaviour by authorizing legal intrusions into their homes and legal controls over their parental behaviour (for example see Donzelot, 1979).

There is one further area which we have already touched on but which merits further discussion as another possible characteristic feature of the modern family: the changing nature of the family as an economic unit. While it is easy to romanticize the family of the past as one in which each contributed in work of one kind or another what he or she could, and all shared in the rewards that might or might not ensue, there is an important element of truth in this picture. Before the educational and technical reforms of the later nineteenth century there were many opportunities for children to contribute to the family economy from an early age; true, the figures of employment which emerge from the **census enumerators' books** seem to show many children unemployed, but this seems to be because many of the activities engaged in by women and children were of a casual and irregular kind—and, in addition, it is clear that at least in some areas the prejudices of the enumerators (or fear of these prejudices among their respondents) led to considerable underenumeration of married women's employment outside the home. The rise of factory textile work with its employment opportunities for women and older children probably conceals a steady decline from the later eighteenth century right up to the Second World War in the full-time employment of women outside the home and in the job opportunities available to younger children. Enclosure of pastures and the use of improved techniques (both reducing the need for children to herd and watch animals), the rising pressure to reduce male dependence on Poor Relief (with as its corollary the reduction of women's employment), the disappearance of domestic spinning, as well as the triumph among the middle classes of ideologies which would place women as the guardians of the home and would see children as tender little plants needing careful nurturing in early life—all served to undermine employment opportunities. And enclosure, restrictions on gleaning and reduced opportunities for it, 'tidier' farming, the attack on poaching, and reduced provision of labourers' smallholdings all restricted women's and children's involvement in the 'foraging' economy in rural areas (Snell, 1987). But in urban areas right to the end of the nineteenth century (if not later) a lively domestic and foraging economy continued, with working-class children filling a whole series of minor service and production niches in the urban economy: carrying, watching, hawking, scrounging, and pilfering (Meacham, 1977). Meanwhile, their mothers stretched their families' incomes not only by careful (and by modern standards enormously time-consuming) housekeeping and purchasing and preparation of food but also by exploiting the opportunities for secondhand or free goods (often including free meals for their children) available through charities and public works (Samuel, 1981). Often, for part of the life cycle, family income was supplemented by taking in lodgers as well. In a very real sense, even when the family did not work together as part of a single producing organization, a productive interdependence existed within the family economy whereby the resources contributed by wage earners (that is, not only the father but also those children who did not leave home and who often in poorer families contributed most of their incomes to the family economy) were complemented by the resources input by the other (in census terms not employed but nevertheless active and essential) members of the household. The interdependence was vital; for both practical and moral reasons it was also often very constraining, limiting freedom to leave home, to marry, or, especially for girls, even to disobey (Thompson, 1975, chapter 5).

Increasingly, however, this pattern was undermined—by technology, which reduced the need for children's employment, and by education and employment legislation, which prohibited it (and indeed which offered to children new visions, new social circles, and new opportunities which they increasingly experienced independently of parental control or even knowledge). In the 1970s only a few years passed between children ceasing education and entering marriages of their own; increasingly, rising living standards and a desire by parents to try to maintain some contact with their children's lives meant that the children's contribution to household resources was minimal even during their unmarried working lives (Millward, 1968; Barker, 1972). While politicians increasingly urged parents to control their children more closely—part of a myth that in the past they had always succeeded in doing so—parents of teenagers had fewer and fewer usable material or cultural means of doing so. Shorter working hours, the increasing percentage of the population living in large cities, and the ready availability of transport out of the local neighbourhood allowed adolescent children (and indeed to some extent their parents too) much more freedom from familial and neighbourhood observation; in a very real sense family members could lead segmented lives, one part secret from another (Anderson, 1979). While long-term sanctions in terms of control over life chances through inheritance had already started to decay in the eighteenth century (though some parents were still able to get their children jobs well into the twentieth), the ability to use short-term sanctions was by the nineteenth increasingly undermined by child protection legislation and by an increasingly pervasive ideology of personal rights and freedoms (Harris, 1974; Anderson, 1979). As for their parents, the products of the enormous consumer durable and food processing industries have allowed, for much of the population, the pursuit by adults of much more independent lifestyles than was ever possible before the Second World War; at its extreme, the potentially conflicting careers of the 'dual-career' family have in many cases made work a source not of cohesive interdependence but of familial disruption.

There is one final point. It would be quite wrong to see the pre-twentieth-century family as one governed totally by collectivism and the need to survive, just as it would be wrong to see the modern family as one governed only by individualism and the pursuit of happiness. But a more stable economic position (and, in general, a more predictable environment) plus a rising emphasis on individual rights at a societal level do seem to have been associated, especially perhaps in the years after the Second World War, with some shift of emphasis towards a family system providing a context for the pursuit of the personal happiness and achievement of its members as a prime goal (Morgan, 1975; Anderson, 1979). Whether this, and indeed many other 'new' features of family life which I have referred to here, will go into reverse in the future for substantial sections of the population only time will tell. The greater stability of the period since the Second World War has, I have argued, been important in underpinning changes in familial patterns and also in producing a greater homogeneity of familial experiences than we have known before. But both could easily change in the harsher, more uncertain, and more diversified economy that we can expect in the 1980s—and the resultant changes would by no means necessarily be for the better.

## Appendix

The data illustrated in figures 3.1–3.5 are preliminary estimates prepared as part of a larger exercise designed to review the wider social consequences of demographic changes in Britain, 1750–1950. Further details, including more information on the methods of calculation and any corrections required in the light of further work, is reported in Anderson (1992). The estimates refer to England up to the mid-nineteenth century and to England and Wales thereafter. All the calculations have been done on a cohort basis, starting with the cohort born in 1681 and repeated for cohorts born at 30-year intervals. The first stage has been to calculate the cohort survival tables, some of which are graphed in figures 3.3 and 3.4. Up to 1871 these take as their starting point the life tables produced for five-year intervals by Wrigley and Schofield (1981) as part of their work of reconstructing English population for the period 1541 to 1871; I am grateful to the authors for providing me with copies of these life tables. The Wrigley and Schofield life tables are for both sexes combined; the sex-specific tables required for the present exercise were produced using as weightings the sex differentials of the Third English Life Table up to age 55 and thereafter the differentials of Coale and Demeny **Model North level 10 Life Table**. After 1871 the Registrar Generals' successive English Life Tables have been used, except that for the 1891 male cohort wartime mortality has been separately estimated from Winter (1976).

Figures 3.1, 3.2 and 3.5 are all derived from estimates which apply **binomial probability** to the survival table results so as to produce joint survival rates; there is an element of inaccuracy here but not enough to vitiate the results. The completed family size estimates of figure 3.1 are derived with suitable adjustments for nuptiality and illegitimacy from the **GRR** estimates of Wrigley and Schofield (1981) and of Wrigley (1969). The present-day mortality and divorce figures graphed in figure 3.2 are taken from Haskey (1983), the earlier divorce figures from Rowntree and Carrier (1958) updated approximately for the 1946 cohort from the annual Statistical Reviews.

The data graphed in figure 3.5 are estimates of the life course of individuals whose vital events and those of their children and grandchildren took place at the median age for the cohorts to which they respectively belonged. It is assumed in the calculations that first and last children survived to marriage and married, and that husbands survived at least to the birth of their last child. A large number of different sources were examined in the production of the timing of marriage and of childbirth estimates, the figures given here being 'best guesses', particularly for the earlier period. Small errors in these figures would not affect the overall argument pursued here. The pre-1831 marriage age data are estimated from Wrigley (1981) and Levine (1977) and thereafter from various sources, including Crafts (1978) and OPCS (1983, table 3.5).

The data used in figure 3.7 are taken from a one-sixteenth sub-sample of the 2 per cent National Sample from the enumerators' books of the 1851 Census. After weighting, the number of cases in the whole sample is 23,628. The data were collected with assistance from the SSRC. The General Household Survey data relate to 1979, the total sample used being 34,121 cases. For both data sets, the number of individuals of each sex for each single year of age (the base for the percentages graphed in the figure) is in excess of 200. The GHS is conducted by the Social Survey Division of OPCS, to whom I am grateful for access to the data.

## References

Anderson, M. 1971. *Family Structure in Nineteenth Century Lancashire*, Cambridge University Press.
Anderson, M. 1977. 'The impact on the family relationships of the elderly of changes since Victorian times in Government income maintenance provision', in E. Shanas and M. B. Sussman (eds) *Family, Bureaucracy and the Elderly*, Durham, NC, Duke University Press.
Anderson, M. 1979. 'The relevance of family history', in C. C. Harris (ed.) *The Sociology of the Family: new directions for Britain*, Sociological Review Monograph, no. 28.
Anderson, M. 1985. 'Urban migration in Victorian Britain: problems of assimilation?' in E. François (ed.) *Immigration et société urbaine en Europe occidentale, XVI$^e$–XX$^e$ siècle*, Paris, Recherche sur les civilisations.
Anderson, M. 1992. 'Changing patterns of household and demography: the social significance', in F. M. L. Thompson (ed.) *The Cambridge Social History of Britain*, Cambridge University Press.
Barker, D. 1972. 'Young people and their homes: spoiling and keeping close in a South Wales town', *Sociological Review*, new series, XX (4), pp. 569–90.
Bell, C. 1968. *Middle Class Families*, Routledge & Kegan Paul.
Clark, P. 1979. 'Migration in England during the late seventeenth and early eighteenth centuries', *Past and Present*, 83, pp. 57–90.
Crafts, N. F. R. 1978. 'Average age at first marriage for women in mid-nineteenth century England and Wales', *Population Studies*, XXXII (1), pp. 21–5.
Davidoff, L. and Hall, C. 1983. 'The architecture of public and private life', in A. Sutcliffe and D. Fraser (eds) *The Pursuit of Urban History*, Edward Arnold.
DHSS. 1974. *The Family and Society: dimensions of parenthood*, HMSO.
Donzelot, J. 1979. *The Policing of Families*, Hutchinson.
Flandrin, J. 1979. *Families in Former Times*, Cambridge University Press.
Frankenberg, R. 1966. *Communities in Britain*, Penguin.

Hajnal, J. 1965. 'European marriage patterns in perspective', in D. Glass and D. E. C. Eversly (eds) *Population in History*, Edward Arnold.

Harris, C. C. 1974. 'Parenthood: a theoretical view from the standpoint of a sociologist', in DHSS, *The Family and Society: dimensions of parenthood.*

Haskey, J. 1983. 'Children of divorcing couples', *Population Trends*, 31, pp. 20–6, HMSO.

Hubert, J. 1965. 'Kinship and geographical mobility in a sample from a London middle class area', *International Journal of Comparative Sociology*, VI, pp. 61–80.

Klein, J. 1965. *Samples from English Cultures*, Routledge & Kegan Paul.

Laslett, T. P. R. 1977. *Family Life and Illicit Love in Earlier Generations*, Cambridge University Press.

Laslett, T. P. R. 1980. *Bastardy and its Comparative History*, Cambridge University Press.

Laslett, T. P. R. and Wall, R. 1972. *Household and Family in Past Time*, Cambridge University Press.

Levine, D. 1977. *Family Formation in an Age of Nascent Capitalism*, Academic Press.

Meacham, S. 1977. *A Life Apart*, Thames Hudson.

Millward, N. 1968. 'Family status and behaviour at work', *Sociological Review*, new series, XVI (2), pp. 149–64.

Morgan, D. H. J. 1975. *Social Theory and the Family*, Routledge & Kegan Paul.

OPCS 1978. *Demographic Review 1977*, HMSO.

OPCS 1983. *Marriage and Divorce Statistics 1980*, HMSO.

Rosser, C. and Harris, C. C. 1965. *The Family and Social Change*, Routledge & Kegan Paul.

Rowntree, G. and Carrier, N. 1958. 'The resort to divorce in England and Wales, 1853–1957', *Population Studies*, XI (3), pp. 188–233.

Samuel, R. 1981. *East End Underworld, vol 2: Chapters in the Life of Arthur Harding*, Routledge & Kegan Paul.

Shanas, E. and Streib, G. F. (eds) 1965. *Social Structure and the Family: generational relations*, Prentice-Hall.

Shorter, E. 1975. *The Making of the Modern Family*, Collins.

Smout, T. C. 1976. 'Aspects of sexual behaviour in nineteenth century Scotland', in A. A. MacLaren (ed.) *Social Class in Scotland: past and present*, John Donald.

Snell, K. D. M. 1981. *Social Change and Agrarian England, 1660–1900*, Cambridge University Press.

Thompson, P. 1975. *The Edwardians*, Weidenfeld & Nicolson.

Vincent, D. 1981. *Bread, Knowledge and Freedom: a study of nineteenth century working class autobiography*, Methuen.

Wall, R. (ed.) 1983. *Family Forms in Historic Europe*, Cambridge University Press.

Winter, J. M. 1976. 'Some aspects of the demographic consequences of the First World War in Britain', *Population Studies*, XXX, pp. 539–52.

Wrigley, E. A. 1969. *Population and History*, Weidenfeld & Nicolson.

Wrigley, E. A. 1981. 'Marriage, fertility and population growth in eighteenth century England', in R. B. Outhwaite (ed.) *Marriage and Society*, Europa.

Wrigley, E. A. and Schofield, R. S. 1981. *The Population History of England, 1541–1871: a reconstruction*, Edward Arnold.

Young, M. and Willmott, P. 1973. *The Symmetrical Family: a study of work and leisure in the London region*, Routledge & Kegan Paul.

# 4

# Do Families Support Each Other More or Less than in the Past?

*Janet Finch*

How have patterns of support between members of the same kin group changed in Britain over time, and especially over the past two centuries? Are the rather variable and unpredictable patterns of kin support [that we see today] of recent origin? Have people lost a clear 'sense of obligation' to assist their kin—a sense that existed in the past? The expansion of the study of family history in recent years, and the coming together of historical and sociological concerns in this field in particular, make it possible at least to attempt answers to these questions in a way that even ten years ago would not have been possible, for lack of appropriate sources of evidence. At the same time, the limitations of the data are very apparent, and mean that the answers to these questions must be partial and to some extent speculative, rather than detailed and authoritative. . . .

## What kinds of assistance did kin give each other in the past?

Proceeding with due caution we can ask: what do we know about patterns of support between kin over the past two centuries? I shall focus here on three types of support: sharing a household, money, and practical support.

### Sharing a household

. . . Household composition is the issue on which much work on the history of the family has been centred. We know that it is fairly

Do families support each other more or less than in the past?
Janet Finch

Abridged from J. Finch, *Family Obligations and Social Change*, Cambridge, Polity Press, 1989, pp. 57–85.

uncommon for adult relatives to share households today: only 12 per cent of households contain three or more adults and not all of these will involve relatives sharing (Central Statistical Office, 1988, p. 36, table 2.2).

The predominant interest of much of the historical work on household composition, especially the early work, was to examine one of the key elements in the idea of a golden age of family support—that in the past it was common for members of the extended family actually to live together, and that a major effect of industrialization was to shrink the household, typically to the nuclear family unit. The earlier work of historical demographers of households was concentrated on examining the simple measure of household size, and they were able to establish by a variety of evidence that the average size remained remarkably constant between the seventeenth century and the twentieth. In fact, the average household size remained between four and five throughout this period and only fell to three during the twentieth century (Laslett, 1972; Wall, 1972). Although the methods used in these studies have been criticized (Berkner, 1975), they have been very influential. Certainly the simple notion that industrialization altered radically the size of the household cannot be correct, since the relatively small change which has actually occurred is of quite recent origin. The large extended family household in any case seems only to have existed for a small minority, if at all.

Although the overall size of households may not have altered dramatically, this still leaves open the question of whether household composition has changed. Did a different [spectrum of] people share a household in the past? Was it more common for at least one or two adult relatives to be added to a household, in addition to a nuclear family unit? That question is more difficult, because of the level of detailed evidence that is required to answer it with certainty.

Wall's evidence (1986) suggests that there have been fluctuations over time in patterns of who shares households, but that these have not been in a single direction. Between the mid-seventeenth and the mid-twentieth centuries there have been three discernible periods, each characterized by different patterns of sharing. The picture is complicated by the existence at certain points in the past of a relatively large number of households containing servants. But people classified as servants could also be kin; for example, older children of a family whose parents could not support them economically sometimes went to live with relatives, and also worked for them (Gittins, 1985, pp. 15–16). Wall's evidence (1986) shows that the really notable change between the mid-nineteenth and mid-twentieth centuries was the [decrease in the] number of people living in other people's homes as servants or lodgers. The number of kin living together rose during the early industrial period (up to the middle of the nineteenth century) and remained fairly constant thereafter. So far as elderly people in particular are concerned, there has been relatively little change in patterns of co-residence with relatives until the later part of the twentieth century; although there have been some fluctuations, the overall pattern shows more continuities than changes. For example, most elderly people who are married have always lived only with their spouses, and small but fairly constant proportions have always lived in residential institutions of one kind or another (Wall, 1984).

If we look at the reasons why kin shared homes with each other in the past, three themes emerge which help us further to understand why there have been fluctuations in co-residence. These are: demographic change, affecting the need to seek accommodation with relatives; the economic circumstances of all parties; changing ideologies of family and household.

Demographic change has affected most obviously the position of elderly people. From about the middle of the twentieth century onwards, the number of elderly people in the population has been rising, and it will continue to rise until the end of the century. This means that there are more people who might need support in old age, including accommodation with relatives. But at the same time the number of available children with whom they might reside is much reduced by comparison, say, with the mid-nineteenth century, because of the reduction in the birth rate. In fact, as many as one-third of all elderly people have no surviving children (Parker, 1985). Thus we now have many more old people and many fewer children with whom they might live, and it is not surprising therefore that the last half-century has been characterized by a reduction in the proportion of single elderly people living with relatives.

Demographic changes of a rather different kind have had the effect of substantially reducing the categories of people who once lived with kin. If we look at the evidence of Roberts's study of Lancashire households between 1890 and 1940 (Roberts, 1984, pp. 72–7), we see that the various categories of kin who co-resided included: unmarried daughters living with parents; unmarried brothers and sisters living with a married sibling; orphaned children; children whose parents were still alive, but who had gone to live with relatives because of parental poverty or lack of space in the parental household. In each of these cases, demographic change, coupled with a rise in living standards, has largely removed the need for these categories of people to live with relatives. Almost everyone now marries at least once and the category of never-married people has virtually disappeared. Increased life expectancy means that it is now a rare occurrence for children to be orphaned. . . .

The economic circumstances of the parties [that might share] seem to offer another important explanation of why it is more common for people to share a home with relatives at some points in historical time than at others. Michael Anderson's work has been particularly important in establishing the significance of considering the material gains for either or both parties, if we wish to understand why people lived with relatives in the past. In his review of the historical data available on household composition in the past, Anderson (1980) emphasizes in particular the distinction between the rural and urban economies. If one takes simply the early industrial period, up to about 1820, it is possible to show that almost one-third of rural households contained servants, typically young people in their early teens who left home to spend about 10 to 15 years in service before marrying. In urban areas this was less common and there seems to have been more opportunity for young people to stay in the parental home for longer, because of the greater availability of work in the locality (Anderson, 1980, pp. 25–6).

Drawing on his own earlier study of Preston in the mid-nineteenth century, Anderson (1972) has also used arguments about economic advantage to examine why the average household size seemed to be larger in the developing cotton towns than elsewhere. Indeed, it is possible to show that there was a marked increase in the number of married children living with parents in cotton towns during the nineteenth century and into the twentieth century—quite the reverse of what one would expect if it were true that industrialization broke up the extended family. Anderson argues strongly that such patterns can be explained only by looking at the material advantages and disadvantages of people living together. He applies [this analysis] to the particular case of young people living with their parents after marriage, by arguing that in the expanding industrial towns there was every opportunity for young people to be wage earners and therefore to be net contributors to the parental household, at a time when wages were at a very low level. In the same period, kin links were an important mechanism for recruiting labour, and so living in the parental household would have given young people increased chances of finding work as well as providing them with accommodation which they might not have been able to afford on their own.

Yet material circumstances alone do not account fully for changes in co-residence. Ideological change, apparently, is a further element in explaining why it is more common to find people living with relatives in some historical periods than in others. Over the past century, there have been ideological pressures—expressed, among other ways, through public policies—to define what constitutes a 'proper' family, and to encourage people to live in such units. As Davidoff puts it (1979, p. 78), '. . . it was during the Victorian and Edwardian periods that "the shape of the private household was being officially defined".' According to Summerfield (1984, chapter 3) 'The desired family form was a household consisting of a married couple and their children, where the man is the breadwinner and the woman a domestic worker. These definitions were consolidated further through public policies put into operation during and after the Second World War.'

These ideological definitions of a normal or proper household are therefore of relatively recent origin. Because they are also incorporated into people's aspirations, they are bound to shape their actions to some extent. . . . They have meant, for example, that housing policies have endorsed the view that each nuclear family should have its own household, and thus increasingly it has become possible for people to take that option. It is now less common for young married couples to begin their married lives in the homes of relatives, except on a very temporary basis.

In summary, the pattern of change in household composition certainly does not involve a simple shrinkage from large to small units. Nor does it entail a straightforward shrinking to the nuclear family unit as a consequence of industrialization. It is the case that typical households in the later part of the twentieth century are much less likely than they were in earlier times to contain anyone other than the conjugal family. The pattern of movement, however, is not wholly in one direction. It seems that people take kin, and indeed non-kin, into their households in situations where this is mutually advantageous, but the balance of those advantages fluctuates over time and varies between different localities in the same historical period. It is also very significantly related to the structure of the population and the composition of families, which affect both the supply of and the demand for shared households.

It is very difficult to say what part is played in these processes by notions of duty to assist kin but, in understanding fluctuations in household composition, the significance of the principle of mutual advantage rather challenges the idea that people took relatives into their own homes solely out of a sense of obligation towards them.

*Financial support*

The evidence about other types of kin support in the past—whether within or across households—is much more fragmented than evidence about household composition. Financial support is perhaps the most accessible to documentation, although even this is not always clear, especially for the great majority of the population who did not codify their financial support for kin through wills and settlements, simply because they lived from hand to mouth.

For the classes who did have enough to bequeath, we have valuable evidence about the patterns of inheritance preferred in the early nineteenth century from a variety of sources, especially a study by Davidoff and Hall (1987) of 622 wills made in two different areas of England during the period 1780–1850. ... Whilst the system of **primogeniture** had been used traditionally by the aristocracy as a way of passing on an estate intact, the expanding entrepreneurial business class of the early industrial period tended to favour partible inheritance. This meant that a man's estate was increasingly likely to be divided between his wife (if she survived him) and his children, although not necessarily in equal measure. One example given by Davidoff and Hall is of Samuel Galton, a wealthy Birmingham banker who had also bought land. When he died, he divided his liquid assets and his land between his sons, having first provided for each of his daughters through setting up trust funds which would provide them with good incomes. This example apparently was fairly typical of the wealthy sectors of the middle class.

It appears that in the earlier part of the nineteenth century a change took place in the kinds of family responsibilities which are implied by inheritance practices. Whereas previously those who had wealth to bequeath typically provided very handsomely for the eldest son, and at a much reduced level for the rest of their children, a practice became common which implied that children had roughly equal claims on a parent's resources, with some distinction made on grounds of gender so that women and men inherited different kinds of property. This idea that parents have equal responsibilities towards their children has remained the dominant one in the twentieth century. ...

Financial support between relatives has one feature that is not shared by other types of support, namely that it has been regulated by the law. This applies most obviously to inheritance, but the law has also been used to regulate financial support within families in a different way, namely through the Poor Law, which has applied to many more people than have ever been affected by inheritance. The vestiges of this remain in the legal requirement that spouses should support each other financially. But until the Poor Law was abolished finally in 1948, the principle of financial support between kin applied more broadly. In particular there was a requirement under English law for children to support their parents financially. Sons carried this legal responsibility throughout their lives; daughters relinquished it when they married. The nineteenth-century origins of these provisions are closely tied into a desire to hold down state expenditure and to ensure that the wealthier classes did not have to dig too deeply into their pockets to support people who could not work for wages. In that sense the Poor Law was a mechanism whereby one class imposed a particular view of family responsibility upon another.

However, we must beware of interpretations that are deceptively simple. ... How do we know whether people gave money to their parents because they felt a sense of duty to support them financially or because they feared prosecution? Does it even make sense to pose the question in this form? Problems of interpreting the historical material are compounded by the fact that contemporary evidence from the nineteenth and early twentieth centuries tends to treat examples of working-class people who did not support their parents as evidence of individuals lacking 'filial affection' (Anderson, 1977). But, of course, people may feel very affectionate towards their parents but be unable to give them money or, indeed, may be able to give them money but feel that this is not the proper thing to do. These issues are difficult enough to disentangle in contemporary research, and there are major problems in gaining access to data that would really enable such distinctions to be made in an historical context.

Nevertheless the evidence that is available does enable us to draw some conclusions. The most important of these is that there seems to be no indication that people assumed automatic responsibility for relatives —including parents—who were old, sick, or in some other circumstances in which they were unable to work to maintain themselves. The evidence suggests that even in the preindustrial period there was no automatic assumption of financial responsibility for elderly parents. This emerges clearly from Clark's discussion (1982) of social security in medieval England, where the emphasis is upon the comparative unimportance of financial support from kin, although this certainly existed. Clark demonstrates that older people tried, where possible, to set up contractually based arrangements (some of them enforceable through the courts) to secure their livelihood and care in old age, through a system whereby they surrendered some of their rights to their land to a specified individual, in return for agreed services such as the provision of a room, fuel and clothing, the washing of clothes, and visiting at times of sickness—'individually arranged pension benefits' (ibid., p. 308). The fact that the transfer of property rights was only partial and conditional provided a guarantee of security in old age, and the people involved in such transactions were not necessarily children or even relatives.

The theme of mutual advantage rather than a sense of duty in financial relationships between kin again emerges from this example; or to put it another way, it suggests that historically, in Britain, financial relationships between adult kin have been regarded typically as two-way exchanges rather than one-way support. One can find examples from the more recent past to support that view: for example, Ross's discussion (1983) of the lifestyle of the working poor in the East End of London, in the period leading up to the First World War, contains evidence about financial relationships between young working adults and their parents, based partly on the surveys of Charles Booth (1892). Ross suggests that the 'board' money which young people paid for living in the parental household was seen as an exchange, especially for daughters: they handed over their wages to their mothers and in exchange their mothers equipped them to enable them to go into service.

The resistance to the idea of one-way financial support can also be deduced from evidence about the circumstances under which people tried to evade legally defined financial responsibilities to kin . . . There are plenty of examples of people 'losing touch' with their elderly parents as a way of avoiding maintenance payments during the period in the late nineteenth and early twentieth centuries when certain Boards of Guardians were trying rigidly to enforce financial liabilities. A rather similar pattern can be seen in the very different circumstances of the inter-war economic depression, when the Household Means Test meant effectively that young working adults living in the same household as their unemployed parents were expected to support them financially. Many young people, with the encouragement of their parents, left home at this time to avoid these responsibilities.

Both these examples raise issues other than the question of whether support is one-way, but they do indicate that there certainly have been historical circumstances in which people have felt that the requirement to provide financial support for parents, in instances where the parents were apparently unable to reciprocate, went well beyond their normal expectations of support between kin. Financial need, even on the part of a close relative, has apparently never been seen as a situation that required an automatic response. Even when people *could* give money to relatives, it has never been obvious that they *should* do so, whatever other circumstances obtained.

We also learn from the historical evidence that **gender** has been an important source of variation in people's experience of financial support within families. In the past, women's capacity to give assistance was even more constrained by their lack of control over financial resources than it is now. This was actually recognized in the Poor Law, which limited women's liability to support their parents to unmarried women, thus reinforcing the idea that a married woman's economic position is complete dependence upon her husband.

*Practical support*

Practical support provides the third example I shall use in this discussion of patterns of support in the past. Childcare is one obvious example, but there are also the many day-to-day tasks that enable households to be maintained and to function at a reasonable level of efficiency. Hareven, in her discussion of early industrial society in America (1978), suggests that this type of exchange was more common than sharing households, but that it could only operate on a reciprocal basis. Between close kin it was possible for the exchanges to be one-way over a longer term, one person being a net 'giver' at a particular point in time because of a reasonable confidence that he or she could be a net 'receiver' at a later stage. But between more distant kin, routine day-to-day assistance had to entail exchange of a two-way kind in the short term because 'the need for reciprocity [was] dictated by the insecurities of urban life' (p. 65). Because of their place in maintaining and servicing a household and its members, it is of course likely that most of these exchanges entailing practical support were between women.

Another interesting feature of exchanges of this type is that, under certain conditions, money could be used to fulfil one part of the bargain, i.e. if practical services were being offered in only one direction, or if those services went beyond that which could be contained in normal, on-going reciprocal exchange. For example, Ross (1983, p. 12) cites evidence of young working adults paying their younger siblings to perform services such as cleaning their shoes. Roberts (1984, p. 180) found examples of women paying their mothers and mothers-in-law to look after their children while they went out to work. She comments that people seemed to feel that childcare was an appropriate service for kin to perform for each other, but also that relatives should not be exploited. In common with other types of support that I have considered here, it seems that practical help, even when on a fairly small scale, has never been given to relatives automatically and without some assessment being made of the wider social context. Reciprocal exchange of services seems to be a particularly important feature of this type of support in the past, as it is in the present.

## Givers and receivers of support

The idea that patterns of support in the past were linked to mutual advantage emerges in relation to all three of the types of support I have considered: sharing households, financial support, and practical day-to-day services. But the picture is incomplete if one thinks solely in terms of undifferentiated 'kin', without asking between *whom* these services flowed. We need to look, therefore, at how the patterns of support varied between those two major divisions within kin groups: gender and generation.

*Women and men*

First, variations by gender. In the past, did different types of support, or varying amounts of support, flow between women and men, and have those gendered patterns changed over time? These obviously are very difficult questions to answer, given the lack of detailed evidence about precisely those kinds of day-to-day support in which gendered patterns are likely to be most apparent. Financial support, however, is relatively easy to document when it concerns those wealthy enough to have money, property, and other possessions to dispose of in wills, or indeed in their lifetimes. As I have already indicated, the evidence here suggests that although English inheritance law traditionally privileged the eldest son, from the early nineteenth century onwards the equal claims of all children began to be acknowledged, although daughters and sons received different *types* of bequest (Davidoff and Hall, 1987). The English Poor Law also allocated different responsibilities to women and men, in respect of giving support to relatives.

Looking at examples of day-to-day practical assistance, it is apparent that women have been involved in exchanging this with other women much more commonly than men have been involved in exchanges with women or with other men. One possible explanation lies in the division of labour between women and men. Because women have been allocated the tasks associated with running households and rearing children as their particular responsibilities, one could argue that they need practical day-to-day support in a way that men do not. It is likely that they will seek this support from other women rather than from men, even their husbands, because the tasks involved have been defined as women's work. Thus, in the past, women had a particular interest in maintaining a pattern of exchanges with female kin, in which they both gave and received day-to-day support. I have made a similar argument [elsewhere] about practical support in contemporary society.

That is a hypothesis about the foundations of practical support between kin in the past which could be tested systematically against historical data, although it would be a major task and certainly is beyond my scope here. However, it is relatively easy to find illustrative examples which suggest that, in the past, the sharing of day-to-day assistance between kin was rooted in the responsibilities allocated to women in their domestic lives. Roberts, in her study of working-class women in three Lancashire towns from 1890 to 1940 (1984, pp. 169–81), demonstrates the importance of women helping other women in extended family networks, through minding children, caring for the elderly, providing clothing, and sometimes taking a relative's child into their own home. Men also provided some support for their relatives, usually minor property repairs or help with an allotment, but the volume of this was much less. Jamieson (1986), in her study of working-class mothers and daughters in urban Scotland in roughly the same period, found that young adult women living in their parental homes would take on domestic work to assist their mothers routinely and extensively, in a way not replicated by their male counterparts. Again, in Ross's study of the East End of London before the First World War, the theme of women assisting other women comes across strongly. With both kin and neighbours, women shared 'extensively and unsentimentally' on the basis of reciprocal exchange (Ross, 1983, p. 6), including sharing such items as food, clothing, domestic items (for example washtubs), and small amounts of money (such as a penny for the gas). There was indeed, she argues, a tendency for women to bypass support from men and to rely on other women as being more dependable sources of support, a tendency found in other cultures of the very poor (p. 6). In such circumstances as these, the main example of men assisting their kin seems to be the use of kin networks to secure employment (Anderson, 1971, pp. 111–23; Roberts, 1984, p. 180).

If the above argument is correct one might expect to find that, in other situations where the division of labour is less fixed, there would be more diverse patterns of kin support across gender lines. . . . Yet even where a less rigid gender division of labour prevails, it seems to be the case that women commonly act as the 'kin keepers', that is to say the people who keep up regular contacts with members of the wider kin group. In so far as women have these contacts rather than men—even if sometimes the contacts are, as it were, on behalf of men—it is likely that they are in a position to mobilize support in a way that men are not. That would lead to a situation where more assistance passes between women than between men even in situations where their 'needs' are more similar than in the examples I have quoted above. Only in the case of money, over which men may retain control even when the domestic division of labour is less rigid, might one expect men to be more actively involved in exchanges of support with kin. Again, this is a hypothesis which would repay systematic investigation in respect of historical examples with contrasting forms of division of labour.

*Older and younger generations*

The second major principle on which kin relations are divided is that of generation. . . . The contemporary evidence suggests predictable patterns in the flow of support between generations. Has this changed over time?

This question cannot be considered separately from the issues of how needs for different kinds of support vary between generations and, for an individual, across a lifetime, and how both of these vary historically. A useful way of considering these issues is to use the concept of the dependency ratio, that is, the ratio of people who are out of the labour market in relation to those who are in it. ... During the last two centuries, changes in the law and in employment policies have progressively excluded both the youngest and the oldest generations from the labour market and, therefore, from the means to support themselves through earning wages. The impact of that has been different for older and younger generations, but it has affected the position of each generation in relation to financial support from relatives and also assistance with accommodation. In the twentieth century it has become increasingly possible for older people who have withdrawn from the labour market to support themselves from resources provided by the state rather than rely on their families; the same has not been true of the younger generation. ...

A key point about the situation of young people is that their need to be supported economically by their parents, and more generally their position in structures of reciprocal support within families, depend to a large extent upon factors outside the control of individual families: laws relating to schooling and employment, and the operation of the labour market. Since these factors can and do change, the position of the younger generation in structures of family support must be seen as specific to particular points in historical time. The major changes in their economic position, which began in the late nineteenth century and have lasted until the present, are essentially responsible for creating the dependence of younger people that now appears such a natural part of human life.

The exclusion of older people from the labour market over the same period has had a somewhat different impact upon their position in reciprocal support within families. However, we can see that their position is also constructed largely by factors that are outside the control of individuals.

Evidence from the middle of the nineteenth century, in Anderson's study of Preston, indicates that older people were involved in structures of family support very much on a reciprocal basis. His work demonstrates that an older person was much more likely to be taken into the household of a relative if he or she were able to contribute something in return, for example by doing domestic work, or looking after children while their mother went out to a job. Of course, it is more likely that women rather than men would be in a position to offer such assistance (Anderson, 1971, pp. 139–44). At the beginning of the twentieth century, Poor Law administrators were still noting that older women seemed more able than older men to survive without any apparent source of income, because of the domestic services they could perform (Roebuck and Slaughter, 1979).

Against the background that people expected support for an elderly person to be reciprocated in some fairly immediate way, the pressure to exclude older people from the labour market was accompanied by a pressure to give them some independent means of support which would prevent their having to rely on their children or other relatives. This was reinforced further by demographic changes, which, by the early years of the twentieth century, already meant that an increasing number of people survived into old age without any children at all. Even if they had been willing to rely on relatives, they could not do so (Anderson, 1977).

The idea that older people should leave the labour force at some point gained ground in the earlier part of the twentieth century with the popularity of ideas about scientific management, which implied that older people were bound to be inefficient workers. Older people were not necessarily unwilling to be excluded, as the existence of 'retirement movements' in various industrialized countries demonstrates (Guillemaud, 1983). The issue of retirement had never been on the agenda previously, quite simply because people died much younger in earlier generations. Now there was considerable pressure for the terms of retirement to be such that older people could maintain economic independence. Although some could do this by using their savings or drawing on insurance policies, many could not, with women much less likely than men to be able to support themselves by these means (Roebuck and Slaughter, 1979). The issue was resolved eventually, in 1908, with the introduction of old age pensions, in a limited form. Only people over 70 were eligible, and initially there was an income test and also a test of good character. People who had been convicted of criminal offences, including drunkenness, and people who had habitually failed to work were not to be supported from state resources. It was, as Thane puts it, 'a pension for the very poor, the very respectable and the very old' (Thane, 1982, p. 83).

None the less the principle of the retirement pension was accepted from that point onwards, and it enabled older people to maintain their position as active partners in structures of kin support, at least in financial terms. Unlike younger people, who have become more dependent upon the 'middle' generation over the last century, the position of older people has moved, if anywhere, in the direction of greater independence. However, the situations of older and younger generations are similar in a different sense, in that in both cases the positions of individuals within those structures are determined very largely by factors outside their control—very obviously so at the time when the issue of old age pensions was first on the agenda.

Thus there *have* been changes over time in patterns of support between generations, but these are not necessarily a result of people's changing beliefs and values about family responsibilities. Indeed, factors such as changes in employment law, in regulations about compulsory schooling, and the introduction of state benefits have very obviously shaped such changes. . . .

## Conclusion: what has changed?

. . . The main point that emerges from considering the historical evidence is that there certainly has been change in the amount and type of support offered [within kin groups], but that this cannot be seen simply as a decline from a high to a low point. The idea that there was a golden age of family obligations in the past was born out of a desire to ensure that increasing numbers of elderly people (and other dependent groups) in the population did not become too heavy a burden financially upon the wealthier classes; hence the anxieties about whether working-class people had an adequate sense of 'filial affection', which can be documented from at least the nineteenth century. But in reality the amount and type of support that kin give each other vary with the particular historical circumstances within which family relationships are played out, so that looking at patterns of support at different points in time means that one is not comparing like with like in quite significant ways: there is variation both in people's need for support and in the capacity of relatives to provide it. . . .

### References

Anderson, M. 1971. *Family Structure in Nineteenth Century Lancashire*, Cambridge, Cambridge University Press.

Anderson, M. 1972. 'Household structure and the industrial revolution: mid-nineteenth century Preston in perspective', in P. Laslett and R. Wall (eds) *Household and Family in Past Time*, Cambridge, Cambridge University Press.

Anderson, M. 1977. 'The impact on the family relationships of the elderly of changes since Victorian times in governmental income-maintenance provision', in E. Shanas and M. B. Sussman (eds) *Family Bureaucracy and the Elderly*, Durham, NC, Duke University Press.

Anderson, M. 1980. *Approaches to the History of the Western Family 1500–1914*, London, Macmillan.

Berkner, L. K. 1975. 'The use and misuse of census data for the historical analysis of family structure', *The Journal of Interdisciplinary History*, 4 (1), pp. 721–38.

Booth, C. 1892. *The Life and Labour of the People of London*, London, Macmillan.

Clark, E. 1982. 'Some aspects of social security in medieval England', *Journal of Family History*, 7 (4), pp. 307–20.

Davidoff, L. 1979. 'The separation of home and work? Landladies and lodgers in nineteenth- and twentieth-century England', in S. Burman (ed.) *Fit Work For Women*, London, Croom Helm.

Davidoff, L. and Hall, C. 1987. *Family Fortunes: men and women of the English middle class 1780–1850*, London, Hutchinson.

Guillemaud, A. 1983. 'Introduction', in A. Guillemaud (ed.) *Old Age and the Welfare State*, London, Sage.

Hareven, T. 1978. 'Family time and historical time', in A. Ross, J. Kagan and T. Hareven (eds) *The Family*, New York, Norton.

Jamieson, L. 1986. 'Limited resources limiting conventions: working-class mothers and daughters in urban Scotland c. 1890–1925', in J. Lewis (ed.) *Labour and Love: women's experience of home and family 1850–1940*, Oxford, Basil Blackwell.

Laslett, P. 1972. 'Mean household size in England since the sixteenth century', in P. Laslett and R. Wall (eds) *Household and Family in Past Time*, Cambridge, Cambridge University Press.

Parker, G. 1985. *With Due Care and Attention*, London, Family Policy Studies Centre.

Roberts, E. 1984. *A Woman's Place: an oral history of working class women 1890–1940*, Oxford, Basil Blackwell.

Roebuck, J. and Slaughter, J. 1979. 'Ladies and pensioners: stereotypes and public policy affecting old women in England 1880–1940', *Journal of Social History*, 13 (1), pp. 105–14.

Rose, E. 1983. 'Survival Networks: women's neighbourhood sharing in London before World War I', *History Workshop*, 15, pp. 4–27.

Summerfield, P. 1984. *Women Workers in the Second World War*, London, Croom Helm.

Thane, P. 1982. *Foundations of the Welfare State*, London, Longman.

Wall, R. 1972. 'Mean household size in England from printed sources', in P. Laslett and R. Wall (eds) *Household and Family in Past Time*, Cambridge, Cambridge University Press.

Wall, R. 1984. 'Residential isolation of the elderly: a comparison over time', *Ageing and Society*, 4 (4), pp. 483–503.

Wall, R. 1986. 'Work, welfare and family', in L. Bonfield, R. Smith and K. Wrightson (eds) *The World We have Gained: histories of population and social structure*, Oxford, Basil Blackwell.

# 5

# Theories of Family Development and the Experience of Being Brought Up

*Lynn Jamieson*

A remarkable variety of academic treatments of family life are in broad agreement as to the processes of development and change occurring within families in the nineteenth and early twentieth centuries. A range of authors identify the same key processes and regard the following as a set of interconnected changes: family household members increasingly come to have a sense of themselves as a distinctive and sacrosanct unit, 'the family', which is separated from the wider social world; emotional relationships within the family household become very intense; gender divisions become more acute, with the sharp demarcation between a housewife/mother role and an earner/father role; respect for the rights of the individual is increased—loyalty to oneself may take precedence over loyalty to the family. . . .

Although there are many different understandings of the source of the changes, there is a general consensus that the causes are deep-rooted major shifts in structural and/or cultural aspects of society, whose origins must be sought in the nineteenth century and before. For these 'classical' historical and sociological treatments of changing family forms, which range from as early as Parsons (1943) to as late as Donzelot (1979), the early twentieth century is crucial. Whatever the structural or cultural causes suggested, those causes were well established by 1900: by then capitalism (or **capitalist patriarchy**) in the advanced industrial countries was relatively mature; a 'modern' industrial occupational structure had emerged; households had had time to elaborate the strategies best suited to a patriarchal wage-earning

Theories of family development and the experience of being brought up
Lynn Jamieson

From *Sociology* 21(4), 1987, pp. 591–607.

economy; the relevant religious changes were long established; and the encroachment of the state on all areas of life had begun.

My aim in this paper is to confront the 'classical' corpus of historical and sociological analysis with a particular set of experiential data—oral accounts of growing up in urban Scotland in the early 1900s gathered by me between 1975 and 1977 (Jamieson, 1983). My respondents' experiences . . . indicate that the processes of change were not all as pervasive at that time as the 'classical' corpus suggests. As such, this paper complements more recent work including that by Harris (1983) and by Gittins (1982). One reading of the revision of the 'classical' analyses, which is suggested by the work of these authors, is to move the processes of change forward in time; thus Harris dates the impact of certain changes in the occupational structure much later than earlier authors suggest; Gittins emphasizes the impact of twentieth-century developments such as the growth of the Welfare State, the cinema, cheap tram travel, and the development of working-class suburbs. Moreover, recent authors have also stressed that the 'classical' corpus over-focused on a single family form, mistakenly identified as *the* emerging 'modern' family. Below, having provided evidence in support of these revisions, I shall suggest that the apparently logical connections assumed in the 'classical' portfolio of changes continue to cast an unhelpful shadow over our analyses.

## The data

The data I am drawing on consist of semi-structured interviews with 64 working-class and 23 middle-class men and women born between 1886 and 1910 and brought up in urban Scotland. The respondents were particularly suitably located, generationally, geographically, and in class background. People brought up in the early 1900s are a suitable generation because that generation lies at the boundary between the nineteenth-century processes focused on by the 'classical' authors and the twentieth-century processes that more recent authors have identi-fied. My interviewees were also suitable geographically because they came from an urban background, and for many authors the deter-minants of change are associated with the shift to an urban capitalist society. Their suitability in terms of class background hinged on the possibility of comparison between classes. A range of 'classical' authors (Ariès, 1973; Stone, 1979) indicate that it was the wealthier sectors of urban society that first experienced these processes of change. The urban bourgeoisie (Lasch, 1977; Shorter, 1977; Zaretsky, 1976) or the urban middle class (Parsons, 1942) are identified as the pioneers of change by some authors, while authors also discuss different determinants and sequencing of events for bourgeoisie and proletariat (Donzelot, 1979; Goode, 1970; Zaretsky, 1976). It is important, therefore, to be able to make comparisons between classes.

I sought out men and women from two types of background: a working-class group who lived close to poverty and a middle-class, well-to-do group who had servants. My working-class respondents were mainly brought up in miners' cottages, or in rented two- or three-roomed tenement flats in Edinburgh and other towns of Scotland's industrial Central Belt. Their households typically consisted of their parents and two, three, or more siblings. A minority of mothers had regular paid employment, usually some form of domestic work. Fathers were manual workers ranging from low-paid, unskilled workers, such as 'scaffies' and labourers, to better-paid, time-served men like tinsmiths, printers, and bookbinders. The middle-class group were brought up in a range of styles from the 'better-class' five-roomed tenement flat with a boxroom for the maid to the grand detached houses of the suburbs with servants' quarters. Their households typically included parents, one or two siblings, and a maid. Their mothers did no paid work, and the majority of fathers were professionals or businessmen.[1] There was, of course, considerable variation in circumstances within each group and some respondents can be identified as at the borderline between the classes.

The middle-class group included seven respondents whose parents were small business proprietors, '**petty bourgeoisie**'. It also included a respondent whose widowed mother ran a sub-post office. These households were marginal in terms of the income and occupational status of the earners. Moreover, several of the petty bourgeois respondents were indistinguishable in relevant aspects of lifestyle from the working-class respondents. Their sons and daughters were, for example, expected to leave school at the minimum leaving age in order to contribute to the family income. On the other hand, a small number of working-class respondents were clearly aware that they were better off than and somehow different from their peers. Although they were the children of skilled workers, there was not a perfect overlap between this group and the small group whose fathers were the most qualified or skilled or who otherwise occupationally bordered on the middle class; four fathers were foremen in their trades, one was a police sergeant, one a mining contractor, and one a proprietor of a second-hand shop.

The types of questions I was asking at the time were influenced by the work of Thompson (1977; for interview guide 1978); I took respondents through their childhood and youth, focusing particularly on their relationships with their parents and more generally on everyday family life. Although this material was not collected with precognizance of the particular purpose outlined here, it is a rich source of information, which allows at least tentative exploration of relevant aspects of the quality of family life: family household members' sense of 'the family' as separated from the wider social world, their experience of gender divisions and emotional intensity within the family, and their sense of loyalty to self being more important than loyalty to the family.

It is only fair to note the limitations of such data[2] and mine in particular. Firstly, since the data are from a single period they can only show how the quality of family life differed from the situation suggested by the 'classical' account; they cannot show whether or not there had been any earlier convergence towards the 'classical' picture. Secondly, experiential accounts are individuals' memories of one slice of the life cycle. A more thorough exploration of quality of family life would involve a picture gathered from several participants in each family household at all stages of the individual life course and family life cycle. Moreover, the kinds of questions I ask of these particular data are sometimes a compromise between what my reading of other authors suggests that I should ask and what my knowledge of the data tells me I can ask. Finally, I have made sparing use of numbers in order to avoid generating an inappropriate sense of accuracy. I do not believe that a single (albeit lengthy and careful) retrospective interview is always sufficient for the precision implied by numbers concerning how many people within the sample had thought, felt, or done this or that.

These difficulties need not be overstated, however; although from only one time period my data offer many possibilities for questioning common assumptions. The interviews contain many details of family life, particularly bearing on the parent/child relationship which, clearly, is centrally relevant. Moreover, although the strategy of using this type of individual account is limited, it is also normal practice. Sociologists of contemporary family life generally construct a picture by interviewing parents with dependent children. A child's (remembered) view has the virtue of giving a different perspective and, if oral rather than documentary evidence of the generation around 1900 is sought, it is all we have to go on. My respondents' parents were all dead. By now, many of the respondents will have died too.

## The 'classical' account

Space prohibits a full review of academic writing on the development of family forms, so in what follows I shall primarily restrict myself to some major analyses (Ariès, 1973; Donzelot, 1979; Goode, 1970; Lasch, 1977; Parsons, 1943, 1959; Parsons and Bales, 1956; Stone, 1979; Zaretsky, 1976). The common ground among these authors' analyses is

so extensive that it is possible to talk of 'the classical account' as identifying a logically interconnected portfolio of changes in family households, although there is not agreement about the causes of change.

In this account, members of the family household come to have a new
sense of themselves as a bounded discrete unit. As Stone puts it, 'the
importance of the nuclear core increased, not as a unit of habitation but
as a state of mind' (1979, p. 93). A gathering stock of perceptions and
practices by family household members elaborated the physical and
social separation of 'the family'; efforts of family members are actively
devoted to constructing the wider social world as 'the outside' and to
keeping 'the family' in and 'the outside' out. Hence, for example, the
Parsonian young couple who carefully keep both their families of origin
equally at a distance. Parsons (1943, 1959) and Parsons and Bales
(1956) talk of the family's 'relative isolation'; for Zaretsky 'the family
became the realm of "private life"' (1976, p. 57); Donzelot talks of the
'tactical constriction' of the bourgeois family and the 'turning back' on
itself of the working-class family (1979, p. 45); Ariès talks of the family
'holding society at a distance' (1973, p. 385), Stone of the shift from an
open to a restricted structure (1979, *passim*).

Authors vary, however, in their characterization of the actors' [in this
case, family members'] perceptions of 'the outside'. Donzelot (1979,
*passim*) tends to see the actors as attempting to protect themselves from
the corruption of the external world and inadvertently shaping the
family into a container which traps its members and makes them
vulnerable to the intervention of outside agents, most notably the state.
Other authors talk more straightforwardly in terms of actors who
perceive the family as a protection from a hostile exterior and/or
protection from an emotional desert—the phrase 'haven in a heartless
world', which Lasch (1977) takes as a title, sums this up.

Of course, different authors also understand the determinants of this
process differently, referring variously to such changes as: the increased
separation of 'home' and 'industrial' employment in the nineteenth
century, combined with the concentration of opportunities for making a
livelihood in urban industrial centres (Zaretsky); a weakening of the
household's connectedness to neighbours and kin, following from either
the decline in feudal patterns of community sociability (Stone; Ariès) or
greater mobility demanded by a modern occupational structure in the
nineteenth or early twentieth centuries (Parsons; Goode). [There is also
reference to] eighteenth- and nineteenth-century changes in architecture (servants' quarters, the dumb waiter, etc.) conducive to greater
privacy for family members of the richer households, despite the
presence of others within the home.

Most authors assume that the process whereby household members gained a new sense of themselves as 'the family' more or less coincided with the development of a sharper gender division of labour, whereby one woman from the household became almost exclusively occupied in the role of housewife/mother. The same cultural and/or structural factors are typically evoked to explain both these processes. For example, this is Parsons's description of the increased division of labour within marriage: 'recent change . . . far from implying an erasure of the differentiation of sex roles, in many respects . . . reinforces and clarifies it. In the first place, the articulation between family and occupational system in our society focuses the instrumental responsibility for a family very sharply on its one adult male member . . . Secondly, the isolation of the nuclear family in a complementary way focuses the responsibility of the mother role more sharply on the one adult woman' (Parsons and Bales, 1956, p. 23).

For a number of authors, increased emotional intensity follows from and may be a consequence of one or both of these linked changes: 'a continuation of the emphasis on the boundary surrounding the nuclear unit . . . of necessity led to a greater stress on internal bonding within the family' (Stone, 1979, p. 411). For example, Parsons, Lasch and Ariès talk of 'holding society at a distance' as a necessary condition for the development of the family as an emotionally intense small group. The authors are not declaring that affection was absent in previous family forms, but that the place of affection was less central to family organization. 'Marriage for love' and the increased importance of sexual expression in marriage are discussed as aspects of a qualitative change in the emotional and sexual relationship between husband and wife. An increase in the emotional intensity of parent/child relationships is outlined: parents are credited with a different form of interest in and devotion to their children; affection, love for their children and their children's love of them, is more routinely sought and valued in itself; parents, but particularly mothers, seek emotional involvement in their children to an unprecedented degree. The term 'child-centred' is used by a number of authors.

'Classical' authors also identify a process of change in terms of how household family members think about their obligations to themselves and to the family unit: the balance between the individual and the family has shifted in favour of the former; to a greater extent, the individual is regarded as 'sole proprietor of his own person and capacities' (Macpherson, 1962, quoted in Lukes, 1973, p. 139) and as 'more important, ultimately, than any larger constituent group' (Macfarlane, 1978, p. 59), including the family. Authors refer to the particular implications this shift has had for the treatment of children: the child is no longer the servant of the family but an individual to be serviced by the family. Ariès, for example, talks of the family helping children to rise in the world 'individually and without collective ambition' (1973, p. 390), that is, without regard to the future of the family as a whole. Parsons (1962, pp. 167–169) talks of 'the family' providing children with a 'training in independence'. Stone (1979) and Goode (1970) talk more generally of the family's accommodation of increased expectations and demands for individual autonomy, privacy and self-expression, while Zaretsky (1976) describes the family as 'the realm of individual freedom'. Lasch (1977) and Donzelot (1979) focus on the new acceptability of state intervention in the family in the name of the individual, and particularly in the name of the child.

In the 'classical account', then, social processes have strengthened the propensity of parents, particularly mothers, to build boundaries around their families and to direct their own energies and emotions inwards towards their children. 'The family' has gained a new sanctity and emotional intensity as the housewife/mother role has become more demarcated. Yet forces have also operated to encourage parents to foster the autonomy and independence of children, who learn to be loyal to themselves rather than to their family. Moreover, the accounts suggest that these processes of change are interconnected and had become well established and pervasive by the early 1900s, although originating within the better-off sections of society.

## Experiential accounts of being 'brought up'

In the remainder of this paper, accounts of being brought up in the early twentieth century are used to construct a picture of the relevant aspects of family life in the 'growing up' stage of the life cycle. They allow us to get a feel for the following: parents' efforts at generating family boundaries, fostering a 'classical' sense of 'the family'; the extent of emotional intensity of respondents' relationships with their parents, particularly mothers; respondents' experience of gender division within the household; and the sense of balance of loyalty between self and the family household.

### Efforts at generating family boundaries

I have looked at the extent to which parents were limiting their children's sphere of activity to the confines of the family and how these limits were justified and experienced. The indicators I have used are: parental prohibitions, incitements, and suggestions concerning when and where to spend time, and concerning those whom children could bring into the family from 'the outside' and when. I also reviewed what evidence I had of state intervention in the family, in response to

Donzelot's notion of the family as a container which facilitates state intervention by encapsulating its members.[3]

My data lead me to conclude that the effort respondents' mothers and fathers put into generating boundaries around their families did not match previous authors' expectations. I start with parental prohibitions and then explore further how respondents felt about them.

There was a universal concern that children should be home by a certain time at night. This was emphasized and enforced by both mothers and fathers. An evening curfew was experienced, at least until their early teens, by all respondents with functioning parents. There were general restrictions placed on bringing friends home, which might also indicate boundary maintenance work on the part of parents. None of the respondents' families were completely 'open door'. Those middle-class respondents and the few working-class ones who were encouraged to bring friends home were to do so at certain times of the day and week. Interestingly, it was the children whose families were on the boundary between working class and middle class who were particularly encouraged to be home-centred in this way, by making part of 'the outside', friends, into 'the inside', family:

> My mother very much encouraged us having friends in the house and, rather than we were allowed to go to other people's houses, she preferred to know what we were up to, where we were. And we could ask half a dozen children in our own age to spend a Saturday afternoon and evening (Liz, born 1899, widowed mother ran a sub-post office).

There were also class differences in the patterns of parental intervention in children's time. Middle-class parents, particularly mothers, were more likely to identify activities as 'unsuitable' than their working-class counterparts. Middle-class girls had the most experience of being told that certain activities were 'unsuitable'. One common but not universal middle-class restriction was the prohibition of 'playing in the street':

> Some of my friends were totally different. I always envied some of my friends because they were allowed to run on the roads alone (Grace, born 189?, father: owner/manager).

Designating activities as 'unsuitable', imposing curfews, and acting as gatekeepers to the household could be parental tools in building a boundary between the family and the outside world—a boundary that cast the outside world as threatening or dangerous. A particularly sharp image of parents containing their children in the family is to be found in the work of Donzelot, who argues that working-class parents unwittingly contributed to the 'policing' of society by learning to keep their children at home, in school, or otherwise safe from the corruption of the wider social world.

Donzelot's account of this draws heavily on official documentary evidence of state intervention in the French family. Similar evidence exists for Britain. For example, the nineteenth century saw a blossoming of occasions on which the state could legally take children into care; various published sources document this and also the scope for action of the personnel involved—School Attendance Officers, school boards, the police, Prevention of Cruelty Officers. The official reports do indeed give the impression of a highly efficient force of state or quasi-state agents patrolling the streets of working-class neighbourhoods. But despite official documentary evidence of their vigour, among my working-class respondents there were very few stories of the Prevention of Cruelty Officers or Attendance Officers.

Nevertheless, 'state agents' in the form of policemen and teachers did have an impact on their lives. Most working-class respondents talked of the hazard that police posed to their street play. For example, Belle told of her local policeman:

> This time we were playing skipping ropes when somebody shouted 'Shot! Here's Tankerbelly' . . . he had gloves and he just 'Wham. Wham. Wham' and whacked us all (Belle, born 1900, father: shoemaker).

Moreover, their parents generally backed up the authority of the police in the event of disaster—like a fine for playing football—but, at the same time, rarely tried to keep children off the street. In other words, while giving some support to the authority of the police, parents did not act in ways that endorsed the state view that children should be 'off the streets'. Similarly parents generally backed up the authority of teachers, smacking children who had been smacked at school:

> 'Someone . . . told your mother so that you got another doing when you got home' (Mickey, born 1895, father: coal miner).

At the same time, a substantial minority of working-class parents were prepared to withdraw a child from school at age 13; about 17 per cent of my working-class respondents left school before 14.[4] A majority of parents were unperturbed by the earlier entry of their children into work through part-time employment while at school. Around two-thirds of the working-class boys and one-third of the girls had part-time or seasonal jobs. Thus, while giving some support to the authorities, working-class parents did not embrace the state view that children should be contained 'at home or in school'.

Class differences in parents' style of intervention in children's leisure may suggest differences in parental concern with separating their children from the wider social world. Working-class children typically maximized the time they spent in the street and free from adult supervision. Parents encouraged this by sending their children on errands which took them out and about in 'the outside' adult world, while their middle-class peers were much more restricted to a special, adult-run world of clubs, societies, and private parties. However, some sense of how respondents experienced these prohibitions, as well as a more detailed picture of their family lives, contradicts this interpretation. For example, the middle-class child's world of adult-supervised sociability was considerably wider than home and family and cannot be characterized as contributing to 'family consciousness'. The respondents most focused on the family were those, like Liz, at the boundary between working class and middle class, whose parents encouraged them to bring friends home. Such a parental strategy could salve concern about children meeting 'suitable' friends and engaging in 'suitable' activities, concern that might not arise in better-off families who had access to such institutions as a local tennis club and a Literary Society.

The dominant message conveyed by parental restrictions was not one of 'the family' as a separated-off haven of home and mother; they offered messages other than or in addition to 'stay home—stay safe' and 'family is best'. These messages sometimes mapped out class boundaries: for example, forbidding children to play in the streets was, I believe, heard more as a statement about class position than about the boundaries between the family and the wider social world. Sometimes middle-class parents explicitly told their children not to do things because they were not in the same undesirable category as those who did them—'it is only low-class people go for walks on Sunday' were the words of one mother. Restrictions placed on children also conveyed messages about parental authority. The curfews imposed by parents sometimes communicated a sense of the dangers of being out late, but the dominant message was often 'I am still the boss here'; the curfew was an aspect of the deference that children, particularly working-class children, were expected to show to their parents.

It is not clear that 'the family' amounted to a state of mind that evoked determined parental action to keep the outside out and the family household in. Unfortunately, it is not possible to speak to the parents directly and to assess how self-conscious they were about their roles as parents and builders of family boundaries. Certainly parents were concerned about the whereabouts of their children, and they wanted them home by a certain time of night, but the motivation for this concern is not necessarily a form of familism that celebrates barriers between the family household and the wider social scene. The leisure time of many children is neither home-centred nor family-centred, and parental restrictions on it often foster neither [the home nor the family as the basis of leisure]. This is not to say that 'the family' is an empty or wholly insignificant category for respondents, but it seems some way removed from 'a haven in a heartless world'.

### Extent of emotional intensity

It seems that the emotionally intense interior of the 'haven in a heartless world' was also largely absent. The ways in which parents intervene in their children's time clearly touches on the quality of the parent/child relationship. I explore the emotional intensity of this relationship further below by looking more generally both at how parents, particularly mothers, spend time with their children and how they exercise parental authority.

Among my respondents many parents, working-class and middle-class, did not spend much of their free time with their children. Time spent on children was predominantly on their physical care or on helping with their formal education. The pattern of activity and interaction between the overwhelming majority of working-class mothers and their children suggests that a mother's priority was good housekeeping, not her children as such. Indeed, for mothers of both classes time spent with children was rarely classifiable as involvement with children as an end in itself. Only two respondents remembered their mothers ever taking part in their imaginative play. Rather, time spent together involved accompanying or assisting mother on her business or leisure, or receiving explicit instruction from her. The prevailing view of a good mother that I received from working-class respondents was that of a busy mother who excelled at housekeeping —making jam and potted meat, in addition to routine high standards of cleaning and cooking. The typical division of labour between middle-class mistresses and the servants suggests that they too shared the same set of priorities, since they were more prepared to delegate childcare than cooking.

The following quotations capture something of the quality of parent/child relationships for most respondents:

> I don't know if you know the golden rule, 'Children should be seen and not heard'. You were not to talk back to elders. You never joined in at the tea table. You were never allowed at the tea table if there were visitors. Children were kept apart (Angus, born 1902, father: tailor).

> We spent a good deal of time with the maid . . . I don't remember getting a lot of attention from my parents. I really can't remember my mother

ever, you know, taking me in her arms or anything like that but we were happy somehow or other (Catherine, born 1902, father: commercial traveller).

Deference was a feature of the majority of children's relationships with their parents. In working-class households, 'good behaviour' meant obedient service and was expected well beyond school-age years— fetching and carrying on demand, performing required domestic tasks and handing over any earnings, including those from part-time and casual work. Although less universal, unquestioning obedience was similarly expected in many middle-class homes; in either case, asking questions of authority was 'giving cheek'. While some children feared or even hated their parents as a result, the majority clearly did regard them with affection. The style of parenting which appeals to the traditional legitimacy of parental authority does not exclude affection between parents and children. But the emphasis in the relationship is on the beneficence of the parent, not the marvel of the child.

'The boss that you love' was not the only image of parents among my respondents. Some talked of their parents as kindly strangers who had little impact on their lives. This was particularly true of middle-class fathers whose occupations meant they were seldom at home:

He was just the man who came to the house for weekends (Elizabeth, born 1897, father: commercial traveller).

Others expressed intense feelings for their self-sacrificing mothers who starved and slaved to protect them from the worst of their circumstances:

I always wanted to help my mother. Her and me were very close (Tilly, born 1890, father: brass finisher).

But in any of these cases, the types of relationship that respondents generally had with their parents do not match an image of child-centred families in which mothers, if not parents, cherish spending time with the children as a valuable and rewarding end in itself, and so strive to make time and space for their families over other concerns. Certainly the majority of respondents grew up in a household with a full-time or near full-time mother/housewife who was the acknowledged orchestrator of the material, financial, and organizational dimensions of family life, whether her domestic work for the family involved daily toil or more lofty supervision. But 'mother', I suggest, even if the most loved in the household, was not necessarily at the heart of the specific complex of feeling and meaning commonly assumed by authors and recently referred to as familism (Barrett and McIntosh, 1982).

*Experience of gender divisions at home*

I have already indicated that the majority of respondents grew up in households where there were clearly demarcated gender roles. The division of parents into mother/housewife and father/earner was the norm. Only a minority of mothers were in full-time employment. The typical gender division was, of course, reinforced by ideas about who should do what: only widows and unfortunate married women worked; housework was women's work (Roberts, 1984; Gittins, 1982). I now turn to the extent to which respondents were forced or encouraged into these 'appropriate' gender roles by their parents.

In school-age years the gender differences approximating to a housewife/earner division were more acute among working-class respondents. Working-class girls almost always *had to* do some housework by about eight years old. Mothers demanded help from their daughters and would not take 'no' or 'wait' for an answer. Boys were asked to do less and did less. Male respondents explained doing nothing by the presence of their sisters in the family:

> No not me 'cause at that time I had sisters (Johnnie, born 1903, father: house painter).

When slightly older, many school-age children had part-time jobs, like delivering milk. However, paid work was more common among boys than girls. Some female respondents explained this by saying that they had had no time to take a job because of the work they were doing at home:

> No I never had a chance 'cause my mother was oot working. I had to be in the hoose with the bairns, washing and everything at 12 and 13 years old (Maggie, born 1899, father: docker).

Differences persisted after leaving school, with young female earners continuing to do housework as well as their full-time paid jobs, while young male earners had far fewer household demands on their time. In some sense, differences were less marked in middle-class households, at least in the school-age years, because daughters were not often asked to carry a heavy burden of housework and neither boys nor girls took part-time jobs. Middle-class young people were generally in full-time education 2–8 years longer than their working-class counterparts, and during this period they were not expected to earn and contribute to the household.

But, of course, these class differences stem primarily from different material and financial circumstances rather than from different developments of gender role demarcation. In working-class households, the enormous burden of domestic work often meant that mothers could not maintain high standards of housekeeping without assistance. The pervasive view that certain types of domestic work were women's work meant daughters were the front-line helpers. The middle-class daughter had a maid-of-all-works between her and the front line; she could still be called upon (Branca, 1975; Dyhouse, 1986), but was rarely burdened with the heaviest toil. Similarly, working-class and middle-class young people had a different relationship to the household income. Working-class young people, male and female, did not expect their parents to be prepared to keep them indefinitely; they always expected to contribute to the household from 14. Although they were not pressed into earning before that age, when they did the money went straight to the household:

> Anything I got for running messages, it was all into the house (Tom, born 1897, father: coal miner).

Young middle-class earners on the other hand typically kept their earnings, or their parents saved them on their behalf:

> The idea was she [mother] stowed it up and when I got married she gave it back to me (Richard, born 1903, father: lawyer).

Indeed, a subset of middle-class parents did not anticipate their daughters *ever* earning; daughters stayed at home and were given allowances while sons started their careers. For these parents work was 'unsuitable' for women of their class and a daughter working was something of a stigma:

> It just wasn't the thing for a girl to take a job (Fiona, born 1901, father: tea merchant).

When it was assumed that daughters would work, the range of 'suitable' occupations was very limited. The fact that financial and material circumstances in the middle-class household did not turn school-age children into houseworkers and earners of the 'appropriate' gender does not then indicate a lesser emphasis on gender-appropriate behaviour.

Parents of both classes did typically treat boys and girls differently in further ways. Girls were given less freedom to come and go than boys, particularly in their teens. Although curfews were imposed on all young people, young women were waited for and watched more closely.

> I used to go the Literary Association meeting at school on Friday nights. If I got home before twelve o'clock, 'jolly good'. But the girls had to be in by nine o'clock or else, which I think was fair enough (Robert, father: owner/manager of nursery garden).

Moreover, young men were typically given more financial independence than young women, whether this was in the form of 'paying digs' rather than handing over all wages and receiving pocket money, [or in the form of receiving] more pocket money or a more generous allowance. The difference in the disposable income of young men and women is partially accounted for by their different earnings. However, parents tended to exaggerate these differences because of a belief that young men needed more money than young women. Part of that 'need' was due to the custom that, when courting, the man paid for the woman; an early form of adoption of the roles of provider and financial dependent by young men and women.

### The balance of loyalties: self versus family

The issue here is whether the 'family' or the 'individual' was regarded as the ultimate unit: where did the emphasis lie—with serving oneself, that is with personal aims as the ultimate guide to action, or with serving the family and family aims? How do we get at this through accounts of growing up? I scrutinized certain life-decisions for indicators of the balance between individual and family. I tried to unravel and weigh up in a small number of key life-course decisions, the elements of personal, self-assertive choice and the elements of serving family needs and goals. In the main the decisions concerned leaving full-time education, entering work, and leaving home. A complicating factor here is the class and gender differences in the extent of individual freedom to make choices because of differential access to resources.

Class differences were particularly marked around the transition from school to work. Working-class respondents at the life-course stage of leaving school and entering work were dominated by family concerns:

> I had to leave the school because . . . we were really needing the money (Nina, born 1903, father: plumber).

The overwhelming majority of exemptions from school at 13 were because their parent(s) 'got them off the school' without seeking their views. Often this was in response to a family crisis, usually the death, illness, or absence of a parent. Many working-class respondents had no notion of what they wanted to do when they left school. They simply knew that they had to work to earn money. Those who did have ideas might be told to take different work if the earnings were considered too low. For example, several women were not allowed to be dressmakers because of the exceptionally poor pay of apprentices. Those respondents who left school early without wishing to do so, or who entered work that contradicted their choice, communicated a sense of no real alternative. If *they* were to survive, *the family* had to survive. At this stage of their life course they had no resources with which to pursue individual interests. Moreover the fact that the child was now, as a full-time earner, making a more substantial contribution to the household did not often bring an *immediate* increase in privileges. Children were still obedient servants and service continued to be demanded of girls.

In contrast, for middle-class children a family's material needs were rarely a factor in shaping the timing of leaving school or the choice of work, although middle-class sons and daughters would probably have come under pressure if they threatened to wound family status by adopting an occupation 'inappropriate' to their class. However, my respondents did not look beyond the 'appropriate' choices available, and cited individual preference and what they were considered to be good at as determinants of their job choices. Moreover, typically, young middle-class earners kept the money earned although still living in their parents' house:

> It was mostly pocket money, what we earned (Catherine, born 1902, commercial salesman's daughter working as a secretary).

It was theirs, an individual possession in a sense that was inconceivable in the working-class family. Of course, not all middle-class young people had an independent income derived from outwith the family; some upper-middle-class young women had no earnings, as they were not expected to earn. However, the receipt of an annual allowance afforded such daughters what might be called an 'independent dependence'. This was a form of independence from which some tried to escape by insisting on having a paid job and keeping themselves. But many accepted the allowance and the freedom to enjoy themselves within the circumscribed area of 'suitable' activities. This did not include the types of services that working-class daughters performed for their parents, although daughters from less well-off middle-class households were expected to do domestic work. In general, however, middle-class sons and daughters experienced a relative absence of family demands on free time[5] and therefore a greater emphasis on personal social life.

This gap between working-class and middle-class respondents in the extent of family demands and individual privilege was much narrower at older ages, as a substantial portion of working-class respondents had experienced increased spending power and freedom from family service, while still contributing financially to the family household. By their early twenties, most young workers had considerably more money to spend than in their first working years although, as noted above, the men generally had more in their pockets, as well as more time at their disposal owing to freedom from housework. For some working-class daughters the greater freedoms of brothers rankled, and they tell stories of 'casting up' their own earning power to parents while arguing for less restrictive and demanding treatment:

> When I came tae nineteen I just let her [mother] ken I wasnae taking any mair orders. I was bringing a wage in tae her, you know (Maggie, born 1899, father: docker).

Indeed, by their early twenties most daughters had considerably more freedom than in the first years of their working lives, even if it did not exactly match that of their brothers.

But for a minority their teens and early twenties, as working-class daughters, still involved levels of domestic work sufficiently extreme to make free time almost non-existent. Similarly, almost all their earnings continued to go 'to the house', leaving no possibility of saving or personal consumption beyond the smallest of purchases. Here perhaps is Tilly's island of 'familistic values' in a tide of increasing individualism (Tilly, 1974). Nevertheless, these respondents explained their apparent devotion to 'the family' in terms of *personal* loyalties, which they *chose* to honour. They talked predominantly in terms of their love for their mothers and the desire to protect the mother from the burden of housework she would otherwise carry. I tentatively conclude that, like the majority of respondents, they accepted the following: children should help their parents, and particularly daughters should help their mothers (since a lot of housework is women's work then daughters do more than sons); help should not ultimately interfere with 'making your own life'; once you are able to have 'your own life' help should be withdrawn unless there is a sense of personal choice and reward attached to the giving.

Working-class and middle-class material circumstances were very different (more conducive to household service in the case of the former and more conducive to the development of individual preferences in the case of the latter), but young people of both classes were able to articulate a sense of themselves as having a right to be proprietor of her or his own person. Even respondents who thought of themselves as delaying 'their own life', those who 'chose' to stay at home and look after an elderly parent, both working-class and middle-class, talked about their decisions in these terms. Yet it remains somewhat unclear precisely what bearing this style of 'individualism' had on family life. Clearly it is not incompatible with behaviour that is similar in consequence to devotion to 'the family'. It was not obviously precipitating the softening of parental authority and greater parent/child intimacy in the working-class family which Goode suggests; the unspoken terms of parents' right to govern generally included acknowledgement that this right diminished over time. Precisely what individualism meant in the middle-class case is perhaps even more unclear. Parents respected their offspring's educational, occupational, leisure, and friendship decisions (provided they did not contradict expectations of appropriate behaviour for their class), and they did not demand service (which they did not require), yet they could remain socially aloof, expecting respect by virtue of their positions as fathers or mothers.

## Conclusion

Much of the portfolio of supposedly interconnected changes anticipated in 'the classical account' was absent in the experience of my respondents. This suggests that in some crucial respects the 'classical' analysis of changes in the family household is mistaken. My respondents were not obviously being pressed into the mould of 'the family' as an inviolable, emotionally intense domain. For them, the social and *perhaps* the emotional focus of children's and young people's lives was not the family. This suggests that it is correct to focus on far more recent changes if trends towards this type of family are to be understood.

One possible response to this, in the light of the tendency to conceive of key processes as beginning in the middle class and diffusing to the working class, would be to hypothesize that the period of my data was that of an intermediate stage in the process of diffusion. But if that were so, then my data should show the relevant processes to be more advanced in the middle class. They do not do so.

A number of authors have suggested that it is necessary to focus on far more recent changes if we are to understand trends towards the type of family form identified as modern by 'the classical account'. Two particularly useful recent accounts are those of Harris (1983) and Gittins (1982). One possible reading of their work leads to the conclusion that the 'classical' authors were not mistaken concerning the key changes and their logical interconnections. Rather, the error is one of timing. Harris (1969), for example, discussed at length how the Parsonian assumption that the modern occupational structure required only geographic and social mobility actually applied to a relatively late stage of industrial capitalist development (see also Harris, 1983). For Gittins, geographic and social mobility is a causal factor in particular recent circumstances: changes in occupational structure, a rising standard of living, the cheap tram and the development of the working-class suburb made more common the isolated suburban housewife/mother who, under pressure from an expanded state, focused her energies on a discrete, emotionally intense family.

One obvious lesson of the mismatch between the experiential

accounts and 'the classical account' is that theoretically presumed logical links between aspects of family life are not necessarily made in everyday living. For example, the development of an emotionally intense, separated-off 'haven in a heartless world' type of family is not tied to the existence of a full-time housewife/mother at home (constrained by beliefs concerning 'appropriate' gender roles and the absence of occupational opportunity). Gender differentiation is deeply rooted but this type of family is not. Physical and social separation of the family household need not lead to a sense of the family as sanctity and haven, nor need a specialized housewife/mother role within a physically and socially separated household translate into a mother who is child-centred.

Recent authors are cautious regarding causal linkage between a specialized housewife/mother role and familism. Gittins, for example, avoids suggesting that the emergence of the socially and physically isolated housewife/mother was the necessary and sufficient condition for the emotionally intense child-centred household. Rather she emphasizes the importance of increased efforts by the state to impose a particular style of motherhood in the years after the First World War. Here she is drawing on a growing literature on the social and historical construction of motherhood. Harris also attributes considerable impact to currents in child-rearing philosophy. I have suggested above that the documented existence of state ideologies (and of state agents trying to implement these ideologies) is insufficient evidence that the desired change in attitude is, in fact, being effected. My own data demonstrate that parental support for state agents need not reflect adoption of the state sanctioned attitudes. Similarly, when relevant changes in attitude to child rearing can be documented, the hegemony of a particular child-rearing philosophy via the state remains a too general explanation as to why ideology is more persuasive at some times than at others.

Harris does go to some length to explain parents' vulnerability to messages concerning their competence as parents. He discusses a shift away from children having significance as economic assets and a narrowing of the opportunities parents, particularly mothers, have of gaining esteem and self-respect, so that the identity of 'parent' becomes more important; parents require 'good' children if they are to be recognized as 'good' parents. However, Harris argues that to attempt to achieve control over the child 'by means of generating a disciplined submission to forms of behaviour will be regarded as impermissible, as it is repugnant to the cultural values of individualism. Hence, the parent must resort to emotional control, which is quite consistent with the cultural emphasis on love as a means to the production of normal adults' (1983, p. 174). Here Harris directly assumes that cultural values of individualism are incompatible with traditional authority, and therefore emotional manipulation has been substituted for 'do as I say'.

'The classical account' also assumes an incompatibility between a pervasive sense of the right of the individual to be proprietor of her or his own person and belief in the traditional authority of parents. They may well be logically incompatible but this does not preclude their coexistence in family households. Respect for 'individualism' and traditional parental authority was not necessarily problematic for my respondents. For many of them, both working class and middle class, parental authority was a traditional right not to be legitimately challenged until at least the late teenage years. At the same time, they recognized that children had ultimately a right 'to make their own lives'. The cultural values of individualism may be deeply rooted, but their postulated interference with parental authority is not.

The intention is not to detract from the work of Gittins or Harris, who have provided us with excellent texts. They take considerable care to dispel any notion of an evolutionary movement towards a single family form, 'the modern family'. They revise the timing of pressure towards the type of family form that 'the classical account' treats as modern and they develop elements wholly or nearly absent from that account. It seems, however, that the 'classical' corpus has left us with a legacy of temptations in the form of too readily assumed relationships between aspects of family life. It is as if certain questions are no longer asked because they are presumed to be already answered. The theoretical assumptions involved are not interrogated by translation into empirical reality. My own limited attempts at moving from the 'classical' academic account to the experiential accounts of respondents suggest that theoretical gains might still be made by further empirical unpicking of the old theoretical stitches.

## Notes

1  Mothers had paid employment while the respondents were growing up in the case of 38 per cent of working-class households. This may be underestimated as I did not probe systematically for this information. In half of these cases the father of the family was dead. In only one middle-class household was the mother in employment; this was a fatherless family. A small number of working-class respondents were brought up by someone other than their parents; 16 per cent had lost a parent before the age of 14; 13 per cent of middle-class respondents had similarly lost a parent, although proportionately more of them lost this parent between the ages of 14 and 20. Of all respondents, 21 per cent lost a parent and 25 per cent lost one or more siblings by the age of 20. Family size differed

notably between the two groups. The median and modal family sizes of the middle-class group were both 4 while the mean was 5. The respective figures for the working-class group were 6, 5, and 7. The overwhelming majority (94%per cent) of working-class children left school at or before age 14, while this was true of only 17 per cent within the middle-class group, predominantly the sons and daughters of shopkeepers. It was these small-business proprietors who were at the margins of the class; they, along with the administrators among my respondents, were the least likely to have resident domestic servants. The high representation of sons and daughters of professionals among my respondents explains the 48 per cent of the middle-class group who stayed on in full-time education after the age of 18.

2  Thompson discusses the technique of oral history at length in *The Voice of the Past* (1978). More recent discussions are to be found in Bertaux (1981), Plummer (1983) and Humphries (1984).

3  Not all possibilities of intervention were fully explored. For example, I did not systematically ask respondents about comments they received from teachers concerning their clothing and footwear (or lack of it). This is one possible route of intervention unexplored. The school medical inspection is another. Through such routes, schools may influence standards of childcare and the experience of motherhood (Lewis, 1986).

4  Efforts to ensure school attendance were standardized in the Education (Scotland) Act of 1883, which established procedures for summonsing parents of absentee children. By the 1890s the average attendance for Scotland as a percentage of school age was 80 per cent; by 1908 it reached 89 per cent, where it remained for some years (Withrington, 1975). Exemption was permitted a year prior to leaving age. The allowable circumstances were further specified and restricted by Acts of 1901 and 1908 (Keeling, 1914; Knox, 1953).

5  Care has to be taken not to overstate this so as unwittingly to produce again the image of the idle middle-class woman. Branca (1975) reminds us that the majority of middle-class mothers did shoulder a considerable burden of domestic work. My data suggest that their demands on their daughters in this direction were, nevertheless, modest. Some upper-middle-class daughters were expected to 'pay calls' (Hamilton, 1982). This was true of only a couple of my respondents. Some talked of the system 'going out'. Davidoff (1973) alerts us to the fact that paying calls is a form of work—the work of maintaining the boundaries of 'society'. Middle-class daughters were still expected to contribute to this work through their manners, their decorum, and their 'suitable' behaviour.

**References**

Ariès, P. 1973. *Centuries of Childhood*, Hardmondsworth, Penguin.

Barrett, M. and McIntosh, M. 1982. *The Anti-Social Family*, London, Verso.

Bertaux, D. (ed.) 1981. *Biography and Society: the life history approach in the social sciences*, London, Sage.

Branca, P. 1975. *Silent Sisterhood: middle-class women in the Victorian home*, London, Croom Helm.

Davidoff, L. 1973. *The Best Circles: society and etiquette and the season*, London, Croom Helm.

Donzelot, J. 1979. *The Policing of Families: welfare versus the state*, London, Hutchinson.

Dyhouse, C. 1986. 'Mothers and daughters in the middle-class home *c*.1870–1914', in J. Lewis (ed.) *Labour and Love: women's experience of home and family, 1850–1940*, London, Basil Blackwell.

Goode, W. J. 1970. *World Revolution and Family Patterns*, New York, Free Press (first published 1963).

Gittins, D. 1982. *Fair Sex: family size and structure 1900–1939*, London, Hutchinson.

Hamilton, S. 1982. 'Interviewing the middle class: women graduates of the Scottish Universities *c*.1910–1935', *Oral History*, 10, pp. 58–67.

Harris, C. C. 1969. *The Family: an introduction*, London, George Allen and Unwin.

Harris, C. C. 1983. *The Family and Industrial Society*, London, George Allen and Unwin.

Humphries, S. 1984. *The Handbook of Oral History: recording life stories*, London, Inter-Action Inprint.

Jamieson, L. 1983. 'The development of "the modern family": the case of urban Scotland in the early twentieth century', unpublished PhD thesis, Edinburgh University, Oliver and Boyd.

Keeling, F. 1914. *Child Labour in the United Kingdom*, London, P. S. King.

Knox, H. 1953. *Two Hundred and Fifty Years of Scottish Education 1696–1946*. Edinburgh.

Lasch, C. 1977. *Haven in a Heartless World: the family besieged*. New York, Basic Books.

Lewis, J. 1986. 'The working-class wife and mother and state intervention, 1870–1918', Lewis (ed.) *Labour and Love*.

Lukes, S. 1973. *Individualism*, London, Basil Blackwell.

Macfarlane, A. 1978. *The Origins of English Individualism: the family property and social transition*, Oxford, Basil Blackwell.

Macpherson, C. 1962. *The Political Theory of Possessive Individualism: Hobbes to Locke*, Oxford, Oxford University Press.

Parsons, T. 1942. 'Age and sex in the Social Structure', *American Sociological Review*, 7, 604–16. Reprinted in Coser, R. L. (ed.) 1974. *The Family: its structure and functions*, London, Macmillan.

Parsons, T. 1943. 'The kinship system of the contemporary United States', *American Anthropology*, 45. Reprinted in Parsons (1964) *Essays in Sociological Theory*, New York, Free Press.

Parsons, T. 1959. 'The social structure of the family', in R. Anshen (ed.) *The Family: its function and destiny*, New York, Harper.

Parsons, T. 1962. 'Youth in the context of American society', *Daedalus*, 91. Reprinted in Parsons, T. 1970. *Social Structure and Personality*, New York, Collier Macmillan/Free Press.

Parsons, T. and Bales, R. 1956. *Family, Socialisation and Interaction Process*, London, Routledge & Kegan Paul.

Plummer, K. 1983. *Documents of Life: an introduction to the problems and literature of a humanistic method*, London, Allen and Unwin.

Roberts, E. 1984. *A Woman's Place: an oral history of working-class women, 1890–1940*, Oxford, Basil Blackwell.

Shorter, E. 1977. *The Making of the Modern Family*. Glasgow, Fontana/Collins (first published in the USA in 1975).

Stone, L. 1979. *The Family, Sex and Marriage in England 1500–1800*, Harmondsworth, Penguin.

Thompson, P. 1977. *The Edwardians: the remaking of British society*, Frogmore, St Albans, Paladin.

Thompson, P. 1978. *The Voice of the Past: oral history*, Oxford, Oxford University Press.

Tilly, L. 1974. 'Comment on Yans McLaughlin and Davidoff', *Journal of Social History*, 7, pp. 453–459.

Withrington, D. 1975. 'Attitudes to truancy: anxieties over withdrawal from school; historical comment', *Research Intelligence*, 1.

Zaretsky, E. 1976. *Capitalism, the Family and Personal Life*, London, Pluto Press.

# 6

# Women and the Domestic Economy, 1890–1970: the oral evidence

*Elizabeth Roberts*

The consideration of women's role in the domestic economy necessarily involves some examination of women's power and influence in both the family and wider society. Here I attempt to answer the difficult question of whether women's role in the family economy in the third quarter of the twentieth century was more or less important than it had been formerly.[1] In the earlier oral history projects, which related to the period 1890–1940 and to the same three towns, Barrow, Lancaster, and Preston,[2] respondents were very anxious to discuss various aspects of working-class standards of living. Many recounted heroic battles against poverty waged by their families, a struggle in which all family members played a part but one in which the mother appeared to have the most crucial role. In the recent project, respondents were asked about their experiences in the period 1940–1970 and a rather different picture emerged. Not only was the epic struggle against poverty over for most (but not all) families but the role of women within the family, and especially with regard to the domestic economy, had undergone sometimes subtle and sometimes substantial changes.

In the earlier part of the century both men and women saw a married  woman's place as being in the home. Working-class men and women were as enthusiastic supporters of domestic ideology as their middle- and upper-class counterparts. But their subscription to this ideology does not mean that it is easy to describe working-class life as patriarchal, nor indeed was it matriarchal. It may have been patriarchal when viewed from the workplace but not when looked at from the

Women and the domestic economy, 1890–1970: the oral evidence
Elizabeth Roberts

This article has been specially commissioned for *Time, Family and Community*.

hearth. Women in many families (indeed, in our survey, the majority) had an important, powerful position. Their power resulted from their key role in the family economy. In this geographical area of north Lancashire, as in other areas, a woman's contribution to the domestic economy cannot be analysed simply in terms of her contribution as a paid worker either inside or outside the home. Within the family economy she had many functions.

Firstly, women were the household managers, the controllers of family budgets. The spending of men's and children's wages as well as any earned by themselves was in the hands of the women. There is of course evidence that this pattern of financial control was not confined to this area. Helen Bosanquet, writing in 1906, said

> There is one most important branch of industrial cooperation which still prevails in the great majority of society; it is that which assigns to the wife the function of manager and spender of the family income . . . while the husband and adult children take the responsibility of providing the income . . . generally speaking they (i.e. the women) expect to have and get the entire management of the family income determining even the amount which the wage earners, husbands, sons and daughters alike may reserve for their own use. (Bosanquet, 1906)

Women decided which food and clothes to buy, what method of saving (if any) to adopt, the rents they could afford, and consequently what kind of houses their families lived in. They sometimes decided to become home owners. It is interesting that only 20 years after the Married Women's Property Act of 1884, some working-class women in Barrow, albeit a small minority, were buying small terraced houses and keeping them in their own names (Roberts, 1984).

Women's skills as consumers were very important. They were required to buy economical but nutritious food. They were also budget managers and had the aim, not always realized, of not falling into debt. Women's skills frequently made all the difference as to whether their families lived with adequate food, clothing, and housing or whether they sank into dire poverty or, indeed, pauperism. These skills in budgeting and household management were important and were viewed as such by the women themselves, by their husbands, and by their children.

It is important to set these skills against the generally low wages for men. Seebohm Rowntree had three attempts at setting a poverty line. In 1901 he published *Poverty: a study of town life*. Basing his conclusions on work he had done in York he suggested that a poverty line of 21s 8d (£1.08) could be drawn for a family of two adults and three children (Rowntree, 1901). In the three towns I have looked at no labourer earned as much as that before the First World War. The top wage appears to have been paid by Lord Ashton, owner of the huge linoleum works in Lancaster, who paid £1 0s 3d (£1.01) per week. Rowntree's second poverty line, published in 1941, was drawn at £2 13s (£2.65) (Rowntree, 1941). This was higher than the other inter-war poverty line of £1 17s 6d (£1.87) suggested by Bowley and Hogg (1925). Labourers' wages were about £2 per week in this period so it would seem that they were just above or just below the poverty line.

In many families, in view of such low wages, competent household management, although vital, was not enough. Married women had to find ways of augmenting the family income. In Preston, as in other textile towns, women found that the labour market needed their services and they needed the wages being offered. According to the 1911 Census, 35 per cent of married women in Preston were recorded as being in full-time work and most of them were textile workers (Census of 1911). (In parentheses it might well be asked how the tradition that married women went out to work could be reconciled with support for domestic ideology. It seems that this work was regarded as a temporary measure and that women regarded their emancipation as returning to the home away from the stresses of doing a full-time job and housework.) The labour market was different in Barrow and Lancaster and there were far fewer opportunities for married women to work full time; in 1911 only 7 per cent were recorded in Barrow and 11 per cent in Lancaster. These figures undoubtedly underestimate women's contribution as paid workers both to the economy at large and to the family economy because the casual work done by them was so often unrecorded or underrecorded by the census enumerators. It is estimated that between 40 and 50 per cent of female respondents and their mothers in our earlier studies worked for wages at some time in their married lives. The characteristics of this work were that it was gender based, it was casual, it had no career prospects, and it was undertaken almost entirely for the purpose of improving the family's economic status. As so many women said, 'we worked because we had to'. Much of the work took place in the women's own homes, it included child-minding, dressmaking, taking in washing, looking after lodgers, and small-scale trading. The latter activity ranged from opening a 'parlour shop' down to making a small range of food items and selling them from the kitchen. Women who did not work in their own homes almost invariably worked in someone else's, as cleaners or as washer-women. Women textile workers could and did earn more than some men, though women doing casual work earned less than their husbands. But these wages could have made all the difference to a family budget; for example, a cleaning woman in the 1930s earned about 3s 6d a morning and two mornings' work could have paid for the rent of many terraced properties. It appears to have been psychologically important to these women that their wages were so important in their families' struggle for survival (Roberts, 1984, chapter 4).

Women's position in the family economy changed in the period after the Second World War. The role of women's work *during* the war has been thoroughly analysed by Penny Summerfield (1984). In a seminal work she concluded that women who were expected to do men's work outside the home had very little support in the form of government policies to help them cope with the double burden of doing a paid job and running a home and family. For me the demands made of women during the war together with the dual role they were expected to play symbolize a bridge between the pre- and post-war world of women. During the war they were expected to be, as they had been earlier in the century, household managers *par excellence*: they were required to feed their families on meagre rations and to clothe them with inadequate supplies of clothing coupons. The war can be regarded as the apogee of the period of married women as household managers. But the other role of women at this time was as important participants in the men's world of work.

It is a truism that social life and consequently social history do not change suddenly, completely, or as a result of one event, however major. The forces of continuity are often as strong as those of change. Consequently some women in the post-war world continued to play a role in their families' economies that was very similar to that played by their predecessors.

For many others, however, there were changes in their role in the domestic economy. Some of these changes were the results of women's changing role in the world of paid work. In this, their position did not change immediately after the war. Indeed, as after the First World War, women lost their jobs at the end of the war and were expected to return to their homes. But the idea that women could and should work outside the home for wages was accepted by an increasing number of women and indeed men. The labour shortage at the end of the 1940s produced a demand for women's work, which many were prepared to accept. It is impossible to know to what extent women were influenced by academic writers of the day; certainly they did not read them but they may have absorbed some of the ideas of writers such as Klein and Myrdal, who argued that it was a woman's duty to work and that housework could not fill all of a married woman's time. 'Our modern economy cannot afford nor our democratic ideology tolerate the existence of a large section of the population living by the effort of others. Whether we like it or not the leisured class has passed into history' (Myrdal and Klein, 1956). Some respondents claim to have felt guilty at being at home; others more simply assumed that as married women they would have paid jobs outside the home, an assumption much less frequently made before the war.

The steady and ever increasing number of married women in paid work outside the home up to 1971 can be seen in tables 6.1 and 6.2 (although there is an interesting dip in Preston in 1971). These figures follow the same trend as those for England and Wales although there are interesting local variations in actual percentages. This trend of more and more married women taking paid jobs is parallel to and undoubtedly related to the rise in prosperity in the period, a prosperity that was very visible in the great increase in the ownership of consumer durables. There is no doubt that married women's paid work contributed to that prosperity, but is it sufficient to record women's increased contribution to the family budget? There are in fact other questions that need to be asked, arising from the changing role many women had in relation to the domestic economy. Most notably, did women have a more important role than previously in the domestic

**Table 6.1**  Married women in paid work

|  | % of population | | |
| --- | --- | --- | --- |
| Year | Barrow | Lancaster | Preston |
| 1901 | 5.8 | 10.2 | 30.5 |
| 1911 | 6.9 | 11.0 | 35.0 |
| 1951 | 14.8 | 38.6 | 45.6 |
| 1961 | 32.6 | n/a | 55.3 |
| 1971 | 40.0 | n/a | 50.2 |

*Source*: Census Returns 1901–1971

**Table 6.2**  Married women economically active in 1971

|  | % of population | | |
| --- | --- | --- | --- |
| Age | Preston | Barrow | England and Wales |
| 16–20 | 47 | 42 | 43 |
| 21–24 | 43 | 43 | 46 |
| 25–29 | 47 | 34 | 35 |
| 30–34 | 55 | 41 | 51 |
| 35–39 | 63 | 51 | 53 |
| 40–44 | 68 | 57 | 59 |
| 45–49 | 70 | 60 | 60 |
| 50–54 | 67 | 50 | 55 |
| 55–59 | 60 | 39 | 45 |
| 60–64 | 29 | 20 | 25 |

*Source*: *Census 1971, County Report, Lancashire*, part I, table 18

economy? I would argue that the whole question is both ambiguous and complex.

What is not ambiguous is that fewer and fewer women were earning money at home. This is reflected in table 6.3, which summarizes childcare arrangements. The washing machine and the launderette rendered the washerwoman redundant. More women preferred to have bought clothes rather than those made by the local dressmaker. Small-scale trading became more and more difficult in the new retailing climate with its emphasis on larger and larger outlets. Women relied less on paid child-minders, preferring either to delay a return to work until their children were at school or to rely on the services of an unpaid relative. Erstwhile lodgers increasingly preferred either to rent or buy homes of their own.

Although women's earnings were increasing, it cannot be argued that they made the major contribution to the improvement in standards of living. Other more important factors were the dramatic rise in real wages (see table 6.4), which affected the wages of men more than those of women, and the generally low levels of unemployment. It can be argued that women's wages were less rather than more important in the matter of family survival when compared with the earlier period. There were of course families whose battle against poverty had not been won. Rowntree, in his third survey (Rowntree and Lavers, 1951), suggested that a poverty line of £5 might be drawn for a family of five, excluding rent. He estimated that only 1.5 per cent of the population existed on or below this line. This should have meant that in our study only one or two respondents and their families should have been living in poverty in about 1950. There were in fact more than this (a conservative estimate gives 11 per cent) and in these families it is clear that women worked, as they had in the past, from dire economic necessity, in order to raise their families above the poverty line.

**Table 6.3**  Respondents' childcare arrangements

| Person providing care | % of total | |
|---|---|---|
| | Pre-war | Post-war |
| Paid minders | 26.3 | 10.6 |
| Unpaid minders | 21.9 | 22.3 |
| Husbands | 5.0 | 12.7 |
| Child at school | 10.5 | 31.9 |
| Child to work with mother | 0 | 6.3 |
| Mother with paid work at home | 31.6 | 10.6 |
| Nursery | 0 | 5.3 |

**Table 6.4**  Average real weekly earnings
(index 1970 = 100)

| Year | Earnings |
|------|----------|
| 1950 | 65.3 |
| 1955 | 73.4 |
| 1960 | 83.8 |
| 1965 | 94.6 |
| 1970 | 100.0 |

*Source*: Pollard, *The Development of the British Economy, 1914–80*, p. 322

However, the majority who worked and who gave as their reason for so doing their need for the money did not need it for basic necessities. The money was spent on such items as 'better' clothes, family holidays, and domestic appliances. Some women put their money towards new cars. Increasingly men's wages were seen as providing all the basic necessities. *Women's* wages, no longer so crucial for the *survival* of the family, were for extras and were therefore somewhat marginalized, in the eyes of both their families and of the women themselves. The term 'pin' money was sometimes used in a rather disparaging way.

Women increasingly worked for other than financial reasons. They considered their own interests and needs more than their predecessors had; they worked in order to meet people and a sizeable number claimed that if they had not gone out to work they would have been seriously depressed or unhappy; a small number went out to work as part of their recovery after a nervous breakdown. Whatever their initial motive for going out to work, many continued to work because they enjoyed themselves and felt happier than when they were at home. They were moving to a situation in which they found an increasing amount of personal satisfaction not in the home but in the workplace.

Yet very few women went to work to build a career. Indeed only two respondents in the period were interested in a career. All the other women sought jobs that were casual, usually poorly paid, gender related, and with few prospects. Above all women looked for jobs that fitted in best with their roles as mothers, and this was as true for the two career women as for the others. A woman's chief preoccupation when looking for work was how it would affect her children. It could be correctly argued that women had always taken badly paid jobs with few if any prospects of advancement, but in earlier days poorly paid work was done as an extra to women's main important work, which was perceived as taking place in the home.

Women's traditional position of power in the home and in the domestic economy as household managers and as budget controllers was weakened after the war. Although some very strong women remained as inheritors of an earlier tradition, managerial skills became less important as prosperity increased. It was, for example, easier and less time-consuming to buy chops and tinned or frozen vegetables than to make a complicated but economical and nourishing broth; skilful budgeting was less important as the amount of a family's disposable income grew; in an increasingly consumerist society, being economical and making something out of nothing was less important than the ability to buy.

Finally, and most crucially, women increasingly lost control of the family budget. The all-powerful female 'Chancellor of the Exchequer' was almost extinct. There were many reasons for this which can only be briefly summarized here. They were both causes and results of rising standards of living, changes in the power relationships in marriage and changes in the perceptions of gender roles.

In many families there was a change in attitude towards the ownership of money. Earlier in the century, with few exceptions, all income coming into a house was regarded as family money, which the wife and mother spent as she thought fit. Although this tradition continued in a minority of families, money was increasingly seen as belonging to the person who earned it. Even before the war young people in more prosperous families had been allowed to 'board' rather than hand all their money over to their mothers. It was their money, they had earned it, they were simply paying their mothers for services. Their earnings were no longer family money to be spent for the benefit of all. After the war, the money earned by children in part-time jobs before they left school was virtually never regarded as family money and they were allowed to keep it for their own use.

More important was the way husbands' and wives' money was viewed. In the post-war period a woman would continue to work after marriage until the arrival of her first child. In many cases their earnings were referred to as 'his' money and 'her' money. It is difficult to escape the conclusion that when some women stopped work the money continued to be seen as 'his'. Some men claimed that, while their fathers had felt obliged to hand over their wages, *they* felt differently as they earned so much more in real terms than their fathers had. Wives no longer needed all their husbands' incomes. Moreover if they earned substantial amounts then they were entitled to spend accordingly. By the 1960s many men were being paid by cheque. No cases were reported, even in families in which previously men had handed over their wage packets, of this being paid into a wife's bank account; the best she could hope for was a joint account.

Some women saw their roles as wives to be different from those of their mothers. These women rejected the image of the powerful, dominating wife and mother and instead cultivated a softer more pliable persona. Greater prosperity meant that there was less need for men to have tough, managerial wives and these attributes were not sought in brides.

Lastly, many couples were influenced by the concept of the companionate marriage. As a result, ideas of sharing and some blurring of gender roles were adopted, however imperfectly. Many couples spoke of sharing the management of the budget. Whether this male involvement in an area in which women had previously held a dominant role should be described as helping and sharing or as interfering and taking over depends on one's own perceptions and it may well be that these are not always in accord with those of respondents.

One is left with the view that the period 1940–1970 was a truly transitional period for married women. Their power in the home and in particular their crucial role in the domestic economy were being eroded. On the other hand, although their participation rates in the labour market were continually rising, they hardly held positions of power within it. By 1970 a new power base for women had not yet developed to replace the old one, which was being so dramatically weakened.

### Appendix: extracts from interviews

*Women and the domestic economy, 1890–1940*

### Mrs Winder (Mrs W.2.1.), born 1910

ER:    It used to be mothers that sort of dominated the home, you know?

R:    Oh yes, I think so and I think in those days that the man passed over the money, much more than he does today. I mean today they sit down and talk it out and there's so much for him and so much for the house. But in those days the wages were so poor that really the man didn't get a right lot out of it unless he was . . .

(Mr J.):    His job was to provide for the family.

R:    Yes, and it was handed over and the wife did the allotting where it went.

ER:    I think they perhaps gave the husband something back didn't they?

R:    Yes, but well in some cases I don't think they got an awful lot. I mean some of these that were always drunk must have got a lot back. I think, they perhaps didn't treat the wives fairly. I mean I can remember when I was smaller when my father was at Williamsons in the Warehouse Office he got a shilling a week to spend, and he only smoked half an ounce of twist, and it was fourpence. And of course he never went to work on a bus or anything, he walked both ways.


### Mr Pearson (Mr P.1.B.), born 1900

ER:    Who decided to come here, was it your mother or dad to this house?
R:     M'mother. M'father wouldn't put his name to anything. He was one of them fellows that said he didn't like anything round his neck.
ER:    A debt you mean?
R:     A debt, yes. No, the house was never in m'father's name. When m'mother died she left the house for him to live in as long as he did but when he died it had to be divided between the children.


### Mr Riley (Mr R.3.L.), born 1890

R:     This is how they had to do it. They were schemers, providers in them days but I'm standing up for the women, the husband had a little wage and it was the women who were the schemers and the providers. There was always something on our table and there was always something to eat and they always had supper.


### Mrs Pearce (Mrs P.1.P.), born 1899

ER:    Did your mother work when you were a little girl? Did she work after she was married?
R:     She used to go out selling things. When she got married my dad was all right at first and then he died when I was quite young. So then she had to start going out what they used to call in them days, hawking. She would go with a basket and pins and needles and tape and things like that. They had to go for miles in the country. Because in towns they were all like us and they wanted to go for the cheapest in these bazaars and things. She had to go out of town where they were a bit better off. She walked miles and miles. Oh it were a terrible day. My sister was only saying the other day, 'Haven't we been awful!' Because I have gone out cleaning. She said, haven't we been daft what we have done. I have had to do it. I've had to go out cleaning when my kids were little. I have been a widow for twenty years. My husband was only a labourer, an out-door labourer. So when it was raining he had to come home. He could have gone on many a time but when it rained the bricksetters said they were doing no more. So he could have earned a bit more. But then he might have gone sooner than he has done working out in that weather. Oh it was terrible days.

**Mrs Morrison (Mrs M.1.P.), born 1898**

ER:    Did you ever make peg rugs?

R:    Of course we did, all of us.

ER:    Before you were married and after?

R:    Yes. My mother and father had a frame. My father used to peg rugs. I had an uncle who never worked, he had epileptic fits, but he used to peg rugs by the dozen and sell them. Everybody had peg rugs. My grandma never came to see us but she brought a peg rug.

ER:    And did you make them after you were married?

R:    Yes.

ER:    When did you stop making them?

R:    I couldn't just say. A friend that I had that worked at a tailor's shop, we used to get the samples and it went into blankets as well as peg rugs. Since the war I've made them.

ER:    That was a good idea making the samples into blankets.

R:    Yes, it was all good cloth. I made three during the war ready for wrapping them up, if we had to go, instead of taking blankets.

ER:    Did you ever make patchwork quilts?

R:    Yes. My mother-in-law always had patchwork quilts.

ER:    It was all very economical, wasn't it?

R:    Oh yes. They are still making them. The lady next door makes them but she sells them for £10 a time. She makes the little tiny ones but we didn't. We used to put whatever we could in big squares and line them with an old blanket and put them on the bed. I remember my mother-in-law putting sheets of brown paper between blankets in winter for warmth.

ER:    I've never heard that one before.

R:    Or a newspaper with brown paper in between the blankets.

ER:    What about bedding, did you have any economical ways of doing sheets and pillow-cases?

R:    Turning the sides to the middle and making pillow-cases out of them. I can show you two little tea-towels made out of my grandmother's linen sheets, the last little bits.

ER:    They went on and on, didn't they?

R:    Yes. Oh yes. I made children's petticoats out of them. My eldest daughter's cradle or cot was made out of a banana crate trimmed with bags that had had cream of tartar in. It was very fine muslin.

ER:    And where did you get those from?

R:    My brother worked for a wholesale grocer and they used to pack this cream of tartar into half pounds and he used to bring the bags home and they were washed. I made curtains all round her cot and it cost me fourpence for a banana crate. I've had a dress made out of dusters. The man next door to us when I was a girl worked for a coal dealer and they used to get bags of clean dusters for polishing their brasses. He used to bring dusters home, spotted muslin and three or four all alike. My mother has made me dresses out of them. I can remember one in particular when we walked to the park with it when Queen Mary was crowned and we all had to walk. There were no buses from the top of Ashton to Avenham Park and we had to walk. I had this cream dress with a blue sash on, made out of three dusters. I have taken things off my own back and made my children things. Necessity is the mother of invention.

## Women and the domestic economy, 1940–70

### Mrs Atkin (Mrs A.3.L.), born 1944

LB: When did you return to work again?

R: Very soon after Peter was born. I didn't intend doing. I wanted one of these continental pushchairs and we'd no money for one and a mother from nursery school said 'Why don't you work in the evenings with me? I'm a telephonist,' and I didn't even know there was a telephone exchange—we'd no phone. She said 'They're taking on summer staff.' So this would be . . . Peter was born January . . . so this would be the same summer. And when I asked Arnold, then he did have views. He didn't want me to work or go out to work.

LB: Why was that?

R: Because he wanted me at home. I'd done my bit and we could manage you see. By this time the house was paid for. I'd stopped giving Arnold's mum my money and he was on more money because he was now a draughtsman and so he didn't agree with it but as I pointed out, we couldn't afford this pushchair, that was a real extra and it was only for six weeks. So he said I could and I was there nine years.

LB: He got used to the idea, did he?

R: Yes. I think it wasn't as inconvenient for him anyway because I was at home all day with both children, because I had Elizabeth as well, and if there was one evening when we wanted to go out together or he needed to go out, you could swop the evening anyway. So it was no bother to him and I think he enjoyed that little bit of time with the children and popped them to bed.

LB: How many hours did you work?

R: Fifteen hours a week including week-ends. So it would be time-and-a-half of Sunday but I didn't like working Sunday days but I could swop them for Sunday evenings. I tried to keep my days free for family and I really enjoyed it. I think I'd still be there only they made us redundant in the end.

### Mrs Kennedy (Mrs K.2.P.), born 1936

ER: How many years were you there?

R: Eleven.

ER: Really! As long as that?

R: Yes.

ER: Oh heavens, I didn't realize.

R: Yes and I only really went for a little bit of spending money for a few weeks, but I finished up there. Because I enjoyed it after you know, I used to look forward to going, there was quite a good crowd.

ER:   How old was the youngest when you went, or was it before the youngest was born?

R:    No, he was three. And I went at night, started at six until nine o'clock. And then when he started school I put in for mornings, so that I would be home for the afternoon. I used to finish at one o'clock.

ER:   Oh I see, so you only did the evenings for quite a little while really. A couple of years perhaps?

R:    Yes a couple of years and then I went on mornings. And they used to stay for their dinners, and it was that I would be at home when they all came home from school, yes.

ER:   Do you think you worked because you enjoyed it all, because the money was useful, or for both?

R:    Well I went for a bit of spending money really, but as things went on I got used to the money and I got that little bit extra you see. And it helps a lot, it did. I mean there was a lot of things I could get then you know, we could save up for holidays and things like that. Plus the company as well.

### Mrs Leighton (Mrs L.2.L.), born 1941

LB:   So who handled the money in your marriage?

R:    Well he did really. Well I mean it was all right while I was working and like I always had my own money, but unfortunately when I wasn't working he sort of handled the money and held the reins really.

LB:   So when you weren't working he was giving you housekeeping money was he?

R:    Yes.

LB:   Who made important decisions in your marriage would you say?

R:    Well we tried to discuss them but he finally—I mean these sort of things come out after you are married. He tended to be one—I mean I could see it as well with his parents, they always gave in, he was just completely spoiled. Obviously I didn't see it beforehand but you know, I mean with being brought up with three there wasn't the money to go around, and I just learnt that I couldn't always have just what I wanted.

### Mr Stephenson (Mr S.9.P.), born 1925

ER:   Just thinking about the budget did your wife look after the everyday spending, or did you decide together what to do with it? I mean different families have different arrangements, you know?

R:    Well we used to just work it out, what we needed, what was best.

ER:   But you did it together, did you?

R:    We did it together, we worked it out together.

ER:   Because in some families the husband just sort of gave the wife the money, and said you get on with it?

R:    Well I always thought that to be a bit cruel, because sometimes it doesn't work out does it? And if you both know what's happening, then you solve the problem together, it's easier that way. And I've always been fortunate to have a motor bike or a car, and with being brought up in the country, a lot of my school day friends later on became owners of farms. So I used to go visiting them and instead of buying five or ten pound of potatoes and having to hump them all the way from town on a bus, which is hard work, I used to go and buy a bag of potatoes, and by buying a bag off friends I used to get them cheaper. I'd buy a bag of carrots, a bag of onions, which in the long term you are saving money. And if I was getting too much, maybe the neighbours would think, Ooh they are cheap, so I would split a bag.

ER:    A very good idea. Where would your wife do her shopping, usually?

R:    Well, when we first got married it was the corner shop sort of thing. But now you have got the supermarkets.

ER:    Well, that's one of the changes. When you moved up to Ashton, where would she shop there?

R:    Well, I used to take her to the supermarket.

### Mrs Maxwell (Mrs M.12.B.), born 1936

ER:    Do you think women work hard?

R:    Oh yes, lots of women yes. Because they go to work, they are doing two jobs aren't they, I don't think it's easy for women but I still wouldn't like to be a man. If I was born again I still wouldn't like to be born a man.

ER:    What do you like about being a woman?

R:    I don't know really. Well it's nice to be sort of taken out and looked after and the door opened for you and, you know, people caring for you. I just like being at home, just the homely things yes.

ER:    Do you reckon you controlled the budget when you were first married or was it more of a joint, you know, we'll spend this and that?

R:    Well when we got married we decided that we wouldn't use my wages, my wages went straight to the bank. Because we said one day we will have to live on one wage so it's best to start from the beginning. So that's what we did. So we discussed matters you know and John decided how much we would put away for gas and electricity and that. He was a budget accountant you see, so he always did that side.

ER:    But that would be different wouldn't it from your mother's generation, where I think the husband earned the money and the wife spent it?

R:    Yes. No, I mean I had my housekeeping but I mean we discussed matters and put it away together you know, what we would do. Whereas mam she had her money and she had to pay the electricity, the rates, the gas, and everything out the money you know.

### Notes

1 Although based partly on official sources, the argument relies heavily on oral evidence collected by myself and Dr Lucinda Beier in the years 1988 and 1989 in the three northern towns of Barrow, Lancaster, and Preston. In all, 99 respondents were interviewed. The project was sponsored by the Economic and Social Research Council.

2  These projects were an investigation into family and social life in Barrow and Lancaster 1890–1930, which was sponsored initially by a Nuffield Small Grant 1972–4 and by the SSRC 1974–6. The second was a similar project in Preston for the period 1890–1940 and was funded by the SSRC from 1978 to 1981. They were carried out under the aegis of the Centre for North West Regional Studies in the University of Lancaster; 170 respondents were interviewed.

## References

Bosanquet, H. 1906. *The Family*, London, Macmillan, p. 199.

Bowley, A. L. and Hogg, M. H. 1925. *Has Poverty Diminished?*, London, King, p. 37.

Great Britain, General Register Office, 1911–15. *Census of England and Wales 1911, County of Lancaster*, table 25.

Myrdal, A. and Klein, V. 1956. *Women's Two Roles*, London, Routledge & Kegan Paul, p. 26.

Roberts, E. 1984. *A Woman's Place*, Oxford, Basil Blackwell, p. 112.

Rowntree, B. S. 1901. *Poverty: a study of town life*, London, Nelson, p. 296.

Rowntree, B. S. 1941. *Poverty and Progress*, London, Longman, pp. 28–9.

Rowntree, B. S. and Lavers, G. 1951. *Poverty and the Welfare State*, London, Longman, pp. 24–5.

Summerfield, P. 1984. *Women Workers in the Second World War. Production and patriarchy in conflict*, London, Croom Helm.

# PART III

MIGRATION AND MOVEMENT

# 7

# E. G. Ravenstein and the 'Laws of Migration'

## D. B. Grigg

It is now 100 years since E. G. Ravenstein's first paper on the laws of migration was published in the *Geographical Magazine*; his later but better known articles appeared in the *Statistical Journal* in 1885 and 1889.[1] His work laid the foundation for subsequent research on migration, and indeed one recent authority has written that 'while there have been literally thousands of migration studies in the meantime, few additional generalizations have been advanced'.[2] Yet geographers paid little attention to his work for three-quarters of a century. However, in 1943 an article by H. C. Darby on nineteenth-century migration within England and Wales renewed interest in Ravenstein's work, which has since become much more familiar to geographers.[3] Ernst Georg Ravenstein was born in Frankfurt-am-Main in 1834 but came to England in 1852: he married an Englishwoman and spent the rest of his life in this country, although he died in Germany in 1913. He worked as a cartographer for the War Office from 1854 to 1872, although he was already writing prolifically. After his retirement he was an active member of the Statistical Society, the Royal Geographical Society, the International Geographical Union, and the British Association for the Advancement of Science. He wrote on many topics, but his best work was on the history of exploration and on population.[4]

This paper has two aims. First, to restate Ravenstein's laws; and second, to review the work which has been done on internal migration in nineteenth-century England and Wales since he wrote his work. The latter might seem a limited task. But to review all the work on migration

E. G. Ravenstein and the 'laws of migration'
D. B. Grigg

From *Journal of Historical Geography* 3, 1977, pp. 41–51.

which Ravenstein's seminal papers have stimulated would be daunting, for there have been, as E. S. Lee has noted, 'literally thousands' of migration studies in many parts of the world since his papers were published.[5]

## The 'laws' of migration

Ravenstein's 'laws' of migration—he also referred to 'principles' and 'rules'—were listed in his article published in the *Statistical Journal* for 1885; he restated them in a second article in the same journal in 1889. But he had published an earlier analysis of migration in the *Geographical Magazine* in 1876. It is worthwhile restating his laws on a number of grounds. First, the 1876 article contains a useful generalization on age and migration which is not referred to in the later and better known articles. Second, the 1885 and 1889 laws differ. No reference was made in the 1889 list to the statement that the natives of towns are less migratory than those of rural areas. Third, two additional laws were enunciated in 1889; that towns grow more by immigration than by natural increase, and that the volume of migration increases as transport improves and industry grows. Fourth, two laws in the 1885 list on the process of absorption and dispersion are subsumed into one in 1889, the 'step by step' law. Fifth, Ravenstein's list of laws in the 1889 article was preceded by a discussion of the motives for migration. E. S. Lee has suggested, with justification, that this be listed as an additional law.[6] Thus the laws may be restated as follows:

1 The majority of migrants go only a short distance.[7]
2 Migration proceeds step by step.
  Ravenstein wrote in 1885[8] 'the inhabitants of the country immediately surrounding a town of rapid growth flock into it; the gaps thus left in the rural population are filled up by migrants from more remote districts, until the attractive force of one of our rapidly growing cities makes its influence felt, step by step, to the most remote corner of the Kingdom'. An almost identical statement had appeared in 1876, with the significant omission of the phrase 'step by step'.
3 Migrants going long distances generally go by preference to one of the great centres of commerce or industry.[9]
4 Each current of migration produces a compensating counter-current.[10]
5 The natives of towns are less migratory than those of rural areas.[11]
6 Females are more migratory than males within the kingdom of their birth, but males more frequently venture beyond.[12]

7 Most migrants are adults: families rarely migrate out of their county of birth.[13]
8 Large towns grow more by migration than by natural increase.[14]
9 Migration increases in volume as industries and commerce develop and transport improves.[15]
10 The major direction of migration is from the agricultural areas to the centres of industry and commerce.[16]
11 The major causes of migration are economic.[17]

## Ravenstein's sources

Ravenstein's laws were based on the place of birth tables published in the British Censuses of 1871 and 1881, together with, in the 1889 paper, similar data from Censuses of North America and Europe. Questions about place of birth were first asked and published in the Census of Great Britain in 1841. It was not until 1851, however, that the place of birth tables showed the county of birth of each resident of England and Wales; at no time did the Census of England and Wales distinguish which county in Ireland or Scotland residents of English and Welsh counties had been born in. Unfortunately, whereas the data on place of enumeration was published for *registration* counties, the county of birth was the *civil* or *ancient* county. As the two counties sometimes had quite different boundaries, these tables have a limited value.[18] However, from 1861 to 1901 the place of birth tables used civil counties for both place of birth and place of enumeration.

The limitations of the place of birth tables are well known. They give no indication of when the migrant moved from place of birth to place of enumeration, nor whether he [or she] proceeded directly or in stages. There is of course no record of those who had left the British Isles.

Ravenstein classified migrants by the distance they had moved. *Local* migrants moved within the county of their birth, and thus go unrecorded in the Census. *Short-journey* migrants moved only from the county of their birth to an adjacent or border county. *Long-journey* migrants went beyond the border counties. Ravenstein used the data to show that the majority of migrants went only short distances. But the varying size and shape of English counties makes comparisons between counties hazardous.

We can now turn to consider what subsequent work has been done upon nineteenth-century English migration, discussing in turn each of Ravenstein's 'laws'.

(1) *The majority of migrants go only a short distance* Although some writers[19] have questioned whether short-distance migration was quite

as important as Ravenstein argued, most have agreed that it predominated in nineteenth-century England, and indeed still does today. Mostly this has been achieved by showing that the majority of the non-natives living in a town or county in a given year were born in the border counties; but the relationship between distance and migration can also be shown cartographically, by relating immigrants to a town or county to either the area or the population of the county whence they came. The predominance of short-distance migration in the nineteenth century has been demonstrated for Cambridgeshire, the West Midlands, London, York, Liverpool, Essex, Barrow, Nottinghamshire, Glasgow, north-eastern England, Northampton, South Shields, Oldham, and South Wales.[20]

All these articles rely upon the printed tables of the Census. However, the Census enumerators' schedules can now be consulted for 1841, 1851, 1861, 1871, 1881 and 1891 and they give the birth place of every *individual* recorded. So far they have been little used for the study of migration, but Anderson has used the 1851 material for Preston.[21] Forty-eight per cent of those enumerated had been born there; of those born elsewhere 42 per cent had been born within 10 miles of the town, and only 30 per cent 30 miles or more away, including 14 per cent in Ireland.

Where only the county of birth is known exact migration distances cannot be derived. However, if migrants are assumed to have moved from the mid-point of the county of birth to the mid-point of the county of enumeration average distances can be cited. This was first done to discuss migration to London,[22] but greatly expanded by Friedlander and Roshier to calculate the average distance moved between all adjacent counties, and from all counties to all non-adjacent counties between 1851 and 1911.[23] They found that the average distance moved between adjacent counties only varied between 45 and 53 miles between 1851 and 1911; movement between all counties and all non-adjacent counties varied between 107 and 114 miles from 1851 to 1911, but rose to 123 miles in the period 1931–51.

This is surprising for it has been suggested that the relative importance of long-distance compared with short-distance migration would have risen in the nineteenth century as the railway net extended and urbanization proceeded.[24] Even more striking differences might be expected between the average distance travelled in pre-industrial England and the period after 1750.

There are of course no place of birth tables before 1841 but two types of evidence have been used to trace migration in England before the nineteenth century. First are various lists of residents of towns which give the place of birth; they include lists of apprentices and freemen, deposition books and settlement certificates, and are invariably a biased sample—freemen coming from the wealthier sections of the population, whilst settlement certificates concerned the very poor.[25] All studies using these data, for various dates from the twelfth to the eighteenth centuries, confirm that short-distance migration was overwhelmingly important in towns in Kent, in Wednesbury, Sheffield, Stratford, Leicester, Sussex, St Helens, Bedfordshire, London, and Birmingham.[26] Unfortunately these data rarely cover a long period and preclude any attempt to discover if the average distance moved rose in the eighteenth and nineteenth centuries.

A second source of evidence is parish registers, which survive for some parishes from the sixteenth century: in some cases they give the place of residence of bride and groom. Although they only indicate a special type of mobility they can demonstrate long-term trends in migration distances. Studies of a number of parishes near Otmoor in Oxfordshire have shown that spatial mobility increased from the sixteenth to the nineteenth centuries.[27] In the early seventeenth century nearly four-fifths of those married were both resident in the parish where the marriage was celebrated, but by the first half of the twentieth century the proportion was less than a fifth. The decline was particularly sharp in the second half of the nineteenth century. When **exogamous marriages** are considered—that is when one or both of the partners were resident outside the parish—the mean marriage distance remained little changed at between four and eight miles until 1850, after which a sharp increase was noted. A similar study of five villages in Northamptonshire and Huntingdonshire from 1754 to 1943 shows that the average distance between a man's place of residence and his place of marriage was 2.9 miles from 1754 to 1843, but 12–16 miles from 1844 to 1943.[28] Similar work on parishes in Northamptonshire and Dorset would also suggest that it was not until the second half of the nineteenth century that there was a significant increase in marriage distances.[29]

Unfortunately, information from marriage registers is not an entirely reliable guide to the general mobility of the population, although it does suggest that the early stages of industrialization did not lead to a dramatic increase in the average distance travelled by migrants. The evidence of the place of birth statistics suggests that for some towns at any rate migrants came from a longer distance after 1851. Thus half the non-natives of the town of Nottingham in 1861 had been born elsewhere in the county; by 1891 this had fallen to only 20 per cent.[30] In 1841 only 10 per cent of the immigrants in Bradford had been born outside Yorkshire, by 1851 over 20 per cent had.[31] The dramatic growth of Middlesbrough led to a fall in the proportion of the population who were Yorkshire-born, from 75 per cent in 1861 to only 50 per cent in 1871.[32]

Although Ravenstein emphasized the effect of distance upon migration, he was aware that ease of access and nearness to other towns were also important.[33] Thus the density of emigrants from Cambridgeshire in 1851 and 1861 declined with distance for the most part; but London, Lancashire and the West Riding exercised a disproportionate attraction.[34] Ravenstein cannot then be seen as one of the pioneers of the **gravity model**; he made no explicit discussion of the influence of distance, the size of the attracting town and the source area of the immigrants. On the other hand, he suggested, in his discussion of the step hypothesis, the idea of 'intervening' opportunities.[35] He did not, and indeed could not, given the nature of his data, suggest, as some contemporary German writers did, that migration proceeded *staffelweise*, from farm to village, village to town, town to city, and city to metropolis.[36]

(2) *Migration proceeds step by step* Ravenstein's assertion that migrants did not proceed directly to their destination but by a series of steps was accepted and indeed publicized by Redford, who wrote in his review of early nineteenth-century migration: 'immigration into any centre of attraction having a wide sphere of influence was not a simple transfer of people from the circumference of a circle to its centre, but an exceedingly complex wavelike motion'.[37] Unfortunately it is difficult to substantiate this from the printed tables of the Census, although Ravenstein devoted much of his 1876 paper to this topic.

Llewellyn-Smith, in his study of late nineteenth-century migration to London, tried to test the hypothesis. He argued that if migrants proceeded by steps, settling for long periods at intervening places, then the average age of migrants from a great distance living in London would be greater than of those coming from near the city; his data for 1861 would appear to bear this out.[38] But the age of migrants in 1861 was not the age at which they arrived in London.[39]

The enumerator's schedules provide one means of testing the step hypothesis, for if families rather than individuals are considered, and the birthplaces of children are noted, the movement of the family group can be traced. Lawton has shown the circuitous manner in which some residents of Liverpool in 1851 must have arrived there.[40] A more sustained analysis has been made by D. Bryant, who has used the birthplace of mothers and their children and their place of residence in 1851 to demonstrate such movements in a number of South Devon parishes.[41] This method could be applied to large towns, although it must be remembered that much migration was by young, single people, rather than by families.[42] At present, it is difficult to confirm the step hypothesis; nor has modern research been able to examine the idea, although it has been shown that 50 per cent of a sample of migrants in Bristol had not come directly.[43] The few writers who have reconsidered the concept have been sceptical of its validity.[44]

(3) *Migrants going long distances generally go by preference to one of the great centres of commerce or industry* Although Ravenstein maintained that the bulk of migrants went only short distances, he recognized that a certain proportion—he estimated 25 per cent—of all migrants went long distances and that they went *directly* to the large industrial or commercial towns.

But there is no reliable means of estimating the proportion of long-distance migrants or of showing that they had proceeded directly to a large town or, as has been noted earlier, of ascertaining whether long-journey migrants increased in relative importance throughout the nineteenth century. Ravenstein, however, recognized a 'special class' of migrants who moved long distances, and there is some suggestion in recent work that long-distance migrants had more skill or education than short-distance migrants, as recent studies of migration in Birmingham, York, and the Peak District[45] have shown, whilst there is some evidence that the volume of long-distance migration varied with fluctuations in the trade cycle.[46]

(4) *Each current of migration produces a compensating counter-current* Even in areas suffering from heavy net out-migration there is always some in-migration. Thus, for example, Huntingdonshire's population fell because of out-migration at every Census from 1861 to 1901. Yet in 1901 there were natives of every English and Welsh county living in the county, whilst Anglesey, whose population had been falling since 1851, also had representatives of all other Welsh and English counties.[47] Ravenstein was thus remarkably perceptive in calling attention to the existence of these counter-currents. There are unfortunately few studies of the areas of in-migration and out-migration for individual counties in the nineteenth century other than Ravenstein's own work, but those that have been done suggest that the areas of in-migration and out-migration were very similar.[48] Hägerstrand has since elaborated this idea and described the *migration fields* of a number of Swedish parishes.[49]

(5) *The natives of towns are less migratory than those of rural areas* Ravenstein stated this as one of his laws only in the 1885 paper, but his statistics are unconvincing; indeed, as has been pointed out, the figures

may be interpreted to show the converse.[50] No subsequent writers on British migration have considered this 'law'.

(6) *Females are more migratory than males within the Kingdom of their birth, but males more frequently venture beyond* Ravenstein noted that in 1871 and 1881 Census tables, more women were found outside the counties of their birth within England and Wales but more men in Scotland and Ireland, and thus argued that females were more migratory than men over short distances, but that more men tended to travel longer distances. This was partly due to the sex ratio in the nineteenth century, and the fact that more men than women migrated overseas.[51] But later work has substantiated the hypothesis.[52] A majority of emigrants from rural Essex went to London, where more Essex-born women than men were to be found. But the female surplus diminished with distance from Essex; in the northern manufacturing towns there were more Essex men than women. The reasons for the greater propensity of women to migrate would seem to be the lack of employment opportunities in rural areas, urban demand for domestic servants, and the fact that it was normally women who moved at marriage.

There were, however, exceptions to the generalization that women were more migratory than men; in some of the rising heavy industrial areas in the late nineteenth century more male than female migrants were recorded, as has been shown for Barrow, the Rhondda, and Middlesbrough.[53] The preponderance of women amongst migrants received special attention in the 1911 Census reports; the comparatively few exceptions amongst the counties and county boroughs were garrison towns, mining areas, ports, and a number of manufacturing towns.[54]

The predominance of women amongst migrants has greatly diminished since the nineteenth century. Within Scotland, for example, there is now little difference in the migratory propensities of men and women, although there are more male immigrants into the country.[55]

(7) *Most migrants are adults: families rarely migrate out of their county of birth* In his 1876 paper Ravenstein briefly considered age and migration, and was able to show that whilst over half the English-born living in their native counties were under 20, only 28 per cent of the men and 25 per cent of the women who lived in English and Welsh counties other than those in which they were born were under 20 years old. With similar data on Scotland and Ireland he concluded that more than two-thirds of the migrants were over 20 years old, and that whole families leave the country of their birth only under exceptional circumstances.[56] He did not return to this issue in his later papers. Nor was he the first to

establish the now widely accepted principle that migrants are predominantly adolescents and young adults, between the ages of 15 and 35. Indeed as the Census at the time simply distinguished between over and below 20 years, this was impossible.

As early as 1851 the authors of the General Report to the Census had noted the much greater proportion of adults than young children who had migrated,[57] but there was no subsequent comment in the reports until 1911, when the Census published, for selected counties and county boroughs, the ages of non-natives. These showed the disproportionate numbers in the 25–35 age-groups when compared with the population as a whole.[58] Earlier, Llewellyn-Smith had shown that migration into London took place mainly at ages between 15 and 30 years,[59] and A. L. Bowley demonstrated that the maximum movement of agricultural labourers out of rural areas took place when they were aged between 17 and 25 years.[60] But it was A. B. Hill's work on migration from Essex that established the predominance of migration in the younger age-groups. He found that in the 1850s the heaviest losses for males were in the age-groups 15–20 and 20–25, amongst girls 10–15 and 15–20, and that the same held true for the period 1901–11. There was little change in the age of migration between the two dates.[61] Nearly all modern studies have confirmed that migrants are predominantly adolescents and young adults, both in Britain and elsewhere in the world.[62]

(8) *Large towns grow more by migration than by natural increase* Ravenstein listed this statement as one of his general conclusions in the 1885 paper, and he has made a similar assertion in the 1876 paper. He offered no evidence to support it yet it was generally believed at the time.[63] There was some evidence to support this belief. In pre-industrial towns mortality was so high that immigration was necessary to maintain numbers. It was once thought by historians that mortality was equally high in the new industrial towns of the nineteenth century, so that their rapid growth could only have been due to migration.[64] Yet natural increase may have been more important in urban growth before 1851 than is sometimes admitted. In spite of the defects of parish registers,[65] they show that growth by natural increase alone had begun in some towns in the second half of the eighteenth century.[66] Thus, according to J. D. Chambers, 'the mid-eighteenth century may be said to represent the dawning of a new urban age'.[67] None the less the growth would have been slow, had it not been for the increased volume of migration. Chambers's study of Nottingham between 1700 and 1801 shows that the town gained by natural increase in every quinquennium after 1745, but in each quinquennium the gain by migration exceeded that

by natural increase.[68] But the role of migration must have been more important than a simple comparison of the increase due to natural gain and to immigration might suggest. Immigrants tended to be young and often unmarried; they married in the towns and their children formed part of the natural increase.

In the first half of the nineteenth century, many towns grew by natural increase—in spite of the high death rates—but the contribution of migration was still more important. Thus the township of Liverpool gained by natural increase 1811–21, 1821–31, and 1831–41 but, in the first two of these decades, migration greatly exceeded natural increase.[69] In Hull there was a small gain by natural increase after 1750 but most of the increase was due to migration.[70] But after 1871 Hull's gain by natural increase consistently exceeded that by migration. Where studies have been made of the relative importance of migration and natural increase in the second half of the nineteenth century, using the Registrar General's figures, they show that natural increase had become far more important than migration in accounting for urban growth.[71]

Comparatively little has been written on the relative importance of natural increase and migration in accounting for the growth of British cities in the nineteenth century. Not only did it apparently vary over time, but there were undoubtedly differences between towns; thus in the 1880s migration accounted for 71.7 per cent of Manchester's population increase, but only 9.4 per cent of Edinburgh's.[72] Further, there were increasingly important differences within cities. The old centres of cities began to lose by migration, whilst the suburbs grew by both natural increase and migration. Here is a major field for research.

(9) *Migration increases in volume as industries and commerce develop and transport improves* Ravenstein believed that the volume of migration was increasing, a view shared by later writers such as Adna Weber.[73] Unfortunately, the place of birth tables have considerable limitations in tracing such changes. They exclude movements within a county, which were probably a majority of all moves; and they refer not to intercensal *net* movement, but to lifetime migration. It is, however, possible to modify the figures to show net intercensal movement between counties by adjusting the place of birth figures. Various methods have been tried to produce corrected net gains and losses for South Wales and for England and Wales as a whole.[74] Only Friedlander and Roshier's figures provide a basis for calculating long-term trends in the volume of migration. Friedlander has subsequently calculated that rural–urban migration increased six-fold between the early 1800s and the 1840s, and thereafter declined[75] (see table 7.1). However, other calculations made by A. K. Cairncross using the census data and the registration of

**Table 7.1**   Rural–urban migration in England and Wales in the nineteenth century (thousands)

| | | | |
|---|---|---|---|
| 1800 | 541 | 1860 | 2,856 |
| 1810 | 883 | 1870 | 2,540 |
| 1820 | 1,094 | 1880 | 2,000 |
| 1830 | 2,336 | 1890 | 1,257 |
| 1840 | 3,380 | 1900 | 1,039 |
| 1850 | 2,217 | | |

*Source*: Friedlander (1969)

births and deaths for the period 1841–1911 suggest that the rural exodus from *rural registration districts* did not reach its peak until the 1880s, declining thereafter.[76]

(10) *The major direction of migration is from the rural areas to the towns* All Ravenstein's data suggested that it was the industrial and commercial counties that were gaining most by migration, and the rural counties that were losing or gaining least. He emphasized, however, the predominance of short-distance migration and therefore did not assume, as some later writers did, that there was a movement of population from the agricultural south and east to the industrial Midlands and north. This had been noted in the General Report of the 1861 Census; 'the tendency of the South Saxon population to emigrate to the North is excessively small . . .'.[77] It was left to Redford[78] to state more categorically that the growing industrial towns of the north recruited their migrants mainly from the north and Midlands, whilst those living south of a line from the Wash to the Severn migrated mainly to London, a pattern well demonstrated by subsequent writers.[79]

Whilst it would seem true that the major flows of migrants were from the rural districts to London and the industrial and commercial towns of the Midlands and the north, by the 1880s another movement was apparent, as was noted by Ravenstein. Commenting on the counter-currents of migration from London to the adjacent counties, he observed that 'many have merely removed to what are actually suburbs and can hardly be said to have left the metropolis'.[80] This was a new direction for British migration and one that has become the major form of movement in modern times.[81] As yet, however, comparatively little is known about the nature of early suburban migration. Did the populations of these early suburbs come from the old city centres or did migrants to London settle initially in the suburbs? Were the suburbs healthier and thus possessed of higher rates of increase? A beginning has been made on such work but much remains to be done.[82]

In demographic terms the nineteenth century ended with the

outbreak of the First World War. In the 1920s and 1930s new directions of flow became important: suburban migration continued in the south-east, and inter-urban flows, particularly from the old industrial regions to London and the Midlands, became more important than rural–urban movement.[83] But little of this was apparent in Ravenstein's lifetime, although by the 1880s some northern industrial towns were already showing a migrational loss.[84]

(11) *The major causes of migration are economic* Ravenstein had little doubt that the main causes of internal migration were the attraction of more jobs and higher wages in the towns, although he did note the significance of 'overpopulation' in rural areas.[85]

Subsequent work would suggest he was right, at least for the second half of the nineteenth century, for fluctuations in the volume of rural–urban migration showed little correlation with prosperity in agriculture, and average wages in industry were above those in agriculture from the middle of the century until the present day.[86] After 1851 there was a continuous decline in the numbers employed in agriculture and widespread rural depopulation.[87] Before 1841 there is little reliable information on migration, and the relation between population growth, migration, and urbanization are not clearly understood. Although it is likely that economic motives predominated it is possible that the 'push' of increasing poverty in the countryside was as important as the 'pull' exercised by higher wages in the towns. Rural England experienced a considerable increase in its population between 1750 and 1850, in spite of the considerable migration to the towns that went on in this period.[88] Much of this increase was absorbed in agriculture down to 1820, both in the reclamation of new land and more intensive use of labour as new methods were adopted. But by the 1820s population growth was outrunning the demand for labour and there is evidence of considerable underemployment, which must have stimulated rural–urban migration.[89]

## Conclusions

It is hoped that this article has shown that Ravenstein's contribution to the study of migration was a very considerable one. His hypotheses about the nature of migration have stimulated a remarkable amount of research on migration in many parts of the world.[90] His work on migration in nineteenth-century Britain, although greatly elaborated by later writers, has not been superseded. This review of subsequent work reveals how much remains to be done. As H. J. Dyos has observed: 'We still know so little, for example, about the ways in which the millions of migrations that comprised the cities were made. Ravenstein's, Redford's and Cairncross's cumulative efforts have been filled out to surprisingly little extent, both for the period before and during that covered by the Census.'[91]

## Notes

1 E. G. Ravenstein's 'Census of the British Isles, 1871; birthplaces and migration', *Geographical Magazine* 3 (1876) 173–7, 201–6, 229–33; 'The laws of migration', *Journal of the Statistical Society* 48 (1885) 167–227; 'The laws of migration', *Journal of the Statistical Society* 52 (1889) 214–301.
2 E. S. Lee, 'A theory of migration', pp. 282–97 in J. A. Jackson (ed.), *Migration* (London 1969).
3 H. C. Darby, 'The movement of population to and from Cambridgeshire between 1851 and 1861, *Geographical Journal* 101 (1943) 118–25.
4 D. Grigg, E. G. Ravenstein, *Geographers* 1 (1976).
5 Lee, 'A theory of migration', 284.
6 Lee, 'A theory of migration', 282–3.
7 Ravenstein, 'The laws of migration' (1885) 199; (1889) 286.
8 Ravenstein, *Census* 202; 'The laws of migration' (1885) 199.
9 Ravenstein, 'The laws of migration' (1885) 199.
10 Ravenstein, *Census* 230; 'The laws of migration' (1885) 199; (1889) 287.
11 Ravenstein, 'The laws of migration' (1885) 199.
12 Ravenstein, *Census* 229; 'The laws of migration' (1885) 199; (1889) 287.
13 Ravenstein, *Census* (1876) 230.
14 Ravenstein, *Census* (1876) 202; 'The laws of migration' (1889) 287.
15 Ravenstein, 'The laws of migration' (1889) 287.
16 Ravenstein, *Census* (1876) 202.
17 Ravenstein, 'The laws of migration' (1885) 181, 198; (1889) 286.
18 Darby, 'The movement of population'.
19 Darby, 'The movement of population'; R. Lawton, 'Geographical analysis of population movements', pp. 60–4 in G. Kuriyan (ed.), *The Indian Geographical Society Silver Jubilee Souvenir and N. Subrahmanyam Souvenir Volume* (Madras 1952); 'The population of Liverpool in the mid-nineteenth century', *Transactions of the Historical Society of Lancashire and Cheshire* 107 (1955) 89–120.
20 Darby, 'The movement of population'; R. Lawton, 'Genesis of population', pp. 120–31 in W. Smith, (ed.), *A Scientific Survey of Merseyside* (Liverpool 1953); Lawton, 'The population of Liverpool'; Lawton, 'Population movements in the West Midlands 1841–1861', *Geography* 43 (1958) 164–77; H. A. Shannon, 'Migration and the growth of London, 1841–1891', *Economic History Review* 5 (1934) 79–86; W. A. Armstrong, *Stability and Change in an English County Town: a social study of York 1801–1851* (Cambridge 1974); A. B. Hill, 'Internal migration and its effects upon the death rates with special reference to the County of Essex', Medical Research Council, Special Report Series, No. 95 (London 1925); J. D. Marshall, *Furness and the Industrial Revolution: an economic*

*history of Furness (1711–1900) and the town of Barrow (1757–1897), with an epilogue* (Barrow-in-Furness 1958); R. Osborne, 'Population and settlement', pp. 341–360 in K. C. Edwards (ed.), *Nottingham and its Region* (Nottingham 1966); A. Redford, *Labour Migration in England, 1800–1850* (Manchester 1926); J. W. House, 'North-eastern England: population movements and the landscape since the early nineteenth century', *University of Durham, King's College, Newcastle, Department of Geography Research Series* 1; P. N. Jones, 'Some aspects of immigration into the Glamorgan coalfield between 1881 and 1911', *Transactions of the Honourable Society of Cymmrodorion* (1969) 82–98; B. Thomas, 'The migration of labour into the Glamorganshire coalfield (1861–1911)', *Economica* 10 (1930) 275–94; J. Foster, *Class Struggle and the Industrial Revolution: early industrial capitalism in three English towns* (London 1974) 77.

21 M. Anderson, *Family Structure in Nineteenth Century Lancashire* (Cambridge 1971); 'Urban migration in nineteenth century Lancashire: some insights into two conflicting hypotheses', *Annales de Demographie Historique* 2 (1971) 13–26.

22 H. Llewellyn-Smith, 'Influx of population', pp. 59–143 in C. Booth (ed.), *Life and Labour of the People in London* 3 (London 1902).

23 D. Friedlander and R. J. Roshier, 'A study of internal migration in England and Wales', part 1, *Population Studies* 19 (1966) 239–79.

24 Darby, 'The movement of population' 124–5; Redford, *Labour Migration* 190.

25 J. Patten, 'Rural–urban migration in pre-industrial England', *University of Oxford, School of Geography, Research Paper* 6 (1973).

26 C. W. Chalklin, *Seventeenth-century Kent: a social and economic history* (London 1965) 33; A. F. Butcher, 'The origins of Romney freemen 1433–1523', *Economic History Review* 27 (1974) 16–27; P. Clark, 'The migrant in Kentish towns 1580–1640', pp. 117–63 in P. Clark and P. Slack (eds), *Crisis and Order in English Towns 1500–1700* (London 1972); J. F. Ede, *History of Wednesbury* (Wednesbury 1962) 172; E. J. Buckatzsch, 'Places of origin of a group of immigrants into Sheffield, 1624–1799', *Economic History Review* 2 303–6; E. M. Carus-Wilson, 'The first half century of the borough of Stratford upon Avon', *Economic History Review* 18 (1965) 46–63; C. T. Smith, 'The growth of Leicester 1670–1835', pp. 191–2 in R. A. McKinley (ed.), *V.C.H., Leicester* 4 (London 1958); J. Cornwall, 'Evidence of population mobility in the seventeenth century', *Bulletin of the Institute of Historical Research* 40 (1967) 143–52; T. C. Barker and J. R. Harris, *A Merseyside Town in the Industrial Revolution: St. Helen's 1750–1900* (Liverpool 1954) 145; N. L. Tranter, 'Population and social structure in a Bedfordshire parish: the Cardington listing of inhabitants 1782', *Population Studies* 21 (1967) 261–82; D. F. McKenzie, 'Apprenticeship in the Stationer's Company, 1550–1640', *The Library* 13 (1958) 292–8; D. V. Glass, 'Socio-economic status and occupations in the City of London at the end of the seventeenth century', pp. 373–85 in A. E. J. Hollander and W. Kellaway (eds), *Studies in London History* (London 1969); J. C. Russell, 'Medieval midland and northern migration to London', *Speculum* 34 (1959) 641–5; W. H. B. Court, *The Rise of the Midland Industries 1600–1838* (Oxford 1953) 47–8; R. A. Pelham, 'The immigrant population of Birmingham 1686–1726', *Transactions and Proceedings of the Birmingham Archaeological Society* 61 (1937) 45–82.

27 C. F. Küchemann, A. J. Boyce and G. A. Harrison, 'A demographic and genetic study of a group of Oxfordshire villages', *Human Biology* 39 (1967) 251–76; A. J. Boyce, C. F. Küchemann and G. A. Harrison, 'The reconstruction of historical movement patterns', pp. 303–19 in E. D. Acheson (ed.), *Record Linkage in Medicine* (Edinburgh 1968).

28 A. Constant, 'The geographical background of intervillage population movements in Northamptonshire and Huntingdonshire, 1754–1943', *Geography* 33 (1948) 78–88.

29 R. F. Peel, 'Local intermarriage and the stability of rural population in the English Midlands', *Geography* 27 (1942) 22–30; P. J. Perry, 'Nineteenth century working class isolation and mobility in rural Dorset, 1837–1936', *Transactions of the Institute of British Geographers* 46 (1969) 115–41.

30 R. A. Church, *Economic and Social Change in a Midland Town: Victorian Nottingham, 1815–1900* (London 1966) 234.

31 J. F. C. Harrison, *The Early Victorians 1832–1851* (London 1971) 147.

32 Redford, *Labour Migration* 189.

33 Ravenstein, *Census* 204; 'The laws of migration' (1885) 206.

34 Darby, 'The movement of population' 124–5.

35 Ravenstein, 'The laws of migration' (1889) 286; S. A. Stouffer, 'Intervening opportunities: a theory relating mobility and distance', *American Sociological Review* 5 (1940) 845–67.

36 A. Weber, *The Growth of Cities in the Nineteenth Century: a study in statistics* (New York 1899) 267.

37 Redford, *Labour Migration* 186.

38 Llewellyn-Smith, 'Influx of population' 69–70.

39 W. A. Armstrong, 'The interpretation of the Census Enumerator's books for Victorian towns', pp. 73–84 in H. J. Dyos (ed.), *The Study of Urban History* (London 1968).

40 Lawton, 'The population of Liverpool' 101.

41 D. Bryant, 'Demographic trends in South Devon in the mid-nineteenth century', pp. 125–142 in K. J. Gregory and W. L. D. Ravenhill (eds), *Exeter Essays in Geography in Honour of Arthur Davies* (Exeter 1971).

42 Armstrong, 'The interpretation of the Census Enumerator's books' 84.

43 C. J. Jansen, 'Migration: a sociological problem', pp. 4–21 in C. J. Jansen (ed.), *Readings in the Sociology of Migration* (London 1970).

44 C. T. Smith, 'The movement of population in England and Wales in 1851 and 1861', *Geographical Journal* 117 (1951) 200–10; B. A. Holderness, 'Personal mobility in some rural parishes of Yorkshire, 1777–1822', *Yorkshire Archaeological Journal* 42 (1970) 444–54; Anderson, 'Urban migration'; J. Saville, *Rural Depopulation in England and Wales, 1851–1951* (London 1957).

45 R. Lawton, 'An age of great cities', *Town Planning Review* 43 (1972) 199–224; Armstrong, *Stability and Change*; R. Hall, 'Occupation and population structure in part of the Derbyshire Peak District in the mid-nineteenth century', *East Midland Geographer* 6 (1974) 66–78.

46 Thomas, 'The migration of labour'.

47 *Census of England and Wales, 1901: Summary tables: Area, houses and population;*

*also population classified by ages, condition as to marriage, occupation, birth places and infirmities*, Session Papers, 1903, 84 (Cd. 1523) 246–7.

48  Darby, 'The movement of population'.

49  T. Hägerstrand, 'Migration and area: survey of a sample of Swedish migration fields and hypothetical considerations on their genesis', pp. 27–158 in D. Hanneberg, T. Hägerstrand and B. Odeving (eds), *Migration in Sweden: a symposium*, Lund Studies in Geography, Series B 13 (Lund 1957).

50  P. A. Sorokin, C. C. Zimmerman and C. J. Galpin (eds), *A Systematic Sourcebook in Rural Sociology* 1 (Minneapolis 1932) 218–9.

51  Saville, *Rural depopulation* 90; N. L. Tranter, *Population since the Industrial Revolution: the case of England and Wales* (London 1973) 59.

52  Hill, 'Internal migration'.

53  Marshall, *Furness and the Industrial Revolution* 353; E. D. Lewis, *The Rhondda Valleys* (London 1959) 239; Ravenstein, 'The laws of migration' (1885) 215.

54  *Census of England and Wales 1911, vol. 9: Birthplaces*, Sessional Papers, 1913, 77 (Cd. 7017).

55  T. H. Hollingsworth, 'Migration: a study based on Scottish experience between 1939 and 1964', *University of Glasgow Social and Economic Studies, Occasional Papers* 12 (Glasgow 1970) 64, 122.

56  Ravenstein, *Census* 230.

57  *Census of Great Britain, 1851: Population tables 2: Ages, general condition, occupations and birth places*, Sessional Papers, 1852–53, 87 (Cd. 1691) civ.

58  *Census of England and Wales 1911, vol. 9: Birthplaces*, Sessional Papers, 1913, 77 (Cd. 7017) xxiv.

59  Llewellyn-Smith, 'Influx of populations' 70.

60  A. L. Bowley, 'Rural population in England and Wales: a study of the changes of density, occupations and ages', *Journal of the Royal Statistical Society* 77 (1914) 597–645.

61  Hill, 'Internal migration'.

62  Hollingsworth, 'Migration'; Jansen, 'Migration'; M. P. Newton and J. R. Jeffrey, *Internal Migration: some aspects of population movements within England and Wales*, General Register Office Studies in Medical and Population Subjects 5 (London 1951).

63  *Census of Great Britain, 1841*, Sessional Papers, 1843, 22 (Cd. 496) 13.

64  C. M. Law, 'The growth of urban population in England and Wales, 1801–1911', *Transactions of the Institute of British Geographers* 41 125–44; E. A. Wrigley, 'A simple model of London's importance in changing English society and economy 1650–1750', *Past and Present* 37 (1967) 44–70.

65  J. T. Krause, 'Changes in English fertility and mortality, 1781–1850', *Economic History Review* 11 (1958) 52–70; P. Razzell, 'The evaluation of baptism as a form of birth registration through cross-matching census and parish register data: a study in methodology', *Population Studies* 26 (1972) 46; B. Hammond, 'Urban death rates in the early nineteenth century', *Economic History* 1 (1928) 419–28.

66  J. D. Chambers, 'Population change in a provincial town: Nottingham 1700–1800', pp. 97–124 in L. S. Pressnell (ed.), *Studies in the Industrial Revolution* (London 1960); P. Deane and W. A. Cole, *British Economic Growth 1688–1959*

(Cambridge 1962) 109; Weber, *The Growth of Cities*; J. E. Williams, 'Hull 1700–1835', pp. 90–173 in K. J. Allison (ed.), *V.C.H., East Riding* 1 *The City of Kingston-upon-Hull* (Oxford 1960); F. Beckwith, 'The population of Leeds during the Industrial Revolution', *Publications of the Thoresby Society* 41 (1948) 120–73.

67 J. D. Chambers, *Population, Economy and Society in Pre-industrial England* (Oxford 1972) 115.

68 Chambers, 'Population change'.

69 Lawton, 'Genesis of population'.

70 J. E. Williams, 'Hull 1700–1835', 191.

71 Shannon, 'Migration'; H. A. Shannon and E. Grebenik, *The Population of Bristol*, National Institute of Economic and Social Research, Occasional Papers 11 (Cambridge 1943); K. Picket, 'Migration in the Merseyside area', pp. 108–48 in R. Lawton and C. M. Cunningham (eds), *Merseyside: social and economic studies* (London 1970); D. V. Glass, 'A note on the under-registration of births in Britain in the nineteenth-century', *Population Studies* 5 (1951) 70–88; M. S. Teitelbaum, 'Birth under-registration in the constituent counties of England and Wales: 1841–1910', *Population Studies* 28 (1974) 329–44.

72 E. E. Lampard, 'The urbanizing world', pp. 3–57 in H. J. Dyos and M. Wolff (eds), *The Victorian City: images and realities* (London 1973).

73 Weber, *The Growth of Cities*.

74 Thomas, 'The migration of labour'; Shannon, 'Migration'; Friedlander and Roshier, 'A study of internal migration'; D. E. Baines, 'The use of published census data in migration studies', pp. 311–35 in E. A. Wrigley (ed.), *Nineteenth-century Society: essays in the use of quantitative methods for the study of social data* (Cambridge 1972).

75 D. Friedlander, 'Demographic responses and population change', *Demography* 6 (1969) 359–81.

76 A. K. Cairncross, 'Internal migration in Victorian England', pp. 65–83 in A. K. Cairncross, *Home and Foreign Investment 1870–1913; studies in capital accumulation* (Cambridge 1953).

77 *Census of England and Wales 1861, vol. 3: General report*, Sessional Papers, 1863, 53 (Cd. 3221).

78 Redford *Labour Migration* 62, 183–7.

79 C. T. Smith, 'The movement of population'; R. H. Osborne, 'Migration trends in England and Wales, 1901–1951', *Geografica Polonica* 3 (1964) 137–62.

80 Ravenstein, 'The laws of migration' (1885) 185.

81 D. Friedlander, 'England's urban transition 1851–1951', *Urban Studies* 11 (1974) 127–41.

82 H. J. Dyos and D. A. Reeder, 'Slums and suburbs', pp. 359–88 in H. J. Dyos and M. Wolff (eds), *The Victorian City: images and realities*, vol. 1 (London: 1973); R. Lawton, 'The population of Liverpool'; J. R. Kellet, *The Impact of Railways on Victorian Cities* (London 1969); Shannon and Grebenik *The Population of Bristol*.

83 Osborne, 'Migration trends'; Friedlander and Roshier, 'A study of internal migration'.

84 Cairncross, 'Internal migration'.

85 Ravenstein, 'The laws of migration' (1885) 181; (1889) 286.
86 Cairncross, 'Internal migration'; J. R. Bellerby, *Agriculture and Industry: relative income* (London 1956).
87 J. R. Bellerby, 'The distribution of man-power in agriculture and industry 1851–1951', *Farm Economist* 9 (1958) 1–11; R. Lawton, 'Rural depopulation in nineteenth century England', pp. 227–56 in R. W. Steel and R. Lawton (eds), *Liverpool Essays in Geography* (London 1967).
88 P. Deane and W. A. Cole, *British Economic Growth, 1688–1959* (Cambridge 1962) 103, 108–9.
89 C. P. Timmer, 'The turnip, the new husbandry and the English agricultural revolution', *Quarterly Journal of Economics* 83 (1969) 375–95; E. L. Jones, 'The English agricultural labour market 1793–1872', *Economic History Review* 17 (1965) 322–38.
90 R. J. Pryor, 'Internal migration and urbanisation: an introduction and bibliography', *Department of Geography, James Cook University of North Queensland, Monograph Series* 2 (1971).
91 Dyos, *The Study of Urban History* 36.

# 8

# Historians and Immigration

## Colin Holmes

In considering migration and British society, we should guard against concentrating exclusively upon emigration. In other words, apart from asking 'Who left Britain and where did they go?', we need to ask 'Who came to Britain and what were the experiences of such groups after their arrival?'

If we begin from this standpoint, and concentrate essentially on the last one hundred years, it soon becomes clear that historians have paid little attention to immigration history. This lack of interest is strikingly evident in texts by Taylor, Bédarida, Robbins and Stevenson.[1] But if the footprints of historians are weak, those left by sociologists are heavy. Indeed, sociologists have dominated academic research on immigration into Britain. However, this sociological literature does not convey any impression of immigration as a continuing process; moreover, the weight of emphasis in these enquiries has centred upon Black and Asian immigrations since 1945. A dissatisfaction with this state of affairs provides some of the motivation for this discussion of historians and immigration. It is also influenced by the reflected experience of writing *John Bull's Island*, which attempted to construct the first comprehensive history of immigration into Britain, concentrating on the years between 1871 and 1971.[2] In writing this type of book, an awareness gradually develops of those issues that need to be kept in mind in future research activity.

Historians and immigration
Colin Holmes

From C. G. Pooley and I. D. Whyte (eds), *Migrants, Emigrants and Immigrants: a social history of migration*, London and New York, Routledge, 1991, pp. 191–207.

## Neglected areas: the Irish

Let us begin by noticing areas of immigration that would repay further attention. The last major general survey of Irish immigrants appeared in 1963 and, to reinforce one of the introductory emphases, it was written by J. A. Jackson, a sociologist.[3] Since that date a number of studies of the Irish minority have been published, including the works of L. P. Curtis, L. H. Lees, R. Swift and S. Gilley, and the useful synthesizing article of M. A. G. Ó'Tuathaigh.[4] However, apart from the last item, these writings are specific studies of parts of the Irish experience in Britain and heavily weighted towards the 'crown of thorns' period in the mid-nineteenth century. The subsequent history of Irish groups has been almost totally ignored. In recovering more of it we should be recapturing details of the largest single immigrant minority living in Britain during the last hundred years.[5] The fact that this fragment of statistical information is not widely known or appreciated is itself significant.

## The continental European dimension

If a wider glance is cast at European groups in Britain other holes soon become visible. But after making this point a degree of qualification is in order. The Jewish immigrants from Russian Poland in the late nineteenth century and the refugees from the Greater Germany in the 1930s have been the subject of numerous enquiries, even if some features of these immigrations still remain obscure.[6] Jewish communities have tended in most countries to recover their history and in Britain the efforts of individual scholars, of varying ideological persuasions, and institutional activity, have all contributed to this process.

Other groups, however, have been less well served. If we retreat into the late nineteenth century, until 1891 the Germans constituted the largest single continental European immigrant minority in Britain. The weight of enquiry into the experiences of Russian Polish Jews has obscured this fact. The result is that we need to know more regarding the reasons behind this movement from Germany. If the lives of certain individuals, such as Ludwig Mond,[7] and the history of specific groups, particularly that of German clerical workers,[8] have provided some evidence on this question, we still await information on German pork butchers, those Germans who worked in the salt industry in Cheshire, indeed on the majority of working-class Germans, including the impoverished German governesses, and also on the ubiquitous German bands that formed a familiar feature of British society before the Great War. A recent study, written incidentally by a specialist in English literature, is helpful in bringing into focus the intellectual and political *émigrés* who came to Britain from Germany before 1914, but it does not assist us much outside these groups.[9] Furthermore, it is only within the last few years that we have started to construct the history of responses towards the German minority during the First World War.[10] The gap which at present exists between the level of such recovery and the relatively lavish treatment of the Jewish refugees from the Greater Germany in the 1930s remains enormous.

If we switch from the Germans to the Italians we soon encounter important omissions. Until recently the Italians in Scotland had been better served by researchers. However, with the appearance of Lucio Sponza's work some of this ground has been clawed back.[11] Even so, none of this research has touched upon the more recent history of the Italians, the fifth largest immigrant minority in the 1950s and early 1960s when the migration flow from Italy was relatively strong. At the moment, the fullest account of these Italians, but a study almost certain to remain unpublished, arises from the efforts of an anthropologist.[12]

At this point it is worth observing that if the Jews who left the Tsar's Empire and settled in Britain have had their history substantially recovered, the same cannot be said of the other smaller groups that left the Russian Empire in the late nineteenth and early twentieth centuries. A start has been made on piecing together the history of the predominantly Catholic Lithuanian minority but the resulting picture of this group, who developed a particularly vibrant community in Lanarkshire, remains patchy and incomplete.[13] Furthermore, in spite of the interest shown by sociologists in Britain's post-war experience of immigration we are still some time away from the likely appearance of any large-scale comprehensive studies of the post-war Polish exiles. The European Volunteer Workers of various nationalities who were recruited by the British Government to assist in the post-war recovery of Britain have also been neglected. Published studies of the Polish minority have been dominated, until very recently, by a process of sociological enquiry which has been re-worked and revised on a number of different occasions. The recent publication of a historical investigation into the post-war Polish group marks a step in the right direction of recovery, even though this particular study takes 1950 as its outer chronological limit.[14] As for the European Volunteer Workers, no full-scale study has appeared since 1958 when a civil servant who had been involved in various EVW schemes worked on the official papers under a privileged access arrangement.[15] Interest has been revived recently in the EVWs, however, partly on account of the possible presence of war criminals among their ranks.[16] Independently of this enquiry, an ESRC-funded exercise led by sociologists at Glasgow University, has also begun to investigate the lives of those men and women who exchanged the dreariness of Displaced Persons camps in Europe for a new uncertain start in Britain.

## Neglected areas: immigration from beyond Europe

If we direct our attention to those groups who come from 'beyond the oceans',[17] it is a sobering thought that for many years the most comprehensive historical study of Blacks in Britain, in other words those groups of Afro-Caribbean origin, came from a social anthropologist, Kenneth Little, whose book *Negroes in Britain*, first published in 1948, constituted the pioneer study of what we might call 'the Edinburgh school'.[18] Work carried out at a later date by Jim Walvin has added to our understanding of the history of the Black minority[19] and paved the way for Peter Fryer's *Staying Power*, which now constitutes the fullest historical account of Blacks in Britain and is particularly useful for its emphasis on the varied but often neglected contributions made by Black men and women to the development of British society.[20] In the case of the minorities from the Indian subcontinent the most comprehensive historical study is the recently published work by Rozina Visram.[21] The books by Fryer and Visram have their strengths and weaknesses. However, both surveys must be welcomed and the fact that these books have been written by people outside the academic world underlines the fact that for many academic historians Blacks and Asians remain invisible people.[22] Such social invisibility applies even more to the Chinese, on whose presence in Britain there is no history.

Where historians have been reluctant to engage in any commitment, sociologists have been particularly busy and their interest in solving social problems has drawn them particularly to the study of Blacks and Asians since 1945. . . . In now considering their activity in more detail, it is worth observing that the bulk of their work is characterized by assumptions, claims, and perspectives against which historians need to be on their guard. Three interrelated emphases have some claim on our attention. In accounting for the hostility experienced by Blacks and Asians, sociological enquiries have placed considerable emphasis upon the role of the folkways, the cultural conditioning process, which is presented as one legacy of the colonial imperial epoch. In short, it has been emphasized that these groups did not step into a neutral ideological world when they arrived in Britain but entered into a society in which colonialism and imperialism had nourished impressions of white supremacy. This emphasis has been particularly pronounced in the work of John Rex and his followers.[23] If we can accept the possibility that such cultural conditioning might be important, we are still left with a number of problems which sociologists have done little to resolve and to which historians should address more attention. For example, are there specific strands within this general set of images upon which we should direct our attention? In addition, can we assess the influence of the weight of the past in relation to the weight of the present in analysing the causes of conflict? In other words, the blanket use of the past as an all-enveloping influence needs to be resisted; at the moment its deployment smacks heavily of speculation.[24]

Closely related to this emphasis on the persistence of the past is the nebulous use of the term racism to describe the hostility encountered by Blacks and Asians. Too often it remains undefined and in many cases has degenerated into little more than a catch-all concept or, in its ultimate degenerative form, into a term of mere abuse. There is also a failure in many accounts to recognize that racism possesses its own complex history and that its definition and social significance change over the course of time.[25]

Finally, and related to this emphasis, when sociologists in the course of their studies indulge in their token reference to historical precedents, they have shown a remarkable tendency to assess the past exclusively through the values of the present. This 'presentism' acts as a distorting mirror to the historical dimension of their work.[26] In short, historians need to be constantly on guard—borrowing indiscriminately from sociologists is a high-risk exercise.

## The numbers game

But do any of these questions and criticisms relate to a significant strand of the British experience? Is it not a fact that the country lacks a tradition of immigration? It has been hinted already that this assumption would be difficult to sustain and at this juncture it can be directly rebutted. In considering such immigration we are not dealing with an episodic phenomenon; on the contrary, we can trace a continual process of entry. Furthermore, we are not restricted to a limited range of immigrant and refugee groups; instead, we can point to a wide range of newcomers. These perspectives need to be emphasized and understood.[27]

So does a qualifying perspective. Over the past one hundred years Britain has tended to be a net exporter of population. At certain times, in the early 1930s and in the years preceding the Commonwealth Immigrants Act in 1962, for example, an opposite pattern can be detected. Nevertheless, the general trend of outward movement which in itself has encouraged an interest in the history of emigration, cannot be gainsaid.[28] Popular remarks dwelling on the prospect of over-population in Britain as a consequence of immigration are often heard. However this emphasis and the related imagery of such discussions, expressed in references to 'waves', 'flooding', and 'swamping', conveniently overlook the net loss factor, the other side of what must be regarded as a two-way process. Even so, we need to return to the emphasis which recognized the continual process of immigration and lay claims to its intrinsic historical importance. After all, which historian would restrict significance to a purely quantitative level? There are in addition other substantial grounds for studying immigration. A consideration of its impact upon the development of British society and a discussion of the responses towards immigration that emerged in Britain, raise points of more than a parochial significance.[29]

## The impact of the newcomers

Many existing discussions of immigrant and refugee groups celebrate the virtues of the newcomers and stress their influence in shaping the contours of British society. In other words we encounter a fair dose of hagiography. Indeed, at times we might be forgiven for thinking that an effete and sinking Britain had been rescued and restored to an even keel by various groups of newcomers. The history of German Jews in Britain provides an excellent illustration of this tendency.[30] It can be readily understood why these emphases emerge. By advancing such claims members of a particular group are saying, in effect, to the majority: 'Look how useful we are; tolerate us.' But it is not only writers drawn from within various immigrant and refugee minorities who offer such emphases. The general transformation of the image of the Ugandan Asian minority is one of the most remarkable developments in recent British social history. This group, which initially ran into widespread opposition, has been showered more recently with lavish praise as the epitome of those qualities of hard work, diligence, and self-help which at present are being strongly asserted in Britain.[31] It is not difficult to understand why minorities are content to bask in this admiring light. In a more cautionary vein, however, we should recognize that no minority possesses a permanent guarantee of admiration. Public opinion can shift with changes in circumstances. Moreover, dangers can lurk in developing the view that the only worthwhile minorities are those that can lay claim to conventional forms of success.

Even so, it cannot be denied that immigrants and refugees have contributed to the development of British society. This observation can be sustained in relation to both the economy and the nation's cultural life.

In concentrating on the theme of economic impact, uncertainties nevertheless continue to surround a number of issues. The role played by the Irish in the industrialization of Britain is a case in point. On the one hand, they have been regarded as indispensable agents in this change: in his general survey Jackson stressed their central role in the industrialization process.[32] A historian's later assessment has sounded a note of caution.[33] The resolution of this difference and the extension of the debate from the period of the Industrial Revolution into later years has not yet been attempted. The economic role of labour from Southern Ireland in the war industries between 1935 and 1945 is one area where more work is required. But it is not only the economic activity of the Irish that remains uncertain. We are told that during the First World War Black workers undertook an important role in the munitions industry.[34] Did they? Where is the evidence of this? What can we unearth on the role of Black workers in the merchant shipping industry in the same period beyond the observation that an increase occurred in their employment?[35] It would not be difficult to provide evidence on similar uncertainties relating to other groups and different periods.

If we move from economic to social or cultural themes, gaps are equally present. The role of the Irish in the Roman Catholic church would repay more attention: it is particularly disappointing that a recent study of the Roman Catholic minority contains only passing reference to the Irish and nothing at all on the Italians and the Ukrainians.[36] Furthermore, the influence of Blacks and Asians upon English literature,[37] to which might be added the contribution of such minorities to the arts in general, continues to escape any systematic historical enquiry.

Any attempt to assess economic or cultural impact poses acute problems, not least because impact is a slippery concept, but that is not a sufficient reason for avoiding the challenge. Studies which have already been completed on the role of Jews in business activity and the number of Jewish scientists admitted to Fellowships of the Royal Society[38] need to find their equivalents in surveys of other groups. Until we engage in such work our understanding of the history of immigration and its relationship to broader currents in British society remains significantly incomplete.

## Responses

In considering the responses that newcomers faced we soon encounter the image of Britain as a tolerant society. Such sentiment forms the stuff not only of much popular and official opinion: its echo can also be found among immigrant and refugee minorities. Hence the observation by Kitty Pistel, a child-refugee from Vienna: 'I am so happy in this free, friendly country, where I experienced so much kindness that it is my biggest wish to remain here for ever.'[39] We shall need to return to this emphasis at a later point. At this juncture, however, it is more germane to remark that one task of the historian is to shift the discussion of response patterns from an emotive to a cognitive level. In doing so we need to probe into the emphasis on toleration.

A comprehensive historical survey of immigrant and refugee minorities in Britain provides a procession of evidence indicating that such groups have encountered hostility, whether at the level of ideas or in the shape of discriminatory action. In its most dramatic fashion it surfaced in various incidents of collective violence. The years between 1911 and 1919, which witnessed attacks on the Chinese in Cardiff in 1911, on the Jews in Tredegar in the same year, on the German minority in 1914–15, on the Russian Poles in 1917, and on the Black minority in 1919, provide some of the most graphic testimony on this score.[40] Violence, however, has not been confined to this period. A group of sociologists, prompted by events in Bristol in 1980, revealed some awareness of this wider canvas but even their account is characterized by a limited chronological range and a concentration upon a restricted range of minority groups.[41] The theme of racial and ethnic violence in Britain still awaits its historian.

## Concluding comment

A consideration of the responses encountered by immigrants and refugees not only provides an opportunity to qualify the image of Britain as a centre of liberal toleration; it also brings to the surface an issue within the academic profession which needs to be aired. There are historians who regard any work on immigration as a diversion. 'Why concentrate on the periphery when there are important tasks at the centre?' is their theme. The study of class conflict is academically respectable: the history of racial and ethnic conflict has not yet attained such status. This negative perception is one reason why so much more work on immigration has been conducted by sociologists, social anthropologists, and geographers. Historians who focus on immigrants, refugees, and minorities run the risk of being blocked in an intellectual cul-de-sac notwithstanding the fact that the distinction between mainstream and peripheral history, which some attempt to draw, is a false antithesis. In order to be effective at the level of analysis the history of immigration needs to be located within the broader swirls and currents of society. For example, the widespread hostility encountered by Russian–Polish Jews in the East End in the late nineteenth century cannot be divorced from the complex changes which affected the housing market during these years. Furthermore, the countrywide attacks on the Irish in Britain in 1882 need to be related to events in Ireland in that year and the broader theme of Irish nationalism. Finally, if the roots of the 1962 Commonwealth Immigrants Act are complex and at the moment particularly uncertain since the official papers are still shielded from public inspection, nevertheless it can be safely claimed that an understanding of the measure needs to transcend the debate about 'race relations' and take on board wider issues such as Britain's retreat from the Commonwealth in favour of a future in Europe and the changing needs of the labour market.[42]

If we do accept the claim that immigration and related issues are proper, respectable neighbourhoods for historians to inhabit, is it possible now to provide some guidelines as to the precise areas into which their research priorities might take them?

'Recover more on the history of European groups' should be one major consideration. Apart from repeating the need to recapture large chunks of the recent history of groups such as the Irish, two examples, drawn from continental European groups, further help to underline the importance of the European perspective. During the First World War, between August 1914 and the spring of 1915, over 200,000 Belgian refugees poured into Britain. The size of this group alone should result in a degree of reflection. The influx of Belgians exceeded the number of Russian Polish Jews who settled in Britain between 1881 and 1914. Yet the history of the gallant Belgians still retains its blank spots. The fullest study, published only recently, is more concerned with the evolution of social policy in the shape of refugee relief work than it is with a rounded study of the refugees.[43] Nevertheless, we should be grateful for what we have on the Belgians: it is not difficult to think of other groups who came to Britain on account of a well-founded fear of persecution on whom even less information exists. The 21,000 Hungarians who entered after the uprising in 1956 constitute one such neglected case.

In recovering this European dimension one general theme also deserves our attention. In contrast to the reiterated importance of the colonial–imperial tradition as a force directing hostility towards Blacks and Asians, the tracing of a tradition through which the British perceived their superiority over Europeans still remains neglected by historians. How closely did the industrialization of Britain influence such perceptions? Can we detect any suggestion of a general hierarchy of toleration? Can it be said that northern Europeans were more likely to be tolerated than southern Europeans? Did further subdivisions exist within these broad groups?[44] At the same time as probing into these questions, we need to assess the influence of such inherited stereotypes alongside immediate pressures, or what Americans often call situational influences, in trying to disentangle and understand the roots of the hostility that European groups have experienced in Britain.

In view of the fact that other social scientists have concentrated their attention almost exclusively on the years since 1945, an important role can also be envisaged for those historians interested in Blacks and Asians. Much more needs to be known about these groups before this period and the same observation applies to those other minorities who came to Britain from beyond Europe. 'Concentrate on recovering the historical dimension of these groups' might be dispensed as timely advice. After all, there is little likelihood of this activity being undertaken by others. In sociology, particularly, the current lack of interest in the historical dimension is likely to be aggravated even more as the subject becomes increasingly policy-orientated.

'Recover more on the history of minorities in Britain' is another emphasis worth bearing in mind, considering the fact that Scotland and Wales have been particularly neglected. Comprehensive studies of those Lithuanians and Jews who lived north of the border have yet to appear. The history of the Irish in Scotland is also in need of revitalization and synthesis.[45] In view of this state of affairs it is to be hoped that the recently established Centre for Migration Research at Glasgow, attached to the Sociology Department, will not neglect the historical dimension of its work. In the case of Wales, there are patches of exhaustive recovery—the history of Blacks and other minorities in Cardiff, particularly those aspects relating to the collective violence of 1919 and the disputes in the shipping industry in the inter-war years, have received detailed attention.[46] However, other groups, such as the Irish, the Jews, and the Poles, have been less well served.

In the case of England, the intending researcher should be urged particularly: 'Recover the history of communities outside London.' The concentration on the capital is understandable. During most periods London has functioned as a magnet, drawing into itself both immigrants and refugees. The East End in particular has recruited many groups of such newcomers over the last hundred years. It is hardly surprising therefore that, for example, we have studies of the Irish in the capital, but it is worth noting that Lees's book *Exiles of Erin*, one of the best known, follows a familiar pattern in concentraing on the mid-nineteenth-century Irish.[47] In the case of the Jewish East End we need to notice Lloyd Gartner's pioneer study[48] and, more recently, and from a different perspective, David Feldman's Cambridge Ph.D. thesis.[49] Moreover, anyone interested in East End Jewry must take account of the works of Bill Fishman who, more than any other historian, has recaptured the ambience of Jewish East London.[50] Sponza's recent work on the Italians reveals that the history of other minorities in the capital has also caught the attention of historians.[51] Even so, it is surprising that, as yet, no one has attempted to construct a general history of immigrants and minorities in London.

Nevertheless, whatever remains to be written on London, even more work is needed on the history of other cities. Bradford is a case in point. Scattered fragments can be found on the Irish and on the more recent history of minorities originating in the New Commonwealth.[52] However, none of this work possesses the feel of completeness. In addition, we certainly need to ask what has happened to the history of the Germans in Bradford, a group celebrated by J. B. Priestley, one of the city's sons, and the visible symbols of whose heyday can still be seen in Little Germany. A similar darkness has settled upon the history of the Poles and the European Volunteer Workers who came to the city after the Second World War. Oral recollections from these and other groups have been compiled by the Bradford Heritage Recording Unit but a historian's firm hand is needed to pull together such material into a coherent whole.[53] This focus upon Bradford is made not because it provides a unique case of supporting evidence for the particular argument that is now being advanced. A similar case can be constructed if our focus is shifted towards other great northern cities such as Liverpool and Manchester. However, the newly established Institute of Irish Studies at Liverpool University should swell our knowledge of the important Irish minority in that city. As for Manchester, one of the most cosmopolitan cities in Britain, an important gap would be plugged by the appearance of the second volume of Bill Williams's history of Manchester Jewry: without it we are lacking information on one of the city's important minority groups.[54] If we leave aside the specifically Jewish dimension of Manchester's history and focus on a more general perspective, it is also surprising that, as yet, there is no overall history of the immigrants and refugees who found their various ways to the city. On standing back from such observations, and reflecting for a moment, we can also envisage the possibility of a potentially important comparative study of Bradford, Liverpool, and Manchester, as centres of immigration into Britain.

'Recover the history of immigration warts and all but with a due regard for the complexity of that history' might be presented as a final consideration. We need to ask ourselves whether we can remain content with celebratory studies, which dilate upon the deeply etched virtues of Britons true, contemplate the pleasure of the country's civilization, and rejoice in the triumph of decency over evil. These assumptions and claims, sometimes shared, it has been noticed, by immigrants and refugees, have acted as a distorting agency in many accounts of immigration. In particular, such work underplays the realities of group conflict which cannot be written out of the script. Indeed, its extent should not be underestimated. Opposition towards immigrants and refugees has surfaced not only from individuals and groups but also in official policies. In other words, the state has disrupted the hopes, aims, and aspirations of such groups, whether through immigration control, internment, the powers it has assumed over deportation, or through the consequences of these developments, in the course of which immigrants and refugees often become stereotyped as 'problem groups'.[55]

Over the past few years considerable emphasis has been placed upon the weight of institutional opposition pressing upon the lives of Blacks and Asians.[56] However, in recognizing the significance of this observation and extending it to other groups, a degree of caution is in order. Some accounts of such hostility towards Blacks and Asians have displayed a particular farouche dimension. A certain wildness of judgement has also extended beyond this particular theme. We can easily lay our hands on texts that portray Britain as a society in which hostility towards immigrants and refugees has been rampant and universal and remains so. In fact, however, attitudes and actions at both official and popular level have often displayed a complexity which cautions against any simple categorization of responses.[57]

If we tackle this issue of complexity from a different angle, liberal writers anxious to promote the view of immigration as a positive force in British society have paid too little attention to the role that immigrants and refugees might have played in the development of hostility.[58] A due degree of caution and a sensitivity to detail and argument are essential in any such exercise but, as in other areas of immigration, the difficulty of the task should not lead to its avoidance. This last observation is also relevant to the themes of inter-minority and intra-minority conflict; these phenomena pose particularly awkward questions, which many investigators are inclined to side-step.[59]

The overall thrust of this discussion has been to draw attention to gaps, problems, and difficulties which face historians interested in immigration. In order to meet these challenges successfully, at a fundamental level historians need to believe in the intrinsic worth of their endeavours. They should resist any tendency to operate from an academic ghetto, whether self-imposed or as a consequence of pressure from other historians. At the same time, they should reach out towards other social sciences and draw discreetly and selectively rather than slavishly upon the insights offered by these disciplines, particularly by sociology and psychology, but without forgetting the additional relevance of political science and geography. By travelling along such lines of enquiry we shall build upon existing strengths. Furthermore, by using whatever material is at hand, whether it comes in the form of traditional printed sources or in the varied shapes of oral and visual artefacts, irrespective of whether these materials are conventionally regarded as 'appropriate' for the historian's task, we shall be able to construct an academic springboard capable of launching us into a 'consistently comparative' analysis,[60] which sets the British experience of immigration against that of other countries. If that point is still some way off and other threads need to be knitted together first, comparative work, the difficulty of which cannot be underestimated, needs to be firmly in our sights in a longer-term vision. After all, the study of immigration is hardly conducive to the perpetuation of an insular tradition of history. Perhaps that is another reason why some historians avoid the topic or reduce it to a residual insignificance? However, the pursuit of that particular argument will have to wait for another occasion.

## Notes

1 See A. J. P. Taylor, *English History 1914–1945*, Oxford, Oxford University Press, 1985; F. Bédarida, *A Social History of England 1851–1975*, London, Methuen, 1979; K. Robbins, *The Eclipse of a Great Power: modern Britain 1870–1975*, London, Longman, 1983; J. Stevenson, *British Society 1914–45*, London, Allen Lane, 1984.
2 C. Holmes, *John Bull's Island, Immigration and British Society 1871–1971*, London, Macmillan, 1988.
3 J. A. Jackson, *The Irish in Britain*, London, Routledge & Kegan Paul, 1963. Some observers prefer to regard the Irish as migrants but custom and practice has the Irish minority in Britain classified as immigrants.
4 L. P. Curtis, *Anglo-Saxons and Celts: a study of anti-Irish prejudice in Victorian England*, Bridgeport, Conn., New York University Press, 1968; L. P. Curtis, *Apes and Angels, The Irishman in Victorian Caricature*, Newton Abbot, David & Charles, 1971; L. H. Lees, *Exiles of Erin: Irish migrants in Victorian London*, Manchester, Manchester University Press, 1979; R. Swift and S. Gilley (eds), *The Irish in the Victorian City*, London, Croom Helm, 1985; M. A. G. Ó'Tuathaigh, 'The Irish in nineteenth-century Britain: problems of integration', *Transactions of the Royal Historical Society*, vol. 31, 1981, pp. 149–73. [For a more recent treatment, see G. Davis, *The Irish in Britain, 1815–1914*, Dublin, Gill and Macmillan, 1991—*Ed.*]
5 *Census 1981, Great Britain, Country of Birth*, London, HMSO, 1983, p. 2.
6 The role of women in both movements would repay more attention.
7 J. Goodman, *The Mond Legacy*, London, Weidenfeld & Nicolson, 1982.
8 G. Anderson, *Victorian Clerks* Manchester, Manchester University Press, 1976, and his 'German clerks in England 1870–1914: another aspect of the Great Depression debate', in K. Lunn (ed.), *Hosts, Immigrants and Minorities: historical responses to newcomers in British society, 1870–1914*, Folkestone, Dawson, 1980, pp. 201–21.

9 R. Ashton, *Little Germany. Exile and Asylum in Victorian England*, Oxford, Oxford University Press, 1986.

10 P. Panayi, 'Germans in Britain during the First World War', Ph.D. thesis, Sheffield University, 1988.

11 L. Sponza, *Italian Immigrants in Nineteenth-century Britain: realities and images*, Leicester, Leicester University Press, 1988.

12 R. C. G. Palmer, 'The Britalians: an anthropological investigation', Ph.D. thesis, Sussex University, 1981.

13 See K. Lunn, 'Reactions to Lithuanian and Polish immigrants in the Lanarkshire coalfield 1880–1914', in Lunn, *Hosts, Immigrants and Minorities*, pp. 308–42; J. D. White, 'Scottish Lithuanians and the Russian Revolution', *Journal of Baltic Studies*, vol. 6, 1975, pp. 1–8; M. Rodgers, 'The Anglo-Russian Military Convention and the Lithuanian immigrant community in Lanarkshire, Scotland 1914–20', *Immigrants and Minorities*, vol. 1, 1982, pp. 60–88.

14 S. Patterson, 'The Poles: an exile community in Britain', in J. L. Watson (ed.), *Between Two Cultures: migrants and minorities in Britain*, Oxford, Basil Blackwell, 1977, pp. 214–41; K. Sword et al., *The Formation of the Polish Community in Great Britain*, London, School of Slavonic and East European Studies, 1989.

15 J. A. Tannahill, *European Volunteer Workers in Britain*, Manchester, Manchester University Press, 1958.

16 See *War Crimes: Report of the War Crimes Enquiry*, Cm. 744, London, HMSO, 1989.

17 V. G. Kiernan, 'Britons old and new', in C. Holmes (ed.) *Immigrants and Minorities in British Society*, London, Allen & Unwin, 1978, p. 54.

18 K. Little, *Negroes in Britain: a study of racial relations in English society*, London, Kegan Paul, Trench, Trubner, 1948: re-issued 1972. Little, Michael Banton, Sidney Collins, and Sheila Patterson are among those researchers associated with Edinburgh University in the early years after the Second World War.

19 See J. Walvin, *Black and White: the Negro in English society 1555–1945*, London, Allen Lane, 1973, re-issued 1988.

20 P. Fryer, *Staying Power: the history of black people in Britain*, London, Pluto Press, 1986.

21 R. Visram, *Ayahs, Lascars and Princes: Indians in Britain 1700–1947*, London, Pluto Press, 1986.

22 One recalls Ralph Ellison's novel *Invisible Man*, London, Victor Gollancz, 1953.

23 J. Rex, *Race Relations in Sociological Theory*, London, Weidenfeld & Nicolson, 1970, pp. 106ff. and his *Race, Colonialism and the City*, London, Routledge & Kegan Paul, 1973. For an attempt to tackle a specific issue against this perspective, see R. May and R. Cohen, 'The interaction between race and colonialism: a cast study of the Liverpool race riots of 1919', *Race and Class*, vol. 16, 1974–5, pp. 111–26.

24 M. Banton, 'The beginning and the end of the racial issue in British politics', *Policy and Politics*, vol. 15, 1987, p. 41, commenting on one specific treatment of the role of the slave trade in fostering images of white supremacy.

25 M. D. Biddiss, 'Myths of the blood', *Patterns of Prejudice*, vol. 9, 1975, pp. 11–19.

26 M. Banton, *Racial Theories*, Cambridge, Cambridge University Press, 1987, pp. xii, xvii and in other publications.

27 See Holmes, *John Bull's Island*.

28 R. K. Kelsall, *Population*, London, Longman, 1979 edition, pp. 29–30, 115.

29 C. Holmes, 'The impact of immigration on British society, 1870–1980', in T. Barker and M. Drake (eds), *Population and Society in Britain 1850–1980*, London, Batsford, 1982, pp. 177–9.

30 H. Loebl, 'Government-financed factories and the establishment of industries by refugees in the special areas of the north of England 1937–1961', M.Phil. thesis, Durham University, 1978. See also C. C. Aronsfeld, 'German Jews in Victorian England', *Leo Baeck Yearbook*, vol. 6, 1962, pp. 313–29.

31 The initial history can be gleaned from E. N. Swinerton, W. G. Kuepper and G. L. Lackey, *Ugandan Asians in Great Britain*, London, Croom Helm, 1975.

32 Jackson, *The Irish in Britain*, p. 93.

33 E. H. Hunt, *British Labour History 1815–1914*, London, Weidenfeld & Nicolson, 1981, pp. 172–4.

34 Little, *Negroes in Britain*, p. 56; Walvin, *Black and White*, p. 205.

35 Little, *Negroes in Britain*, p. 56.

36 M. Hornsby-Smith, *Roman Catholics in England: studies in social structure since the Second World War*, Cambridge, Cambridge University Press, 1987.

37 S. Rushdie, 'The Empire writes back with a vengeance', *The Times*, 3 July 1982.

38 H. Pollins, *Economic History of the Jews in England*, London and Toronto, Farleigh Dickinson University Press, 1982; R. N. Salaman, 'The Jewish Fellows of the Royal Society', *Miscellanies of the Jewish Historical Society of England*, Part 5, 1948, pp. 146–75.

39 Harris House Diary, Testimony of Kitty Pistel from Vienna: MS 2845. Manchester Central Reference Library.

40 See Holmes, *John Bull's Island*, chapters 1 and 2.

41 H. Joshua et al., *To Ride the Storm: the 1980 Bristol 'riot' and the state*, London, Heinemann, 1983.

42 C. Holmes, *Anti-Semitism in British Society 1876–1939*, London, Edward Arnold, 1979, chapter 2 on the East End and *John Bull's Island*, pp. 41, 58, and 60 (on the Irish) and 261–3 (on the 1962 Act).

43 P. Cahalan, *Belgian Refugee Relief Work During the Great War*, New York, Garland Press, 1982.

44 M. D. Biddiss, 'Racial ideas and the politics of prejudice, 1850–1914', *Historical Journal*, vol. 15, 1972, p. 572.

45 The pioneer work of J. E. Handley, including *The Irish in Scotland 1798–1845*, Cork, Cork University Press, 1943; *The Irish in Modern Scotland*, Cork, Cork University Press, 1947 and *The Navvy in Scotland*, Cork, Cork University Press, 1970, constitutes an excellent base.

46 By Neil Evans, particularly in 'The South Wales race riots of 1919', *Llafur*, vol. 3, 1980, pp. 5–29, and 'Regulating the Reserve Army: Arabs, blacks and the local state in Cardiff 1919–45', *Immigrants and Minorities*, vol. 4, 1985, pp. 68–115.

47 Lees, *Exiles of Erin*.

48  L. P. Gartner, *The Jewish Immigrant in England 1870–1914*, Detroit, Wayne State University Press, 1960.

49  D. Feldman, 'Immigrants and workers: Englishmen and Jews: Jewish immigration to the East End of London, 1880–1906', Ph.D. thesis, Cambridge University, 1985.

50  W. J. Fishman, *East End Jewish Radicals 1875–1914*, London, Duckworth, 1975 and *The Streets of East London*, London, Duckworth, 1979 for text and photographs, and *East End 1888*, London, Duckworth, 1988.

51  Sponza, *Italian Immigrants*.

52  See, for example, C. Richardson, 'Irish settlement in mid-nineteenth century Bradford', *Yorkshire Bulletin of Economic and Social Research*, vol. 20, 1968, pp. 40–57 and M. Le Lohé, 'The effects of the presence of immigrants upon the local population in Bradford 1945–77', in R. Miles and A. Phizacklea (eds), *Racism and Political Action*, London, Routledge & Kegan Paul, 1979, pp. 184–203.

53  R. B. Perks, '"A feeling of not belonging": interviewing European immigrants in Bradford', *Oral History*, vol. 12, 1984, pp. 64–7, provides a sample of oral evidence.

54  B. Williams, *The Making of Manchester Jewry 1740–1875*, Manchester, Manchester University Press, 1976.

55  See Holmes, *John Bull's Island* on these various points and his *A Tolerant Country? Immigrants, Refugees and Minorities in Britain*, London, Faber, 1991.

56  K. Leech, '"Diverse reports" and the meaning of "racism"', *Race and Class*, vol. 28, 1986, pp. 82–8.

57  Recognized by Paul Rich in his review of *John Bull's Island*, which is described as 'a sober historical assessment of an emotive issue which has frequently given rise to polemics', *History Today*, vol. 39, April 1989, p. 48.

58  Following the guideline of J. Higham, 'Anti-Semitism in the gilded age', *Mississippi Valley Historical Review*, vol. 43, 1957, p. 566.

59  See Holmes, *John Bull's Island*, p. 413, note 172 for a number of examples.

60  Higham, 'Anti-Semitism', p. 569.

# 9

# Migration and the Social History of Modern Europe

*James H. Jackson, Jr. and Leslie Page Moch*

Since 1700, Europe has been transformed from a sparsely settled rural society to one characterized by densely populated urban centres and significant overseas settlements. Europe's population recovered its early fourteenth-century levels, then growth accelerated after the mid-eighteenth century, owing apparently to declining mortality rates and changes in marriage patterns.[1] What are not so clear, however, are the causes of population concentration and the social meaning of city growth. More specifically, in what ways was human migration responsible for this change from a rural to an urban society, and how were these movements played out? The answers to these questions are central to historians' view of the European past as well as to their understanding of the contemporary world.

The original answer to the questions of migration and urbanization was formulated by the social observers of the late nineteenth and early twentieth centuries, who saw the shift in population from the agricultural countryside to the crowded and alien worlds of the city and the factory as the root cause of contemporary social problems.[2] They perceived an increase in the total volume of migration; thus these critics of urbanization assumed that more individuals were suffering from the effects of residential dislocation. In this perspective, migration was an irreversible phenomenon that enabled the demographically moribund and decaying city to exist by draining the vitality from rural migrants, leaving them hollow vestiges of their former robust selves. Within this context, fraught with contemporary urgency, governmental agencies

From *Historical Methods* 22 (1), 1989, pp. 27–36.

continued to collect descriptive information that enabled scholars, such as the statistician E. G. Ravenstein and the German social scientists Rudolph Herberle and Fritz Meyer, to sketch a basic outline of migration behaviour in the nineteenth and early twentieth centuries.[3] Ferdinand Tönnies, Georg Simmel, Max Weber, and Friedrich Engels created powerful stereotypes of community and society that continued to animate and circumscribe sociological research well into the twentieth century, partly because they did not view migration merely as a problem of demographic calculus.[4] Rather, they helped to set our research agenda by focusing attention on the social meaning of migration for individual lives and for the collectivity.[5]

Since the nineteenth century, migration has been viewed as a hallmark of modern life. Indeed, geographic mobility has been incorporated into the **modernization paradigm**. The hypothesis of a 'mobility transition' distinguishes pre-modern sedentary societies from modern ones and articulates the idea that migration is an important component of modernity.[6] A corollary argument asserts that individuals who are willing to move are more 'modern' than those who do not leave home.[7]

## An emerging consensus

The conventional analysis of the link between migration and urbanization declared that city growth in the nineteenth century was caused by the movement of rural dwellers, who were irreversibly drawn from their sedentary villages into the city, and that this signalled a transition to the modern urban–industrial era. A new perspective on migration is emerging, however, that is profoundly different from the modernization paradigm. Neither the presumed destructive power of migration nor the irreversibility of rural–urban moves plays an important role in the alternative view. Rather, this view emphasizes the continuities and regional networks in migration history.

The origins of a new analysis of migration are to be found, first, in an ideological and methodological reaction to the modernization paradigm. Critics have pointed to the ethnocentric social and political assumptions of such theories of development, as well as to the imprecision of the presumed tension between the major variables of 'tradition' and 'modernity'.[8] Students of migration are particularly disturbed by the ignorance of rural lifeways displayed by modernization theory, which reads sedentary qualities into rural life and overlooks rural migration patterns.

A second source of alternative assessments of classic migration theory springs from studies of contemporary migration in the Third World.

Using survey techniques as well as census data, researchers have placed the assertions of the conventional wisdom into a cross-cultural perspective and have begun to reveal the complex interplay of migration, social mobility, housing, and employment. For example, Janice Perlman's investigation of the migrant shantytowns of Rio de Janeiro reveals networks of kin and friendships that created a vital urban community where outsiders saw only poverty and disorientation.[9]

The third source of this revision of the conventional wisdom includes a plethora of case studies and a few surveys of broader bodies of data, which are based upon newly explored migration records, including the population registers of Sweden, Belgium, and Italy, and the impressive German migration statistics.[10] Population registers and migration records provide the most accurate information about the levels and flows of human mobility in the past. Scholars of other areas of Europe that have no such migration records, such as England and France, are also contributing to a new analysis of migration by asking new questions of traditional sources, such as parish records or bureaucratic surveys —questions that are not bound by assumptions about the presumed sedentary nature of pre-modern life or about the necessary connection of migration and social disorder.[11]

The clearest conclusion of this new analysis of migration is that Europeans have always moved in considerable numbers. European populations have never been as sedentary as we once thought; rather, several distinct kinds of movement have characterized the countryside since at least the seventeenth century. Most closely tied to the agricultural seasons were the great annual migrations undertaken by groups of harvest labourers, construction workers, and pedlars within the powerful reaches of Rome, Milan, Paris, and, to a lesser extent, London, the North Sea coast, Provence, and Madrid.[12] In addition, many men travelled long distances within their own nations, such as the northern English who flocked to London for apprenticeships and less certain fortunes in the seventeenth century.[13] The movements of seventeenth- and eighteenth-century Europeans appear to have been particularly intense between mountain and plain, city and hinterland. Poor mountain areas, hard pressed to support their residents all the year round, quickly developed traditions of temporary out-migration. They could spare the manpower needed for the most onerous and difficult lowland tasks, especially in the winter months.[14]

Besides these long-distance movements, many of which were seasonal and temporary, rural Europeans regularly travelled shorter distances. Those most likely to do so were cultivators who moved from one large estate to another; in such cases, the majority might leave their home villages.[15] Sharecroppers moved by a similar pattern—entire families moved together to work for a new landlord.[16] Although landowning peasants were less likely to move, they also disappeared from parish records at a much greater rate than was once thought.[17] The most important form of rural migration primarily involved single persons. Young men and women—even those who would eventually inherit a farm or be a mistress of one—worked as farmhands, hired out by the year. From as early as age 10 until their mid-twenties, many young peasants moved annually from one service position to another.[18] In the eighteenth century, in areas where farm servants were commonly used, as many as 70 per cent of the young men aged 20 to 24 (and half of the women) moved to a new parish annually as they changed masters.[19]

Many of those who did not go into rural service worked in the nearest market towns as day-labourers, domestics, or apprentices. Families in areas surrounding cities could spare their daughters; cities attracted these young women to work in urban kitchens, shops, inns, and ale-houses.[20] Extant urban records from seventeenth- and eighteenth-century cities of Germany, England, and France unanimously show that men also came to the preindustrial city—from elite and wealthy merchants to apprentices—from surrounding regions.[21] ...

Thus a multitude of case studies suggests that the modernization paradigm, which characterizes migration as a comparatively recent phenomenon, fundamentally distorts the historical experience of Europeans. Both temporally and socially, migration appears to have been an established pattern; it is part of all recorded periods in early modern and modern Europe and was experienced by elite bureaucrats and peasants, by the landless and unlucky, by women as well as men. After 1750, when the demographic pattern of the old regime began to break down, geographic mobility enabled European societies to adapt to changing growth patterns and to adjust their labour forces to new opportunities in agriculture and manufacturing. The implications of this new research on preindustrial migrations suggest that a reassessment of the relationship between and social meaning of migration and urbanization in the nineteenth century is essential—a revaluation that recognizes the continuities of human mobility.[22]

## Problems and unsolved puzzles

In the light of this accumulating evidence, we can no longer view geographic mobility as a unilinear and mechanistic phenomenon. Clearly, a preoccupation with only one piece of migration—whether that is movement into a city or departures from a rural area—seriously truncates our understanding of the process and its central place in

European history, both before and after 1750. In addition, the tendency to use 'migration' interchangeably with 'urbanization' has obscured our understanding of both city growth and migratory behaviour. A thorough reconsideration has been stimulated not only by a growing body of research but also by colleagues who suggest that social historians strive to 'illuminate the complex interplay between large structural changes . . . and routine social life', including mundane geographic wanderings.[23] Several problems and unsolved puzzles stand in our way, however.

Formidable technical and source problems present the greatest difficulty in discovering the volume and rhythms of historical migration. Necessity forces us to depend upon varying bureaucratic definitions of migration, which makes comparisons difficult. The second quandary results from the quality of migration data. Few major sources allow the reconstruction of an individual's migration history over an entire life course. . . .

More difficult than determining the magnitude of historical migration, which better sources would allow, is the task of defining the mechanisms and social meaning of geographic mobility. For the purposes of this essay, we have organized this analytical task into five interrelated questions. How did migrant selectivity operate? What motivated people to leave their homes and take a chance on new surroundings? What was the character of migration streams? What was the impact of migration on places of origin and destination? Finally, how did individual migrants respond to residential change?

First and most fundamental, our knowledge of the operation of *migrant selectivity* is sketchy. Migrants were not a random sample of either their places of origin or their destinations. Rather, migration was selective on a wide range of variables, particularly age, gender, landholding status, education, and income. Young males, the landless, and the educated were generally the most likely migrants in historical Europe. It is clear, however, that this selectivity worked differently in one labour market and geographic location compared with another. On the question of gender, for example, Ravenstein stated that the 'woman is a greater migrant than man', but he also observed that women moved shorter distances within Britain than men.[24] Indeed, during the nineteenth century women moved in droves—many of them to commercial cities where they could find work as domestics. Other migration streams were clearly male; for example, men were more likely than women to make their way to coal-mining towns, and the great majority of seasonal harvest labour—both in modern Africa and in historical Europe—was male.[25]

Migration selectivity by demographic and social traits, such as education or landholding status, is fairly clear and relatively easy to analyse. It is more difficult to analyse individual migrant psychology and attitudes, specifically the degree to which a person is an innovator or open to change.[26] From the viewpoint of sending communities, the migration of their more innovative citizens may deprive them of future social leadership. Migration does not necessarily require a pioneering spirit, however. Those interested in preserving a traditional way of life do migrate; indeed, the desire to finance land purchases in order to maintain peasant families sent European rurals temporarily to both distant fields and cities to earn cash. Moreover, well-established migration systems forged by leaders carry their share of followers.[27]

A second area of migration research concentrates on the *motivation* for geographic mobility.[28] Historical studies suggest that landholding and demographic patterns, seasonal organization of work, migration traditions, political upheaval, and religious intolerance all caused people to migrate. Clearly, we must scrutinize a broad range of perspectives in order to understand why people moved and how they chose a destination. Migration patterns respond primarily to a need for labour and to political and religious persecution. Within this framework, the social organization of migration explains the impetus to migrate, the timing, and the destinations for a large proportion of historical actors. Indeed, the flow of information among migrants offers the best explanation for such large-scale movements as migration from Britain to North America.[29] In the view of many migration scholars, the perceptions of migrants about opportunities in different places are more significant in the decision to move than objective economic reality.[30] The personal information field that each potential migrant possesses about possible destinations, employment opportunities, and social support explains why people are attracted to certain destinations and jobs.[31] Information is exchanged within many kinds of institutions. Occupational traditions and employing organizations weighed heavily in determining the peregrinations of travelling apprentices and bureaucrats.[32] In addition, students of the family economy have found that the family, rather than the individual migrant, made migration decisions in its economic interest.[33] Migrants tend to go where neighbours have gone; therefore, traditions of migration have been created between home towns and particular destinations.[34] Chain migration thus linked the Auvergne to Catalonia and Westfalia to Holland in the seventeenth century and Sicily to North America and Anatolia to Germany in the twentieth century. Although it appears that information flows and social contacts create migration systems, this insight has yet to be integrated into a broad theoretical understanding of migration and historical change.

A third area of geographic mobility research concerns flows of movers *within* a migration system. Based on published statistical sources, some migration studies have focused on the impact of net population movements on gross population characteristics and have analysed the biased character of flows between sending and receiving areas.[35] Other studies have recognized the relationship between distance and the character of the migration stream and have employed various gravity models to describe the friction of distance.[36] Additional research has attempted to delineate the pattern of inter-area population flows and to identify hierarchies of migration destinations.[37] What is most lacking in studies of migration streams is an analysis of return migration and multiple moves.[38] These factors offer keys to the lives of proletarians in Europe and to their struggles with economic dislocation, as well as to the peregrinations of bureaucrats and church officials. If we could better understand multiple moves and returns home, migration would be integrated more realistically with the social history of Europe.

A fourth theme of migration studies emphasizes *the impact of geographic mobility on the places people left and on their destinations*. This is tied directly to the compositional effects of migrant selectivity. The young male migrants who flooded Paris before 1848 created a concern regarding urban social problems such as prostitution, drunkenness, and theft.[39] The experience of the Austrian city of Graz, with its heavy influx of retiring civil servants during the late nineteenth and early twentieth centuries, illustrates the ways in which the demographic and occupational structures as well as the political life of a town can be deeply influenced by migrants. Likewise, rural areas underwent demographic restructuring when they lost young people to urbanization; these regions lost some of their most highly educated children.[40] Intriguing questions remain about the impact of migration on historical populations at origin and at destination. Studies of villages from which young men migrated in great numbers in times of economic stress, for example, show a boom in the number of unwed mothers.[41] How typical are these Portuguese and French parishes, and what other social effects might such villages illustrate? The answer to these questions would tie migration more realistically to the social history of Europe.

The fifth and final area of migration studies focuses on the *consequences of migration* for the individual mover. Much of this work responds to studies of urban crime and to nineteenth-century observations that migrants became disoriented and uprooted people, prey to revolution and mental disorders. The pessimistic view of the conventional wisdom has been challenged by scholars whose work attempts to explore the social context or auspices of migration.[42] From Marseilles and Nîmes in southern France, from Duisburg in the Ruhr Valley, and from London and Preston across the English Channel come reports that migrants found structures of stability that cushioned their adjustment to the urban world.[43] On the other hand, one recent analysis of criminal convictions reports that not everyone who left home became a social and economic success; thus, although not all migrants were criminals, a disproportionate number of urban criminals were migrants.[44] As Olwen Hufton observed, it is unlikely that the poor could always stay on the right side of the law in their efforts to survive.[45] Thus, the issue of social deviance lingers, often becoming embroiled in insoluble definitional disputes. Is migration disorienting simply because a typical nineteenth-century migrant might change residences 15 or 16 times during a lifetime? Because two-thirds of these moves are made during the young adult years and permit a migrant long stretches of residential stability, does migration lack disruptive power?[46]

The division of migration analysis into these five basic emphases is useful in order to set our research agenda. None the less, this topical compartmentalization must not obscure the fact that the most significant historical issues in the study of geographic mobility encompass all five categories. Historical questions are multifaceted in another sense as well: their resolution requires the perspectives of sociologists, geographers, social psychologists, and economists, as well as historians. The three primary *historical* issues in European migration studies illustrate these scholarly axioms. They deal with the relationship between migration and social change—first with cottage industry, then with the development of factory production and concomitant urbanization, and finally with the transition from one to the other.

The implication of cottage industry for migratory behaviour is the central conundrum for the eighteenth and early nineteenth centuries. A growing body of evidence suggests that long-run shifts occurred in migration trends in the eighteenth century. The relationship between these shifts and simultaneous economic and demographic change has yet to be established, however. In England, long-distance migration slowed, and levels of migration decreased in the countryside. Expanding rural industry that employed people at home, declining rates of population increase, and implementing strict residency requirements for poor relief are three factors that slowed migration, but the role of each has yet to be determined.[47] The continent, on the other hand, exhibited contradictory patterns during a time of relative peace and population increase following 1750. Population pressure forced increasing numbers of long-distance migrants to leave mountainous regions and find temporary work in provincial cities and prosperous countrysides; some would never return home.[48] Areas of expanding rural industry are said to have absorbed their own prolific populations, but there are no investigations to confirm this. In some such areas, rural mobility seems actually to have increased as proto-industrial villages were infused with newcomers.[49] These contrasting patterns have not been adequately confirmed; nor have they been analysed as part of a continental system of mobility.

A second historical problem is the nature of the connection between migration and urbanization in the time between the onset of factory industry and the outbreak of the First World War. How much migration was there? Did it increase to previously unreached levels? The best German data show that a peak of migration in and out of cities was reached in the decades preceding the war, but there are no reliable comparisons with migration rates of earlier times. Moreover, a simulation of migration and urbanization from 1500 to 1800 suggests that the nineteenth-century migration rates may not have been unprecedented.[50] Did migration make the cities grow? To a degree, yes; but cities were less deadly than they had been in the seventeenth and eighteenth centuries so that migration may have been much less important to the growth of some important administrative and commercial capitals than contemporary observers believed. This is partly true because many people departed from the cities as well as entered them, and these departures have rarely been recorded. German sources that recorded the actual volume of migration (as opposed to net migration figures) revealed large numbers of moves in and out of cities for every person permanently added to the urban rolls.[51]

In addition, the existence of long-standing regional and local exchanges of population illustrates the complex relationship of migration, industrialization, and urban growth in the nineteenth century. This finding suggests that the people who came to industrial cities were not strangers from alien rural cultures. Miners alternated between agricultural pursuits and ore extraction; factory workers moved between fields and workshops, as long as employers tolerated or required seasonal absences.[52] Clearly, in many areas, rural dwellers balanced themselves between urban life and the fields. Researchers must try to disaggregate earlier preindustrial fluctuations of population and newer patterns that accompanied the commercial and manufacturing revolutions of the nineteenth century.[53] Moreover, we must explain new and unexplored patterns within the nineteenth century, such as the precipitous decline in overseas migration and the simultaneous unprecedented acceleration of internal migration in Germany in the 1890s.[54]

The issues of migration that surround rural industry and the growth of urban production do not fall neatly into separate temporal categories. On the contrary, it is increasingly obvious that some forms of domestic production persisted long after the 1840s; in many regions, domestic rural industry existed simultaneously with factory production. The relationship between these two becomes the third major issue of European migration studies. What kinds of population movements did the de-industrialization of the countryside mobilize? What role did the collapse of rural industry and the resulting agricultural crises play in rural–urban migration? There are some indications that rural residents left home only when necessary and that they balanced their lives between urban and rural areas as long as possible, but there is little direct evidence of this.[55]

Thus, the links between migration, industrialization, and urbanization remain sketchy. They will be clarified by interdisciplinary work that acknowledges a variety of perspectives while allowing the historical picture to be complicated by a variety of insights into issues such as selectivity, the social organization of migration, and the merging of human motivation and social consequences with large-scale change. If these issues can become part of historical studies of migration, the social history of Europe will be enriched.

## A systems approach

The application of a systems framework to the migration experience suggests one means to meet the need for a comprehensive perspective by providing a strategy to overcome topical compartmentalization.[56] By seeing migration as a circular self-modifying system and a complex of interacting elements, individual movers can be placed in the context of their places of origin and destination, the structural context can be specified, and the long-term implications of migration for that structural environment can be defined.[57] Systems analysis can

1 demonstrate how interrelated social, political, economic, and technological forces converge to stimulate geographic mobility;
2 uncover the social tensions unleashed by those moves;
3 show how countervailing migratory trends emerge. . . .

The systems framework is not the only logical method of investigating the impact of migration. Moreover, there are problems in collecting the varieties of data that are needed for an analysis of changes in social and economic structures. None the less, the systems approach does provide a strategy of analysis and also has the virtue of forcing us to deal with the feedback aspects of migration systems, requiring that we see the effects and causes of migration as well as the long-term structural concomitants in combination. Although we may continue to analyse general notions about migration by studying its individual components, the systems approach can help us identify the significance of our particular study in acquiring an understanding of a larger social process.

## Conclusion

Our brief survey offers fundamental observations about European migration studies. First, many descriptive studies of migration still need to be done. Second, scholars from many disciplines can fruitfully contribute to this task—geographers, with their grasp of spatial matters; anthropologists, with their understanding of values; demographers, with their expertise at specifying impacts; and economists, with their perceptions regarding flows of labour and capital. Such disciplinary and interdisciplinary endeavours will enrich our understanding of the fundamental processes of social change in the past three centuries, challenging conventional views of cultural, economic, and institutional change since 1700. The high volume of preindustrial mobility, for example, conflicts with the durable stereotype of pre-modern society as being immobile, a stereotype that distorts both historical research and findings. The fact that movement into urban industrial jobs did not necessarily involve disorienting changes adds an important perspective to our concepts of industrial labour force formation. In addition, we can attempt to unlock a basic dilemma of human society: how can individual stability exist simultaneously with aggregate disruption? In this view, migration is the motor force behind the creation of subcultures that offer supportive networks and at the same time create social friction.[58]

None the less, we cannot allow our concern for understanding migration as a core historical phenomenon to blind us to its link with distinct regional and national histories. If migration is a significant connector of social processes, we must link it to the most important questions of social history in each nation of Europe. What is the link between France's migration experience and its relatively limited development of factory production? Can geographic mobility help us to understand the unique elements of German social and political development during the nineteenth century? In seeking to comprehend migration as a historical process, we must also see it in relation to the polity and national history.

Finally, our view of migration will be impoverished if we neglect the fact that it is a human process—not the shuffling of economic atoms but rather the movement of historical actors embedded in systems of family, politics, religion, education, and sociability. If we ignore the experiences of ordinary people and attach ourselves instead to the passive implications inherent in the language of migration 'flows' and 'streams', of 'push' and 'pull', we will be neglecting an excellent opportunity to deepen our understanding of the historical process.

Likewise, common people can be obscured from view by the haze of ideological and methodological controversy.[59] Our assessment of migration is increasingly following the same patterns as the debate concerning the standard of living during the Industrial Revolution. Pessimists—from Friedrich Engels, Barbara Hammond, and John L. Hammond to Eric J. Hobsbawm and Edward P. Thompson—have used literary evidence to describe the pernicious qualities of early industrial life and indict industrial capitalism.[60] Optimists, including George R. Porter, Thomas S. Ashton, Ronald M. Hartwell, and Arthur J. Taylor, have assembled statistical data in order to explore the concrete dimensions of workers' lives, demonstrating the material benefits of capitalism.[61] This debate can serve as a warning to migration scholars, partly because it demonstrates the limits of both quantitative and literary evidence and the powerful undertow of ideology. The contentiousness of these optimists and pessimists also illustrates how easily we can isolate the economic and social sides of migration from one another. Only by embracing such complexity can ordinary citizens of the past be endowed with their role as active agents of change in the urban-industrial world we have gained.

### Notes

1 A general discussion of these developments can be found in Weber, A. F. 1899, *The growth of cities in the nineteenth century: a study in statistics*, Ithaca: Cornell University Press; Thistlewaite, F., 1960, Migration from Europe overseas in the nineteenth and twentieth centuries, *XIe Congrès international des sciences historiques, Stockholm 1960*, 5:32–60; Wrigley, E. A., 1969, *Population and history*, New York: McGraw-Hill; Roebuck, J., 1974, *The shaping of urban society: a history of urban forms and functions*, New York: Scribner's; Lees, A. and L. Lees, eds., 1976, *The urbanization of European society in the nineteenth century*, Boston: Heath; Vance, J. E., Jr., 1977, *This scene of man: the role and structure of the city in the geography of western civilization*, New York: Harper's; Lee, W. R., ed., 1979, *European demography and economic growth*, London: Croom Helm; Wrigley, E. A., 1983, The growth of population in eighteenth-century England: a conundrum resolved, *Past and Present*, 98:121–50; Teuteberg, H. J., ed., 1983, *Urbanisierung im 19. und 20. Jahrhundert: historische und geographische Aspekte*, Cologne: Bohlau Verlag; de Vries, J., 1984, *European urbanization, 1500–1800*, Cambridge, MA: Harvard University Press; Hohenberg, P. and L. Lees, 1985, *The making of urban Europe, 1000–1950*, Cambridge, MA: Cambridge University Press; Tranter, N. L., 1985, *Population and society 1750–1940*, London: Longman.

2 For a review of these ideas, see Schorske, C. E., 1963, The idea of the city in

European thought: Voltaire to Spengler, in *The historian and the city*, edited by
O. Handlin and J. Burchard, 95–114, Boston: MIT Press; Fischer, C. S., 1976,
*The urban experience*, New York: Harcourt, Brace, Jovanovich; Berry, B. J. L.,
1981, *Comparative urbanization: divergent paths in the twentieth century*, New York:
St. Martin's; Smith, M. P., 1980, *The city and social theory*, Oxford: Basil
Blackwell.

3  Ravenstein, E. G., 1885 and 1889, The laws of migration, *Journal of the
Statistical Society*, 48:167–227, 52:241–301; Heberle, R. and F. Meyer, 1937,
*Die Grossstädte im Strome der Binnenwanderung*, Leipzig: Hirzel.

4  Tönnies, F., 1957, *Community and society*, East Lansing, MI: Michigan State
University Press; Simmel, G., 1903, Die Grossstädte und das Geistesleben, in
*Die Grossstädte: Vortrage und Aufsatze sur Stadteausstellung*, edited by T.
Petermann et al., 183–206, Dresden: Zahn und Jaensch; Weber, M., 1894, *Die
Lage der Landarbeiter im ostelbischen Deutschland*, Abteilung 1: Schriften und
Reden, Band 3, in *Max Weber Gesamtausgabe*, edited by M. Riesbrodt,
Tubingen: J. C. B. Mohr; Weber, M., 1958, *The city*, New York: Basic Books;
Engels, F., 1974, *Zur Wohnungsfrage*, Frankfurt/Main: Marxistische Blätter.

5  See the work of the Chicago school of sociology, especially that of Park, R. E.,
1916, The city: suggestions for the investigation of human behavior in the urban
environment, *The American Journal of Sociology*, 20:577–612; Park, R. E., 1928,
Human migration and the marginal man, *The American Journal of Sociology*,
33:881–93; Werth, L., 1938, Urbanism as a way of life. *The American Journal of
Sociology*, 44:1–24. For a review of these perspectives, see Fischer, C. S., 1975,
Toward a subcultural theory of urbanism, *The American Journal of Sociology*,
80:1319–41.

6  Zelinsky, W., 1971, The hypothesis of the mobility transition, *Geographical
Review*, 61:219–49.

7  See, for example, Anderson, B. A., 1980, *Internal migration during modernization
in late nineteenth-century Russia*, Princeton: Princeton University Press.

8  The most recent critique of modernization theory from a migration scholar is
Hochstadt, S., 1987, Temporary migration and rural social science history,
paper presented at the annual meeting of the Social Science History
Association, 30 October, New Orleans. See also: Frank, A. G., 1967, Sociology
of development and underdevelopment of sociology, *Catalyst*, 3:20–73; Gusfield,
J. R., 1967, Tradition and modernity: misplaced polarities in the study of social
change, *American Journal of Sociology*, 72:351–62; Tipps, D. C., 1973, Modernization theory and the comparative study of societies: a critical perspective,
*Comparative Studies in Society and History*, 15:199–226.

9  Perlman, J. E., 1976, *The myth of marginality: urban poverty and politics in Rio de
Janeiro*, Berkeley: University of California Press; Todaro, M. P. 1976, *Internal
migration in developing countries: a review of theory, evidence, methodology, and
research priorities*, Geneva: International Labor Office; Simmons, A., S. Diaz-
Briquets and A. A. Laquian, 1977, *Social change and internal migration. A review
of research findings from Africa, Asia, and Latin America*, Ottawa: International
Development Research Center.

10  de Vries, *European urbanization*; Gutmann, M. P. and E. van de Walle, 1978,

New sources for social and demographic history: the Belgian population registers, *Social Science History*, 2:121–43; Hochstadt, S. L., 1983, Migration in Germany: an historical study, Ph.D. diss., Brown University; Hochstadt S. L. and J. H. Jackson, Jr., 1984, 'New' sources for the study of migration in early nineteenth-century Germany, *Historical Social Research/Historische Sozialforschung*, 31:85–92; Kalvemark, A.-S., 1979, The country that kept track of its population, in *Time, space, and man: essays in microdemography*, edited by J. Sundin and E. Soderlund, 221–38, Atlantic Highlands, NJ: Humanities Press; Kertzer, D. and D. Hogan, 1985, On the move: migration in an Italian community, 1865–1921, *Social Science History*, 9:1–24.

11 Among the best studies are Souden, D., 1984, Movers and stayers in family reconstitution populations, 1660–1780, *Local Population Studies*, 33:11–28; Térrisse, M., 1974, Méthode de recherches démographiques en milieu urban ancien (XVIIe–XVIIIe), *Annales de Démographie Historique*, 249–62.

12 de Vries, *European urbanization*; Hochstadt, S., 1983, Migration in preindustrial Germany, *Central European History*, 16: 195–224; Lucassen, J., 1987, *Migrant labour in Europe 1600–1900*, London: Croom Helm; Poitrineau, A., 1985, *Les Espagnols de l'Auvergne et du Limousin du XVIIIe au XIXe siècles*, Aurillac: Malroux-Mazel.

13 Clark, P. and P. Slack, 1976, *English towns in transition, 1500–1700*, London: Oxford University Press, 64–5; Clark, P. and D. Souden, 1982, Rural–urban migration and its impact in early modern England, *Proceedings of the Eighth International Economic History Congress, Budapest*, B8:1–7.

14 Blanchard, R., 1925, *Les Alpes françaises*, Paris: Colin; Hufton, O., 1974, *The poor of eighteenth-century France*, Oxford: Oxford University Press; Poitrineau, A., 1983, *Remues d'hommes: essai sur les migrations montagnardes en France aux XVIIe et XVIIIe siècles*, Paris: Aubier Montaigne; Perrenoud, A., 1970, Les Migrations en Suisse sous l'ancien régime: quelques problèmes, *Annales de Démographie Historique*, 251–9.

15 Gaunt, D., 1977, Pre-industrial economy and population structure, *Scandanavian Journal of History*, 2:183–210.

16 Todd, E., 1975, Mobilité géographique et cycle de vie en Artois et en Toscane au XVIIIe siècle, *Annales: E. S. C.*, 30:726–44.

17 Macfarlane, A., 1984, The myth of the peasantry: family and economy in a northern parish, in *Land, kinship, and life-cycle*, edited by R. M. Smith, 333–50, Cambridge: Cambridge University Press; Souden, Movers and stayers.

18 Kussmaul, A., 1981, *Servants in husbandry in early modern England*, Cambridge: Cambridge University Press; Schofield, R., 1970, Age-specific mobility in an eighteenth-century rural English parish, *Annales de démographie historique*, 261–74.

19 Todd, Mobilité géographique, 730.

20 Chatelain, A., 1969, Migrations et domesticité féminine urbaine en France, XVIIIe siècle–XX siècle, *Revue d'histoire économique et sociale*, 47:506–28; Poussou, J.-P., 1983, *Bordeaux et le sud-ouest au XVIIIe siècle: croissance économique et attraction urbaine*, Paris: Editions de l'Ecole des Hautes Etudes en Sciences Sociales; Souden, D., 1984, Migrants and the population structure of late

seventeenth-century provincial cities and market towns, in *The transformation of English provincial towns, 1600–1800*, edited by P. Clark, 133–68, London: Hutchinson.

21 Clark and Slack, *English towns in transition*; Hochstadt, Migration in preindustrial Germany; Poussou, *Bordeaux et le sud-ouest*.
[ ]

22 Hochstadt, Migration in preindustrial Germany; Jackson, J., Jr., 1980, Migration and urbanization in the Ruhr valley, 1850–1900, Ph.D. diss., University of Minnesota.

23 Zunz, O., ed., 1985, *Reliving the past: the worlds of social history*, Chapel Hill, NC: University of North Carolina Press, 6.
[ ]

24 Ravenstein, The laws of migration, 48, 1885: 19.

25 Bell, M., 1980, Past mobility and spatial preferences for migration in East Africa, in *The geographical impact of migration*, edited by P. White and R. Woods, 84–107, London: Longman; Lucassen, *Migrant labour*.

26 Galtung suggests that innovators can only be identified in terms of their origin communities and that they may be very traditional in the context of destinations. Galtung, J., 1971, *Members of two worlds: a development study of three villages in Western Sicily*, Oslo: Universitetsforlaget.

27 Petersen, W., 1975, *Population*, 3rd ed., New York: Macmillan, 317–27; Tilly, C., 1986, Transplanted networks, New School for Social Research, Center for Studies of Social Change, working paper no. 35.

28 For a general overview of this problem, see De Jong, G. F. and R. W. Gardner, eds., 1981, *Migration decision making*, Elmsford, NY: Pergamon Press.

29 Baines, D., 1985, *Migration in a mature economy: emigration and internal migration in England and Wales, 1861–1900*, New York: Cambridge University Press.

30 Wolpert, J., 1964, The decision process in a spatial context, *Annals of the Association of American Geographers*, 54:537–58; Wolpert, J., 1965, Behavioural aspects of the decision to migrate, *Papers and Proceedings of the Regional Science Association*, 15:159–69; Isnard, W., 1960, *Location and space economy*, Cambridge, MA: Harvard University Press, chapter 3; Bogue, D. J., 1977, A migrant's-eye view of the costs and benefits of migration to a metropolis, in *International migration: a comparative perspective*, 167–82, New York: Academic.

31 Hagerstrand, T., 1957, Migration and area, *Lund Studies in Geography*, ser. B, 13:27–158.

32 For an analysis of the migration of artisans, see Scott, J. W., 1974, *The glassworkers of Carmaux*, Cambridge, MA: Harvard University Press. Discussions of the geographic mobility of bureaucrats are found in Tilly, C., 1978, Migration in modern European history, in *Human migration: patterns and policies*, edited by W. McNeil and R. Adams, 48–72, Bloomington: Indiana University Press; Dupeux, G., 1973, Immigration urbaine et secteurs économiques, *Annales du Midi*, 85:209–20; Moch, *Paths to the city*; Sewell, W. H., Jr., 1985, *Structure and mobility: the men and women of Marseilles, 1820–1870*, Cambridge: Cambridge University Press. For an overview of economic problems migration analysis, see Willis, *Problems in migration analysis*, chapter 2; Mueller, C. F., 1982, *The economics of labor migration*, New York: Academic, chapter 2.

33  Berkner, L. and F. Mendels, 1978, Inheritance systems, family structure, and demographic patterns in Western Europe, 1700–1900, in *Historical studies of changing fertility*, edited by C. Tilly, 209–23; Moch, L. P., 1986, The family and migration: news from the French, *Journal of Family History*, 11:193–203; Moch, L. P. et al., 1987, Family strategy: a dialogue, *Historical Methods*, 20:113–25; Tilly, L. A. and J. W. Scott, 1978, *Women, work, and family*, New York: Holt, Rinehart and Winston.

34  See, for example, Brettell, C., 1986, *Men who migrate, women who wait*, Princeton: Princeton University Press; Poitrineau, *Remues d'hommes*. Transatlantic traditions are best known; see Baines, *Migration in a mature economy*; Barton, J., 1975, *Peasants and strangers: Italians, Rumanians, and Slovaks in an American city, 1890–1950*, Cambridge, MA: Harvard University Press; Franke, E., 1936, *Das Rurhgebiet und Ostpreussen: Geschichte, Umfang und Bedeutung der Ostpreussen-Wanderung*, Essen: Walter Bacmeisters Nationalverlag.

35  Kollmann, W., 1974, *Bevölkerung in der industriellen Revolution*, Göttingen: Vandenhoeck und Ruprecht.

36  Hagerstrand, Migration and area.

37  Ogden, P. E. and S. W. C. Winchester, 1975, The residential segregation of provincial migrants in Paris in 1911, *Transactions, Institute of British Geographers*, 65:29–44.

38  Hoerder, D., ed., 1985, *Labor migration in the Atlantic economies*, Westport, CT: Greenwood Press.

39  Chevalier, L., 1973, *Laboring classes and dangerous classes in Paris during the first half of the nineteenth century*, New York: Fertig.

40  Hubbard, W. H., 1984, *Auf dem Weg zur Grossstadt: eine Sozialgeschichte der Stadt Graz, 1850–1914*, Munich: R. Oldenbourg. For a historical view of rural loss, see Pitié, J., 1971, *Exode rural et migrations intérieures en France*, Poitiers: Norois. For current studies of migration, see Browning, H. L. and W. Feindt, 1969, Selectivity of migrants to a metropolis in a developing country: a Mexican case study, *Demography*, 6:347–57.

41  Brettell, *Men who migrate, women who wait*; Gullickson, G. L., 1986, *Spinners and weavers of Auffay: rural industry and the sexual division of labor in a French village, 1750–1850*, Cambridge: Cambridge University Press.

42  Darroch, A. G., 1981, Migrants in the nineteenth century: fugitives or families in motion? *Journal of Family History*, 6:257–77.

43  Anderson, *Family structure in nineteenth-century Lancashire*; Jackson, J. H., Jr., 1982, Migration in Duisburg, 1867–1890: occupational and familial contexts, *Journal of Urban History*, 8:235–70; Lees, L. H., 1979, *Exiles of Erin: Irish migrants in Victorian London*, Ithaca: Cornell University Press; Moch, *Paths to the city*; Sewell, *Structure and mobility*.

44  Sewell, *Structure and mobility*, chapter 8.

45  Hufton, *The poor of eighteenth-century France*, 367.

46  Jackson, Migration and urbanization in the Ruhr Valley.

47  Clark and Slack, *English towns in transition*; Clark and Souden, Rural-urban migration and its impact in early modern England; de Vries, *European urbanization*; Houston, R. and K. D. M. Snell, 1984, Protoindustrialization? Cottage industry, social change, and industrial revolution, *The Historical Journal*,

27:473–92; Levine, D., 1977, *Family formation in an age of nascent capitalism*, New York: Academic; Souden, Movers and stayers.

48 Poitrineau, *Remues d'hommes*; Poussou, *Bordeaux et le sud-ouest au XVIIIe siècle.*

49 Goubert, P., 1960, *Beauvais et le Beauvaisis de 1600 è 1715*, Paris: SEVPEN. For an overview of the theory of protoindustrialization, see Clarkson, L. A., 1985, *Proto-industrialization: the first phase of industrialization*, London: Macmillan.

50 de Vries, *European urbanization*, 233:6; Hochstadt, Urban mobility in Germany.

51 de Vries, *European urbanization*, 233–4; Hochstadt, S., 1981, Migration and industrialization in Germany, *Social Science History*, 5:445–68.

52 Hanagan, M., 1986, Agriculture and industry in the nineteenth-century Stephanois: household employment patterns and the rise of a permanent proletariat, in *Proletarians and protest: the roots of class formation in an industrializing world*, edited by M. Hanagan and C. Stephenson, 77–106, New York: Greenwood; Schomerus, H., 1981, The family life-cycle: a study of factory workers in nineteenth-century Wurttemberg, in *The German family: essays on the social history of the family in nineteenth- and twentieth-century Germany*, edited by R. J. Evans and W. R. Lee, 175–93, London: Croom Helm; Scott, *The glassworkers of Carmaux.*

53 Anderson, M., 1971, *Family structure in nineteenth-century Lancashire*, Cambridge: Cambridge University Press; Chevalier, L., 1950, *La Formation de la population Parisienne au XIXe siècle*, Paris: Presses Universitaires françaises; Kertzer and Hogan, On the move; Moch, L. P., forthcoming: The importance of mundane movements: small towns, nearby places, and individual itineraries in the history of migration, in *Migration in modern France: population mobility in the nineteenth and twentieth centuries*, edited by P. E. Ogden and P. E. White, London: George Allen and Unwin; Sewell, *Structure and mobility.*

54 Bade, K. J., 1984, Die deutsche überseeische Massenwanderung im 19. und frühen 20. Jahrhundert: Bestimmungsfaktoren und Entwicklungsbedingungen, in *Auswanderer-Wanderarbeiter-Gastarbeiter: Bevölkerung, Arbeitsmarkt, und Wanderung in Deutschland seit der Mitte des 19. Jahrhunderts*, edited by K. J. Bade, 259–99, Ostfildern: Scripta Mercaturea Verlag; Hoerder, *Labor migration in the Atlantic economies.*

55 Hochstadt, S., 1987, Urban migration in Imperial Germany: towards a quantitative model, *Historical papers/Communications historiques*, 1986:197–210.

56 von Bertalanffy, L., 1950, An outline of general system theory, *British Journal of the Philosophy of Science*, 1:134–65; von Bertalanffy, L., 1956, General system theory, *General Systems Yearbook*, 1:1–10; von Bertalanffy, L., 1962, General system theory—a critical review, *General Systems Yearbook*, 7:1–20.

57 A few studies have taken this approach. See Demko, J., 1969, *The Russian colonization of Kazakhstan, 1896–1916*, Bloomington: Indiana University Publications, Uralic and Altaic Series; Mabogunje, A. L., 1970, Systems approach to a theory of rural–urban migration, *Geographical Analysis*, 2:1–18; Briggs, J. N., 1978, *An Italian passage: immigrants to three American cities, 1890–1930*, New Haven, CT: Yale University Press; Piore, M., 1979, *Birds of passage*, New York: Cambridge University Press.

[ ]

58 Fischer, *The urban experience.*

59 See, for example, the history workshop movement in England and the controversy among German social historians regarding the relative merits of 'structural' and 'experiential' history. Samuel, R., ed., 1981, *People's history and socialist theory*, London: Routledge & Kegan Paul; Gerhard, P. and B. Schössig, eds., 1985, *Die andere Geschichte*, Cologne: Bund-Verlag; Heer, H. and V. Ulrich, eds., 1985, *Geschichte entdecken*, Reinbek bei Hamburg: Rowohlt; Kocka, J., 1986, Sozialgeschichte zwischen Strukturgeschichte und Erfahrungsgeschichte, in *Sozialgeschichte in Deutschland*, I, edited by W. Schieder and V. Sellin, Göttingen: Vandenhoeck und Ruprecht; Borscheid, P., 1987, Alltagsgeschichte—Modetorheit oder neues Tor zur Vergagenheit? in *Sozialgeschichte in Deutschland*, III, edited by W. Schieder and V. Sellin, Göttingen: Vandenhoeck und Ruprecht.
60 Engels, F., 1971, *The conditions of the working class in England in 1844*, translated by W. O. Henderson and W. H. Chaloner, Oxford: Basil Blackwell; Hammond, B. and J. L. Hammond, 1926, *The rise of modern industry*, London: Methuen; Hobsbawm, E. J., 1964, *Labouring men*, New York: Basic Books; Thompson, E. P., 1963, *The making of the English working class*, New York: Pantheon Books.
61 Ashton, T. S., 1954, Economics responsible for living conditions, in *Capitalism and the historians*, edited by F. A. Hayek, 33–155, Chicago: University of Chicago Press; Hartwell, R. M., 1961, The rising standard of living in England, 1800–1850, *Economic History Review*, 13:397–416; Porter, G. R. 1847, *The progress of the nation*, London: John Murray; Taylor, A. J., 1960, Progress and poverty in Britain, 1780–1850: a reappraisal, *History*, new series, 45:16–30.

# PART IV

A SENSE OF COMMUNITY?

# 10

# 'Community' and the Social Geography of Victorian Cities

## *Richard Dennis and Stephen Daniels*

Quantitative studies of nineteenth-century cities have made rapid advances in the last decade [the 1970s] in terms of both the complexity of techniques and the range of sources to which techniques have been applied. Simple representations of material from the census enumerators' books like graphs and pie diagrams have been superseded by location quotients, indices of segregation, and factor analyses. Synchronic descriptions of urban structure have been supplemented by assessments of change (for example, of residential persistence and mobility) and analyses of relationships (for example, journeys to work and marriage patterns). Researchers have ventured beyond the census to examine other nominal listings—in directories, electoral registers, ratebooks, and church records—often using record linkage techniques to check or supplement information from one source with that from another. Our enthusiasm to apply new techniques to new sources has often left us exposed to Anderson's criticism that 'we have been paying too little attention to the question of why we are measuring what we are measuring'.[1] Many quantitative historical geographers justify their enterprise as the testing of modern theory on such subjects as migration and modernization.[2] Some such theories, particularly those concerned with Sjoberg's and Burgess's stereotypes of preindustrial and industrial cities and the 'transitional' nature of Victorian cities, are little more than rough generalizations and some urban historians have been more than sceptical about them.[3] Certainly the retrospective application of the methods, concepts, and theories of contemporary social research is a

'Community' and the social geography of Victorian cities
Richard Dennis and Stephen Daniels

From *Urban History Yearbook 1981*, Leicester, Leicester University Press, pp. 7–23.

critical issue. In this paper we consider the significance of 'what we are measuring' for a particularly contentious concept, that of 'community'. We assess the usefulness or relevance of more sophisticated methodological techniques to the identification and investigation of communities in Victorian cities.

The concept of community is used to perform many different functions in the description and analysis of society. There have been as many definitions of community as there have been writers interested in the subject, and so little consensus that some writers have suggested we should abandon the concept entirely. Historically the concept of community has evolved with both a descriptive meaning, indicating a particular social group living in a certain area, and an evaluative meaning, indicating a positive neighbourly quality of social relationships. Raymond Williams remarks that 'unlike all other terms of social organization (state, nation, society, etc.) it seems never to be used unfavourably'. From the nineteenth century onward the concept's 'sense of immediacy or locality was strongly developed in the context of larger and more complex industrial societies'.[4] The contrast between a community and the realm of impersonal, indirect, and instrumental social relationships informs many critical descriptions of nineteenth-century cities. In 1887 Tönnies formalized this contrast as that between *Gemeinschaft* and *Gesellschaft*. Concepts of community in writings on the 'condition of England question' were often manifestly ideological; middle-class supervision and influence was usually seen as a precondition of community feeling.[5] What were treated in such writing as symptoms of disorganization and disharmony—segregated homogeneous working-class districts—are more often seen by modern social investigators as likely **paradigms** of community feeling.[6] Yet the sense of contrast, often historicized in such a way that communities are seen to be in a state of permanent decline, still informs descriptions of such places. Consider, for example, Robert Roberts's vivid autobiographical account of slum life in Edwardian Salford.[7] 'The classic slum' has many characteristics that are commonly identified as typical of working-class communities: the containment of life within a clearly marked territory, a greater publicity of life than in middle-class districts, an immobile population which is socially homogeneous and whose lifestyle is conservative. Yet the account is of Roberts's pre-teenage experiences. Either he had a remarkably vivid memory or he was more dependent on secondary sources than his eyewitness style suggests. It was written more than 50 years after the life it describes and after its author had become aware of and perhaps influenced by the literature of community studies.

The social and perceptual boundaries of Roberts's childhood community were well defined in terms of physical features—railways, gasworks, bonded warehouses, tramlines—a situation which was actually exceptional in the conurbation of which it was a part.[8] Modern community investigators have found it difficult to identify geographical boundaries. Peter Mann argued that it was less important to establish where communities begin and end than to study social relationships in their own right.[9] Terence Lee found it equally difficult to unravel individual perceptions of neighbourhood to define commonly accepted boundaries between neighbourhoods.[10] F. W. Boal's study of interaction patterns along the Shankill–Falls divide in Belfast suggested that a shared perception of boundaries did develop in situations of conflict and threat.[11] Margaret Stacey suggested that we should abandon the purely descriptive study of unique communities in favour of comparative analysis of 'local social systems', the residents of which are related by bonds of kinship, occupation, class, religion, and politics. Where some bonds are missing there is either no local social system or, more usually, a partial system.[12] Stacey's complete local social system represents an elaboration of an earlier sociological concept—the 'urban village'— where employment and services are provided within a confined area and where individuals and families remain for long periods, sometimes for whole lives and several generations.[13]

We can use nineteenth-century sources to establish where people lived, near whom they lived, how often and to where they moved, with whom they socialized, whom they married, to whom they were related and how they were employed. We can infer or reconstruct with varying degrees of confidence other characteristics such as place of work and social status. But do these findings have any value as evidence of community life? Geographers have made numerous studies of where people lived and whom, occupationally and ethnically, they lived near, but their research has not really helped us to understand community structure. The calculation of segregation indices imposes a static pattern on a fluid reality, in which segregation changed by the hour or the day of the week as well as secularly through the century;[14] nor is the most appropriate scale at which to measure segregation at all clear;[15] and we have already noted that some contemporaries assumed that 'community' required social mixing and therefore declined as segregation intensified, whereas modern writers assume that 'community' is based on class and therefore more likely to develop as segregation increases. Because segregation has attracted a substantial literature in recent years, we have chosen to concentrate on five other types of 'evidence': residential persistence, residence–workplace patterns, kinship, patterns of marriage, and special-interest groups. Nevertheless, many of the problems that surround the interpretation of segregation indices apply to these indicators too.

# Persistence

Inevitably, different persistence studies based upon a variety of sources have been unable to follow a common method of calculating persistence rates. Their diversity reflects the periodicity of different sources, from censuses every decade to ratebooks compiled as often as every six months, and the quality of the information they contain. For example, some census enumerators recorded insufficiently precise addresses for us to ascertain whether a household was occupying the same or a different dwelling in the same street in successive censuses. Most researchers have investigated persistence with objectives other than the study of local community structure foremost in their minds. For their purposes, persistence at the same address or within the same city may be the most appropriate scales to record. For the present purpose, persistence at some intermediate scale may be more significant.

Several researchers have calculated one-year persistence rates *at the same address* of 60 to 80 per cent and ten-year rates of 13 to 20 per cent.[16] Some of these variations depend on whether sample populations have been traced forwards or backwards through successive listings. A study in 1844 traced families backwards, revealing that 77 per cent of labouring families in York had lived in their present residences for at least a year.[17] This procedure yields higher persistence rates than the more usual forward tracing of individuals through censuses, directories, or electoral rolls, since there are no losses attributable to death. Pritchard estimated that about 4 per cent of dwellings in Leicester fell vacant each year following the death of the householder, and Pooley calculated that mortality accounted for the loss of a quarter of adults in Liverpool from directories during the course of a decade.[18]

The York sample confessed to be 'principally of the Labouring Class', but recent studies have reflected the bias of electoral registers and directories towards the better-off. Although Pooley included labourers in his samples, they were generally those living in streets that were principally inhabited by the middle classes and so attracted the attention of directory compilers. Consequently, they may have been unrepresentative of their status. In theory, census linkage should be free from bias since the census included everybody. In practice, it favours married men with families, who can be linked on the evidence of their wives' and children's names and ages, even if they have changed their occupation, and even if information on their own ages or birthplaces has been inaccurately recorded. Census linkage discriminates against single people, especially if they possessed a common name or were occupationally *and* geographically mobile, and the illiterate, whose names may have been recorded differently by different enumerators. These problems can be ignored if our aim is only to determine whether individuals are still present at the same address. They become acute when we try to locate the new addresses of absentees.

Persistence rates of less than 20 per cent over a decade are much lower than we find nowadays, but they do not necessarily indicate an absence of community consciousness in the past. We may make different interpretations of equal persistence rates in the past and at present, because the social and financial implications of moving house have changed, particularly as owner-occupation has replaced private renting as the dominant form of tenure. Pritchard argued that mobility in the past was facilitated by high vacancy rates, while low rates of mobility today may reflect an inability to move, because of the costs involved in buying and selling property or the bureaucracy involved in moving between council houses: immobility does not reflect a state of satisfaction with present housing or neighbourhood.[19] If Pritchard's correlation of mobility and vacancy rates is correct we should find that persistence rates fluctuated in accord with local building cycles, yet we could not argue that people's attachment to their local community fluctuated equally violently! So it may be an area's *comparative* level of persistence that marks it out as a geographical community, not its absolute persistence rate. Finally, while many households did not stay at the same address for very long, they rarely moved far. The evidence of contemporaries such as Charles Booth and of modern researchers confirms that short-distance and circular mobility was characteristic of working-class areas. In Preston 14 per cent of males in Anderson's sample area inhabited the same houses in 1851 and 1861, but another 26 per cent could be traced to houses less than 200 yards away.[20] Of 271 households in Leeds that Ward could trace somewhere in the city in successive censuses, 34 per cent remained at the same address and 36 per cent had moved less than a quarter of a mile.[21] In Liverpool one-third of within-city moves were of less than a quarter of a mile.[22] Frequent short-distance mobility may have been treated as casually in the nineteenth century as we regard regular commuting to work nowadays. At the least, therefore, it may be better to measure persistence *in the same area* than *at the same address*.

Even this calculation is difficult to interpret because tenants and owner-occupiers held different attitudes towards residential mobility. In West Hill Park, Halifax, a model estate financed by the Halifax Building Society with the specific objective of encouraging owner-occupation among skilled artisans, and where the rate of owner-occupancy was indeed high at 59 per cent, 33 per cent of household heads (67 out of 205) remained at the same address from 1871 to 1881. In an area of cheap back-to-backs and terraces immediately to the north, almost all rented, the equivalent persistence rate was only 17 per cent (41 out of 242).[23] For the residents of West Hill Park, persistence at the same address may have denoted an attachment to the dwelling as 'home' rather than to neighbours or neighbourhood. For renters, with little emotional attachment to their dwellings and minimal removal costs, continued residence in the same house was more likely to signify commitment to the locality. But short-distance mobility may be more powerful evidence of community for owner-occupiers than for renters. For the latter, it may indicate only the heterogeneous nature of the local housing stock and the inefficient flow of information about housing vacancies over long distances: renters moved locally because they only knew about vacancies near their existing homes and because they did not need to search more distant localities to find accommodation of the right size or cost. For owner-occupiers, employing a more extensive information network of newspapers, solicitors, and agents, short moves were more likely to be positive expressions of choice, reflecting the desire to continue living locally.

Probably the least ambiguous measure of persistence is the ratio of local moves to all moves. What percentage of those who moved did not move very far? Even then we cannot distinguish between moves influenced by attachment to the local area and moves influenced by the spatial bias in information on housing and employment vacancies. Nor does this calculation allow for the movement of communities *en masse*, for which a sense of group solidarity survives its relocation, as in the migration of some ethnic minorities from inner city to suburbia. Moreover, this proposal still leaves us to determine the most appropriate scale for measuring persistence 'in the same locality'. How *do* we 'ensure that our geographical spaces are also relevant social spaces'?[24] There is a danger of prejudging the issue by assuming that arbitrarily defined enumeration districts or wards comprise the building blocks of 'communities'.

An alternative, adopted in directory-based research, is to assume that the names used by directory compilers to describe different localities in a city had some real local meaning. Ward used such areas in his study of segregation in Leeds and Dennis partitioned late-Victorian Huddersfield on the same basis.[25] In his study of persistence rates in Cardiff, Daunton divided the city into eight areas defined as far as possible by physical features such as rivers and railways that hindered movement across the city. Interestingly, he found that the area with the lowest level of same-address persistence (Canton, 11 per cent over ten years) had the highest rate of same-area persistence (37 per cent), whereas North Roath, with the highest same-address rate (23 per cent) had a surprisingly low same-area rate (32 per cent).[26] These figures lend themselves to various interpretations, in terms of local differences in rates of new housebuilding, mixes of house types and sizes, levels of owner-occupation, social status, and multiple occupancy. Evidently, no single hypothesis can account for all the area variations in persistence. We really require complete coverage at the **individual scale** rather than 10 per cent sample data at the **ecological scale** if we are to make further progress at explaining persistence. For present purposes, however, it is less important to explain these variations than to consider their consequences for the nature of community life. Was Canton, with its high rate of internal mobility, more of a local community than North Roath, where people either stayed in the same house or moved out of the area completely?

Ten-year persistence within the whole city of Cardiff was 41 per cent, while within particular areas of the city it varied between 24 and 37 per cent. The fact that few of those who left their local areas moved to another part of the same city implies that Cardiff functioned as a series of relatively self-contained geographical communities. The same inference can be made from estimates of within-city persistence for other cities. We might expect these rates to be low in small cities, where there were few opportunities to move locally to obtain alternative housing or employment, and high in large cities, where the occupationally mobile could change both home and job and still remain within city limits. Yet persistence rates proved to be higher in Huddersfield (population 60,000) than in Liverpool (population 400,000).[27] For Huddersfield further evidence that the town comprised relatively independent communities is provided in figure 10.1, which plots the 1851 addresses of household heads enumerated in two districts of the town in 1861. Even in the case of a newly built suburb, Primrose Hill, which attracted families moving out from the town centre and from the same sector of Huddersfield, there were few cross-town movers from other suburbs.

An alternative method of identifying geographical communities is to group together sub-areas (e.g. streets, blocks, enumeration districts) which had high rates of internal mobility and strong bi-directional flows of movers between one another. Pritchard used this technique in his study of Leicester,[28] and figure 10.2 exemplifies its use in intercensal linkage in Huddersfield.

All this empirical work relates to unplanned communities and to the modern concept of working-class urban villages. But we must also consider the relevance of persistence to the nineteenth-century ideal of planned communities, on peri-urban or rural sites. Population mobility was an important issue in the programme of some nineteenth-century community builders. At his model mill village of Styal, Samuel Greg

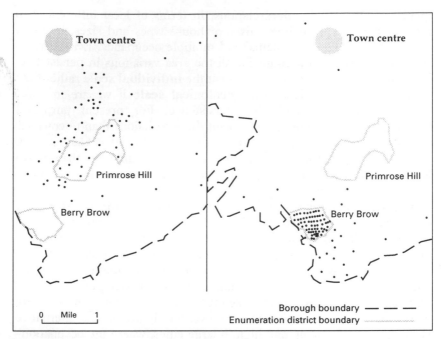

**Figure 10.1**  1851 addresses of residents living in selected districts of Huddersfield in 1861: *left* Primrose Hill; *right* Berry Brow. (One dot represents one household head) *Source*: Census enumerators' books.

provided decent houses and gardens for his workers to 'fix them to the spot and to wean them from those unsettled and migratory habits so peculiarly characteristics of the manufacturing population'.[29] Edward Akroyd was prepared to make a low return on model houses let at modest rents to secure 'an attached and contented population' at his rural mill colony of Copley. Yet of the 72 household heads living in Copley in 1851 only 28 (39 per cent) were living in the colony on census night ten years later, 19 (26 per cent) in the same house. What may have mattered more to the residents of Copley than the rate of population turnover were the origins of newcomers. Most of the first residents were born within walking distance of the village and many had worked near by at Luddenden Foot in a mill which Akroyd closed when he opened the mill at Copley in 1849. The numbers and proportion of household heads born outside Yorkshire increased progressively from 3 (3 per cent) in 1851 to 14 (12 per cent) in 1861 and 24 (19 per cent) in 1871. Most came from the Midlands and south of England and were not employed in the mill. In 1880 a local newspaper reported that the older residents 'allege that these foreigners have brought with them habits of

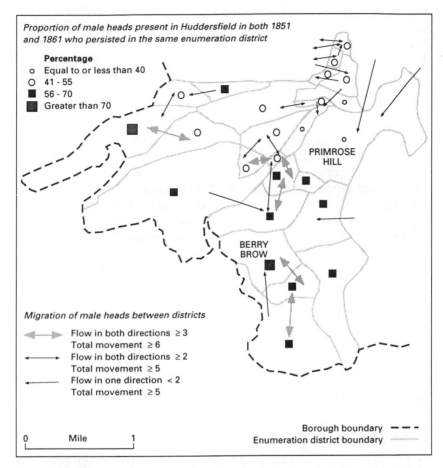

Proportion of male heads present in Huddersfield in both 1851
and 1861 who persisted in the same enumeration district

**Percentage**
o  Equal to or less than 40
O  41 - 55
■  56 - 70
▨  Greater than 70

PRIMROSE
HILL

BERRY
BROW

*Migration of male heads between districts*

◄▨▨▨►  Flow in both directions ≥ 3
        Total movement ≥ 6
◄——►   Flow in both directions ≥ 2
        Total movement ≥ 5
◄——    Flow in one direction < 2
        Total movement ≥ 5

0        Mile        1

Borough boundary  — — -
Enumeration district boundary ▨▨▨▨

**Figure 10.2**  Persistence and intra-urban migration in south-west Huddersfield, 1851–61
*Source*: Census enumerators' books.

unthrift and intemperance . . . and that they are not so clean and tidy in
their household affairs as become true citizens of a village so select'.[30]
The most celebrated model mill colony in Victorian England was
Saltaire, which grew to a resident population of over 4,000. It is
instructive to compare its intercensal persistence rate for 1861–71 with
that of a much smaller and unrenowned mill colony of 600 inhabitants
living in ordinary back-to-backs next to Well Croft mill in the
neighbouring village of Shipley. Thirty-five per cent of the 1861
household heads of Saltaire were listed as living in the colony ten years
later, 12 per cent in the same house. In the Well Croft colony 30 per
cent of 1861 household heads were listed as living in the same house

and 40 per cent in a colony which offered much less opportunity for movement, in terms of total housing stock, than did Saltaire. We might infer from these figures that there was a greater sense of belonging in the Well Croft colony, but in the absence of information on the policy of house allocation, the state of local housing and job markets, and the attitudes of residents, such an inference cannot be made with much confidence. Saltaire was publicized as a select enclave of highly skilled and respectable workers—there were proportionally fewer unskilled household heads than in neighbouring mill colonies and virtually no Irish—and in a village dedicated to the improvement ethic, social and moral exclusiveness may have been more significant for community consciousness than the stability of its population.[31]

It is apparent that persistence, at whatever scale, is an ambiguous and imperfect indicator of community structure. Just because we regard residential stability as a prerequisite for community formation in modern society we cannot assume that it was necessary in the past, especially in situations of close social control—in model communities —or of acute deprivation—in slum communities. Where the poor had no official state help in times of crisis, dependence on neighbours might develop very quickly of necessity. Nevertheless, persistence is a useful index taken in conjunction with other measures of community structure, discussed below, particularly if apparently similar social or cultural environments are being compared or the same area is being studied through time (making allowance for the downward secular trend to mobility over long periods).

## Employment

As with residential mobility so with the relationship between residence and workplace some unsystematic interest was shown by contemporary observers. At the turn of the century, Lady Bell reported on employees at the ironworks on the north bank of the Tees, opposite Middles-brough.[32] She found that of over 260 workers who lived close to the works in an isolated settlement on the north bank, at least 93 (36 per cent) had worked there for more than 20 years, while of 585 workers who commuted from Middlesbrough proper only about 65 (11 per cent) had worked there so long. However, we cannot conclude that employees preferred to work near their homes and that those who did were reluctant to change their workplace. If anything, the relationship worked in reverse. A dwelling on the north bank was provided by the company as a reward for faithful service. It was counted a privilege to live in this strange, wild settlement. But once there a sense of community developed: 'many of the dwellers in the place have as deeply rooted an attachment to it as though it were a beautiful village . . . more than one who has left it has actually pined to be back again.'[33]

More recently, several historical geographers have tried to reconstruct journey to work patterns. A. Dingsdale analysed trade-union records for workers in the Halifax carpet industry.[34] At the end of the nineteenth century 27 per cent of the trade union members lived within a quarter of a mile of their workplace and less than 10 per cent travelled more than a mile to work. By comparison, in 1851 37 per cent of Halifax carpet workers lived less than quarter of a mile from Dean Clough Carpet Mills and less than 3 per cent lived more than a mile away. From this and other fragmentary evidence, Dingsdale concluded that journeys to work did lengthen during the second half of the century, but that they increased more for professional people than for labourers. For 1851, Dingsdale used the manuscript census record of occupation and assumed that those who lived in Halifax must have worked there. Since Dean Clough was the only carpet mill in Halifax, journeys to work could be estimated with confidence, unless carpet workers travelled very long distances to work in other towns or worked outside the factory system.

Other studies suggest a much closer relationship between residence and workplace in 1851. In Huddersfield, over 60 per cent of silk workers lived within a quarter of a mile of Edward Fisher's silk mill, and many of the 18 per cent who lived more than a mile away probably worked at smaller factories elsewhere in the town.[35] In Chorley, 59 per cent of industrial workers lived less than a quarter of a mile from a place where they could have pursued their stated occupation, and in Halifax, 68 per cent of cotton workers lived within a quarter of a mile of their nearest cotton mill.[36]

We might suppose that the uniqueness of the carpet industry in Halifax made it unrepresentative of journey to work patterns among the mass of industrial workers in the town. It was difficult for a carpet worker to change his employer without changing his trade unless he moved away from the town. Consequently he had an extra incentive to find a home close to his only possible workplace. Workers in other trades could move to new firms more easily and might exhibit less loyalty to any locality as well as to any particular employer. In fact, Halifax carpet workers seem to have lived farther from their place of employment than other workers. Perhaps this apparent difference shows how unlikely it was that anything like 59 per cent of Chorley's industrial workers or 68 per cent of Halifax cotton workers *did* work at their nearest possible workplace.

In the case of Crossley's Dean Clough Mills, literary evidence sheds further light on the relationship between home and workplace. In 1880 an old employee recalled that many were prepared to walk long distances to work at the mill because of its good working conditions and industrial relations: 'it was the mill of the day in the district.' In 1903 another employee who lived in a village outside Halifax and who had worked for Crossleys for 40 years described how in his youth 'employment at Dean Clough was considered a very great privilege and a very great honour and also a distinct step in the social advancement of those who were favoured with it.' We should perhaps be sceptical of this testimony, which appeared in the firm's centenary brochure, but there is no doubt that Crossleys commanded the respect of local working people. In the election of 1847 they voted for the Chartist candidate and established a fund of goodwill in the town by taking on those dismissed by local mill owners for Chartist activism. Subsequently they sponsored a variety of self-help institutions and in 1863 set up a pioneering profit-sharing scheme.[37]

This example suggests that the role of workplaces in fostering community consciousness depended less on whether the workers lived near by than on the state of industrial relations. Indeed, we could treat the workplace as a community in its own right, asking whether relationships inside the mill were reflected outside. Were differences of skill reflected in residential patterns and did foremen and overlookers hold positions of authority in social and religious institutions? In his article on Lancashire factory politics, Joyce claimed that some mill owners enjoyed an influence that extended beyond the factory into the surrounding residential area. In the workplace 'the structure of authority was itself often directly political and figures of authority in the factory were often prominent in the social and political landscape of those outside it.'[38] Joyce argued that voting behaviour in the 1868 elections in factory neighbourhoods in Blackburn and Bury demonstrated popular support for the politics of local factory owners and that this political consensus grew out of the 'community of shared experience'.[39]

Most studies of the relationship between residence and workplace have detached the workers from the households to which they belonged. Vance distinguished between determinative ties (employment that determined where families lived) and contingent ties (employment for other family members that was contingent on where they had decided to live)[40] and the workforces discussed earlier in this section will have included workers with both sorts of tie. Presumably, the workplace would have played a more influential role in the social relations of those with determinative ties, yet it is difficult at this remove to decide just who those workers were. We would normally assume that the job of the household head constituted that household's determinative tie, but in families in which the head was self-employed or worked at home the need to find employment for spouse or children may have determined where the family lived. Conventional wisdom tells us that the nineteenth century witnessed the disintegration of the family as the unit of work, yet in practice we do not know how often different members of a family worked in different places. The analysis of residence–workplace links also assumes stability of employment, but many workers must have changed jobs or employers as frequently as they moved house. The interpretation that we place on these changes will depend upon both the type of employment (whether factory, workshop, or domestic, permanent, casual, or itinerant) and the state of the labour market. Among casual labourers the absence of permanent links with a specific workplace may have generated *more* dependence upon neighbours prepared to help in crises and local tradesmen prepared to extend credit during temporary unemployment. Workplace and locality may have been alternative, rather than mutually reinforcing, communities.

## Kinship

It has been suggested that areas are more likely to function as 'urban villages' if their inhabitants are also kin. Several studies have demonstrated that the numbers of co-resident kin (excluding the nuclear family of the household head) increased substantially during the Industrial Revolution. In 100 preindustrial settlements discussed by Laslett only 10 per cent of households contained co-resident kin; in 1851, 17 per cent of households in Cardiff, 22 per cent in York, and 23 per cent in Preston included resident kin.[41] Relatives found both housing and employment through family contacts. In return, working kin either pooled their income with that of the household head to help feed, clothe, and heat the entire household, or paid rent to the head if they were treated as lodgers. The proportion of households with lodgers also increased. Many shared the same birthplaces as members of the family with which they lodged and it is probable that many described in the census as 'lodgers' were also kin. Unemployed kin, especially elderly relatives, acted as unpaid child-minders, so letting mothers go out to work to increase the household income.

There is also evidence that close relatives, such as parents and married children, lived nearer to one another than would be expected if a random allocation of families to dwellings had occurred. Anderson identified relatives by linking names in three successive censuses.[42] He was able to link persons who had been living in the same household in one census, and whose relationship was therefore known, but who were members of different households in another census. In this way we can measure the residential propinquity of parents and children or brothers and sisters, although women are difficult to trace unless marriage registers are used to identify surname changes. The result is an absolute lower limit of the degree to which neighbours were also kin, since we cannot positively identify kin who never lived together under the same roof. In Preston, Anderson found more than twice as many kin living less than 200 yards apart than he would have expected by random processes. In Huddersfield, of 97 sons living with their fathers in 1851 but in their own household ten years later, only five had moved more than a mile from their parents and nearly 70 per cent were living less than a quarter of a mile away. Fifteen sons were enumerated in 1861 with census schedule numbers adjacent to those of their fathers.

However, this evidence of kin living with or near one another is as ambiguous as the other indices we have considered. In Cardiff, co-resident kin lived most frequently in households of relatively high social status, suggesting that the arrangement benefited the kin more than the household head, who would not have been desperate for the additional income. It could even be argued that resident or neighbouring kin were used as child-minders or to help in crises because other, unrelated neighbours were *not* prepared to help out. In these circumstances the presence of kin would be evidence of the absence of a geographically defined community. More probably, the propinquity or co-residence of kin may reflect merely the limited circulation of information on housing vacancies so that married children, for example, did not move far from their parents, regardless of any positive desire to live near by.

Many more studies have plotted the geographical distributions of groups from the same birthplace. Not only national minority groups that had migrated long distances, such as East European Jews and Irish, but also groups from nearby rural origins lived together in the city. But only in very small areas—individual courts or streets—were migrants sufficiently concentrated to constitute a majority of the population. Thus Lees noted that the London Irish lived in enclaves inside English working-class territory, worked in English areas and traversed English areas to visit other Irish enclaves: although they married endogamously and expressed an allegiance to the Catholic church, their community was essentially ethnic rather than geographical.[43] While many ethnic areas, if not their inhabitants, remained stable over time, we know little about areas inhabited by short-distance migrants. On the edge of Huddersfield, Taylor Hill and Newsome accommodated 62 migrants from Westmorland in 1851. Between 1851 and 1861 three moved to other parts of Huddersfield and 22 others were 'lost'. By 1861 the 37 survivors had been joined by 7 new arrivals from Westmorland but only one person had moved in from elsewhere in Huddersfield. Of the 37, only 3 had definitely moved house, although the imprecise address evidence in the census suggests that another 5–10 had probably moved without crossing enumeration district boundaries. The evidence indicates a stable, but decaying, community, with above-average persistence rates, little contact with communities of migrants from Westmorland living in other parts of Huddersfield, and suffering gradual collapse as older folk died and younger members married and left. A particular problem in this research concerns the identification of second-generation migrants other than children still living with their Westmorland-born parents. Even in Taylor Hill and Newsome, the Westmorland-born formed a tiny minority, but we do not know how many of their neighbours actually had links with Westmorland. It is difficult to imagine that the social contacts of this small migrant group were restricted only to their Kendal-born neighbours.

In all the situations described above, we require more positive evidence of patterns of interaction before we can define the geographical, social, or cultural boundaries of communities. It is not enough to know that neighbours were kin, shared the same birthplace or the same occupation. Did they also talk, drink, or worship together, did they intermarry?

## Marriage

Marriage registers, recording the ages, occupations, and addresses 'at the time of marriage' (which may differ from addresses at time of first meeting) of brides and grooms have been used by sociologists, geographers, and social historians to test a variety of often contradictory hypotheses. For example, historians have measured the 'social distance' between the occupational status of bride's and groom's families, inferring social mobility as a consequence of marriage; or they have assumed that marriage partners perceived one another as social equals, in which case marriage patterns could be used to reconstruct the composition of social classes.[44] If mill-workers' sons married shop-keepers' daughters more frequently than would have occurred had partners been selected without regard for occupation, then it could be concluded that mill-workers and shopkeepers belonged to the same social class. Likewise, the cultural isolation of ethnic minorities has been examined by considering the extent to which their marriages exhibited ethnic endogamy.[45] Unfortunately, this type of argument ignores the geographical setting in which partners met: the scale and extent of residential segregation and the ease with which prospective marriage partners could overcome the friction of distance. Irish migrants in Liverpool may have married other Liverpool Irish simply because they lived in all-Irish areas and never had the opportunity to meet non-Irish.

Geographical analyses of marriage patterns have focused almost exclusively on the numbers of marriages contracted over different 'marriage distances' (the geographical distances separating the premarital addresses of partners), checking the validity of **'distance decay' models** of social interaction, and measuring the impact of improved communications, more leisure time and an improved standard of living on marriage distances.[46] Most studies have considered rural areas where it is assumed that there was no residential segregation to distort the distribution of 'opportunities' for marriage. In urban areas, however, we must allow for changes in the distribution and perception of 'opportunities' as the scale of segregation increased and as class was redefined. It could be argued that although new forms of public transport allowed people to travel further to make friends, they did not need to do so since the enlarged scale of residential segregation provided sufficient opportunities for interaction with social equals close at hand.[47] Thus the close-knit community structure of working-class urban villages from the late nineteenth century onwards was a consequence of modern urban structure, not an anachronistic survival from preindustrial or early industrial 'workplace communities'.

We can test this interpretation using grouping methods as illustrated in the section on persistence, or related techniques of **social network analysis**, but it would be misleading not to acknowledge substantial problems in these methods:

1 the assumption that marriage was typical of other forms of social interaction, and that it held the same meaning for different people;
2 the difficulty of obtaining marriage registration data, short of purchasing it piece by piece, or restricting attention to church weddings for which duplicate registers remain in church hands, but which may yield an unrepresentative sample, especially in industrial towns where nonconformity and the Register Office accounted for increasing numbers of marriages;
3 the problem of interpreting 'address at time of marriage';
4 the problem of imprecise address information, e.g. 'of this parish'. If samples of marriages solemnized in the months immediately following a census are selected, the names of marriage partners may be linked to entries in census enumerators' books, but this severely limits the size of sample that can be taken. Linkage to other listings—ratebooks, electoral rolls, directories—is pointless, since few newly-weds will already have been household heads and are unlikely to feature in such listings;

5 despite a decrease in the age at first marriage and an increase in
the proportion of the population ever married, most people in
Victorian cities got married only once. Hence the need to apply
techniques that were designed to identify links between *individuals*
and predetermined, geographically defined *groups* of individuals-
—whole streets, blocks, or enumeration districts— which are
assumed to function as a single unit.

The use of techniques such as **transaction flow analysis** on
Huddersfield data supported the hypothesis that working-class communities became more clearly defined towards the end of the century,
but it also demonstrated that ethnicity operated independently of spatial
proximity. For example, two Irish districts, geographically separated by
the town centre, formed one 'marriage community' throughout the
period of study (1850–80). The intensification of geographically defined
communities in the later nineteenth century could therefore be seen as
an indirect consequence of the reduction of working hours and
improvements in public transport that are normally associated with a
**declining frictional effect of distance** and the growth of '**non-place
community**'. These changes, which gradually enabled workers to live
further from their work, also allowed them to live in one-class areas
alongside the social equals with whom they had always, even at a
distance, chosen to interact.

## Special-interest groups

The records of local clubs and churches are another attractive source of
information on community structure but again problems arise in their
use. We have concentrated in this paper on the existence of working-
class 'urban villages', but most special-interest groups, especially those
such as nonconformist churches that have preserved records of their
activities and membership, are usually assumed to have been predominantly middle class. It is dangerous to assume that membership was
regarded in the same way by all the members of an organization, or that
the membership of different organizations was regarded equally. Some
church members who valued their church for its companionship as
much as for its theology may have been happy to attend the nearest
church, whatever its denomination; others, for whom doctrinal differences were more important, may have travelled distances to church that
were quite unrepresentative of their other forms of social interaction.
Nor does the fact that different individuals belonged to the same
organization necessarily mean that they knew one another at all

personally. Finally, the assumption that special-interest groups helped
to define geographical communities conflicts with the usual sociological
interpretation of them as substitutes for non-sectarian community spirit.
For example, Warner argued that between 1830 and 1860 'all
Philadelphians, of every class and background, reacted in the same way
to the loss of the old patterns of sociability and informal community.
They rushed into clubs and associations.'[48]

Interestingly, Warner suggests that organizational life was for 'every
class and background', not only for the middle classes. Yet for most
slum-dwellers in British cities social life continued to focus on the
doorstep or the pub or shop at the corner of the street. Subscription to a
sick or burial club or children's attendance at Sunday School could
hardly be regarded as support for special-interest groups. But the
middle-class nature of church and club membership can also be
exaggerated. Not only the 'under-world of religion' but even those
denominations usually regarded as solidly middle class often included a
majority of artisans and small tradesmen among their members. In 1851
most full members of one of the most prestigious churches in
Huddersfield, Highfield Congregational Chapel, were shopkeepers,
skilled craftsmen, or textile workers and their families: not poor, but not
the cream of the middle class. Less than 20 per cent of members whose
status could be ascertained from the census boasted obviously middle-
class occupations, such as merchant, gentleman, or annuitant.

Nor can it be argued that religious groups encouraged secondary
relationships or 'association' at the expense of 'community'. Churches
offered not only Sunday services and the life-cycle events of baptism,
marriage, and burial, but also many mid-week social and educational
activities, e.g. mutual improvement associations, libraries, dramatic
societies. Best observed that 'recreation, excitement and amusement
(not to mention the contacts with the opposite sex which could lead to
marriage) were available within all such religious communities as
sanctioned them (i.e. all but the severely puritanical) and were often
ample enough to fill a member's time'.[49] Dyos extended the argument
to non-members, writing that most churches 'probably became focal
points for the social activities of a larger proportion of the communities
they served than the statistics of strict church attendance would
suggest'.[50] So we may interpret the proliferation of churches and church
organizations as an attempt to maintain a sense of localism, not as
destructive of local community structure. Certainly this thinking lay
behind both the Anglican church's policy of creating new suburban
parishes and the parallel strategy of nonconformists in opening
suburban chapels. In Huddersfield, Congregationalists opened three
new suburban chapels during the 1860s, each initially drawing support

almost entirely from its immediate vicinity. Of course, the greater choice that became available, at least for the geographically mobile, could in time destroy the localism that neighbourhood churches had been intended to foster. When members moved house they might retain membership of the congregation near to their old homes. New members would be recruited from further afield, perhaps as existing members introduced workmates who lived in other areas. Over time, processes of selective recruitment reinforced the occupation, class, or age bias of those doing the recruiting, producing interest groups based more in particular sectors of social and demographic space and less upon limited geographical areas.

Even if we accept that the geographical extent and density of support for special-interest groups, and especially religious congregations, are valid indicators of local community structure, we have to cope with substantial practical problems in the use of church and club records. In Huddersfield, a variety of 'membership lists' were available, either still in the custody of local churches or, in the case of dead, dying, or historically conscious congregations, in the local history archives. Some churches produced annual yearbooks with printed lists of the names and addresses of members, but usually all that was available was a continuously updated list of members, recording name, address, date of admission to membership and date of death, resignation, or expulsion. In the case of deaths, age was also often given, providing useful additional information in an attempt to link church records to the manuscript census. Problems arise where an old address has been deleted and a new address substituted. While this provides interesting evidence of residential mobility, it is usually impossible to date the change of address and therefore some error will be unavoidable in plotting the distribution of members at any particular moment. A final problem in comparing different churches lies in the definition of membership. Some lists record 'members', others 'communicants', others 'seat-holders'. Where more than one of these categories is recorded it is clear that they did not coincide.

Used in conjunction with newspaper accounts, yearbooks, and published histories that provide information on the range of activities in which churches were involved, membership records can be employed to test a variety of hypotheses on the changing relationship between church and neighbourhood. Figure 10.3 shows the beginnings of dispersal among the membership of one Huddersfield church, founded in 1865. In 1871 a number of members, mostly single females, were attracted from districts in the town centre, but by 1893 this source had dried up and more distant members were recorded with addresses in areas that were nearer to other churches of the same denomination, some

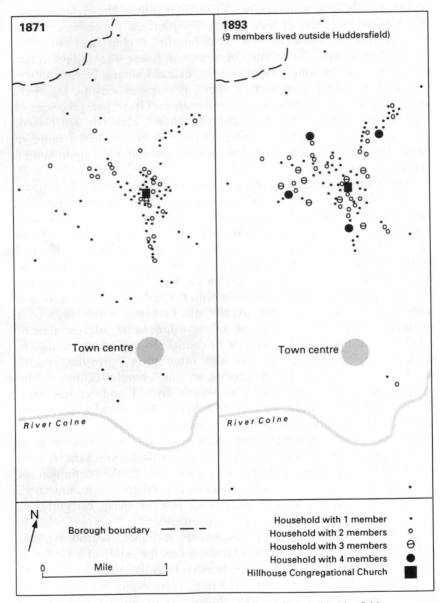

**Figure 10.3**  Membership of Hillhouse Congregational Church, Huddersfield
*Source*: Church yearbooks.

completely outside Huddersfield. Almost all of these people had first joined the church when they were living much nearer to it, and their continued presence on the membership roll does not necessarily indicate the decay of a geographically defined community in Hillhouse, particularly since we do not know whether they were still active, worshipping members. The overriding message of Figure 10.3 is that the church continued to function as a *local* church. This is one occasion when different sources, on segregation, marriage, and church member-ship, support the same interpretation: the existence of stable, close-knit 'urban villages' in respectable working-class and lower-middle-class areas in the last quarter of the nineteenth century. Elsewhere, the conflict of different sources warns against the assumption that all areas underwent the same experience, but in other respects leads to the same conclusion: we need to use different sources together to build up a consistent interpretation.

## Conclusion

Taken in isolation every statistical index of community structure is ambiguous and taken together different indices may be contradictory. We do not conclude that quantitative study should be abandoned, rather that a more adequate context of interpretation should be established. At present there are too few figures to make reliable comparisons. The purposes of the studies from which they are derived vary, as do the methods of data collection and analysis. At the very least we need agreed procedures. In any single study different calculations could be related, for example rates of persistence and indices of segregation and patterns of marriage and institutional membership. In general the more indices of community life that are available the more advantaged we are to assess the significance of any one.

Inferences may vary according to the type of neighbourhood and type of population being studied. For example a persistence rate may take on a different meaning in a planned industrial colony than in an area of speculative housing with a greater variety of employment. Statistical sources favour the regularly employed. The sizeable population of wayfarers in Victorian cities, who worked casually or seasonally and who slept rough or in lodging houses, are the subject of many literary descriptions but often evaded more standardized accounts. By contrast, the 'respectable' working class who are more readily identified in statistical sources rarely figure in the graphic descriptions of social investigators. Too great a reliance on these descriptions hardens our image of all working-class neighbourhoods as disorderly slums. Even for 'respectable' citizens we need to know much more about their varying experiences of moving house, marrying, commuting, and joining institutions before we can satisfactorily interpret the rates and distribu-tions calculated for these activities. It is a truism that statistics are insensitive to the fluency, complexity, and ambiguity of social life. Communities may be characterized as much by antagonism, jealousy, fear, and suspicion as by more neighbourly attitudes and relationships. In Roberts's Salford 'close propinquity, together with cultural poverty, led as much to enmity as it did to friendship.'[51] Questions of community consciousness require attending to more fragmentary and impressionist 'literary' sources.

In summary, we need community studies that bring into relation many types of evidence on many aspects of social life. To those who have spent decades renouncing the practice of regional geography this may seem a retrograde step. But regional geography need not be idiosyncratic. As quantitative evidence may be qualified by a holistic understanding of social attitudes and relationships in particular places, so it can provide a basis for a general understanding of community life that may in turn illuminate specific studies.[52]

## Notes

1 M. Anderson, 'Indicators of population change and stability in nineteenth-century cities: some sceptical comments', paper presented to SSRC Seminar on 'The internal structure of nineteenth-century British cities', Lancaster (1978).

2 See, for example, two collections of papers by urban historical geographers: 'Change in the town', *Trans. Inst. Brit. Geographers*, N.S. 2 (3) (1977), 257–416; 'The Victorian city', *Trans. Inst. Brit. Geographers*, N.S. 4 (2) (1979), 125–319.

3 See the reviews of the two IBG collections by M. W. Beresford, *J. Hist. Geography*, 5 (1979), 346–8; D. Cannadine, *Urban History Yearbook* (1980), 105–6; M. J. Daunton, *J. Historical Geography*, 6 (1980), 332–3.

4 R. Williams, *Keywords* (1976), 65–6.

5 B. I. Coleman, *The Idea of the City in Nineteenth-century Britain* (1973); B. Disraeli, *Sybil* (1845), books II and III, and *Coningsby* (1844), book IV, chapter 3.

6 C. Bell and H. Newby, 'Community, communion, class and community action', in D. T. Herbert and R. J. Johnston (eds), *Social Areas in Cities* (1978), 283–301.

7 R. Roberts, *The Classic Slum* (1971) and *A Ragged Schooling* (1976).

8 See T. R. Marr, *Housing Conditions in Manchester and Salford* (1904), which includes a map of land uses and house types on which Roberts's community stands out like the proverbial sore thumb!

9 P. H. Mann, *An Approach to Urban Sociology* (1965), 155.

10 T. R. Lee, 'Cities in the mind', in Herbert and Johnston, *Social Areas*, 253–81.

11 F. W. Boal, 'Territoriality on the Shankill–Falls divide, Belfast', *Irish Geography* (1969), 6, 30–50.

12 M. Stacey, 'The myth of community studies', *Brit. J. Sociology*, 20 (1969), 134–47.

13 J. Connell, 'Social networks in urban society', in B. D. Clark and M. B. Gleave (eds), *Social Patterns in Cities* (1973), 41–52. For examples of 'urban villages' see

M. Young and P. Willmott, *Family and Kinship in East London* (1957) and H. Gans, *The Urban Villagers* (1962).

14  R. J. Dennis, 'Why study segregation? More thoughts on Victorian cities', *Area*, 12 (4) (1980), 313–7.

15  H. Carter and S. Wheatley, 'Residential segregation in nineteenth-century cities', *Area*, 12 (1) (1980), 57–62; D. Ward, 'Environs and neighbours in the "Two Nations" residential differentiation in mid-nineteenth-century Leeds', *J. Hist. Geography*, 6 (1980), 133–62. For a critique of American studies, see O. Zunz, 'Residential segregation in the American metropolis: concentration, dispersal and dominance', *Urban History Yearbook* (1980), 23–33.

16  M. J. Daunton, *Coal Metropolis: Cardiff 1870–1914* (1977); C. B. Pooley, 'Residential mobility in the Victorian city', *Trans. Inst. Brit. Geographers*, 4 (2) (1979), 258–77; R. M. Pritchard, *Housing and the Spatial Structure of the City* (1976); M. Anderson, *Family Structure in Nineteenth-century Lancashire* (1971); J. T. Jackson, 'Housing and social structures in mid-Victorian Wigan and St Helens' (Ph.D. thesis, University of Liverpool, 1977).

17  *First Report of the Commissioners for inquiring into the State of Large Towns and Populous Districts* (1844, XVII), Appendix, 108.

18  Pritchard, *Housing*, 51; Pooley, 'Residential mobility', 261.

19  Pritchard, *Housing*, especially 115–22. For the modern housing market, see A. Murie et al., *Housing Policy and the Housing System* (1976); R. Dennis and H. Clout, *A Social Geography of England and Wales* (1980), chapter 8.

20  Anderson, 'Family structure', 41–2.

21  Ward, 'Environs and neighbours', 157.

22  Pooley, 'Residential mobility', 270. A more detailed discussion is included in C. G. Pooley, 'Migration, mobility and residential areas in nineteenth-century Liverpool' (Ph.D. thesis, University of Liverpool, 1978).

23  S. Daniels, 'Moral order and the industrial environment in the woollen textile districts of West Yorkshire, 1780–1880' (Ph.D. thesis, University of London, 1980), 226.

24  Anderson, 'Indicators of population change'.

25  Ward, 'Environs and neighbours', 143; R. J. Dennis, 'Community and interaction in a Victorian city' (Ph.D. thesis, University of Cambridge, 1975), 145–6.

26  Daunton, *Coal Metropolis*.

27  R. J. Dennis, 'Intercensal mobility in a Victorian city', *Trans. Inst. Brit. Geographers*, N.S. 2 (1977), 349–63; Pooley, 'Residential mobility'; R. Lawton, 'Mobility in nineteenth-century British cities', *Geographical J.*, 145 (1979), 206–24.

28  Pritchard, *Housing*, 54–60.

29  S. Greg, *Two Letters to Leonard Horner* (1840), 16.

30  Daniels, 'Moral order', 172–3.

31  ibid., 278–9.

32  F. E. E. Bell, *At the Works* (1911).

33  ibid., 40–1.

34  A. Dingsdale, 'Yorkshire mill town: study of the spatial patterns and processes of

urban industrial growth and the evolution of the spatial structure of Halifax' (Ph.D. thesis, University of Leeds, 1974).

35  Dennis, 'Community and interaction', 323–9.

36  A. M. Warnes, 'Early separation of homes from workplaces and the urban structure of Chorley, 1780–1850', *Trans. Hist. Soc. Lancs. Ches.*, 122 (1970), 105–35; Dingsdale, 'Yorkshire mill town'.

37  Daniels, 'Moral order', 201.

38  P. Joyce, 'The factory politics of Lancashire in the later nineteenth century', *Hist. J.*, 18 (1975), 525–53.

39  See also J. D. Marshall, 'Colonisation as a factor in the planting of towns in north-west England', in H. J. Dyos (ed.), *The Study of Urban History* (1968), 215–30. For a case study, see O. Ashmore and T. Bolton, 'Hugh Mason and the Oxford Mills and Community, Ashton-under-Lyne', *Trans. Lancs. Ches. Ant. Soc.*, 78 (1975), 38–50. For a discussion of the factory as community in modern society see B. Jackson, *Working Class Community* (1968).

40  J. E. Vance, 'Housing the worker: determinative and contingent ties in nineteenth-century Birmingham', *Economic Geography*, 47 (1967), 95–127.

41  P. Laslett, 'Size and structure of the Household in England over three centuries', *Population Studies*, 23 (1969), 199–223; A. Williams, 'Family, household and residence since the eighteenth century', paper presented to Anglo-Canadian Historical Geography Conference, Danbury (1977); W. A. Armstrong, *Stability and Change in an English County Town: a social study of York*, 1801–1851 (1974); Anderson, 'Family structure'.

42  Anderson, 'Family structure', 56–62.

43  L. H. Lees, *Exiles of Erin: Irish migrants in Victorian London* (1979), chapter 3.

44  J. Foster, *Class Struggle and the Industrial Revolution* (1974); R. Q. Gray, *The Labour Aristocracy in Victorian Edinburgh* (1976); G. Crossick, *An Artisan Elite in Victorian Society* (1978).

45  Lees, *Exiles of Erin*, chapter 6; Pooley, 'Migration, mobility and residential areas'.

46  For example, P. J. Perry, 'Working-class isolation and mobility in rural Dorset, 1837–1936', *Trans. Inst. Brit. Geographers*, 46 (1969), 121–41; P. E. Ogden, 'Marriage patterns and population mobility', *Univ. of Oxford School of Geography Research Papers*, 7 (1973).

47  R. J. Dennis, 'Distance and social interaction in a Victorian city', *J. Hist. Geography*, 3 (1977), 237–50.

48  S. B. Warner, *The Private City* (1968), 61.

49  G. Best, *Mid-Victorian Britain, 1851–75* (1971), 197.

50  H. J. Dyos, *Victorian Suburb* (1961), 163.

51  R. Roberts, *The Classic Slum* (1971), 47.

52  A recent affirmation of the writing of historical and regional syntheses is C. Harris, 'The historical mind and the practice of geography', in D. Ley and M. Samuels (eds), *Humanistic Geography* (1978), 123–37.

# 11

# Natives and Incomers: the symbolism of belonging in Muker parish, north Yorkshire

*Scott K. Phillips*

In memoriam: P. A. Lienhardt, 1928–86

How did Muker people represent themselves as belonging to Muker?[1] People can belong to their locality, after all, in different ways; the awareness and idiomatic expression of these various ways of belonging are among the main means whereby Muker people distinguish between locals and incomers.

This distinction entails a notion of cultural boundary: one either belongs as a born-and-bred local *of* the parish or one is an immigrant who has *settled in* the locality but whose roots lie elsewhere. The boundary between locals and incomers, however, is anything but hard and fast. Moreover, the characters, or stereotypic markers, for expressing the idea of a cultural boundary are not fixed in their meaning. Rather, the boundary is flexible; this is so because the markers whereby local identity is symbolized are several, and their significance varies in and through time depending on the context of social interaction.

My purpose here is less to describe social and economic differences between locals and incomers in Muker than to show how these differences are typically expressed and experienced by Muker people. My purpose, in short, is to reveal the symbolism of belonging to a local culture in rural Britain.

Idioms of local identity, I suggest, constitute what Holy and Stuchlik (1981) call 'folk models'—that is, complexes of people's ideas about and perspectives on their social identities and relationships. My account will

Natives and incomers: the symbolism of belonging in Muker parish, north Yorkshire
Scott K. Phillips

From A. P. Cohen (ed.), *Symbolising Boundaries: identity and diversity in British cultures*, Manchester, Manchester University Press, 1986, pp. 141–54.

stress that in Muker there is not one but a multiplicity of such idioms through which people present themselves to themselves and to others as they organize, adapt and make sense of their everyday lives. Before focusing on these folk models of local identity, it is necessary to say something about the changing economy, ecology, and society of Muker parish itself.

## Muker

Muker is a **civil parish** in upper Swaledale, which lies in the north-west corner of the Yorkshire Dales. Its 265 residents [in 1981] inhabited 30,000 acres (or 80 square miles) of uplands situated between 1,000 and 2,500 feet above sea level. The parish is bounded by Tan Hill (1,876 feet) to the north, Wensleydale to the south, Melbecks parish to the east, and Great Shunner Fell (2,506 feet) to the west. Its upland landscape is bleak, wet, cold, and windy, and in winter it is covered by deep drifts of snow.

Although Muker is unsuitable for arable agriculture, its gritstone and limestone moors provide an ideal environment for hardy hill sheep. Economic activity in Muker is typical of British upland ecology in that it is concerned mainly with sheep breeding. There is no industry in the parish. As part of Swaledale, Muker falls within the Yorkshire Dales National Park (designated in 1954). Since the creation of the National Park the Yorkshire Dales have seen an increase in motorized tourism.[2] In Muker, local shopkeepers, guest-house proprietors, and the publican earn their livings, in part, by catering for tourists' seasonal needs ... Even so, tourism has created few new jobs: there are no more guest houses in Muker today than there were before the Second World War, and the same is true for the whole of Swaledale.

Muker is also typical of the British uplands today in being a popular location for holiday and retirement cottages. In this article I will concentrate mainly on the usually resident population of locals and (mainly retired) incomers.

Like many upland parishes in Britain, Muker has experienced a gradual depopulation throughout this century, from a population of 615 in 1891 to 265 in 1981. This pattern of decline was precipitated by the closure of local lead mines and coal pits in the late nineteenth century. Families who had until then eked out a living by combining hill farming on small holdings (less than 50 acres) with jobs in mining increasingly migrated to Durham and Lancashire in search of industrial work. Those farming families that remained in upper Swaledale survived by gradually amalgamating their own farms with previous small holdings to make larger, more viable units.

Amalgamation of farms has gone hand in hand with the development of capital-intensive methods of farming. The mechanization of hill farming since the 1950s has further reduced work opportunities in Muker. Hill farms today provide employment only for the household head and one son: there is no such thing any more as a family farm supplemented by seasonal hired labour during haytime.

Nevertheless, sheep breeding and, to a lesser extent, cattle rearing constitute the backbone of the parish economy. Farming provides employment for 55 per cent of the 123 economically active residents. The other main sources of gainful activity are catering and retailing, in which 18 per cent find work, and other service industries and small businesses, which employ the remaining 27 per cent.[3]

The quality of privately and publicly owned services in Muker has gradually improved over the previous quarter century, but in the last decade some basic services have dwindled or have been discontinued altogether. Muker is supplied with electricity, telephones, water, sewerage, and television reception. But its two village schools, weekly banking service, the post office in the village of Keld, and the twice-daily bus service between Keld (at the top of Swaledale) and Richmond (the major market town at the foot of the dale) proved too expensive in the face of less demand from a declining population. Today there is one sub-post office; most banking is done by correspondence; and people without cars must rely on neighbours and relatives for lifts to the nearest bus stop, which is in Gunnerside (six miles from Muker village). Muker children attend the primary school in Gunnerside; for their secondary education they travel 20 miles down the dale to Richmond Comprehensive School.

## Dualistic and scalar markers of belonging

Although locals acknowledge these changing aspects of their parish, they hold and express notions about Muker being a community with distinctive traditions. These traditions are conceived as intrinsic to 'Dales life', that is the larger cultural context of the Yorkshire Dales. None the less, locals feel committed personally to Muker as such: they share a sense of belonging to a distinctive parish community whose families, dialect, and history are *different* from those of the resident incomers, *different* from those of towns and cities further afield. It is this complex awareness of cultural difference that informs the collective representations of Muker people (incomers as well as locals) of what is, and what is not, typical of 'Dales life' generally, and Muker life particularly.[4]

The **markers of cultural difference** are several and they are used by Muker people, depending on context, in two quite distinct ways. Before examining these various uses, we should look more closely at the markers themselves.

*Kinship* is one of the central markers of difference in Muker. When talking with me about the parish community, local people often stressed their links with other Swaledale families. Incomers also represented the community as, among other things, an exclusive body of kin. The idea that 'everyone's related to everyone' is a collective representation of the local community which Muker people present to people from the outside world. Kinship is depicted as being at once a mechanism of inclusion in, and exclusion from, the core set of locals.[5]

Another common marker of difference derives from ideas about an *instinctive feel for farming and the land,* which is considered as peculiar to local farming families. A further distinction relates to *employment*: locals typically work as farmers, or in trades or catering jobs; incomers typically are retired, urban, middle-class couples. Yet another character concerns *language difference.* The possession of a distinct regional language, such as Welsh, or a local dialect, 'Swardal' in Muker, as well as an ability to use standard English, enables the members of regional or local cultures to exclude incomers from some areas of life and include them in others. In Muker, locals speak dialect among themselves, but switch to speaking 'proper English' when incomers are present and engage them in conversation. For Muker people, dialect constitutes a cultural boundary, that can be manipulated depending upon context. Finally, a distinction is made in terms of a person's *length of association with the locality.* Some local families, and incomer couples, have been in Muker longer than others.

These, then, are the main markers of cultural difference which inhere in Muker people's collective representations of their local identity. [As already noted] they are used in two quite distinct ways. When Muker people, natives and immigrants, represent their local identity to people from 'the outside world' . . . they use their various markers of identity in a dualistic manner. Dichotomous discriminations allow Muker people to portray a stereotypical identity: locals were born in the parish, incomers were born away; locals speak dialect, incomers do not. During my fieldwork, I found that when people were interviewed they often summarized how they belonged to Muker in this dichotomous manner. Used in this way the local/incomer idiom is a cultural shorthand: a symbolic typification of people through notions of regional cultural distinctiveness. There is also a cultural longhand whereby locals and incomers portray themselves to each other in everyday conversations and gossip. In these local conversational contexts, people represent themselves and others as belonging to the community less in dualistic terms and more in qualified ways. They place themselves and their families at various points along a scale of localness, ranging from 'real Yorkshire Dalesfolk' at one end to 'people from away' at the other. Such scalar qualifications usually entail temporal distinctions. There is, for example, a difference drawn between the 'real' Muker families (of three or more generations in Muker) and other local families who have been in Muker for only two generations. There is also a distinction made between a 'new incomer' and an 'old incomer' who, after many years' residence in the parish, is counted as 'a local now'. It is the 'now' which is significant: it suggests that continuous and contiguous residence in the locality is as important a character of local identity as descent.

We may look more closely now at how Muker people express and experience their individuality *within* the local community. It is at the level of allocating individual identities that Muker people emphasize the *variability* of the stereotypic markers, or characters, of local identity. We shall consider the various characters in turn.

*Kinship*

Kinship connection is a fundamental character of local identity—a marker of difference between the core set of locals and the peripheral set of incomers. Yet the value of kinship as an index of localness varies depending on the circle or degree of kinship that people appeal to when reckoning their own and other people's identities.

As elsewhere in Britain, kinship in Muker is conceived of in terms of widening circles and degrees.[6] The most immediate circle of kinship for any individual is his or her natal family. It encompasses people of whom one usually speaks with the pronoun 'our': 'our lad Alan' (brother/son), 'our lass Angela' (sister/daughter). People usually include their spouses in this circle and refer to them as 'our ——'. Children refer to their parents usually with the pronoun 'me' (for 'my'): 'me Mum' and 'me Dad'.

The next and larger circle of kin comprises relatives, of whom one speaks in varying degrees of distance. Included in this are one's aunts, uncles, and first cousins. Also included are affines, half-brothers and half-sisters (i.e. individuals who have a parent in common) and more distant cousins such as second cousins (i.e. children of one's parents' first cousins) and quarter cousins (a vague category variously used to refer to children of one's second cousins and of one's half-brother and half-sister). Williams (1956, p. 69) rightly observes that 'the ties which unite relatives are not always fixed'. As in the Cumbrian village of Gosforth, so in Muker the ties and sentiments between half-brothers are expressed in vague terms. In Muker, an air of embarrassment shrouds references to half-brothers born of one's mother out of wedlock. Also, in Muker (as in Gosforth) the relative positioning of distant cousins is vague: little distinction is made between, say, one's grandfather's first cousin and one's father's second cousin (p. 70).

The furthest circle of kinship connection—a circle that is in some ways mythical—is that of one's 'fore-elders' (or ancestors). Reference to 'fore-elders' is expressive of a widespread concern with family origin. Those individuals who are counted, and who count themselves, among the 'real' or 'old' or 'big' Muker families trace their links to the locality and to other 'old' families through fore-elders who were among the 'original' Swaledale families. No one can specify with any certainty who these 'original' families are. But reference is usually made to at least one of five or six predominant local families whenever people trace their inter-relationships. A middle-aged Muker man, for example, told me that his relationship to everybody 'in the closed community of local families' is traceable through his fore-elders in 'two big Swaledale families': the Manns and the Avians.[7]

Herein lies the variability of the character of kinship as a marker of local identity. If kinship is reckoned in terms of one's natal family and affinal ties, someone who belongs to a local family that has been living and working in Muker for three generations may count themselves, and be counted by others, among the set of locals. If, however, kinship is reckoned by reference to one's family's fore-elders, that same person may be counted as less local if their fore-elders are associated with another part of Swaledale (e.g. Reeth, which is lower down the valley than Muker) or another part of Britain (e.g. Wales). As the positioning of an individual's fore-elders within or beyond the dale varies, so does his or her claim to greater or lesser inclusion within the core set of 'old' Muker families.

## Instinctive feel for farming and the land

Another character of local identity concerns the naturalistic notion that people born of Muker farming families possess an instinctive feel for farming and the upper Swaledale environment. Yet this, too, is evidently variable. Not everyone born of a farming family goes into farming, if for no other reason than that most farms are only large enough to occupy one son besides the father. Those who go from school into apprenticeships and into jobs in shops develop different attitudes to the land from those of their 'young farmer' counterparts.

Feel for the land varies, therefore, along occupational lines. One farmer's son, who has continued the family farm since his father died, described farming as his life, his career, and his hobby. Like other Muker farmers, he is devoted to his stock, interested in the fortunes of his farming neighbours, and a regular attender at agricultural markets and shows. Quite different attitudes are expressed by those farmers' sons who have entered trades and retailing. One such man commutes daily to Catterick Army Camp, some 20 miles away, where he works as an electrician. He admitted to me that as his work takes him beyond the dale he is uninterested in the fortunes of the farmers and the seasonal activities taking place in their fields. The dale and its farms have become for him, he says, an area through which he drives as a commuter. He and other farmers' sons who have paid 'jobs' also stress that they believe the money and hours are better in a job than in farming. One farmer's son who works in an agricultural supplies store in Hawes, Wensleydale, best summarized these attitudes: 'Everyone who had a job seemed to be getting more money than farmers. So I got a job. But, looking back, I wouldn't mind farming. I like sheep, and I like shows like Tan Hill. Still, I like my job; it's only selling really, and it's good money.'

Feel for the land among farmers' sons may decline as they choose non-farm work and develop commuter attitudes to their native locality; or it may be transmuted in work connected with farming but which pays more money than a farmer's son might expect from his father.

*Employment*

A distinguishing character of local identity is that locals see themselves as 'hard-working' people engaged in either paid employment ('jobs') or self-employment (farming, guest-house keeping); they regard incomers as 'idle' people who are happily retired. However, this is an ideal-typification of what is actually a more variable situation. To some extent, the typification engenders a self-reinforcing situation. Locals are seen as 'hard-working', so jobs in the locality are usually 'given to' (even 'reserved for') local people. Incomers, on the other hand, are considered to be lazy and untrustworthy, making their chances of finding employment more difficult.

Employment has varying significance in and through time. All middle-aged and young locals are employed [in 1981], either in farming or in non-farming work. But there is a qualitative difference drawn between the two types of employment. Young farmers, for instance, commonly represent farming as 'hard work', whereas they regard paid jobs as less strenuous and less time-consuming. And this is bound up with local people's consciousness of class differences among themselves. Implicit in the class perspectives of Muker people is the notion that the less work a person has to do, the higher his or her social class.

Among older generation Muker people the distinction between employment and retirement is vague, to say the least. Old farmers, who have handed their farms over to their sons, may none the less still work on the farm or supervise certain tasks. Retired farmers usually attend the weekly auction markets; they sometimes take charge of selling their sons' rams at the annual October sales. Incomers, although they are retired, frequently start small businesses (a village shop or a woollens store) or find part-time work, as 'an interest', in these ventures. Such people have retired from their career positions, but have created employment for themselves, partly out of a desire to be occupied, and partly for extra money to boost their fixed-income superannuations. The line between employed and retired, 'hard-working' and 'idle' is vague and fluid.

*Language difference (dialect)*

One of the ideal-typical notions of Dales identity is that each dale has a distinct dialect. Muker people reinforce this collective idea when they remark upon, and value, the distinctiveness of Swaledale's dialect from those of neighbouring dales (Arkengarthdale and Wensleydale). Likewise they locate their parish community within Swaledale by noting the considerable variation in the dialect up and down the valley. The generally agreed axiom is that the further one goes up the dale from Richmond (at the foot of Swaledale) the broader and—so Muker people imply—the more authentic the dialect becomes, and vice versa. Locals, in fact, consider that there are 'two Swaledales', each having a distinct culture history, landscape, and economy. People in and below Reeth (a village situated midway along the dale) are described by Muker locals as speaking 'in a more civilized way' than Muker people. They occupy and work a broad-based valley floor, which is partly arable but is used mainly for growing silage and rearing cattle. The narrower and steep-sided valley above Reeth is what Muker people often refer to as 'the real Swaledale'. People are conscious of the Norse and Scottish elements in the dialect and place names of the upper dale—elements that are absent from the toponymy of the lower dale, which was settled mainly by Romans and Anglo-Saxons.[8] The dale is collectively represented, therefore, less as a homogeneous cultural entity and more as a cultural continuum, with Reeth as the pivotal reference point. The broad speakers in Muker constitute one end of that continuum; the residents of the market town of Richmond, whose dialect and accent are recognizably distinct, represent the other end.

The dale-wide axiom 'lower = less broad; upper = broader' is applied in Muker parish itself. So, for example, Thwaite villagers are considered, and see themselves, as broader speakers than Muker villagers who live a mile down the road from Thwaite; the inhabitants of Angram, a half mile up the road from Thwaite, are broader than Thwaite villagers, and so on up the dale. Individuals, too, gain an aspect of their identity from dialect idiosyncrasies. Certain old men are noted for being very broad. One is considered so broad as to be virtually unintelligible to middle-aged and young locals.

Further evidence about the variability of a character of local identity such as dialect is provided by the speech behaviour of middle-aged and young locals. Local children attend Richmond Comprehensive School. This comprises several Richmond schools, which most Muker children's parents started attending in the mid-1940s. In mixing with Richmond children, Muker youths have been labelled 'woolly backs' and 'hill people', and derided for their dialect pronunciation. As one Muker girl explained: 'We say "buke"; they say "book". We say "muir"; they say "moor".' She and other children have responded by adjusting their speech style at school. But they revert to dialect forms back home in the dale. Young locals who have paid jobs in Richmond admit to playing down their dialect at work. They, too, revert to more local styles of speaking when they meet friends in Muker at the pub or at the village hall for badminton and other recreations. Not to speak in a local manner would be to risk sounding like someone 'from away'. Some young farmers think that their fellows whose jobs are outside the dale speak less dialect because they have adjusted their speech to where they work. Dialect is increasingly represented by the old and young farmers alike as 'dying out'.

Dialect within Muker, therefore, at the level of allocating *individual* identities, is used less as a character of cultural integrity and more as an index of social changes across and within generations. 'Swardal' is still considered as a marker of the *collective* distinctiveness of locals from incomers who speak with different accents. Locals frequently told me that they speak dialect among themselves but switch to speaking 'proper English' when they talk with incomers. The actual variations and adjustments of dialect from place to place, between generations, and between locals and incomers not only mark distinctions between people today; they also distinguish an idealized and immutable past (when all local people spoke dialect) from the actual and altered present (when dialect is 'dying out').

### Length of association with the locality

Finally, it is notable how such a character as lengthy of association with the dale, when applied to an incomer who has lived in Muker since the mid-1940s/early 1950s, makes the difference between that person being classified as an 'old incomer' (or 'a local now') and a 'new incomer'. There is, then, a close resemblance between 'locals' and 'old incomers' on the basis of continuous and contiguous residence in the locality. Association with the dale is a cumulative attribute. The longer an incomer resides in the parish, the more likely it is that she or he will be counted among the set of locals by other locals and new incomers.

## Overview of the markers of local identity

A careful examination of the above-mentioned stereotypic characters of local identity thus reveals that each of them is far from being an immutable marker of a distinct cultural boundary between locals and incomers. Rather, the attributes themselves and their social significance are variable with situation, and across generations and among different kin groups and occupations. Moreover, it is precisely this internal variation which is used by locals to discriminate between 'real' and 'not so real' locals, and by incomers and locals alike to differentiate between 'old' and 'new' incomers.

The attributes, in other words, are symbols, in that they are, as Geertz says of symbols, 'vehicles for a conception' (1973, p. 93). The conception is that of localness, of belonging to a locality; the variability of the attributes enables people to discriminate between degrees of belonging by marking cultural boundaries; and these boundaries are expressive of a complex sense of difference between people of the dale ('locals') and people settled into it ('incomers'), between long-standing residents ('locals', 'old incomers'), and more recent residents ('new incomers'), between people who work on the land in the locality ('farmers') and people who work in trades and shops outside the locality (people with 'jobs').

In brief, stereotypic attributes provide people with a model of Muker Dalesfolk and their variability provides Muker people (locals and incomers) with a model for allocating individual identities along the continuum from 'real Dalesfolk' at one end to 'people from away' at the other. Despite their sense of difference, however, Muker people are also attached to 'community' and 'neighbourly' practices; these serve largely to overcome differences and to stress people's sense of solidarity. I will now attempt to illustrate the process of emphasizing local solidarity with respect to the notions and practices of 'community' and 'neighbourliness'.

## Idioms of solidarity

Whenever Muker people cross each other's paths they usually exchange greetings and address each other with first names or nicknames. In this everyday practice one sees how the *representational* notion of the Dales community as a familiar social world in which everyone knows everyone also serves as a *normative* notion: it shapes and informs people's customary behaviour; it implies that everyone *should* know everyone and therefore should act as if they do (Holy and Stuchlik, 1983, pp. 81–106). Locals explained to me how it is a Dales principle that people should acknowledge each other and pass the time of day. Incomers frequently commented upon the custom of exchanging greetings as an aspect of 'the community' that they value greatly. The principle that informs the custom explains, in part, why locals adjust their speech to 'proper English' when they speak to incomers: one adjusts one's speech according to the person being acknowledged. This is very much the folk explanation: locals say that to include incomers in conversations and greetings they have to speak in ways that incomers will understand.[9] To speak in a dialect that incomers do not understand would be rude. This alternation between 'Swardal' and 'proper English' may be compared with an identical norm in the Welsh community of '**Pentredewaith**'. Frankenberg (1957) observed that although Welsh people value the Welsh language as a symbol of their ethnic identity, they consider that speaking Welsh in the presence of someone in the village who does not understand it is a form of rudeness (pp. 29–31).

The normative notion that everyone should know and acknowledge everyone may thus be seen to express a principle that stresses the fellowship and integrity of the community over categories of individuals. In short, the 'community' principle energizes a custom that overrides and transforms linguistic differences between locals and incomers.

Another 'community' practice is that of 'neighbouring'—giving and receiving help and hospitality.[10] Here too it is readily apparent that the representational notion of the local community as a familiar world wherein people help each other also constitutes a normative notion. That is, it is largely because locals believe that they should feel free to walk into one another's homes and to borrow from one another that they do act in those ways. Incomers often remarked during interviews that when they first arrived in Muker they were made to feel welcome through the hospitality that locals extended to them in their homes. Moreover, since moving into Muker they have been offered and rendered help by locals when it is necessary. Help and hospitality, then, are practices that express the principle of mutual aid among neighbours. They are symbolic acts constitutive of a local community boundary within which incomers as well as locals are included. It is this neighbouring principle that overrides differences among locals (e.g. farmers/non-farmers, 'old'/'not really old' families) and differences between locals and incomers (especially kin/not kin). Association with the locality and its inhabitants, through common residence, means that a person becomes a 'neighbour'. The obvious point about being a neighbour is that one must act like one. And in acting like a neighbour one reinforces a shared sense of community solidarity.

Finally, the practice of 'mucking in' also served either to overcome or actively to use differences between locals and incomers so as to engender community solidarity and ensure the continuity of local ways. Locals muck in in such neighbourhood organizations as the Muker Silver Band, the Gunnerside Football Club, the Women's Guild, and the Muker Badminton Club. It is emphasized by locals that mucking in is the way incomers will be accepted by them, and is in fact proof of such acceptance. One Mukerman put this view succinctly: 'People talk about incomers being foreign for 20 years or more, but that's not so. We accept people if they muck in and do what we do. We don't like people coming and telling us what we should be doing. "When in Rome, do as the Romans do."' That incomers are expected to take their behavioural cues from the locals, and that they should not presume to alter local ways, indicate the implicit asymmetry of the relationship. The principle that incomers should muck in in ways that conserve traditional practices ensures that neighbourhood organizations are safeguarded against take-overs by would-be leaders with the urban middle-class values of assertiveness, explicit styles of communication, and formal methods of decision making noted by Forsythe in Stormay, Scotland (Forsythe, 1980, pp. 296–8). Leadership and participation in organizations stress consensus and equality.

Incomers recognize that mucking in on *local* terms is both a means and a symbol of acceptance. One new couple have involved themselves gradually in neighbourhood organizations such as the Women's Guild (Secretary) and the Silver Band (Treasurer). They explained their strategy in the following way: 'We didn't try to get ourselves into things. We waited till the village came to us. We firmly decided not to come in and try to reorganize things or take things over.' After about three years they were asked to join organizations and do things. As one local told them: 'If the locals ask you to do something, it means they've accepted you.'

The social significance of mucking in was also revealed during the Tercentenary Celebrations of the endowment of Muker's elementary school. At the end of the 'Week of Events' (21–26 May 1978) the then headmistress (an incomer who married a local man in 1954) delivered her closing address—'Involvement and Benefits Derived'. In it she emphasized how everyone had been involved in the celebrations. And she noted how 'community involvement' had overridden the sense of difference between locals and incomers:

The villagers were all involved: each received an invitation to attend functions, but also a request to do a duty of some kind or other and to produce exhibits. . . . Eight people (officially) were on duty whenever the exhibition was open, but there were always more there only too eager to assist with any task however menial. This in itself had repercussions: so-called 'incomers' were equally involved, and all united to show others with pride what 'Our Village' could do.[11]

On certain occasions, incomers are included in local activities precisely, it would seem, *because* they are incomers. The new couple mentioned above, for instance, have also been invited by the Muker Show Committee to judge the children's fancy dress competition. In a community where the children's parents are often related, the placing of such responsibility on the shoulders of non-kinsmen diminishes the possibility of ill feeling arising over an unbiased yet inevitably unpopular decision. A similar device has been described by Frankenberg in his ethnography of 'Pentredewaith' (1957, pp. 17–18, 65, 152–5). There he revealed how Pentre people used 'strangers' in local organizations to make unbiased decisions, thereby reducing tension among themselves. Frankenberg compared this with similar roles performed by strangers in other cultures—leopardskin chiefs among the Nuer, stranger groups among the Sanusi of Cyrenaica, and strangers in the early monastic settlements of North Wales (p. 155). 'Mucking in' in Muker serves to include incomers in the activities of the local community whilst, at the same time, preserving community solidarity.

To summarize: balancing the differences between locals and incomers there exists a range of 'community' and 'neighbouring' idioms whereby Muker people can and do transform their sense of difference into a sense of social integrity. Through the practices of acknowledging, neighbouring and mucking in, people express and experience their collective notions of being a community and belonging to it. If the categories of 'local' and 'incomer' are used to explain and emphasize differences between people, the archetypal ideas of 'community' and 'neighbourliness' inform and pattern everyday practices that stress solidarity.

## Conclusion

In this article I have described the ways in which Muker people (natives and incomers) express and experience their sense of belonging to their locality. My account has revealed how people use the characters, or stereotypic markers, of their local identity both as a cultural shorthand, to express a typified 'Dales' cultural identity, and as a cultural longhand, to allocate individual identities within the local 'arena of distinctiveness' (to use Cohen's definition of culture, 1982). Furthermore, this

investigation shows that the most obvious categories of local identity—
'local' and 'incomer'—are only two of several idioms for expressing and
evaluating a Muker person's social identity. Ideas about 'community'
and 'neighbouring' enable people to conceive of more inclusive modes
of association; notions of 'community' and 'neighbouring' create and are
the creative principles for people's sense of belonging.

More generally, this article has sought to examine how local identity
is similar to ethnic identity with regard to fundamental symbolic
boundary processes of social life. The outcome of the analysis is that
there are no objective differences between categorical sets of people;
rather the categories and their markers are variable, polysemic, and
ambiguous. Depending upon the context, a person's social identity can
be either an embarrassing stigma of social marginality and geographical
peripherality, or a valuable resource for the maintenance of cultural
distinctiveness.

## Notes

1 In this article (based on fieldwork for my doctorate at Oxford University, which
was funded by a Commonwealth Scholarship) I use the term 'Muker people' to
refer to people living in the civil parish of Muker, whether they are native to the
locality or not. Where it is necessary to distinguish them I use the ethnic terms
'locals' and 'incomers'.

2 See *Report of the National Parks Review Committee* (1974), para. 5.41.

3 Census 1981 Small Area Statistics: 10% Sample, pp. 5–6. Where it is noted
that many of the jobs in retailing and service industries lie in the nearby market
towns of Hawes and Richmond, which are beyond the civil parish, it is clear that
farming is the main source of employment in the locality itself.

4 The importance of focusing on this awareness of difference, in doing the
ethnography of locality, has been emphasized by A. P. Cohen in the second
section of his essay 'Belonging: the experience of culture' (1982, pp. 2–9).

5 Frankenberg (1957, p. 50) makes a similar point about people's ideas about
community in rural Wales. More recently, so does Strathern (1981, p. 4).

6 Comparative evidence concerning the way that kinship is conceived of by people
in other British rural communities is available. See Rees (1951, p. 73); Williams
(1956, p. 71); and Strathern (1981, p. 149). All these writers reveal how people
think of kinship in terms of widening circles and degrees.

7 All names used in the text are pseudonyms, in order to protect the privacy of my
informants.

8 The collective representation of 'two Swaledales' would seem to derive from and
express two distinct culture histories in the valley. As much is clear from recent
local historical researches reported by Fieldhouse and Jennings (1978) and
Jensen (1978).

9 Speech adjustment by 'locals' in the face of 'incomers' is a complicated
phenomenon. To some degree, it can be accounted for in class terms, in that

locals apparently feel embarrassed by their parochial language and lack confidence in the ability of outsiders to grasp their meaning should they speak in local idioms. By adjusting their speech to 'proper English', locals admit (implicity) that they should speak according to the speech styles of middle-class urban dwellers, rather than insist that these outsiders learn to speak in local ways.

10 I have elsewhere enquired into the principles underlying neighbouring in Muker, with reference to the maintenance of dry stone boundary walls shared by Muker hill farmers. See Phillips (1984).

11 This is taken from a typescript of the closing speech, made available to me by the headmistress (now retired). I wish to acknowledge her kindness and co-operation.

# References

Cohen, A. P. 1982. 'Belonging: the experience of culture', in A. P. Cohen (ed.) *Belonging: identity and social organisation in British rural cultures*, Manchester, Manchester University Press.

Fieldhouse, R. and Jennings, B. 1978. *A History of Richmond and Swaledale*, London, Phillimore and Co.

Forsythe, D. 1980. 'Urban incomers and rural change: the impact of migrants from the city on life in an Orkney community', *Sociologia Ruralis*, 20 (4), pp. 287–307.

Frankenberg, R. 1957. *Village on the Border: a social study of religion, politics and football in a North Wales community*, London, Cohen & West.

Geertz, C. 1973. *The Interpretation of Cultures*, New York, Basic Books.

Holy, L. and Stuchlik, M. (eds) 1981. *The Structure of Folk Models*, ASA monograph, London, Academic Press.

Holy, L. and Stuchlik, M. 1983. *Actions, Norms and Representations: foundations of anthropological inquiry*, Cambridge, Cambridge University Press.

Jensen, G. F. 1978. 'Place names and settlement in the North Riding of Yorkshire', *Northern History*, 14, pp. 18–46.

Phillips, S. K. 1984. 'Encoded in stone: neighbouring relationships and the organisation of stone walls among Yorkshire Dales farmers', *J. Anth. Soc. Oxford*, 15 (3), pp. 235–42.

Rees, A. D. 1951. *Life in a Welsh Countryside: a social study of Llanfihangel yng Ngwynfa*, Cardiff, University of Wales Press.

*Report of the National Parks Review Committee*, 1974.

Strathern, M. 1981. *Kinship at the Core: an anthropology of Elmdon, Essex*, Cambridge, Cambridge University Press.

Williams, W. M. 1956. *The Sociology of an English Village: Gosforth*, London, Routledge & Kegan Paul.

# 12

## Avoiding the Ghetto:
## Pakistani migrants and settlement
## shifts in Manchester

*Pnina Werbner*

The dynamics of Asian immigrant settlement in British cities have been regular and predictable, yet they remain almost entirely unrecognized. The omission is twofold: both ethnographic and methodological. There has been a veritable flood of static descriptions of immigrant residential distributions in various cities, mostly based on the bare demographic 'facts' contained in census reports. In the desire to arrive at hard and fast facts, these distributional patterns have been accepted in place of less systematic but more subtle analyses of settlement as a process, and its relation to the understandings that immigrants themselves have of the urban environment. Yet in Manchester, not only has the immigrant enclave been shifting, but Pakistanis seldom settle down permanently in a [particular] house or neighbourhood. Their settlement patterns are characterized by an exploratory, persistent seeking of more valuable or advantageous properties in better neighbourhoods. This propensity to move has, however, been mostly ignored in the literature. Even more striking has been the lack of detailed analyses of changes in settlement patterns since the arrival of immigrants' families.

The hiatus is partly due to the prevalent stereotyped view that 'middle-class' Asians live in the inner suburbs while 'working-class' Asians of village background live in inner-city 'ghettos'. This is perceived to be a permanent, unchanging situation: the 'working-class' Asian seeks safety in numbers; his social encapsulation prevents him

Avoiding the ghetto: Pakistani migrants and settlement shifts in Manchester
Pnina Werbner

From *New Community* 7 (3), 1979, pp. 376–89.

from venturing forth from the ghetto. Abandoning the ghetto is synonymous, according to this view, with rejecting one's own community—in other words, with 'assimilation'.

Contrary to this stereotype, Asians—whatever their background— may be regarded as strategic house-owners, highly conscious of the way the housing market operates. Moreover, their ghettos may be characterized as 'open' rather than 'closed' ghettos. They are constantly escaping the ghetto, which just as inexorably closes around them once again. Residence in this open type of ghetto has been characteristic of European immigrant groups such as Jews and Poles, and the process has been voluminously documented for cities in the United States.[1] The settlement patterns of such immigrants contrast, perhaps, with those of Black ghetto dwellers, whose ability to encroach into hitherto White areas appears to be far more restricted. Consequently they have fewer choices, a less flexible pattern of movement and a tendency to remain longer in the ghetto.

The lack of analyses of immigrant residential movement is all the more surprising when considered in the light of the attention given to this phenomenon in the American urban literature. This paper[2] seeks to show that movement rather than stability is the distinctive feature of Pakistani immigrants' settlement patterns in Manchester. Understanding this is vital to any analysis of their social relations, for the fact that Pakistanis are persistent and indefatigable 'movers' is associated with a tendency on their part to remain encapsulated in highly exclusive social networks composed almost entirely of fellow Pakistanis. Hence the paper looks at movement in its social setting. The first part describes the background of Pakistani immigrants in Manchester and reconstructs their residential movements in the city. In the second part the moves and social network of a single immigrant of village background and working-class occupation are discussed.

## The history of movement in the city

It is commonly believed by local Pakistanis in Manchester that the first Punjabi Muslims to arrive in the city were two well-known local figures, one of whom came in 1927, the other in 1937.[3] They settled in terraced housing near the University, around Oxford Road, and were joined by a small trickle of others, some of whom came over in response to reports about Manchester that [the two] sent home. After the partition of India and [the birth of] Pakistan in 1947, the families of these early migrants [which were still in East Punjab] were forced to move as refugees into the newly created state (some had moved of their own volition into the 'Canal Colonies' of Pakistan even before partition). By that time many

of the Manchester-based Pakistanis had ventured into private enterprise—mainly door-to-door peddling, market trading and wholesaling
(in the case of the two earliest arrivals mentioned above).[4]

At that time, and in particular during the 1950s, their businesses
began to prosper and they brought their sons over to help run these
enterprises, as well as a large number of relatives and friends. In 1948, I
was told, there were only 'a few hundred of our people', all living in
the Chorlton-on-Medlock area just south of the centre, beside the
University. Like the two early arrivals, most originated in East Punjab
(now Indian Punjab)—mainly from the Jullundur District, some from
Hoshiarpur (see figure 12.1).[5] The majority were also members of the
*Arain* Muslim caste, which had a large population in Jullundur.[6]

The arriving immigrants lived in crowded quarters, sharing
accommodation and living expenses. A now prosperous businessman
told me that living expenses at that time came to £1 a week: the rest of
his income, around £5 a week, could be saved. The early arrivals were
linked to each other by previous ties of neighbourliness, kinship, or
friendship, and—even more importantly—by the intensity of relationships generated by the small size of the community at that time. Even
today [in 1979, the year this paper was written, and thereafter], these
early comers continue to retain close links with one another, and to set
themselves apart from other Pakistani migrants.

*The 'bachelor houses'*

For a long time migrants continued to live in 'bachelor houses', four or
five to a room, sharing expenses. This pattern of bachelor housing, the
relationships between landlord and lodgers, and those between lodgers
have been carefully documented by a number of anthropologists
(Dahya, 1974; Desai, 1963, pp. 39–55; Aurora, 1967, pp. 35–49).[7] A
man on his arrival was provided with free lodging until a job could be
found for him. After he had saved enough money he would buy a house
of his own, often with the help of an interest-free loan from his former
landlord or from friends, and would himself become a landlord to
arriving newcomers. During the 1950s, terraced housing was extremely
cheap and was perceived to be a desirable investment, since it also
increased the standing of the house-owner and the dependence of
others upon him. In Manchester a similar but parallel pattern also
evolved with regard to relationships between wholesalers and market
traders: wholesalers helped market traders go into business and thus
created for themselves a clientele, until the market traders set up as
wholesalers themselves.

From accounts given to me by various people, the pattern of bachelor
housing in Manchester appears to have conformed to that described for

**Figure 12.1** Immigrant sending districts in Pakistan

Bradford and the Midlands. By 1976–7, there were only a few of these bachelor houses left, scattered throughout the city. In them the old pattern—so common in the 1950s and 1960s—of camaraderie, sharing and weekend sessions of card games, political debates, and, in

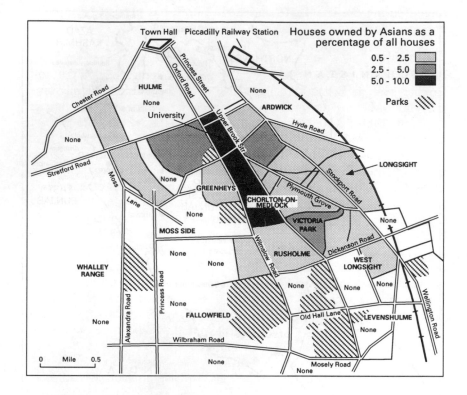

**Figure 12.2**   The central residential cluster, 1963

some cases, drinking (prohibited according to Islam) was still followed. Most men had, however, brought their families over to Britain, while even single men had purchased their own houses. Since the flow of migration was stopped following the progressive tightening of immigration controls during the 1960s, the waves of newcomers to fill these [bachelor] houses had disappeared. Most men owned their own houses by then, or shared them with kinsmen or friends. Others lived with married relatives.

During the 1950s the main arrivals—apart from relatives and friends of the early comers—were students coming to study at the various institutions of higher education in Manchester. They too settled around the University and Victoria Park (see figure 12.2; for a discussion of figures 12.2–12.4, see the Appendix). Many came from the same area of origin as the early migrants, i.e. from the same districts of East Punjab,[8] and were often linked to them by kinship and family friendship. The link between students turned professionals and the early migrants, forged during the late 1950s and early 1960s, has persisted and is an important feature of leadership in the community.

## The second wave of migrants

By 1958 some of the Jullundur men were bringing their wives and families over to Britain. At about that time the number of migrants arriving in Manchester increased dramatically reaching a climax during the early 1960s. Many of the migrant men I know came to Britain during this period. This second wave of migrants, unlike the earlier one, came from all over West Punjab and even from Karachi (see figure 12.1). The migrants came from Gujarat and Jhelum Districts, and from the Canal Colonies of Lyallpur, Sahiwal, Multan, and Bahawarpur; a few came from Gujar-Khan sub-district (*tahsil*) in the Rawalpindi District, from Mirpur in Azad Kashmir, and from Campbellpur in the North-West Frontier. One large kindred group came from Gujranwala via service in the British army. Migrants also came from the big cities—Lahore, Rawalpindi, Lyallpur, Sahiwal, and Karachi—but many of these had originally come from villages or towns in East Punjab, their families having moved to these cities at the time of partition.[9] Just as migrants in Manchester come from different parts of Pakistan, so too they belong to different Muslim castes, so that today a large number of different castes are represented in the city.

A move southwards from the University area was precipitated by this new influx of migrants in the early 1960s. Housing in south Manchester tends to improve as one moves south (Lomas and Monck, 1975), and the city's '**ecological zones**' can be seen to be arranged roughly in concentric circles around the city centre, in a way reminiscent of American cities such as Chicago (Park et al., 1923; Wirth, 1928). As in Chicago, too, each wave of immigrants to the city has tended to replace the former wave in its innermost cheap housing areas. Unlike Chicago, however, differences in neighbourhood housing prices are not too extreme (Lomas and Monck, 1975, pp. 34–5). By the time of the great influx of migrants in the 1960s, the early migrants had established themselves financially and were moving out of the earlier area of settlement in search of separate accommodation for their newly arrived families, and—in the case of the more successful migrants—in search of superior housing to match their improved material position. As numbers increased, migrants also began living in neighbourhoods adjacent to the University area and the number living in Victoria Park rose. Victoria Park was a somewhat more attractive area than that immediately around the University, with better houses and longer leases. It had traditionally been an immigrant area and had once been a superior middle-class suburb (Williams, 1976, pp. 80–1). Migrants also moved into Moss Side and Rusholme, where West Indians had been living for a number of years.[10] These were neighbourhoods of poor housing, which became a continuation of the 'twilight zone' around the University. In 1963 most Asians still lived around the University (roughly, Manchester districts 13 and 15), and it appears to have been a typical lodging area: it was overcrowded, run down, and neglected (Patterson, 1963, pp. 157–91; Rex and Moore, 1967).

Figure 12.2 shows the distribution of Asian house-owners (rate-payers) in 1963. The ratepayers' list (City of Manchester Ratepayers' List, 1963) indicates that there was some residential concentration by criteria of ethnicity or religious persuasion. Thus, the majority of Sikhs were living west of Oxford Road (in Manchester 15) at the time, and a number of streets there had a high Sikh population. The Sikh temple was also in the area. Punjabi Muslims followed a similar pattern east of Oxford Road: while most lived scattered throughout the area (and, indeed, the different Asian communities intermingled), some streets had a far higher proportion of Pakistani house-owners than others. One reason for this unevenness probably lay in the fact that in some streets whole blocks of terraced houses were owned either by the Council or by private property companies. Moreover, a certain amount of discrimination was said to have been experienced in house-buying in the early days. But even more importantly, there was (and is) a general tendency, marked in later years as well, for immigrants to seek to live in the midst of fellow migrants, though some prefer to live slightly removed from their fellows. I discuss this phenomenon in more detail below.

In 1963 the commercial centre of the Asian community was on Oxford Road and Upper Brook Street, near the main Asian residential cluster at the time, although Asian restaurants (usually owned by Bengalis) and some delicatessens were more widely scattered. There were five established hosiery wholesale houses on Oxford Road, four owned by Pakistanis, one by an Indian. The owners of three of these wholesale houses, two of whom were the earliest arrivals mentioned above, have dominated the organization of the Pakistani community in south Manchester since the early days.

*Urban renewal and southward movement*

In the early 1960s the City Corporation began a large-scale urban renewal scheme and the whole area that at the time constituted the main Asian residential cluster—Hulme, Greenheys, Chorlton-on-Medlock, and, later, Moss Side and Rusholme—was cleared during the following ten years. This precipitated a gradual fan movement southwards as one area after another was demolished. Immigrants began buying small family houses south of the area of initial settlement, and West Longsight in particular gradually became the heart of the immigrant residential cluster.

Longsight is an area of three-bedroom, terraced or semi-detached houses. Most Pakistanis [at the time of writing in 1979, and even into the 1990s] live in the central part of the area where there are no gardens and little greenery to alleviate the drabness of the surroundings. Nevertheless, most of the housing in the area is in reasonable condition and surrounding it are leafy streets with bigger houses. Neighbouring Victoria Park too has remained an important immigrant centre in the 1970s. Its houses are in better condition than those of other early immigrant areas and it has been turned into an improvement area by the City Council.

The urban renewal scheme was extremely advantageous to many of the immigrants who had purchased their own houses early on. The Corporation compensated them very adequately and the money they received was used by most of them to invest in better-quality, more expensive housing, often with the help of a private building society or council mortgage.[11] The renewal scheme happened to come at a time when many immigrants began bringing their families to Britain, so they bought small, three-bedroom, terraced or semi-detached houses in place of the large Victorian terraces preferred for house letting. After house prices in Manchester began to rise dramatically towards the end of 1970 (to double in 1971 and then again in 1972) many migrants saw a more valuable property than they had originally owned multiply in value within a short time. For many who were house-owners, houses turned out to be an extremely profitable investment: on the whole, the houses they own today are in fair or good condition, making it worthwhile to invest further in home improvements. Many are in attractive, tree-lined neighbourhoods, and some have gardens. The houses have continued to maintain their relative value on the local market and those which have been extensively improved have increased in value.

The urban renewal scheme was an important factor precipitating the scattering of the immigrant population. By 1977 there was no 'ghetto' area in Manchester for Asian immigrants. There were only two adjacent neighbourhoods—Victoria Park and West Longsight—with a relatively high Asian population, which I call the 'central residential cluster'. But most Pakistani immigrants in Manchester live outside this cluster, although relatively close to it.

The movement into Longsight demonstrates clearly the gradual move southwards. Thus, the number of Asian migrants living in the western part of this neighbourhood, immediately south of Victoria Park (electoral areas 27 and 28 of Longsight constituency) increased dramatically during the 1960s. In 1963 there were only three ratepaying households in the area,[12] as compared with 200 listed on the electoral roll in 1976–7. Between 1969 and 1975 alone, the number of Asian households listed on the electoral roll of the area increased by one-third, but in 11 of the 26 roads in the area the total more than doubled: from 53 enumerated in 1969 to 125 in 1975. By the 1970s, West Longsight and Victoria Park formed the centre of the Pakistani residential cluster. Even so, the proportion of adult Asian immigrants (mainly Pakistanis) resident in the heart of this neighbourhood was only about 20 per cent of the total adult population, and [Asian immigrants] constituted only 16 per cent of the households in the area. In the more predominantly immigrant streets only about one-third of the population was Asian, with the exception of one street in which, in 1976–7, the adult Asian population was 66 per cent of the total. These calculations do not include West Indians or other immigrants, who were, in any case, far less numerous than Asians in the area. In contrast with Longsight, Victoria Park still had many immigrants of other back-grounds living there—Poles, Ukrainians, Jews, Italians, Chinese, and (a few) West Indians. Many Pakistani immigrants were already moving south of Longsight to avoid the residential cluster. Their movement took a fan-like shape as they settled into areas immediately adjacent to those in which they had been living previously.

Figure 12.3 shows the distribution of Asian households (in which there were voters) in some of these areas in 1976–7. It is evident that outside Victoria Park, West Longsight, and perhaps a part of Levens-hulme—the current [1979] area of intake for migrants moving outwards—the proportions of immigrants in the total populations of other areas were very small, and reached at most 4 per cent. In new council housing areas, where house ownership was not allowed in that period, the number of Asian immigrants was only about 1 per cent of the population, and they were widely scattered. By the early 1970s, this area of council housing covered most of the initial areas of settlement of Asian immigrants.[13]

The movement south in the late 1960s started from a single area around the University and had three prongs: to the south-west, to the south-east, and due south (see figure 12.4). Of the early immigrants who had lived around the University and had moved out in the early 1960s, some first moved to Moss Side and then, following the urban renewal scheme and improved economic conditions (which happened to coincide for many in the late 1960s), they moved further out into the inner suburbs of the city—to Whalley Range, Chorlton-cum-Hardy, and West Didsbury (a sample of the electoral roll in 1976–7 indicates that 4 per cent of the population around Alexandra Road in Whalley Range were Asians). Others moved due south through Rusholme to Fallow-

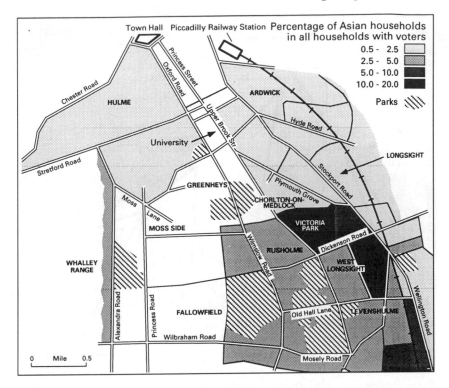

Town Hall   Piccadilly Railway Station   Percentage of Asian households
in all households with voters

0.5 - 2.5
2.5 - 5.0
5.0 - 10.0
10.0 - 20.0

Parks

**Figure 12.3**   The central residential cluster, 1976–1977

field and Withington. From Victoria Park, migrants followed the path
south-eastward through such places as West Longsight, Levenshulme,
Burnage, Ladybarn, and into Stockport.[14] The fan-like movement of
immigrants is exemplified by the Sikh community's movement from east
of Oxford Road in a south-west direction to Whalley Range and
Chorlton-cum-Hardy, where they now [1979] have their main temple.

## Scattering and clustering

The scattering was facilitated in part by the great diversity of housing
types prevailing in most southern neighbourhoods, with a parallel
diversity in prices. Because house prices do not differ excessively
between one neighbourhood and another in Manchester (as they do in
London, for example), it is possible to buy a slightly smaller house in an
area considered 'better' for the price of a bigger house in a lower-class
area. Neighbourhood price differences for equivalent houses only
increase significantly on moving to the outer suburbs of north Cheshire.
This has allowed migrants to choose both the neighbourhood and the

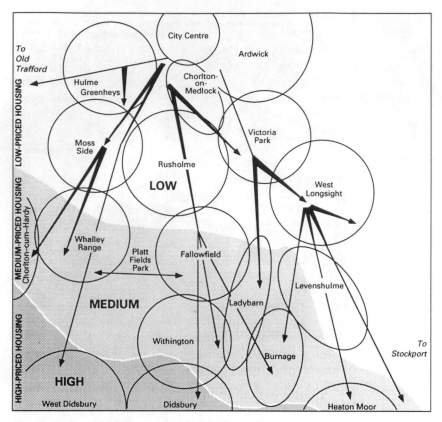

**Figure 12.4**  Schematic representation of the pattern of movement of Asians in south Manchester

house price that suit their social and financial requirements. Since very cheap terraced housing is widely distributed, immigrant clusters have formed in many different parts of Manchester.

'Twilight zones' of deteriorating properties turned into lodging houses were no longer prominent in south Manchester in the late 1970s, mainly because most slum areas had been entirely demolished, and with no new immigrants there was less demand for rooms in lodging houses. One must also remember that the city has never had a restrictive policy regarding lodging areas, as appears to have been the case in Birmingham (Rex and Moore, 1967). Much of the student lodging is, in fact, located in middle-class areas of the city—in Didsbury and Chorlton-cum-Hardy—and immigrant lodging, too, appears to be widely scattered.

By 1976, and indeed since the late 1960s, the commercial centre of the Asian community had shifted about a mile down the road southwards to Rusholme, as the shops on Oxford Road and Upper Brook Street were demolished. By the late 1970s, this had become a thriving shopping centre with travel agencies, banks, material and clothes shops, record shops, furniture shops, cafés and sweet shops, and a number of delicatessens, some selling ritually slaughtered *halal* meat. [At the time of writing in 1979] many other delicatessen shops serve neighbourhood needs and an alternative, although smaller, concentration of Asian shops exists on the eastern periphery of the central residential cluster, on Stockport Road and Wellington Road. [This situation is even more pronounced in the 1990s.] The Rusholme centre is common to Asian groups of all religions and areas of origin. Although located at walking distance from the central cluster, the centre serves migrants throughout Manchester, and many of the shoppers there live as far as ten miles away from it.

The wholesale houses have also shifted, following the expansion of their businesses and the demolition of their premises in Oxford Road. They have been moved to the area around Thomas Street and Lever Street in the heart of the city, which has always been the traditional wholesale district of Manchester. Small wholesaling has expanded remarkably in this district during the past decade [the 1970s], with the appearance of numerous small wholesale houses alongside the bigger ones. In 1977 there were at least 50 Asian wholesale houses in that area alone. Others were moved to another traditional wholesale district, Cheetham Hill and Bury New Road in Salford, just north of the city centre. This is also the wholesale centre for electrical goods, and Asians entered this branch of the trade as well. In addition to wholesaling, Pakistanis have also founded a large number of clothing factories relying mainly on outworkers and these are located not far from the wholesale districts, on the periphery of the town centre. The availability of suitable premises for wholesaling and manufacturing in Manchester facilitated the expansion of these activities in the city, along with retailing, and by the 1970s it was the most important distribution centre for cheap clothing in the north, catering for small retailers and market traders in Scotland, Ireland, and the north of England. Once again, residence was not dependent on work location, and most wholesalers and manufacturers live over five miles from the business centre.

Unlike the business and shopping centres, the Central Manchester Mosque has remained in the same place throughout the years of transition and outward movement. It is situated in Victoria Park, not far from the shopping centre, in an area of large and beautiful Victorian mansions set in their own grounds. Most of these houses have been converted into public institutions and student hostels. The mosque was initially bought and run by the whole Muslim community in Manchester. At first a separate Pakistani mosque of grand proportions was set among terraced houses in the cheap area of Rusholme, bought with funds raised mainly by prosperous Bengali restaurateurs but, as the West Pakistani community grew in numbers and spread into Victoria Park and West Longsight, its members came to dominate the Central Mosque. Today, although officially the Central Mosque serves the whole Muslim community, it is controlled by West Pakistanis, and each of the other Muslim communities has its own mosque. The Central Mosque has been entirely rebuilt, with the bulk of the contributions coming from prosperous West Pakistanis. A smaller West Pakistani mosque is located in the Cheetham Hill area, but there has not been an efflorescence of mosques belonging to the West Pakistani community in south Manchester, and this is extremely important for an understanding of the wider organization of the community. The location of the Central Mosque has continued to provide a focus around which the community has grown and spread.

*Pioneers, elites, and occupational–residential differentiation*

On the whole, migrants tended to follow their relatives and friends from the old neighbourhoods into the new areas of settlement, which explains the fan-like pattern the movement took, but it must be emphasized that the 'pattern' is merely a tendency. As people prosper or make new friends they shift neighbourhoods: Withington, Chorlton-cum-Hardy, and a section of Whalley Range are the centres of residence of more affluent Pakistanis (Nowikowski and Ward, 1978). For migrants from Jullundur who all moved outwards at about the same time, the move did not disrupt their existing set of social relations. This was the case even though they are now residentially more scattered and do not concentrate in particular streets in the new neighbourhoods. Migrants who had previously shared the same lodgings or lived in the same street can today be found living scattered within a single neighbourhood, and they rely more heavily on cars and telephones for keeping constantly in touch with one another. Many are, in addition, involved in business together and they have also developed a complex set of ritual relationships.

Migrants are still moving today, in the late 1970s: in the electoral areas of Longsight mentioned, only 80 per cent of the migrant households remained in the same hands between 1975–6 and 1976–7. The movement was even greater if changes in household composition are taken into account. For the new wave of migrants that has been moving out of the poorer housing areas in the 1970s, the movement into non-immigrant areas is often associated with a loss of the supportive, neighbourly environment of the central residential cluster and with a period of relative isolation in so far as casual visiting and day-to-day neighbourliness are concerned.

This last movement exemplifies the problems encountered by immigrant 'pioneers' moving into new areas. As mentioned, for the earlier migrants who moved outwards the move did not result in a far-reaching disruption of their social networks. In the mean time, however, the community has become more stratified and more stable in its internal social relations. For the current wave of migrants moving outwards this has a number of implications. In the first place, they are leaving a neighbourhood which has already become established as a small, close-knit community, composed of families rather than of single men. Although the central residential cluster is an area of low-priced housing, its residents nevertheless lead a thriving and vibrant social life. Many of them prefer to remain living there and do not follow those moving outwards immediately. In the second place, the new wave of migrants moving out of the central cluster are following in the footsteps of earlier migrants who have established themselves as the elite of the community by virtue of their longer residence in the city, their wealth, and their control of community institutions. For those moving out of the central cluster today the move represents a chance to enhance their social status by establishing new friendships or acquaintances with immigrants of higher status, while attempting not to lose former friends.

Hence, men living in Longsight who have succeeded in business tend to move directly into inner-suburban neighbourhoods where other businessmen live. By contrast, factory workers, rather than moving directly to these suburbs, prefer to move into low- or medium-priced houses still within walking distance of the central residential cluster. The types of job these factory workers have appear to enable them to live outside the residential cluster. Mainly they work in factories that employ relatively few immigrant workers. They are therefore scattered among other British workers and as a result they acquire some proficiency in English and a knowledge of British customs and etiquette.[15] Mill workers, by contrast, prefer not to venture beyond the central cluster. It seems, then, that the familiarity of migrants with other Mancunians at work facilitates their moves into non-immigrant areas. Their ability to speak English enables them to strike up neighbourly relations with non-Pakistanis living nearby and to expect to cope independently with the various contingencies which might arise. These immigrants form the vanguard of the new move from the poorest areas towards the better neighbourhoods.

However, this second wave of immigrants that arrived in the 1960s seems doomed to trail behind the earlier arrivals from East Punjab. For as they have begun to move outwards, the elite, composed of these early arrivals, has already embarked on a new move, this time from the inner suburbs of the city to the 'exclusive' outer suburbs of Greater Manchester. Like those moving out of Longsight, the pioneers of this move are experiencing some isolation, for they too are living away from the majority of their friends and relatives. Some even move back into the centre's middle-class neighbourhoods, but the trend outwards has nevertheless been gaining momentum. In a few years one may expect to find 'golden ghettos' of Pakistanis in these outer suburbs, as friends and relatives join the early pioneers (Kramer and Leventman, 1961).

## Living on the periphery—a case study

I turn now to the movements of one immigrant, Iftahar (a pseudonym), a factory worker of village origin. Iftahar moved to Manchester from a small Lancashire town in 1969. At first he and his wife lived as lodgers in the house of migrants from the same area of origin in Pakistan, in the heart of West Longsight. After a year they bought a house on T. Road, then the *periphery* of the central residential cluster. Iftahar spent a great deal of effort and some money improving and redecorating the house. A relative of his former landlord, Naim, also bought a house near by, on the same road. During the following few years the Asian population of T. Road increased dramatically, so that in 1975 they constituted 66 per cent of the residents in the road. Many of the migrants came from Jhelum District.

In 1974 Iftahar moved out of T. Road, having sold his house there for a large profit. He first moved to an entirely non-Pakistani area in Stockport, where he bought a modern house on an estate. But his wife found the isolation there hard to bear, and when his car broke down he sold the house and moved back, once again to the periphery of the central cluster—in Levenshulme. There he could rely on a regular lift to work. The street he lived in was about 15 minutes walk from T. Road, where two close family friends remained. The road he was currently living on had only two other resident Pakistani families.

The distinctive lifestyle of Iftahar and his friends is associated, I would argue, with residence on the edge, or periphery, of the main residential cluster. What is striking about their choice of residence is that living on the periphery is associated with the avoidance of intense sociability. There are even some migrants who remain living in the central cluster while still attempting to avoid major social commitments. This attempt is usually far less successful than that of migrants living on the periphery, as women in particular tend to get caught up, in due course, in elaborate transactional relations with neighbours and acquaintances. Outside the residential cluster, women often lead lonely lives, although they usually have one or two friends in the neighbour-hood, and visitors do sometimes drop by at weekends. Men tend to have more casual callers, but often days go by without a knock on the door. Life for these migrants follows an uneventful routine, and dinners and other celebrations, when they do occur, are remarkable and significant for their rarity.

Competition for social status amongst migrants in Manchester takes a number of different forms. For migrants living on the periphery, status is clearly regarded as synonymous with wealth and education. Their residential movement is related to this perception, for they are aware that the immigrants' residential cluster has gradually been shifting southwards and, like most Mancunians, they associate living outside it with increased status. They consider most immigrants living in the residential cluster to be of low status, while high-status migrants are known to live in middle-class neighbourhoods, such as Chorlton, outside the cluster. They do not seem to feel that the price they pay—the lack of neighbourly relations with other Pakistanis—is significant. The main reason for this is that the men, the main decision makers, do not rely primarily on a residentially based network. Indeed, the men find the lifestyle of the residential cluster, surrounded by the constant sociability of women, uncongenial. This lifestyle is character-ized by intense interaction between neighbours, friends, and kin, accompanied by a continuous flow of ceremonial prestations [gifts], and regular participation in domestic rituals. Consequently it is associated with female-dominated networks.

Iftahar and his friends prefer not to involve themselves in the excessive giving and hospitality that is at the core of friendship relations in other sections of the community. Instead they share an *ethos* of frugality and saving, and friendships are valued in so far as they uphold this *ethos*. Although they appear to spend a good deal on consumer items, to compete through 'respectable' living, this expenditure may in fact serve to maintain or increase the values of their properties. A negative instance is afforded by the case of the friend Naim, still resident on T. Road, who refused to spend much on decorating his house or moving to a better house, despite friends' attempts to persuade him. He and his wife were intending to return to Pakistan and remitted money home regularly. A couple of years later, Naim's house was found to have serious structural defects, and the family, with five young children, was living in very bad conditions. In general, however, among Iftahar's friends the ideal of 'respectable' living was a predominant one, and the material lifestyle aspired to was highly consonant with British tastes and preferences.

Movement to the periphery is also a way of gaining capital in the form of housing. Migrants buy and redecorate houses and then sell them at a profit. Many have moved a number of times, each time to the periphery of the residential cluster as it 'catches up' with them. They recognize that renovated houses appreciate in value disproportionately to the cost of their redecoration, and they are therefore prepared to invest a great deal of money in high-quality wallpaper, paint, and wall-to-wall carpeting. They do most of the repairs and decorating themselves, with some help from friends.

An idea of the scale of profit possible is given by the moves of Iftahar, who bought and sold a house outside the residential cluster within a two-year period. With the profits of £500 plus savings and returned debts he sent his wife and three young children to Pakistan for several months. The wife took with her £1,000 for his brother there, who was taking care of his older children from a former marriage. He was left with sufficient funds for a down payment on a new house, one much cheaper than the one he had sold, together with redecorating costs of over £1,000. The new house, a semi-detached with a large garden, was in a very bad condition and he had bought it at a bargain price of £5,700, initially without a mortgage. A year later, after more than £1,000 had been invested in improvements, it had appreciated in value to between £8,000 and £9,000. This was at a period (during 1975) when house prices were at a standstill! In 1979 the house was worth at least £16,000. Even in 1975 he had made a clear profit of over £1,000. Not all migrants are as capable as Iftahar in this respect, while some are now directing their resources into market trading. Yet the pattern is not, moreover, uncommon; while, for migrants starting businesses, it is easier to save when living on the periphery. Migrant men also help each other through long-term, interest-free loans (Dahya, 1974).

Iftahar still relies heavily on the network of friends he built up during his residence in the central cluster, as well as on friends made at work.[16] His wife has made only one new friend since their move to Levenshulme, since many of the Pakistani residents there are more educated and sophisticated than she is. Nevertheless, the couple are proud property owners and feel they have improved their lot. Many of their friends have also moved out of the central cluster, although not all of them have moved to Levenshulme. Since the factory [where they worked] closed down in 1976, most of them have become market traders or manufacturers, some quite successful. None of them, however, can be said to be currently sharing the constant excitement and involvement which is the lot of those still resident in the 'ghetto'.

# Conclusion

In his classic study of the ghetto (1928), Louis Wirth discusses the movement of Jews in Chicago out of the ghetto and into the areas adjacent to it, whither they are followed by fellow deserters, only to find that a new ghetto has risen up around them. He describes the isolation and sense of loss of these peripheral residents, and the contradiction in which they are caught between the old criteria, of status and value, and the new. In this paper I have shown how a similar process has been taking place among Manchester Pakistanis; this has led to a similar fan movement out of the immigrant enclave, which itself has been moving outwards. I have indicated that the first arrivals, now resident in the inner suburbs, have established themselves as the elite of the community by virtue of their affluence and control of its institutions. I have also discussed briefly how later migrants, although neither educated nor wealthy, are attempting to raise their status through residence outside the enclave. Although they remain encapsulated in exclusive social networks of fellow Pakistanis, they do pay a price in social terms when living on the periphery of the ghetto. Gradually, however, the ghetto is surrounding them once more as other migrants move out of the existing ghetto to join them.

### Appendix

The information on figures 12.2–12.4 is based on the City of Manchester Rate-payers' List of 1963 and the Manchester Voters' Electoral Rolls of 1969–70, 1975–76 and 1976–77. I wish to thank T. Gluckman for assisting me in the laborious task of copying the entries in the electoral rolls. Asians and Pakistanis were identified in both cases by their names and this, of course, introduces a margin of error into the figures. In 1963 few Asians were British citizens and therefore there was little point in examining the electoral rolls for this earlier period. However, migrants who had come to Manchester in the 1950s already owned their houses, a fact reflected in the Ratepayers' List. The percentages presented in figure 12.2 are unlikely to represent the actual number of Asian migrants in the total population, since each property owned by an Asian would be likely to house a large number of single men as paid lodgers. Significance must be attributed, therefore, primarily to the relative *distribution* of Asians in the various neighbourhoods, rather than to their actual proportion in the population. By 1969, and particularly by 1975–7, most Asian men had acquired British citizenship and it was felt that the electoral rolls would give a reasonably accurate picture of their relative distribution in different neighbour-hoods. The rolls were checked for accuracy by looking up people I knew personally, and were found in all cases to list them, although there was a time lag of about a year in recording their movements. Once again, the percentages given may not be entirely accurate and the *relative* distribution is the most significant fact to emerge.

The picture compiled through these two sources was found to reflect accurately the impressions and memories of Asians regarding their settlement patterns, and this gives it additional validity. The percentages given do not reflect the fact that the Asian population in the inner city tends to be younger than the non-immigrant population, with more children of school age. This fact is more evident in the proportions of Asian children attending local schools (see the article by Auriol Stevens in the *Observer*, 8 July 1979).

## Notes

1 Williams (1976) does discuss the movement of Jews in Manchester in the eighteenth and nineteenth centuries; cf. also Mason (1978) on the settlement shifts of various ethnic minorities in northern Manchester.

2 This paper is based on research in the Manchester Pakistani community conducted with the aid of a Social Science Research Council grant during 1975–1978. [For a more recent treatment of the subject, see Werbner [1990]; an extended version of this paper appears as chapter 1 in that volume.]

3 I know of one other who came to Manchester earlier, but he is not a man of local reputation.

4 See Desai's (1963) discussion of Indian pedlars in the Midlands in the late 1950s (pp. 64–7).

5 The impetus towards labour migration from the Jullundur area is discussed by Aurora (1968, pp. 24–34) and Marsh (1967, pp. 2–9). Migrants appear to have originated from families of small landholders whose land and standing were threatened by fragmentation but who could afford to send one son overseas.

6 See the *Punjab Gazetteer*, Jullundur District, 1935. The *Arain* population constituted over a third of the Muslim population there.

7 Rex and Moore (1967) also discuss relations in lodging houses in Birmingham and describe the mutual visiting of Pakistanis on weekends (p. 122). Their discussion focuses on the bad living conditions prevalent in these houses and the 'landlordism' of Pakistanis. This was less common in Manchester, where market trading appeared to offer more attractive opportunities for further investment. The 1963 City of Manchester Ratepayers' List seems to indicate that few Asians owned more than one house at that time.

8 According to Wilber (1964), many of the high posts in the Pakistan Government are occupied by members of refugee families from India (p. 121). This gives some indication of the relative educational attainments of Muslims in India and Pakistan.

9 According to Wilber (p. 5), 45 per cent of the urban population of West Pakistan in 1951 were refugees, mainly from East Punjab.

10 Victoria Park was at first a lodging-house area of large Victorian houses with relatively short-term leases, although longer than in areas around the University. Most tenants in the area appear to have been Asians, and later the area was transformed back into a family residential area. Moss Side, before its virtual demolition, was a 'mixed' area, with a predominance of West Indians.

11 Because Asians prefer to own their own houses, they did not apply for council housing, nor did they appear to experience much discrimination in house-

buying outside so-called 'twilight zones' (Fenton, 1977). Rex and Moore's arguments about immigrants in the inner city (1967) appear therefore to be somewhat inapplicable to this phase of migration (See also Dahya, 1974).

12  A household as defined here includes all persons living in a separate house, and may thus be composed of more than one nuclear family, and may include lodgers and friends living in the house.

13  Other works on immigrants and residence in Manchester include Nowikowski and Ward (1978), Fenton (1977), Flett (1977), Flett and Peaford (1977), and Lomas (1975). The last work makes no distinction between West Indian and Asian immigrants and this results in an inaccurate picture of the situation of Asian housing, a fact clearly demonstrated by the research of Fenton and Flett.

14  These are the areas where I know people. I do not know the path taken by migrants to Old Trafford and the west, nor do I know the movements of immigrants living in north Manchester, especially in the Cheetham Hill area, nor in Stockport and in the east (Hyde, Ashton-under-Lyne, etc.). Many of these probably moved to be near their jobs, since most big factories are located in these areas rather than in Manchester proper. Migrants do, however, travel great distances to work from the main residential cluster.

15  Factories may be divided into 'low grade' and 'high grade' according to the type of work performed in them and the proportion of immigrants in the labour-force. Where work is low-paid and dirty, there is often a high proportion of immigrants in the work-force (see Marsh 1967, pp. 17–21; Wright, 1968; Patterson, 1963).

16  I discuss Iftahar's social network and present detailed matrices of it in Werbner (1979). [See also Werbner, 1990.]

**References**

Aurora, G. S. 1967. *The New Frontiersman*, Bombay, Popular Prakashan.

City of Manchester Ratepayers' List, 1963.

Dahya, B. 1974. 'The nature of Pakistani ethnicity in industrial cities in Britain', in A. Cohen (ed.) *Urban Ethnicity*, ASA Monograph 12, Tavistock.

Desai, R. 1963. *Indian Immigrants in Britain*, Oxford University Press.

Fenton, M. 1977. 'Asian households in owner-occupation', Working Papers on Ethnic Relations, no. 2, SSRC.

Flett, H. 1977. 'Council housing and location of ethnic minorities', Working Papers on Ethnic Relations, no. 5, SSRC.

Flett, H. and Peaford, M. 1977. 'The effect of slum clearance on multi-occupation', Working Papers on Ethnic Relations, no. 4, SSRC.

Kramer, J. R. and Leventman, S. 1961. *Children of the Gilded Ghetto: conflict resolutions of three generations of American Jews*, Yale University Press.

Lomas, G. B. G. and Monck, E. M. 1975. *The Coloured Population of Great Britain: a comparative study of coloured households in four county boroughs*, The Runnymede Trust.

Manchester Voters' Electoral Rolls 1969–70, 1975–76, 1976–77.

Marsh, P. 1967. *The Anatomy of a Strike*, Institute of Race Relations.

Mason, T. 1978. 'Residential succession, community facilities and urban renewal at Cheetham Hill, Manchester', *New Community*, 6 (1–2), pp. 78–87.

Nowikowski, S. and Ward, R. 1978. 'Middle class and British? An analysis of South Asians in suburbia', *New Community*, 7 (1), pp. 1–10.

Park et al. 1925. *The City*, University of Chicago Press.

Patterson, S. 1963. *Dark Strangers*, Penguin.

*Punjab Gazeteer*, Jullundur District, 1935.

Rex, J. and Moore, R. 1967. *Race, Community and Conflict: a study of Sparkbrook*, Oxford University Press for the Institute of Race Relations.

Werbner, P. 1979. 'Ritual and social networks: a study of Pakistani immigrants in Manchester', PhD thesis, Manchester University.

[Werbner, P. 1990. The Migration Process: capital, gifts and offerings among British Pakistanis, Oxford, Berg.]

Wilber, D. N. 1964. *Pakistan: its people, its society, its culture*, Survey of World Cultures, HRAF Press.

Williams, B. 1976. *The Making of Manchester Jewry 1740–1875*, Manchester University Press.

Wirth, L. 1928. *The Ghetto*, University of Chicago Press.

Wright, P. L. 1968. *The Coloured Worker in British Industry*, Oxford University Press for the Institute of Race Relations.

# 13

# Community and Nation in the Past: perception and reality

*Dennis Mills*

Through illustrative examples, an attempt is made in this article to tease out some characteristics of the relationships between local, community, and national history. In such a small compass a broad-brush treatment has necessarily been adopted, and I hope this will be forgiven in the pursuit of a rounded view.

Leaving on one side for the time being the distinction between 'local' and 'community', I begin by considering how national trends in industrialization and urbanization over the last two centuries have affected local communities, initially with a brief case study of the Lincoln area, written in a deliberately descriptive and personalized form to encourage readers to think about parallel developments elsewhere, and then moving to a broader plane, setting local changes in a national context.

Here I concentrate on matters economic and technological, in which the state at first played relatively little direct part, but the scene then shifts to a consideration of the issue of state involvement in matters of social policy. The examples chosen—the Poor Law and the building of hospitals—are intended to demonstrate contrasts between strong and weak state involvement. I end by drawing a distinction between local history broadly defined and the sharper focus that becomes possible when the 'community' is used conceptually as well as descriptively.

## Industrialization and urbanization: a local case study

A very important national theme for the historian of communities over the last two centuries is the urbanization of the population, followed by

Community and nation in the past: perception and reality
Dennis Mills

This article has been specially commissioned for *Time, Family and Community*.

its **suburbanization**. These processes wrought immense changes on the socio-occupational structure and geographical shape of existing communities, and created wholly or almost wholly new communities in many parts of the country. Industrialization was the driving force behind these changes.

By 1851 Britain had become the first modern nation with more than half its population living in towns. By the end of the century that proportion had reached about 80 per cent. In the present century the tide has turned in the opposite direction, with population dispersing from the great **conurbations** and even towns of modest size into both contiguous and far-flung suburbs. The distinction between urban and rural, clear in 1914, is now so blurred that some scholars deny its existence. I propose to continue this theme through the medium of a local and personal example before turning to its formal analysis.

For me, rural–urban contrasts became sharply evident in 1945 when I went to live in Canwick, an **estate village** only 1½ miles from the centre of Lincoln. From our cottage windows we could see the cathedral on the opposite hilltop, whilst laid out in the Witham valley below were the railways and foundries created in the Victorian period (see figure 13.1). Down there, work-forces of thousands lived in terraced streets within earshot of works' buzzers, belonged to working men's clubs, walked in droves to see Lincoln City FC promoted to Division 2, played in their own works' teams, and voted Labour (a bundle of related characteristics subsequently referred to as '**Fordism**').

On the hill at Canwick we were still doffing our caps to Major the Honourable Dudley Roger Hugh Pelham, DSO, JP, DL, drinking untreated milk from a village farm, and wondering how long it would be before the cricket club dare play on Sundays. During the eighteenth and nineteenth centuries Canwick had been developed as an estate village by the Sibthorps, who for a long time represented Lincoln in Parliament. Their principal residence, Canwick Hall, faced the cathedral symbolically across the Witham valley, and was surrounded by pleasure grounds, park, and kitchen gardens. Within the village all cottages and farmsteads gradually came under Sibthorp control and they built a dower house within a separate walled enclosure also containing stables, garden, and greenhouse (Mills, 1959, 1973).

In 1929 the last male Sibthorp died and the incidence of estate duties led the family about 10 years later to sell their property in Canwick and elsewhere in the county to Jesus College, Oxford. Major Pelham and his wife (née Sibthorp) rented the Dower House from the College, and Lord Liverpool, looking for a smaller residence than hitherto, leased the Hall in 1939. The Victorian social hierarchy was crumbling fast when the war started.

**Figure 13.1**    Lincoln from the south, 1958. This view is similar to that mentioned in the text, the bottom half of the photograph being taken up with railways, foundries, and related housing. A swathe of housing had recently been demolished for the construction of the Pelham Bridge, which eliminated a crossing over several railway lines. The top half shows the medieval city dominated by the cathedral, the Edwardian water tower, and the castle. Below the cathedral is the shopping and business area, with occasional medieval survivals; and behind the cathedral on the flat hilltop most of the houses are of inter-war construction
*Source*: Aerofilms

In 1946, after the wartime occupation of the village by the Royal Signals, the tempo quickened. Jesus College turned the Hall and Canwick House into flats. When building controls were relaxed in the early 1950s they began to sell off quarter- and half-acre plots. Canwick soon became a high-income and functional suburb of Lincoln, although it still remains outside the city boundary. The change from deeply rural to suburban seemed to take no more than 20 years (see figure 13.2).

To the south-west is Bracebridge, two miles from the centre of Lincoln, and still outside the city boundary when my family lived there *c.* 1910–15. Unprotected by a large estate owner, it had already felt many urban pressures. To put myself in an appropriate frame of mind to write what follows, I went and stood on the hilltop at Red Hall above the old village. On the hilltop eastwards of my vantage point is the new 'village' of Bracebridge Heath, still entirely agricultural with only three farmsteads until 1852, when the opening of the County Pauper Lunatic

**Figure 13.2**   Canwick from the north, 1969. In the centre of the photograph is the Dower House, with a huddle of estate cottages on three sides of its wall. Within the wall four new houses have been built, and a fifth site awaits attention. To the left is Canwick House, built by the Sibthorps for a Victorian gentleman-vicar, with the churchyard further left still. To the left and above the church are the kitchen gardens of the Hall, vacated by the writer's father in 1965, and built on in about 1980. Nearby the pleasure grounds of the Hall are already built on in 1969, as is much of the remaining ground in the photograph. The Hall itself is off the photograph to the left
*Source*: *Lincolnshire Echo*

Asylum brought the first residential element. Further development came during the First World War with the building of an aircraft factory, since used for a wide variety of industrial and commercial enterprises, which have added to the demand for housing, the latter also stimulated by proximity to Lincoln.

Down the hill westwards of Red Hall I viewed a great sea of housing where tens of thousands of people live today in Bracebridge, Boultham, and other areas of suburban Lincoln (see figure 13.3). At the end of the eighteenth century the scene would have been entirely rural: in 1801 Bracebridge and Boultham villages, on either side of the river, had populations of only 145 and 73 respectively; in the distance two miles to the north the cathedral completely dominated the city of only 7,205 people (see figure 13.4). In the late eighteenth century the two main roads connecting Lincoln to London, one passing through Bracebridge, had been **turnpiked**. Improvements had also occurred on the two main

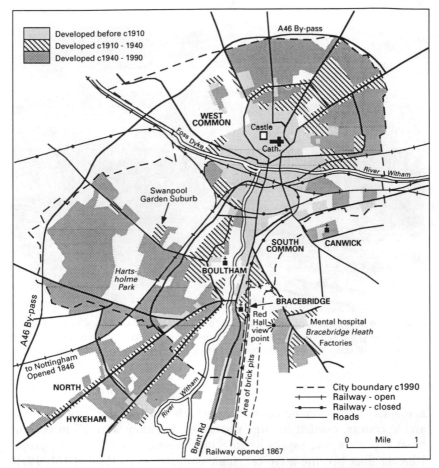

**Legend:**
- Developed before c1910
- Developed c1910 - 1940
- Developed c1940 - 1990

A46 By-pass

WEST
COMMON

Foss Dyke

Castle
Cath.

River Witham

Swanpool
Garden Suburb

SOUTH
COMMON

CANWICK

Harts-
holme
Park

BOULTHAM

BRACEBRIDGE

Red
Hall
view
point

Mental hospital
*Bracebridge Heath*
Factories

A46 By-pass

to Nottingham
Opened 1846

NORTH

Witham

Area of brick pits

HYKEHAM

River

Brant Rd

Railway opened 1867

- – – – City boundary c1990
- +—+ Railway - open
- ●—● Railway - closed
- —— Roads

0        Mile        1

**Figure 13.3**  Lincoln's development in the twentieth century. Included in developed land are derelict land, cemeteries, and sewage works; excluded are the principal recreational spaces and abandoned clay and gravel pits
*Source*: Dennis Mills

navigations into Lincoln, the River Witham to Boston and the Foss Dyke to the Trent, but in 1800 Lincoln was still basically only a market town, made bigger by being head of a large county and a still larger diocese (see figure 13.5).

Modern factory industry arrived only with the railways. The first to enter the city was built from Nottingham in 1846 and still crosses my view in the middle distance. By 1850 all the major railway connections were in place and by 1860 all the main foundry firms of Victorian Lincoln had become established. They specialized in agricultural

**Figure 13.4** A woodcut of Bracebridge, *c.*1867, with Lincoln Cathedral in the distance, demonstrating the rural past of the village. To the right of the Saxon church is the vicarage, demolished for council houses; the brick-clay area lies off the photograph, immediately to the right
*Source*: Local Studies Collection, Lincoln Central Library

machinery and pumping equipment, which Lincolnshire, as a low-lying arable county, needed in large quantities; but they were all to become great exporters too, especially to South America and Eastern Europe. Lincoln thus became a typical single-industry town (Hill, 1974, 1979; Wright, 1982).

Recruitment of the expanding work-force was achieved partly by the natural increase of population, partly by in-migration. Hill calculated that 69 per cent of the population over 20 years of age had been born outside the city, divided about 6 : 4 between Lincolnshire and out-of-county birthplaces (1974, p. 126). A recent study has traced migrants of six nearby villages in the Lincoln census enumerators' books (CEBs): 219 in 1851 (compared with a population at the same date of 4,361 in the six villages) and 537 in 1881 (cf. 4,859). Despite the importance of heavy engineering in Lincoln, most migrants from these villages were female, and even men were spread over a wide range of occupations (Graves, 1992, pp. 6–8, 11–14). There are indications that similar figures might be discovered for many free-standing towns in Victorian England.

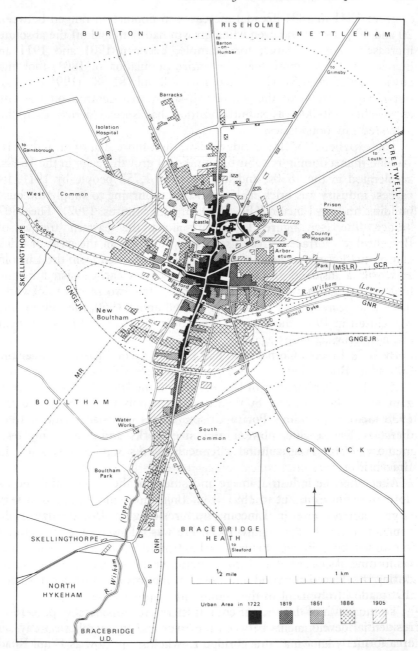

**Figure 13.5**  The growth of Lincoln's built-up area, 1722–1905, including Bracebridge old village
*Source*: Wright, 1982

From 1841 to 1881 decadal increases in population ranged between 20 and 40 per cent and even when growth had flattened off the absolute increases were still large; for example, between 1901 and 1911 an increase of 8,500 (more than the entire population of 1801) took the city's population to 57,000. Today it is still only 81,987 (1991 census), but the population of the journey-to-work area centred on the city approaches 150,000, as suburbanization has spread across even the extended city boundaries.

The experience of Bracebridge was at first more that of an industrial satellite than a dormitory suburb. Significant growth began in the 1840s, accelerated in the 1850s, and had reached 1,752 people by 1911. Its earliest industry was brick-making and lime-burning to supply the busy building trade in Lincoln (Hill, 1974, p. 125; Squires, 1992). The 1867 branch line (see figure 13.4) ran along the eastern fringes of Bracebridge's terraced streets, separating them from the strip of brick clay on the lower reaches of the hill. This was worked from the Lincoln end over a distance of two miles, a process clearly assisted by the building of the railway. In recent years all but two of the brickworks have disappeared; brick production ceased about 1960; the railway line was closed in 1966; the clay pits have been filled in and most of them are now growing crops again.

By 1872 Lincoln Corporation had built its second gasworks near the railway at Bracebridge and two gasholders are still visible (see figure 13.6). My earliest memory of Bracebridge in the late 1930s was the twin gauntlet of the gasworks, by then the sole supply for Lincoln, and the 1938 factory of Smith's Potato Crisps, across the road. White's 1891 directory lists a glue, powder and size works and, within my own memory, Battle's agricultural chemicals works was also situated in Bracebridge.

Altogether the industrial image and smells of the village inhibited its dormitory function, but in 1891 J. C. Bainbridge, the owner of a very large drapery store in Lincoln, was residing at Bracebridge Hall, completed in 1883 (see figure 13.7). He was followed by a man always known locally as Blood Mixture Clarke, from the product that had made his fortune. As elsewhere, Lincoln's main businesses were locally owned during the Victorian period and their owners resided within a distance that made involvement in the community a possibility.

To the south of the ancient church there are considerable post-1945 residential developments between the river and the derelict railway, an area formerly known as Bracebridge Lowfields, but now as Brant Road to make property more saleable. Many houses occupy the sites of market gardens and nurseries established in the last century to supply the expanding Lincoln market. White's 1872 directory lists only one

**Figure 13.6** Bracebridge High Street, *c.*1914, showing gasholder, tram, Victorian terraces. Short streets led off as in the right foreground, abutting on the river to the left, the railway to the right
*Source*: L. Tindall and Local Studies Collection, Lincoln Central Library

market garden, but by 1891 there were ten, and in 1919 Kelly listed 14. By 1891 the large firm of Pennell and Son had moved its main nursery to the Lowfields from a site within half a mile of the city centre, and since 1960 it has again gradually transferred its stock and business to two sites at the extreme limits of the current built-up area. Such a progression marks the rise of land values as the suburbs grew.

Bracebridge is only a fraction of the suburban development to the south-west of Lincoln, for on the far (west) bank of the Witham other wide swathes of housing can be seen from Red Hall. Although Boultham had been an estate village, development began in the 1920s for lower-middle-class and working-class housing (see figure 13.8). Also in Boultham is Swanpool Garden Suburb, a 1920s development of 113 houses and Lincoln's most important contribution to town planning history (Mills, 1989, pp. 201–3). Boultham was incorporated into Lincoln in 1920, along with Bracebridge. In 1898 the latter reached the status of an Urban District Council, but both had to succumb to the city's territorial ambitions through a failure to solve the problem of sewage disposal.

North Hykeham stands further out and is still outside the city

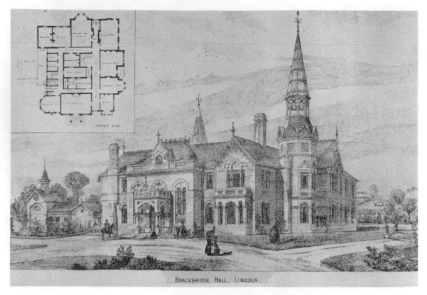

**Figure 13.7**   Bracebridge Hall, print from architect's drawing, the florid Gothic style typical of residences of Victorian self-made men
*Source*: Local Studies Collection, Lincoln Central Library

boundary, although contiguous with Boultham. Its population was 551 in 1901, 9,551 in 1971, and about 11,000 according to 1990 planning estimates. Westwards and over the tracks of the 1846 railway line, large-scale development did not come until the 1960s, when Lincoln Corporation acquired large parts of a Second World War aerodrome and brought it within the city boundary from Skellingthorpe parish.

Table 13.1 shows that despite boundary extensions, Lincoln's population rose relatively little during the first three-quarters of this century. The growth of the built-up area is substantially the result of higher living standards, which demand larger houses and gardens, more recreational and school land, bigger sites for factories, and so on. Equally important is the steep reduction in average household size in England and Wales from 4.4 persons in 1901 to 2.89 persons in 1971 and 2.46 in 1990–1 (*Social Trends*, 22, 1992, p. 40). Together these factors have made it necessary to divert a great deal of suburban development into the surrounding villages.

Finally, it is worth mentioning that the western boundary of the city is now marked by the A46 bypass, which has encouraged the growth of industrial estates, including the electronics factories now more typical of Lincoln than its traditional heavy engineering. A few miles further west

**Figure 13.8**    Boultham Park Road—'then' and 'now' illustrations typical of those found in many pictorial histories covering different parts of the country: (a) the drive to Boultham Hall on the point of being turned into Boultham Park Road in the early 1920s (note members of the road-making gang in the background); (b) Boultham today is mainly residential and has both private dwellings and council housing. (Note the road makers are still at it!)
*Source*: (a) Hodson, 1982; (b) Dennis Mills

**Table 13.1**    Growth of population in the Lincoln area, 1901–1971

|  | 1901 | 1971 | Increase | |
|---|---|---|---|---|
|  |  |  | Number | % |
| Lincoln, including population absorbed by boundary changes | 48,784 | 74,269 | 25,485 | 52.2 |
| Villages within six miles | 13,590 | 48,980 | 35,390 | 260.4 |

*Source*: Mills, 1989, p. 31.

and almost on the skyline are several power stations along the course of the River Trent, reminding us that the main source of power as well as the main means of transport has changed since the beginning of the century.

## Industrialization and urbanization: the national context

I will now attempt to put my local example into the national context of economic, demographic, and social change. Conventionally defined as the period 1760–1830, the Industrial Revolution led to a concentration of industrial activity on the coalfields encouraged by the introduction of steam power and the switch from charcoal to coke in the smelting of iron. Hitherto, manufacturing had been dispersed across large parts of rural Britain, and the equation 'rural = agricultural' only became true for the country as a whole during the nineteenth century.

Although by 1830 the growth industries were well established on the coalfields and at the ports (where raw materials could meet coal supplies), the *typical* workplace was still a workshop, rather than a factory, and most towns were still quite small. For some time turnpikes and navigations had been contributing to the freer movement of goods, but a fully integrated national market only came with the building of the main railway network between, say, 1830 and 1860. It was then that the factory really took over, and large-scale industry was also established in many towns away from the coalfields, including Lincoln.

As the Victorian period progressed, rural domestic industries declined rapidly, and the rural craftsman also found himself steadily losing the battle against mass-produced goods. Each area now had a speciality of some importance nationally, whilst local self-sufficiency declined. The local–national relationship could be described as top-downwards, although against this it should be noticed that some developments of nation-wide significance had begun on a purely local basis. For example, the idea of the rail*way* developed as a means of getting coal from the collieries of County Durham to the coast for shipment to London.

Concurrently with the adoption of coal as a new motive force in the middle of the eighteenth century, population began to rise rapidly, breaching thresholds that previous upward fluctuations had left untouched. The relationship between demography, economics, and technology is complex, but in some respects it is possible to think of demographic growth as an independent variable. It occurred in rural areas without obvious new forms of employment, as well as on the coalfields and in the burgeoning towns. So individual communities had to run fast to stand still in relation to the general growth of both urban and rural population in the period 1750–1850.

In England and Wales the population approximately doubled between 1700 and 1800 (with the bulk of the increase in the second half of the century); it doubled again between 1801 and 1851 and again between and 1851 and 1911; and then came the flattening off as the birth rate plunged in the 1920s. In the rural areas much of the natural increase (births minus deaths) was migrating to the towns by the second quarter of the nineteenth century, and by the third quarter most rural areas were losing population in absolute as well as relative terms.

Agricultural employment declined rapidly especially in arable areas from the last quarter of the century, as the long agricultural depression (late 1870s to late 1930s) coincided with the widespread adoption of labour-saving machinery. Even in the more prosperous times since 1940, farming has continued to shed labour, and even in so-called rural areas those who work on the land are usually a small minority. This is one sense in which 'rural' is thought to have all but lost its meaning.

The opposite side of the coin is that urban growth romped ahead in both absolute and relative terms during the railway period, say 1830– 1920. The concentration of large populations in small areas led to many environmental and social problems, which can be analysed at community level. Despite the bad reputation of the Victorian city, it was far more prosperous than any that had come before and was, therefore, able to introduce new amenities such as gas lighting, water sewerage, urban transport, dispensaries and hospitals, universal schooling, and so forth. Some of these amenities did not go beyond urban boundaries, thus sharpening urban–rural contrasts that developed also because the growth of towns cut off their populations from the countryside, and because the decline of rural industries meant there was less in common between rural and urban areas, in terms of occupation.

The idea of the railway had been developed further because there was a demand for the better transport of goods than that provided by turnpikes and canals. Likewise, towards the end of the nineteenth century the continuous geographical spread of built-up areas promoted the development of forms of transport especially designed for the movement of people: the horse-bus, the horse-tram, the electric tram, the underground railway, the motor omnibus, and the car. The introduction of bus services, coinciding with more serious thought about 'homes fit for heroes', contributed to a sea change in suburban development after the First World War. Council houses were built in large numbers for the first time, and both they and contemporary private developments were at more generous densities than those enjoyed by most ordinary townspeople before 1914.

Commuting from free-standing settlements into nearby cities had begun before the First World War in areas, such as the Home Counties, where demand was high enough to promote suitable railway services. The bus extended this practice away from railway routes and into many provincial districts. It enabled rural workers to stay in their homes when they took jobs in a nearby town just as much as it made rural living a possibility for many people who had hitherto both worked and lived in a town. Suburbanization was no longer limited to areas contiguous with a town. In the 1930s, and more especially from the 1950s, the car continued and extended the process begun by the bus.

The inversion of the social composition of a rural population took no more than 50 years. Whereas in the Edwardian period most male villagers had been farm labourers or village craftsmen on modest wages, by 1960 they were predominantly middle class. The movement of the middle class from town to village reduced their influence on the affairs of urban, especially inner-city, communities, where amenities and community welfare have declined. In some cities this trend has been halted when housing has been '**gentrified**' or slums have been replaced by modern housing attractive to childless professionals wishing to avoid a car journey to work: such people are sometimes known as 'centralists', to distinguish them from the suburbanites and the ex-urbanites, the latter commuting from beyond the continuously built-up areas.

Although rural deprivation has not disappeared altogether, it is no longer so evident; and most villages now have local amenities of an essentially urban character. There are street lights and they often stay on all night; the village hall is centrally heated; there is secondary schooling for all children; refuse collection is taken for granted. However, the number of village organizations has probably declined and certainly their objectives have changed under the influence of radio and television, of greater mobility, including the late return of people from work, and of the increasing numbers of married women in employment.

At the beginning of the period community might be defined largely in terms of territory. This was modified by smaller villages depending for services on larger villages, and all rural communities were dependent to some degree on nearby towns. It is also possible to distinguish several communities, often overlapping, in the Victorian town. Now most people live in more than one territory, more than one community: home, work, school, professional organization, sports team, leisure activity, shopping are often based in different places, sometimes quite large distances apart. For example, I have more in common with Dr Rees Pryce, an Open University staff tutor living in Rhiwbeina, a suburb of Cardiff, than with some of the residents of my own street in Branston, a commuter village four miles from Lincoln. In 1800 only members of a very small upper class could have considered making such a statement.

So far I have concentrated on territorial aspects of communities and concurrent changes in socio-occupational composition. I now turn towards particular aspects of everyday community life.

## The Poor Law: history made from the top downwards?

The Poor Law is taken as an example of the top-downwards mode by which, it can be asserted, some of our community history has been made. It is counterbalanced in the next section by a discussion of the development of voluntary dispensaries and hospitals, where local initiative is seen to predominate. Although the simple dichotomy of top-downwards and bottom-upwards proves to be inadequate on its own, it is a useful starting point in the dialectical analysis of change within communities.

Up to 1834 the poor in England and Wales were relieved (i.e. maintained) largely under the provisions of the Elizabethan Poor Law. The relevant statutes were part of a large body of legislation introduced by Henry VIII and Elizabeth I, aimed at strengthening royal control over the affairs of the nation, at the expense of the aristocracy and what remained of Roman Catholicism. With the sovereign at its head, the Protestant Church of England became effectively a department of state, with an agency in every parish in the form of the **vestry meeting**. Although day-to-day administration of the Poor Law was carried out by parish overseers on behalf of vestries, they were subject to the supervision of the Justices of the Peace, usually local gentry, themselves appointed by the Crown. The office of JP had been created by Henry expressly to keep the peace and to administer the law on the basis of *national* standards.

Whilst the Elizabethan Poor Law appears to have codified some existing practices, there is also one particular way in which it represented a top-down view taken by the authorities in London. Thus, the statutes placed responsibilities on the parish, probably because those who framed it were thinking in terms of a model of community that suited the rural parts of southern England. But the parish was an unsuitable unit of administration in the many towns where there were several (sometimes quite large numbers of) separate small parishes, between which the poor might easily circulate. Conversely, in rural areas of the Midlands and the north of England, as well as in Wales, parishes sometimes extended over large districts containing anything from two to a dozen or more distinct settlements. Usually these villages and hamlets had the status of independent townships, each with their own systems for regulating agricultural and related affairs.

In towns and many rural areas, therefore, the community historian is likely to find that the Elizabethan statute was not applied literally or had been amended. For example, by the 1620s the municipality of Nottingham was taking measures to employ the poor of both parishes in the town (Chambers, 1932, p. 235). Keith-Lucas has summed up the situation as one in which 'for practical purposes a parish may be taken to be a place making a separate poor rate'. In particular, the township became the usual unit of administration in rural areas and not the ecclesiastical parish, unless it was coterminous with a township. Parliament even went so far as to enshrine this practice in an Act of 1662 in relation to the counties of Cheshire, Derby, Lancashire, York, Westmorland, Cumberland, Durham, and Northumberland (Keith-Lucas, 1980, p. 77). In the end, a bottom-upwards view was made to prevail in this particular respect.

The Old Poor Law was amended a great deal before being subjected to a root-and-branch transformation by the New Poor Law in 1834. Of special interest in the present context is the innovation by the JPs of the Speenhamland district of Berkshire in 1795. Across the whole of the rural south of England the natural increase of population had for some time not been matched by equivalent increases in employment, with the consequence that farm labourers' wages fell. As a result, the rise in the prices of corn and bread brought on by the wars against France did not take long to produce crisis conditions, in which the labourers looked certain to starve.

Parliament equivocated, but the Speenhamland magistrates responded by issuing instructions to overseers that men in work, and therefore not eligible for poor relief, should be given allowances to make up their wages to a subsistence level. A sliding scale based on family size and the price of bread was devised. Other districts introduced similar measures, and it is difficult to know how much they took their cue from Speenhamland and how much that district owes its fame to **Eden's**

**treatise** of 1797 (Fraser, 1973, p. 33). From the present standpoint what matters is that state action was found wanting and that the most threatened localities used their own initiative to find humane solutions.

In the long run, the allowance system and the more general principle of outdoor relief (i.e. relief given to paupers in their own homes) brought the Old Poor Law into disrepute. The Poor Law Amendment Act of 1834 probably instigated an even bigger change than the Elizabethan Poor Law. Parliament set out to impose a uniform solution across the whole of England and Wales, namely that paupers would receive relief only in workhouses, and admission would be made so unattractive that applications from the able-bodied would dry up overnight. Full-time professionals were to be based in workhouses serving Unions of about 25 parishes each (Bruce, 1961, p. 84).

Local political control of Union affairs was set up in the form of Guardians elected by the ratepayers of each parish, but they and their officers were subject to supervision in minute detail by the Poor Law Commission in London. Until it was transformed into the Poor Law Board in 1847, with a minister at its head, the Commission was itself free of direct political and democratic control (Fraser, 1973, p. 49). However, it soon transpired that a solution capable of introduction in the rural south was not sensible in the industrial north. Here the trade cycle was the main cause of distress, not underemployment in agriculture. When business was slack hundreds of men and women could be put out of work, or onto short time, for relatively short periods, and through no fault of their own. No purpose would be served in building workhouses capable of coping with large numbers in single-industry towns and villages. The expense was prohibitive and no one could reasonably claim that work-shyness was the problem.

Attempts by Poor Law Commissioners who went 'down' from London to set up Unions in some parts of Lancashire and Yorkshire met with stiff resistance, including riots. In neither county had any of the new Unions been set up by 1841 (J. L. and B. Hammond, 1934, pp. 100–4) and the problem rumbled along into the 1850s in some towns such as Leeds (Fraser, 1973, p. 49). Problems were not confined to the industrial north and the Midlands, since a study in Portsmouth shows that there had to be give and take between the Commissioners and the local Guardians (Ogborn, 1992, p. 222–3).

The authorities generally had to bend to local opinion, including that of magistrates and employers. In particular, the Outdoor Labour Test Order promulgated by the Commission in 1842 made permissible the use of outdoor relief, provided men showed a willingness to do some work on what would now be called job creation schemes (Bruce, 1961, p. 90). The result was that by 1854, 84 per cent of paupers were on outdoor relief (Fraser, 1973, p. 48). Thus, in practice, the bottom-upwards view had achieved a substantial victory, even though the main principle of the 1834 legislation survived.

It also needs saying that the original amendments of 1834 did not fall on the country through a sudden brainwave on the part of Edwin Chadwick, even though he was the architect-in-chief of the New Poor Law. The Poor Law Commission collected a great body of evidence, running into perhaps a couple of dozen huge '**blue books**', from all parts of the country, not only analysing 'the problem', but also describing the many possible solutions already in operation locally, under the framework of the Old Poor Law. Mention should be made of two in particular.

First, the concept of the 'New Bastilles', as the Union workhouses came to be known, owed a great deal to the work of George Nicholls at the Southwell and Bingham workhouses in Nottinghamshire. Later he was to become a member of the Commission and an important historian of the Poor Law. His approach was essentially to be as harsh as possible, with the deterrent workhouse 'looked upon with dread by our labouring class' (Fraser, 1973, p. 38). His success in bringing down poor rates in his area provided the proof the Commission needed to transfer a local experiment to the national arena.

Second, as at Southwell and Bingham, many areas had already set up Unions well ahead of the 1834 Act, which adopted the principle for the country as a whole. As already mentioned, Nottingham was operating what in effect was a Union for the whole town as far back as the 1620s. Bristol operated a scheme from 1696, influential elsewhere, under which the city parishes combined to set up a 'pauper manufactory' (Fraser, 1973, p. 32). Incorporations of town parishes appear to have been more common than those of country parishes, but in Suffolk and Norfolk 468 parishes combined into 13 Unions, based on the **hundreds,** or traditional administrative areas, and 89 local Acts were passed between 1722 and 1797 in various parts of the country (Keith-Lucas, 1980, pp. 93–5).

In addition, two private members' Acts of 1722 (Sir Edward Knatchbull) and 1782 (Gilbert) made it possible to set up Unions, of a certain pattern, without recourse to a separate Act, and by 1834 67 'Gilbert Act' Unions had been created from a total of 924 parishes (Keith-Lucas, 1980, p. 93). (There were 15,600 'poor law' parishes in England and Wales in 1835 (Poor Law Commissioners, 1835, p. 6).)

Like the Incorporations, the Gilbert Unions made use of full-time, professional, paid officials operating at a central workhouse, in place of the voluntary, unpaid, and amateur work of the parish overseers. Some of both types of Union survived the 1834 Act or became the basis for larger Unions fitting into the overall Poor Law geography of their parts of the country. The New Poor Law, therefore, already had many local precedents for imposing the Union workhouse on the whole country from the top.

This section can usefully end on three rather broader points for the community historian. First, there was a continual dialogue between central and local opinion, involving many shifts of emphasis and power which need to be analysed. One should not assume that the state of play remained static between such great upheavals as the passing of the 1834 Act. Secondly, the central authorities were often willing to concede that general principles of policy could be interpreted with some flexibility to suit local conditions. And thirdly, as the next section demonstrates, the local–national relationship varied from one aspect of social policy to another. (This paragraph owes much to the summary discussion of nineteenth-century central–local relations by Ogborn, 1992.)

## Voluntary dispensaries and hospitals: a case of history made from the bottom upwards?

Voluntary dispensaries and hospitals, whilst also aimed at the lower classes, had a history that contrasts sharply with the history of the Poor Law, since in earlier centuries many people could not afford significant medical care, yet failed to qualify for help from parish overseers. By the middle of the eighteenth century, scientific knowledge and living standards were improving modestly and the upper classes had come to the conclusion that it was in their own interests that rudimentary medical facilities should be extended down the social scale in order, amongst other things, to reduce the risk of epidemics. The upper class, of course, could afford to engage medical men and buy from apothecaries whatever was prescribed. More significantly, they did not need hospitals because the simple equipment of contemporary surgeons made it possible for operations to be carried out in the privacy of a well-to-do person's home.

Broadly speaking, dispensaries and hospitals were opened earliest in London and the large provincial centres, their establishment gradually diffusing down the **urban hierarchy** to places of smaller size (Abel Smith, 1964; Cherry, 1980; Pickstone, 1985). However, local initiatives, or lack of them, clearly disturb the general pattern and voluntary hospitals were probably more numerous than free-standing dispensaries.

For example, in Lincolnshire, 17 voluntary hospitals were opened at a wide range of dates from 1769 to 1924, whereas only seven towns ever had a separate dispensary. The establishment of the latter was also confined to a shorter period, 1789 to 1856, probably because the vogue for dispensaries was overtaken by a wave of hospital building. Thus, there appears to have been a complex relationship between dispensaries and hospitals. To take extremes, the County Hospital in Lincoln opened in 1769 but the city had no separate dispensary until 1828; whilst Horncastle was the first town to have a dispensary in 1789 but the last to open a hospital in 1924 (Mills, in Bennett forthcoming).

The very first voluntary dispensary to be established on a charitable basis opened in London in 1770. It is rather surprising that Horncastle, with a population of only 2,015 in 1801, should be but 19 years behind the metropolis. The explanation is that the dispensary originated from a public meeting called by Sir Joseph Banks on 28 October 1789. He was one of the most prominent scientists of the time and also a local landowner and lord of the manor of Horncastle. He was concerned by annual outbreaks of smallpox. The meeting was attended by local gentry, clergy, two outstanding physicians, and other luminaries who fell in with the wishes of Sir Joseph and jointly subscribed to the setting up of a dispensary for the free treatment of the poor of Horncastle and its substantial market catchment (Clarke, 1981, pp. 5, 8).

The importance of variation in local initiative can also be demonstrated in relation to voluntary hospitals. Within Lincolnshire the most striking case is that of Gainsborough, which had to wait until 1913 before it acquired a hospital, by which time the population had passed 20,500. During the period 1870–1900 the more typical threshold for establishing a hospital was around the 10,000 mark.

By this time voluntary hospitals were accepting middle- and upper-class patients on a fee-paying basis, as medical advances around the middle of the nineteenth century had brought an end to the majority of home operations. However, in many areas they did not accept pauper patients in most medical categories. This situation had arisen from circumstances prevailing in the early part of the century, when paupers were given medical treatment as part of normal Poor Law provision, thereby being mostly excluded from the terms of admission to voluntary dispensaries and hospitals.

The scene shifts from voluntary effort and local initiative towards state provision, but not necessarily towards a top-downwards mode of provision. The Guardians were obliged to set up Poor Law infirmaries, as adjuncts to their workhouses. The range of facilities varied greatly, however, depending on local circumstances, such as population density and the initiative shown by individual medical officers working for the Guardians. The provision of medical care for paupers was less chaotic than provision in the voluntary sector, but did not have the regularity that was supposed to characterize the administration of poor relief. By the 1920s significant numbers of Poor Law infirmaries had become leading hospitals in their localities and were used by large numbers of non-paupers (Pickstone, 1985, p. 213).

Meanwhile, local authorities had been charged with the task of setting up isolation hospitals and sanatoria for tubercular patients, thus adding a third hospital sector. This mixture of local initiative and national legislation led to such complications that rationalization was almost bound to occur when advances in medical technology caused funding difficulties, especially in the voluntary hospitals. So in 1930, when the Guardians were abolished, the Poor Law infirmaries came under local authority control. Where they were well equipped, they became the chief surgical hospitals for their areas. This merging of two hospital sectors can now be seen as a preliminary step towards the National Health Service, within which in 1948 the local council hospitals and nearly all the voluntary hospitals entered into unified state ownership. A coherent national system had evolved out of 200 years of the most varied local initiatives mixed with two kinds of state provision.

The discussion of the Poor Law and hospital and dispensary provision has demonstrated a dialectical relationship between the local and the national, with much see-sawing between the two power bases. Thus, though the community historian must take account of national developments and government edicts, this should be done in the light of local responses to local circumstances. Put another way, local developments should be analysed against the yardstick of central government intentions. By so doing one can assess the contributions of each within a particular area.

## Local history and community history

Now the time has come to draw a distinction between local history and community history. *Local* history is concerned with the history of any aspect of human endeavour at the local level: railways, graveyards, hospitals, street furniture, cricket clubs, airfields, friendly societies, and so on almost *ad infinitum*, have all claimed the attention of historians somewhere or other. Moreover, while the more academic forms of local history have often concentrated on 'important' aspects of the subject, such as farming and industry, religion, and politics, there is no one agreed hierarchy into which the branches of enquiry can be fitted.

*Community* history, it could be claimed, has begun to focus more sharply on a particular group of concepts, although as yet there is no clearly defined set of community historians practising self-consciously within recognizable guidelines. They can be set out as follows:

1 concepts relating to the problems of *defining* communities;
2 those related to the study of *relationships* between individuals and households *within* communities;
3 those used in the study of *relationships between* communities.

Beginning with the second group, there are a number of dimensions along which intra-communal relationships may be observed and in some cases quantified. For instance, the extent to which marriage partners were found from within the community can be discovered from parish registers; trade directories can be used to discover something about economic relations through the information they give on occupations. Political groups might be identified from **poll books** or from the reporting of particular political events and the often closely connected relationships between religious groups. But all these examples and others can be interrelated in various ways. The pursuit of these complex webs of activity forms one of the hallmarks of community, as opposed to simply local, history.

Community history is therefore similar to some views of social history 'as a total historical approach. Even when a limited topic is dealt with, the image of what was happening in the broader society can be kept in mind' (Stearns, 1977). This call for a 'total historical' approach is made rather less demanding when the historian researches at the level of an individual community, but it is still something of a counsel of perfection. Nevertheless, the historian who works on the documents relating to, say, an event in which the dramatis personae are identifiable, or to a particular form of economic activity, will make a much greater contribution to community history if he or she uses other sources to relate this research to the general history of the locality.

The best starting point for community history in the nineteenth century might be the CEBs, since these uniquely record the particulars of everyone resident on census night. But several kinds of document may be expected to list all or very nearly all the names of householders, e.g. many tithe awards, most ratebooks, and some urban trade directories, to quote the most obvious examples. Data from these can therefore be added to a census database, from which the most rewarding analyses will be those of family, household, and social structure, especially where data from the parish registers have also been integrated.

The history of the family is basic to the history of community both in terms of practicality and of concepts, since a community can readily be treated as a collection of families. And, as Wrigley has observed (1985,

p. 2): 'the family may lay fair claims to being the most fundamental of all human institutions, at once the most nearly universal and the most pervasive.'

The next step in writing the total history of a community will vary substantially with the circumstances, but work has very high claims, if only because the community would not exist had it not been able to get a living from local resources. Moreover, occupations are an indispensable tool in the study of social structure and social stratification. From work it is only a short step to the study of power and politics. For those who controlled the local economy were usually powerful in other ways.

The harsh world of economic reality might be sublimated in a number of ways, through religion, social policy, education, and leisure activities, studies of which can follow on from the basic enquiries already noted. **Nominal record linkage** can be very important, as in a study of nineteenth-century Lewes, where the membership of the **'bonfire societies'** not only indicated their importance in leisure activities, voluntary work, and local politics, but also demonstrated the existence of several communities within the town (Etherington, 1990).

Those who have studied communities through the records of family and household have naturally enough been much influenced by practical considerations, not least by the fact that nominal record linkage between and within populations of, say, 1,000 at each census are very time-consuming, even with the aid of a computer. Administrative definitions of 'community' have, therefore, been prominent, and accepted by implication, rather than explicitly justified. The criticism has often been made that **family reconstitutions** originating in this way are biased towards persons who remained in observation from baptism to marriage, and on through their reproductive years, if not until death. Results, then, reflect the experiences of the geographically stable element of the population, whilst for technical reasons those of the often large, mobile population are left out of account. For the latter, perhaps the true definition of 'community' was not the urban parish but the whole town, not the rural parish but the group of villages and hamlets within which they moved. The definition of a community as a face-to-face territorial group may not then be as simple as it at first appears.

Phythian-Adams has considered the various geographical scales at which the analysis of community needs to take place if the gap between local history and national history is to be bridged successfully (1987, especially chapter 2). All sorts of overlapping groups of villages might be significant communities depending on the criteria used. Thus a study of **marriage horizons** might produce quite different catchment areas from those served by particular nonconformist chapels with congregations scattered across several Anglican parishes. Or they might be similar because one is acting on the other, but which is cause and which effect? To go back to the three groups of concepts mentioned above, it can be seen that here each overlaps with the other two. A study of marriage horizons is one way of looking at intra-communal relationships, but it soon spills out into a study of the relationships between communities. It might even call into question the original definition of community on which the project was initially based, or at least raise the question that people lived simultaneously in several forms of community.

To continue up the scales mentioned by Phythian-Adams, it can be seen that the country town acted as the focal point for the rural population within its hinterland for many purposes beyond its basic function of marketing. Each year farm and domestic servants may have attended the statutory hirings there in order to find new employment. Such towns too were often the headquarters of Poor Law Unions, and many Methodist circuits were organized across the surrounding countryside from them. So was the population of a country town hinterland functioning as a community?

There are many other units and scales that could be used self-consciously by the community historian, but it would be impossible for individual historians to work at all the levels in any depth. However, research will be better informed if they are kept in mind, if communities are not studied as if they were entirely self-contained. The 'functioning entity', to use Wrigley's phrase (1985, p. 1), whatever its scale, needs to be put in the forefront of the community historian's thinking. He or she will then be in a good position to order his or her priorities, and to make a more significant contribution to the understanding of national trends on the basis of research undertaken at the 'local' level.

### References

Abel Smith, B. 1964. *The Hospitals 1800–1948: a study in social administration in England and Wales*, London, Heinemann.
Bennett, N. and Bennett, S. (eds) (forthcoming). *Historical Atlas of Lincolnshire*, Hull, Hull University Press.
Bruce, M. 1961. *The Coming of the Welfare State*, London, Batsford.
Chambers, J. D. 1932. *Nottinghamshire in the Eighteenth Century*, London, Frank Cass.
Cherry, S. 1980. 'The hospitals and population growth: the voluntary general hospitals, mortality and local populations in the English provinces in the eighteenth and nineteenth centuries', *Population Studies*, 34, pp. 59–75, 251–65.
Clarke, J. N. 1981. *Horncastle Dispensaries and Hospitals, 1789–1981*, Horncastle: The League of Friends to Horncastle Hospital.
Etherington, J. E. 1990. 'The community origin of the Lewes Guy Fawkes night celebrations', *Sussex Archaeological Collections*, 128, pp. 195–224.

Fraser, D. 1973. *The Evolution of the British Welfare State*, London, Macmillan.

Graves, A. 1992. 'Victorian migration between six rural villages and Lincoln', unpublished A-level project report, copy in Lincoln Central Library.

Hammond, J. L. and Hammond, B. 1934. *The Bleak Age*, Harmondsworth, Penguin Books.

Hill, Sir Francis, 1974. *Victorian Lincoln*, Cambridge, Cambridge University Press.

Hill, Sir Francis, 1979. *A Short History of Lincoln*, Lincoln, Lincoln Civic Trust.

Hodson, M. B. 1982. *Lincoln Then and Now*, vol. 1, p. 52, 30 Malton Road, North Hykeham, Lincoln LN6 8HR, Hodson.

Keith-Lucas, B. 1980. *The Unreformed Local Government System*, London, Croom Helm.

Mills, D. R. 1959. 'The development of rural settlement around Lincoln', *East Midland Geographer*, 11, June 1959, pp. 3–15 (reprinted in Mills, 1973).

Mills, D. R. (ed.) 1973. *English Rural Communities: the impact of a specialised economy*, London, Macmillan.

Mills, D. R. (ed.) 1989. *Twentieth-century Lincolnshire*, History of Lincolnshire, vol. XII, Lincoln, Society for Lincolnshire History and Archaeology.

Ogborn, M. 1992. 'Local power and state regulation in nineteenth-century Britain', *Transactions of the Institute of British Geographers*, news series 17, pp. 215–26.

Phythian-Adams, C. 1987. *Re-thinking English Local History*, Leicester, Leicester University Press (Department of Local History, Occasional Papers, fourth series, no. 1).

Pickstone, J. V. 1985. *Medicine and Industrial Society: a history of hospital development in Manchester and its region*, Manchester, Manchester University Press.

Poor Law Commissioners, 1835. *First Annual Report*, London, British Parliamentary Papers.

*Social Trends* 22, 1992. London, HMSO for Central Statistical Office.

Squires, S. 1992. 'Cross O'Cliff Hill Brickworks, Lincoln', *Lincolnshire History and Archaeology*, 27, pp. 48–9.

Stearns, P. 1977. 'Coming of age', letter to *Social History Newsletter*, autumn 1977.

Wright, N. R. 1982. *Lincolnshire Towns and Industry 1700–1914*, History of Lincolnshire, vol XI, Lincoln, Society for Lincolnshire History and Archaeology.

Wrigley, E. A. 1985. *The Local and the General in Population History*, the sixteenth Harte Lecture, Exeter, University of Exeter.

# Glossary

This glossary has been compiled on a minimal 'need-to-know' basis, specific to this volume.

**Binomial probability** The probability or likelihood of one of two possible outcomes (either/or relation).

**Blue books** British Parliamentary Papers (i.e. reports of commissions, committees of enquiry, etc.): so called because published between blue paper covers.

**Bonfire societies** Societies in the Sussex town of Lewes, based in different areas of the town, that exist primarily to take part in 5 November (Guy Fawkes) celebrations.

**Capitalist patriarchy** Stage of capitalism in which one income, supplied by the male head of the family, is dominant.

**Categories** *Perceptual*: family; kin. *Analytical*: class; status.

**Census enumerators' books** Books into which nineteenth-century British census enumerators copied the householders' schedules, plus certain other information (e.g. addresses, descriptions of dwellings).

**Chain migration** Process whereby migration continues from one place to another because the earlier migrants, by maintaining links with their places of origin (hence the description 'chain'), encourage and facilitate further migration.

**Civil parish** A parish created for civil as opposed to ecclesiastical administration.

**Cohort** A group of individuals for which some selected characteristic or activity is observed at intervals over a period of time; for example, a group born or married in a particular year may be studied, hence *birth cohort* or *marriage cohort*, and such cohorts may then be compared. A *cohort life table* gives the likelihood of death at specific ages for a particular birth cohort.

**Conjugal family** A couple, with their children if any.

**Conurbation** A predominantly urban area formed when towns grow and merge into what is in some respects (e.g. physically, though not necessarily politically) a single entity.

**Cross-sectional data** Data obtained from a one-off survey or census; in effect a 'snapshot' and therefore containing no information over time (in contrast to a **Longitudinal study**).

**Declining frictional effect of distance** Distance tends to inhibit migration; this is known as the frictional effect of distance. Improvements in communications reduce this effect. (See also **Distance decay model**.)

**Distance decay model** Theoretical models in which the interaction between locations decreases as the distance between them increases.

**Ecological scale** The level or scale of magnitude that relates to areas (rather than to individuals). See **Individual scale**.

**Ecological zone** The area occupied by a specific group or activity.

**Eden's treatise** *The State of the Poor*, published by Sir Frederick Morton Eden in three volumes in 1797: an early analysis of poverty, including an attack on the Speenhamland system.

**Estate village** A village, usually planned, built and controlled by a landowner on his or her estate.

**Existential relationship** A relationship that is distant or indirect.

**Exogamous marriages** Marriages taking place between people who are not from the same group or locale.

**Experiential data** Information drawn from individuals' experiences; often obtained through interviews.

**Family reconstitution** A technique used by historical demographers to calculate ages at marriage, death, etc., in order to determine rates of fertility, nuptiality, and mortality in a particular community. It involves linking together entries in the registers of baptisms, marriages, and burials for a parish, using the names of individuals as the linking device (hence the term **nominal record linkage**). Once the links have been made for each recorded individual, the information can be drawn together to give the demographic experience of families, then the different family experiences can be aggregated to give the demographic experience of the community as a whole. See Wrigley, E. A. (ed.) 1973, *Identifying People in the Past*, London, Edward Arnold; Wrigley, E. A. et al., *English Population History from Family Reconstitution*, Cambridge, Cambridge University Press (forthcoming).

**Fordism** Process of mechanized mass production pioneered by Henry Ford with his car assembly line in the early twentieth century; the term also embraces the associated lifestyles.

***Gemeinschaft*** and ***Gesellschaft*** Terms distinguishing the kinds of social relationships supposed to predominate in villages from those supposed to predominate in towns—the former (*Gemeinschaft* or community) based on kinship, organic ties, and a common belief system, and the latter (*Gesellschaft* or association) on individualism, competitiveness, anomie, etc.

**Gender** Characteristics (other than biological) associated with femaleness or maleness.

**Gentrified** Describes houses in working-class parts of a town that have been bought, 'done up', and occupied by members (usually young) of the middle class.

**GHS** General Household Survey. As the name suggests, a survey of domestic trends in Britain. Begun in 1972–3 and now carried out annually by the Office of Population Censuses and Surveys (OPCS).

**Gravity model** A theoretical model in which the movement between two places is assumed to be directly proportional to their sizes; based crudely on Newton's law of gravity.

**GRR** Gross reproduction rate. A measure of fertility, indicating the average number of live *female* births per woman who survives through her entire fertile period.

*Halal* **meat** Meat from an animal killed according to Muslim law.

**Hundred** Former administrative subdivision of a county. In the north of England the term 'Wapentake' was used for a comparable area.

**Individual scale** The level or scale of magnitude that relates to individuals, i.e. people or households (rather than to areas).

**Industrialization** The process involved in the change-over from a society dominated by its agricultural sector to one dominated by its (or another's) industrial sector.

**Industrial revolution** (also, with initial capitals **Industrial Revolution**) Profound economic and social change brought about by rapid economic growth over a relatively short period, resulting in a change-over from a society dominated by its agricultural sector to one dominated by its industrial sector. The concept has been much disputed. See Hudson, P. 1992, *The Industrial Revolution*, London, Edward Arnold; O'Brien, P. and Quinault, R. (eds) 1993, *The Industrial Revolution and British Society*, Cambridge, Cambridge University Press.

**Kinship** Relationships (actual or presumed) based on blood or marriage, with those so related being *kin*.

**Life course** Although often used to mean 'life cycle', life course differs from the latter in its emphasis on the contingent in a person's experiences from birth to death.

**Longitudinal study** A study in which characteristics of interest in a group of individuals or things are observed at intervals so as to monitor the development of those characteristics over time.

**Markers of cultural differences** Features, characteristics, or indicators taken as identifying a particular social grouping. *Dualistic markers* are of the either/or type, i.e. one has or has not a certain characteristic. *Scalar markers* range along a scale, i.e. from a lot to a little of a certain characteristic.

**Marriage horizons** The distances over which people find their marriage partners.

**Median** When a set of observations (e.g. ages, incomes, heights) are placed in order by size, the observation that lies in the middle (i.e. where half the observations are bigger and half smaller than it) is called the median. The median is useful when some extreme values in a distribution of age, income etc. have a disproportionate effect on the mean.

*Mentalité* Usually used to refer to the mental attitudes of a group.

**Model North level 10 Life Table** A life table, paradoxically, is a record of mortality at different ages (hence 'table') and is based on the assumption of an unchanging birth rate. By incorporating 'changing' birth rates one can produce model life tables that, over the short term, are closer to real life. The best known set of these is to be found in Coale, A. J. and Demeny, P. 1966, *Regional Model Life Tables and Stable Populations*, Princeton, Princeton University Press. The Model North level 10 Life Table is one of this set.

**Modernization paradigm** New patterns of thought and behaviour, resulting from (or, some would say, preceding) the processes associated with the Industrial Revolution.

**Nominal record linkage** A method of gathering information about an individual from different sources by using his or her name as the linking device, as in **family reconstitution** or genealogy.

**Non-place community** A grouping identified by some factor other than location, as in, for example, 'immigrant community' or 'community of scholars'.

**Paradigm** Term used to describe ways of viewing and studying social phenomenon, e.g. Marxist paradigm, **Modernization paradigm**.

**Parish registers** Books in which a church officer (usually the vicar) registers the baptisms, marriages, and burials occurring in a parish.

**Partible inheritance** An inheritance divided amongst all the children of the testator, usually in equal portions, though sometimes with sons getting larger shares than daughters.

**Pentredewaith** A name coined by Ronald Frankenberg for the village he studied in North Wales. Some social anthropologists follow this procedure of changing place and proper names in order to protect their sources.

**Petty bourgeoisie** Lower middle class, especially shopkeepers and small traders.

**Phenomenological approach** An approach that focuses on the meaning of human actions and rejects the objective observation and measurement of social phenomena. See **Positivistic style of research**.

**Poll books** Before the Secret Ballot Act of 1872, British electors cast their votes in public at parliamentary elections. Local printers frequently recorded these, together with other information about each elector (e.g. name, address, occupation, and published them in book form, hence poll books.

**Positivistic style of research** Often used to describe research based on the observation and measurement of empirical social phenomena and the testing of hypotheses as in some of the natural sciences. See **Phenomenological approach**.

**Primogeniture** The principle whereby the whole of an inheritance goes to the first born, often, in the past, the first-born male.

**Sampling error** The difference between the statistical value of a characteristic in a sample taken from a population and the value of that characteristic in the whole population, i.e. a measure of the extent to which the sample is unrepresentative of the whole. As used here, the word 'population' refers to anything that is being sampled, and thus includes things (e.g. cars, apples, incomes, etc.), not just people.

**Sampling without replacement** In this context the term refers to the taking of a sample, based on an electoral register, of which those not contactable at first are then ignored. The result is a sample possibly biased towards the less mobile members of the population.

**Social network analysis** The study or analysis of a social system in which all individuals are linked in some way and so form a network, e.g. a kinship group.

***Staffelweise*** Literally 'stepwise'. Used to describe a type of migration that proceeds by steps or stages, e.g. from village to nearby town then, after a while, to larger town, and so on.

**Structural domains** Various social groupings (some overlapping) in which an individual may participate, e.g. the immediate co-resident family, wider kin, work colleagues, leisure-time associates.

**Suburbanization** Process whereby residential areas (suburbs) grow up outside a town centre (hence 'inner suburbs' and 'outer suburbs') and an associated lifestyle develops.

**Synchronous change** Concurrent changes, e.g. getting married and simultaneously leaving the parental home.

**Trade directory** A handbook for a particular town or area in which tradesmen, public servants, and (in some cases) leading inhabitants are listed.

**Transaction flow analysis** A technique used to measure the extent of contacts or transactions (e.g. marriages, letters, sporting activities) between spatially separate places.

**Turnpike** Roads developed under the authority of private Acts of Parliament, which permitted charges to be levied on those using such roads.

**Urban hierarchy** The ranking of towns in a region or country according to the range of facilities they offer.

**Urbanization** Literally the growth of towns in absolute terms or relative to the proportion of the population living in the countryside. More usually the term embraces the associated social and economic changes.

**Vestry meeting** Meeting of those responsible for the civil administration of a parish, i.e. for roads, policing, care of the poor. So called because it was often held in the church vestry.

# Recommended reading list

## General

Allan, G. 1985. *Family Life: domestic roles and social organization*, Oxford, Blackwell.

Anderson, M. 1980. *Approaches to the History of the Western Family 1500–1914*, London, Macmillan.

Ariès, P. 1962. *Centuries of Childhood: a social history of family life*, translated by Baldick, R., New York, Vintage; London, Cape.

Berger, B. and Berger, P. L. 1983. *The War over the Family: capturing the middle ground*, London, Hutchinson.

Cohen, A. P. 1985. *The Symbolic Construction of Community*, London, Tavistock.

Demos, J. and Boocock, S. S. (eds) 1978. *Turning Points: historical and sociological essays on the family*, Chicago, Chicago University Press.

Hareven, T. and Plakans, A. (eds) 1987. *Family History at the Crossroads: a* Journal of Family History *reader*, Princeton, Princeton University Press.

Harris, C. C. 1983. *The Family and Industrial Society*, London, Allen and Unwin.

Laslett, P. and Wall, R. (eds) 1972. *Household and Family in Past Time*, Cambridge, Cambridge University Press.

Medick, H. 1976. 'The proto-industrial family', *Social History* 1, pp. 291–315.

Netting, R. M., Wilk, R. R. and Arnould, E. (eds) 1984. *Households: comparative and historical studies of the domestic group*, Berkeley, University of California Press.

Parke, R. D. (ed.) 1984. *The Family*, Chicago, University of Chicago Press.

Rabb, T. K. and Rotberg, R. I. (eds) 1976. *The Family in History: interdisciplinary essays*, New York, Octagon Books.

Shorter, E. 1976. *The Making of the Modern Family*, New York, Basic Books.

Stone, L. 1981. 'Family history in the 1980s: past achievements and future trends', *Journal of Interdisciplinary History*, 12, pp. 51–87.

Tilly, L. A. and Cohen, M. 1982. 'Does the family have a history? A review of theory and practice in family history', *Social Science History*, 6, pp. 131–80.

Tilly, L. A. and Scott, J. W. 1978. *Women, Work, and Family*, New York, Holt, Rinehart and Winston.

Wachter, K. W. et al. 1978. *Statistical Studies of Historical Social Structure*, London, Academic Press.

Wrigley, E. A. 1987. *People, Cities and Wealth: the transformation of traditional society*, Oxford, Blackwell.

**Britain and Ireland**

Abbott, M. 1993. *Family Ties: English families, 1540–1920*, Routledge, London.
Anderson, M. 1971. *Family Structure in Nineteenth-century Lancashire*, Cambridge, Cambridge University Press.
Arensberg, C. and Kimball, S. 1940. *Family and Community in Ireland*, Cambridge, Mass., Harvard University Press.
Armstrong, A. 1974. *Stability and Change in an English County Town: a social study of York 1807–1851*, Cambridge, Cambridge University Press.
Bohstedt, J. 1983. *Riots and Community Politics in England and Wales, 1790–1810*, London, Harvard University Press.
Brown, A. 1992. *Computing in Local and Regional History*, Leicester, Leicester University Press.
Bushaway, B. 1982. *By Rite: custom, ceremony and community in England, 1700–1880*, London, Junction Books.
Campbell-Lease, J. A. 1989. *A Companion to Local History Research*, Sherborne, Alpha Books.
Cox, J. 1982. *The English Churches in a Secular Society: Lambeth 1870–1930*, Oxford, Oxford University Press.
Drake, M. and Finnegan, R. (eds) 1993. *Sources and Methods for Family and Community Historians: a handbook*, Cambridge, Cambridge University Press.
Dymond, D. 1988. *Writing Local History: a practical guide*, London, British Association of Local History.
Finnegan, R. and Drake, M. (eds) 1993. *From Family Tree to Family History*, Cambridge, Cambridge University Press.
Foster, J. 1974. *Class Struggle and the Industrial Revolution: early industrial capitalism in three English towns*, London, Weidenfeld & Nicolson.
Golby, J. (ed.) 1993. *Communities and Families*, Cambridge, Cambridge University Press.
Guy, S. 1992. *English Local Studies: a guide to resources*, Exeter, University of Exeter Press.
Harkness, D. and O'Dowd, M. (eds) 1981. *The Town in Ireland*, Belfast, Appletree Press.
Hey, D. 1987. *Family History and Local History in England*, London, Longman.
Higgs, E. 1989. *Making Sense of the Census*, London, HMSO.
Lees, L. H. 1979. *Exiles of Erin: Irish immigrants in Victorian London*, Manchester, Manchester University Press.
Levine, D. 1977. *Family Formation in an Age of Nascent Capitalism*, New York, Academic Press.
Levine, D. (ed.) 1984. *Proletarianization and Family History*, New York, Academic Press.
Levine, D. 1987. *Reproducing Families: the political economy of English population history*, Cambridge, Cambridge University Press.
Lewis, C. 1989. *Particular Places: an introduction to English local history*, London, British Library.

Macfarlane, A. 1977. *Reconstructing Historical Communities*, Cambridge, Cambridge University Press.

Mills, D. R. (ed.) 1973. *English Rural Communities: the impact of a specialized economy*, London, Macmillan.

Mills, D. R. 1980. *Lord and Peasant in Nineteenth-century Britain*, London, Croom Helm.

Moody, D. 1986. *Scottish Local History: an introductory guide*, London, Batsford.

Moody, D. 1988. *Scottish Family History*, London, Batsford.

Moody, D. 1992. *Scottish Towns: a guide for local historians*, London, Batsford.

Phythian Adams, C. 1987. *Re-thinking English local history*, Leicester, Leicester University Press.

Pryce, W. T. R. (ed.) 1993. *From Family History to Community History*, Cambridge, Cambridge University Press.

Riden, P. 1983. *Local History: a handbook for beginners*, London, Batsford.

Riden, P. 1987. *Record Sources for Local History*, London, Batsford.

Rogers, A. 1977. *Approaches to Local History*, 2nd edition, London, Longman.

Rogers, A. (ed.) 1977. *Group Projects in Local History*, Folkestone, Dawson.

Rogers, L. D. and Smith, J. H. 1991. *Local Family History in England 1538–1914*, Manchester, Manchester University Press.

Rowlands, J. et al. (eds) 1993. *Welsh Family History: a guide to research*, Aberystwyth, Association of Family History Societies of Wales.

Steedman, C. 1984. *Policing the Victorian Community: the formation of English provincial police forces 1856–80*, London, Routledge & Kegan Paul.

Swan, P. and Foster, D. (eds) 1992. *Essays in Regional and Local History: in honour of Eric M. Sigsworth*, Beverly, Hutton Press.

Tiller, K. 1992. *English Local History: an introduction*, Stroud, Alan Sutton.

Urdank, A. M. 1990. *Religion and Society in a Cotswold Vale: Nailsworth, Gloucestershire, 1780–1865*, Berkeley, University of California Press.

## Europe

Åkerman, S. et al. (ed.) 1978. *Chance and Change: social and economic studies in historical demography in the Baltic area*, Odense, Odense University Press.

Alter, G. 1988. *Family and the Female Life Course: the women of Verviers, Belgium, 1849–1880*, Madison, University of Wisconsin Press.

Bell, R. 1979. *Fate and Horror, Family and Village: demographic and cultural change in rural Italy since 1900*, Chicago, University of Chicago Press.

Bretell, C. B. 1984. *Men who Migrate, Women who Wait, Population and History in a Portuguese Parish*, Princeton, Princeton University Press.

Czap, P. Jr. 1982. 'The perennial multiple family household, Mishino, Russia, 1782–1858', *Journal of Family History*, 7, pp. 5–26.

Evans, R. J. and Lee, W. R. (eds) 1981. *The German Family: essays on the social history of the family in nineteenth- and twentieth-century Germany*, London, Croom Helm.

Evans, R. J. and Lee, W. R. (eds) 1986. *The German Peasantry: conflict and community in rural society from the eighteenth to the twentieth centuries*, London, Croom Helm.

Flandrin, J. L. 1979. *Families in Former Times: kinship, household and sexuality*, Cambridge, Cambridge University Press.

Forster, R. and Ranum, O. (eds) 1976. *Family and Society*, Baltimore, Johns Hopkins University Press.

Goody, J. 1983. *The Development of the Family and Marriage in Europe*, Cambridge, Cambridge University Press.

Goody, J., Thirsk, J. and Thompson, E. P. (eds) 1976. *Family and Inheritance: rural society in western Europe*, Cambridge, Cambridge University Press.

Kertzer, D. 1984. *Family Life in Central Italy 1880–1910: sharecropping, wage labour and co-residence*, New Brunswick, NJ, Rutgers University Press.

Mitterauer, M. and Sieder, R. 1982. *The European Family*, Oxford, Blackwell.

Netting, R. M. 1982. *Balancing on an Alp: ecological change and continuity in a Swiss mountain community*, Cambridge, Cambridge University Press.

Plakans, A. 1984. *Kinship in the Past: an anthropology of European family life 1500–1900*, Oxford, Blackwell.

Ransel, D. (ed.) 1978. *The Family in Imperial Russia: new lines of historical research*, Urbana, University of Illinois Press.

Segalen, M. 1983. *Love and Power in the Peasant Family: rural France in the ninteenth century*, Oxford, Blackwell.

Segalen, M. 1985. *Fifteen Generations of Bretons: kinship and society in lower Brittany, 1720–1980*, Cambridge, Cambridge University Press.

Segalen, M. 1986. *Historical Anthropology of the Family*, translated from the French by Whitehouse, J. C. and Matthews, S., Cambridge, Cambridge University Press.

Sundt, E. 1980. *On Marriage in Norway*, translated from the Norwegian by Drake, M., original edition 1855), Cambridge, Cambridge University Press.

Sundt, E. 1993. *Sexual Customs in Rural Nineteenth-century Norway*, translated from the Norwegian by Anderson, O. W. (original edition 1863), Ames, IA, Iowa State University Press.

Tilly, L. A. 1979. 'The family wage economy of a French textile city: Roubaix, 1872–1906', *Journal of Family History*, 4, pp. 381–94.

Wall, R., Robin, J. and Laslett, P. (eds) 1983. *Family Forms in Historical Europe*, Cambridge, Cambridge University Press.

## North America

Baum, W. K. 1971. *Oral History for Local Historical Society*, 2nd edition, Nashville, American Society for State and Local History.

Burton, O. B. 1985. *In My Father's House are Many Mansions: family and community in Edgefield, South Carolina*, Chapel Hill, University of North Carolina Press.

Cherlin, A. J. (ed.) 1988. *The Changing American Family and Public Policy*, Lanham, MD, University Press of America.

Clubb, J. M., Austin, E. W. and Kirk, G. W. Jr. 1989. *The Process of Historical Enquiry: everyday lives of working Americans*, New York, Columbia University Press.

Conzen, K. N. 1980. 'Community studies, urban history and American local history', in M. Kammen (ed.) *The Past Before Us*, Ithaca, Cornell University Press, pp. 270–92.

Elder, G. H. Jr., 1974. *Children of the Great Depression*, Chicago, Chicago University Press.

Felt, T. W. 1976. *Researching, Writing and Publishing Local History*, Nashville, American Association for State and Local History.

Gordon, M. (ed.) 1983. *The American Family in Social-historical Perspective*, 3rd edition, New York, St Martin's Press.

Gouldrup, L. P. 1987. *Writing the Family Narrative*, Salt Lake City, Ancestry Inc.

Hareven, T. (ed.) 1977. *Family and Kin in Urban Communities*, New York, New Viewpoints; London, Croom Helm.

Hareven, T. (ed.) 1978. *Transitions: the family and the life course in historical perspective*, New York, Academic Press.

Hareven, T. K. 1982. *Family Time and Industrial Time: the relationship between the family and work in a New England industrial community*, New York, Cambridge University Press.

Hareven, T. K. and Langenback, R. 1979. *Amoskeag: life and work in an American factory city in New England*, London, Methuen.

Hareven, T. K. and Vinovskis, M. 1978. *Family and Population in Nineteenth-century America*, Princeton, Princeton University Press.

Kammen, C. 1986. *On Doing Local History: reflections on what local historians do, why, and what it means*, Nashville, American Association for State and Local History.

Katz, M. B. 1975. *The People of Hamilton West: family and class in a mid-nineteenth-century city*, Cambridge, Mass., Harvard University Press.

Pleck, E. H. 1980. *Black Migration and Poverty: Boston 1865–1900*, London, Academic Press.

Russo, D. J. 1974. *Families and Communities: a new view of American history*, Nashville, American Association for State and Local History.

Russo, D. J. 1988. *Keepers of Our Past: local historical writing in the United States 1820s–1930s*, London and Westport, Greenwood Press.

Yans-McLaughlin, V. 1982. *Family and Community: Italian immigrants in Buffalo 1800–1930*, Urbana, University of Illinois Press.

# Index

N.B. *Italicised* page references refer to diagrams or illustrations